D0443273

The City of Joy

DOMINIQUE LAPIERRE

The City of Joy

TRANSLATED FROM THE FRENCH
BY KATHRYN SPINK

All that is not given is lost.
Indian proverb

DOUBLEDAY & COMPANY, INC., GARDEN CITY, NEW YORK

1985

A portion of the proceeds from the sale of this book will go toward helping the author's friends in the City of Joy.

The author and his wife have founded *Action Aid for Lepers' Children of Calcutta,* whose headquarters are at 26, Avenue Kléber, 75116 Paris, France. Donations received by the association, which has over 5,000 members throughout Europe and the United States, go toward supporting a home for 250 children of lepers, in Calcutta.

DESIGNED BY WILMA ROBIN

Library of Congress Cataloging in Publication Data
Lapierre, Dominique.
The city of Joy.
1. Conduct of life. 2. Altruism. 3. Calcutta (India)
—Description. 4. Calcutta (India)—Social conditions.
5. Refugees—India—Calcutta. I. Title.
BJ1595.L2713 1985   954'.14
ISBN: 0-385-18952-4
Library of Congress Catalog Card Number: 85-10128

To Tâtou, Gaston,
Pierre, François, James,
and to "the lights of the world"
of the City of Joy.

Contents

AUTHOR'S NOTE

During frequent stays in Calcutta I was fortunate enough to meet some exceptional human beings. They have given me so much, and have had such an impact on my life, that I decided I wanted to tell a story about their lives, in a remarkable area of the world called the City of Joy.

This story concerns men, women, and children who have been uprooted from their homes by implacable nature and hostile circumstances, and thrown into a city whose capacity for hospitality has been pushed beyond imagining. This is a story about how people learn, despite incredibly difficult odds, to survive, to share, and to love.

My story about the City of Joy is based on two years of extensive research in Calcutta and various areas of Bengal. I was given access to personal diaries and correspondence, and the bulk of my research consisted of over two hundred lengthy interviews, conducted through interpreters in various languages including Hindi, Bengali, and Urdu. These interviews, which I transcribed into English and French, are the basis for the dialogues and testimonies in this book.

The protagonists of the City of Joy wished to remain anonymous. Therefore, I have purposely changed the identities of some characters and certain situations. The story I tell here is, however, true to the confidences that the people of the City of Joy have shared with me, and to the spirit of this unusual place.

This book, though the fruit of extensive research, does not pretend to speak for the whole of India. I have enormous affection for India, and great admiration for its intelligence, its achievements, its tenacity in overcoming difficulties. I know well its vir-

xii AUTHOR'S NOTE

tues, grandeurs, and diversity. The reader should not extend to the country as a whole impressions he gathers here of one small corner of it—a small area of Calcutta called the City of Joy.

Dominique Lapierre

The City of Joy

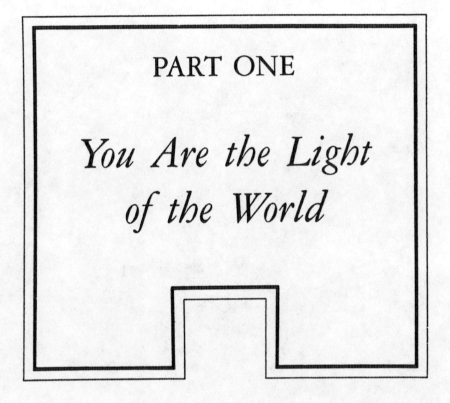

PART ONE

You Are the Light of the World

1

HE HAD THE APPEARANCE of a Mogul warrior: thick shock of curly hair, sideburns which met the drooping curve of his mustache, a strong, stocky torso, long muscular arms and slightly bowed legs. Yet thirty-two-year-old Hasari Pal was merely a peasant, one of the five hundred or so million inhabitants of India who were looking to the goddess Earth for their livelihood.

He had built his two-roomed hut with mud walls and a thatched roof; it was a short distance away from the village of Bankuli, West Bengal, a state in northeast India almost as large as the State of Indiana and five times as populated as Illinois. His wife, Aloka, was a young woman with a clear complexion and the look of an angel. The wing of her nose was pierced with a gold ring and her ankles were ornamented with bangles that jangled as she walked. She had given him three children. The eldest, twelve-year-old Amrita, had inherited her father's almond eyes and her mother's peach skin. Ten-year-old Manooj and six-year-old Shambu were two sturdy boys with black tousled hair who would far rather chase lizards around the pond than guide the buffalo into the family rice field. In the peasant's home there lived also Hasari's father, Prodip, a gaunt man with a lined face, barred with a thin, gray mustache; his mother Nalini, a bent old woman as wrinkled as a walnut; his two younger brothers with their wives and children—in all, sixteen people.

Openings set very low in the framework of the hut maintained a certain degree of coolness in the torrid summer, and a little warmth during the chilly winter nights. Shaded by red-and-white bougainvilleas, a narrow veranda ran the length of two of the hut's sides.

Seated beneath a sloping porch roof, Aloka was pedaling at a kind of wooden seesaw with a pestle fixed to its end, a machine which served to husk the rice. Tick-tack, tick-tack, as the pedal for the rice machine rose and fell, her daughter, Amrita, pushed new handfuls of grain under the pestle. The rice, removed from its husk, was picked up and sorted by the grandmother. As soon as she had a basketful she went to empty it at the *gola*, a small silo, set on piles in the middle of the courtyard. Its loft was on two levels and served simultaneously as a granary and a dovecote.

All around the hut the golden rice plantations stretched as far as the eye could see, sprinkled with the dark green of mango orchards, the light green of palm tree clusters and the soft green of bamboo groves, set at far distances from each other. Like sparkling lacework reflecting the blue of the sky, irrigation canals stitched the landscape tightly into squares. Footbridges formed delicate arabesques over pools covered with lotuses, hyacinths, and ducks. Children with sticks drove great shining buffalo across the small dikes, stirring up an ocher-colored dust as they went. At the end of this stiflingly hot day, the reddening disk of Surya, the Sun god, was sinking beyond the horizon, and a welcome breeze was blowing in from the sea. From the vast, flat expanse of land resounded the joyous cry of a myriad birds swooping low over the rice tips in salute to the oncoming night. Bengal was indeed the celebrated jewel of troubadours and poets, a paradise where on moonlit nights the god Krishna came to play his flute with the *gopis*, his playmates, and to sweep his beloved wife, Radha, into his dance.

With the disappearance of the sun, came "the hour of the cow dust," the time when the cattle came back from their grazing, the men returned from the rice fields, and the chickens came home to roost. With his cotton loincloth tucked up between his legs to make it easier for him to walk, Hasari Pal whistled as he ambled peaceably along, carrying his wooden plow over his shoulder. As the night drew on, the doves redoubled their circling and cooing. In the tamarinds a tribe of mynahs, India's sparrows, struck up a deafening concert. Two squirrels striped with the "three-finger marks of the god Rama" scampered about in the papaya. Herons and egrets made hastily for their nests. A mangy dog sniffed at the ground in search of a suitable place to spend the night. Then, gradually, the high-pitched squeak of the cicadas faded away. There was the last tick-tack of the rice machine—then silence, a silence that was almost immediately broken as the frogs started up their chorus. And above that there rose the rhythmic croak of a buffalo toad.

In less than five minutes, the tropical night had descended upon the land. As she did every evening, Hasari's wife, Aloka, blew into a conch shell to greet the goddess of the night. One of her sisters-in-law rang a small bell to chase away the evil spirits, especially those who lived in the hundred-year-old banyan tree at the end of the road. The cow was tied up in the shanty that served as a stable. For a while a recalcitrant goat forced everyone to scatter about, trying to catch it. Eventually, however, order was restored and Hasari pulled a barbed gate across the entrance to the courtyard, to keep out jackals and foxes. Then his mother performed a ritual as ancient as India itself—she filled the oil in the lamp which burned before polychrome pictures of the tutelary gods: Rama and his wife Sita, goddess of the fruits of the earth; Lakshmi, the goddess of prosperity seated on a lotus blossom; and Ganesh, the elephant-headed god of good fortune. Two other pictures, discolored by the years, showed the childlike face of Krishna, greedily swallowing a bowl of butter, a popular representation of the Cowherd god most dearly loved by the Hindu people; and the Monkey god, Hanuman, a legendary hero of some of the most prodigious adventures of Indian mythology.

While the womenfolk cooked the meal outside over a clay oven, Hasari and his two brothers came and sat down beside their father under the veranda. The heady fragrance of a jasmine bush embalmed the night that was pinpricked with the elusive lights of dancing fireflies. In a sky studded with stars a thin crescent moon was shining. It was "Shiva's moon," the new moon of the benefactor of the world, the thousand-eyed god of prosperity. The four men were sitting, deeply immersed in silent meditation, when Hasari noticed his father observe his sons one after another. Then he heard the old peasant murmur as if to himself, "Coal doesn't change its color when you wash it. What can't be cured must be endured."

*

The old man couldn't remember how many generations of lotuses had bloomed and faded in the pond since he was born. "My memory is like camphor. It evaporates with time," he would say. "There are so many things that I've forgotten. I am well advanced in years now and I do not know how many of the baskets of rice, filled by the gods of life at my birth, are left to me." What Prodip Pal did remember, however, was that he had once been a prosperous peasant. He had owned as many as six granaries full of rice and eight acres of fertile land. He had been able to provide for the future of his sons and give his elder daughters generous dowries to procure them good husbands. For himself and his wife in their old age, he had kept the strip of land and the house he had inherited from his father. "The pair of us should be able to live there in peace," he had promised her, "until the day when Yama, god of the dead, comes to claim us."

The old man had been wrong in his expectations. That plot of ground had been given to his father years ago by a *zamindar*, a large landowner, in recognition of his devotion. One day this benefactor's heir laid claim to the land. Prodip Pal refused to return it; the matter came before the courts. But the young *zamindar* had bought the judge and the peasant was obliged to abandon his land and his house. To pay the legal costs, he even had to sacrifice the dowry saved for his last daughter and the plots of his two youngest sons. "That dishonest landowner had a heart harder than a jackal's," he had remarked.

Fortunately his eldest son had been able to rescue the whole family under his own roof. Hasari was a good son. He did his utmost to convince his father that he was still the head of the family. The old man was indeed more familiar than anyone else with everyone's rights and duties, the local ways and customs and the boundaries of the rice fields and pastureland. He alone could maintain harmonious relations with the large landowners—a trump card of prime importance for the survival of a family of peasants. "Fishes can't afford to live on bad terms with the crocodiles in the pool," he often liked to say. Nevertheless, the fact

remained that this man venerated by his children had lost everything. He was no longer under his own roof.

"And yet I couldn't complain," he would concede. "It was true
that I was a ruined man but I still had my three sons. What a
blessing those sons were!" Thanks to them he still enjoyed those
things which, for an Indian peasant, constitute wealth: a small rice
granary, a stack of straw, two cows and a buffalo, a piece of land, a
little grain kept in reserve in earthenware jars in case of hard times,
even a few rupees in a money box. And what of his sons' wives?
They too had brought happiness into the household. They were all
three as beautiful as Parvati* and would all three make worthy
mothers for the Pandavas.† The Pals might well be poor, but they
were happy. Tomorrow the lotuses would be moist with dew. The
time for the harvest would come and with it the season of hope.
And on the old *mowa* trunk, the orchids would proclaim the glory
of God.

* Wife of the god Shiva.
† Five brothers, heroes of the great epic, the Mahabharata.

2

YET FURTHER TERRIBLE trials lay in store for Prodip Pal and his family. Just as ten or twelve million other Bengali peasants during this second half of the twentieth century, they were to become the victims of that endemic phenomenon known to economists as the cycle of poverty—that unavoidable process of descending along the social ladder by which the farmer became a sharecropper, then a peasant without land, then an agricultural laborer, then, eventually forced into exile. It was no use even dreaming of climbing a step in the opposite direction. Here everyone had to fight merely to defend his existing status, which was under constant threat. Improvement of that status was quite inconceivable, for poverty can only engender greater poverty. If it is true that coal does not change its color when washed, it is equally true that poverty painted in even the most dazzling colors remains forever poverty.

Their legal wrangles with the *zamindar* had left the Pals with only half of an acre of good land, on which to produce ten to twelve hundred pounds of rice. That constituted barely a quarter of what was actually necessary to feed the family. To make up the deficit, Prodip Pal and his sons managed to sharecrop another plot of land. Although some owners demanded three quarters of the harvest in payment, Prodip was able to retain half of it. This arrangement was of vital importance. When they would run out of rice, they would survive on the fruits from the three coconut trees and on the vegetables from the high ground that required very little irrigation, such as the "serpent gourds," a kind of cucumber that measured up to six feet in length, marrows, and giant radishes.

There were also the fruits from the jackfruit tree, some of which weighed nearly four pounds. The Pals were thus able to survive for two years. They even managed to buy two goats. And they regularly gave thanks to the gods, taking offerings to the little temple built at the foot of the most ancient banyan tree in the village.

During the third year, however, disaster struck once more. A parasite destroyed the entire field of rice in midgrowth. To overcome this catastrophe, the father set out on the path that led to the only brick house of the village. Its tiled roof dominated the other huts.

Nearly all the inhabitants of Bankuli had been compelled at some time or other to call on the *mahajan,* the jeweler-usurer, a potbellied man with a skull as smooth and shiny as a billiard ball. No matter how much distaste he provoked, the *mahajan* of Bankuli was, here as elsewhere in India, the key person in the village. He was its banker, its moneylender, its pawnbroker, and, very often, its vampire. By mortgaging the family field, Hasari's father obtained the loan of four hundred pounds of rice on condition that he would return six hundred after the first harvest. It was a year of great deprivation for the Pals. But "as the tortoise moves forward with difficulty to attain his objective," they succeeded in "turning the page of the god of life." Because of his debts and the inability of buying enough seed, the two following years were nothing short of a nightmare. One of Hasari's brothers had to give up his sharecropping and take a job as an agricultural laborer. By this time the cycle of poverty had really begun to strangle the Pals. Bad weather added to their plight. One night in April, a storm brought down all the mangoes and coconuts. Consequently they had to sell the buffalo and Rani, one of the two cows, despite the fact that they were so useful during the working season. Rani obviously did not want to leave. She strained at her rope with all her might, uttering the most heart-rending bellows. No one could fail to read in her reaction a bad omen, a sign that Radha, beloved of the Cowherd god Krishna, was angry.

The departure of the animals deprived the Pal family of part of their precious daily milk and, above all, of the indispensable dung, which when mixed with chopped straw and fashioned into cakes was dried in the sun and used as fuel for cooking food. Every day Hasari's daughter and her cousins had to go out in search of replacement dung. Manna as precious as this, however, did not simply belong to anyone who cared to pick it up, and the villagers chased them away. And so they learned to be secretive and steal it. From dawn to dusk, Amrita's brothers scoured the countryside, with their elder cousins, in search of anything to eat or turn into cash. They picked fruits and wild berries. They collected dead wood and acacia twigs which Indians use to clean their teeth. They caught fish in the pools. They made garlands of wild flowers. And they took these meager treasures to the market which was held three times a week, seven miles from their house.

Two further incidents were to aggravate the Pals's financial difficulties. Weakened by the lack of food, Hasari's youngest brother fell ill. One day he began to cough blood. For such poor people illness was more of a curse even than death. A doctor's fee and the cost of medicine could take several months' income. And so, to save his brother, Hasari resorted to the only remaining course of action: he broke open his baked clay money box and ran to the village priest begging him to intervene with destiny, by celebrating a special *puja*, a ceremony of offering to the gods.

The boy regained sufficient strength to take part in the second event of that year which was to sink his family a little further into destitution: the marriage of his youngest sister. The girl's aging father had at last found her a husband, and nothing was to prevent the wedding festivities from proceeding according to the traditional ritual. How many millions of Indian families, for generations, have been ruined by the marriages of their daughters? First there was the dowry, an ancestral custom officially abolished since Independence, but one that still prevailed in practice. The small farmer with whom Hasari's father had negotiated the marriage of his last daughter had demanded one bicycle, two cotton loincloths, a transistor, and half an ounce of gold, plus a few jewels for the young bride—all under the guise of a dowry. In total his requirements amounted to a good thousand rupees (some one hundred U.S. dollars).

Custom required, furthermore, that the girl's father, alone, covers the cost of the ceremony, which meant finding another thousand rupees to feed the families and their guests, and buy presents for the officiating Brahmin. For these poor people it was a cruel bloodletting, but the marriage of a daughter is a sacred duty for a father. Once his last daughter had left home, the old man would have completed his task on earth. Then at last he would be able to await in peace the visitation of Yama, god of the dead.

Prodip Pal went back to the usurer to ask for a new loan of two thousand rupees. As collateral, he took with him his family's only assets, his wife, Nalini's last remaining jewels: a pendant with matching gold earrings and two silver bracelets. The old woman had received these ornaments on the occasion of her own marriage, according to that same custom of the dowry. If it was a cruel system, it was also a form of provision for the future, in fact the only method of family savings in India. The sum loaned by the *mahajan* represented only half the actual value of the items, at a rate of interest that was astronomical: 5 percent per month, 60 percent for one year! The poor woman had little hope of seeing her jewels again—jewels that she had worn with such pride on feast days during the forty years of her life with Prodip Pal.

Next Prodip Pal asked his sons to cast their nets into the pool and fish for all the available carp and *ruyi*. Thanks to the celebrated harvest which preceded the war with China, Hasari, the eldest son, had been able to buy a few dozen fry to spawn in his water reserve. The fish had multiplied and grown so that now each one weighed several pounds. Kept until now as a provision against total famine, they would provide a surprise dish at the wedding banquet.

"Twilight is near," the old man kept telling himself, "but the sun still glows red. Our *chakra*, the wheel of our destiny, has not yet completed its turn."

*

"It was very pale, alluvial earth," Hasari Pal would recall. "But it was our earth, Mother Earth, Bhu-devi the goddess Earth. I had never known earth that was any other color and I loved it just as it was, without question. Don't we love our mother just as she is, whatever her complexion or faults? We love her. And if she suffers, we suffer with her.

"It was the month of May, the very heart of the Bengali summer. The air seemed to shimmer over the overheated countryside. Every day I gazed long and confidently at the sky. It was gradually assuming the tints and shades of peacock feathers. According to an announcement made by the Brahmin priest of the village, one more moon and the monsoon would be with us. The Brahmin was a very wise and knowledgeable man. He was also very old and he knew all the villagers as if they were members of his own family, even though that was quite impossible because he was of high, noble birth, far above any caste we might belong to. On the first day of each new year our father and all the other family heads in the village used to go and consult him as to what the coming twelve months held in store as far as men, cattle, and the harvests were concerned. Like a good many of his caste, our elderly Brahmin knew the laws of the seasons and the paths pursued by the heavenly bodies. He was the one who fixed the dates for the agricultural work and the family ceremonies. No one knew quite how he made his calculations but he studied the movement of the planets and prescribed which days were most auspicious for sowing seeds, for harvesting, and for getting married. The wedding season was over for this year. Now was the time for the earth to be impregnated. The Brahmin had predicted a year of exceptional riches, a year blessed by the gods, a year such as only occurs once in ten years—or even longer; a year without drought or epidemics or cockchafers or locusts or any other calamity. He knew, our Brahmin priest."

So the time to sow had come and each family went to make its *puja* to the gods. Hasari, with his father and his brothers, presented himself at the little altar at the foot of the banyan tree which stood at the entrance to the fields. "Gauri, I offer you this grain," his father recited, placing a grain of rice in front of the image of the wife of the god Shiva, protectress of peasants. "Give us plenty of water and return it to us a hundredfold." Three days later, sure enough, some beneficent storms came to soak the seedlings.

Hasari was certain that this year the gods were at one with the Bankuli peasants. His father had not hesitated to borrow from the bald-headed usurer an additional two hundred rupees against a proportion of the prospective harvest. Hasari had used twenty-five of these rupees to hire a team of oxen to plow the field. About forty rupees went for seed; the rest had been spent to buy manure and pesticides. This would be one of the greatest harvests they had ever had and, since the premonsoon rains had fallen at the requisite time, the Pals could spare themselves the hiring of a water pump. Fortune was smiling indeed, for that would have cost them six rupees an hour, the equivalent of the price of four pounds of rice—a small fortune!

Every morning Hasari went with his father and brothers to squat at the edge of the field. For hours on end he stayed there, contemplating the growth of the soft, young green shoots. The beginning of the monsoon was predicted for Friday, June 12. Friday is not a very auspicious day in the Hindu calendar. It did not matter really: the monsoon was the monsoon and its arrival each year was the gift of the gods to the people of India.

3

EVERYONE—men, women, children, and even the animals—
were anxiously staring at the sky. Usually a violent wind gets up a
few days before the monsoon breaks. The sky darkens suddenly as
clouds invade the earth, rolling one on top of the other like rolls of
cotton and skimming across the surface of the fields at extraordinary speed. Then other enormous and seemingly golden-edged
clouds succeed them and a few moments later a tremendous blast
of wind explodes into a hurricane of sand. Finally, a further bank of
black clouds, this time without their golden edges, plunges the sky
and the land into darkness. An interminable roll of thunder shakes
the air and the stage is set. Agni, the Fire god of the Vedas, protector of men and their hearths, hurls his thunderbolts. The large,
warm raindrops turn into cataracts. Children fling themselves stark
naked into the downpour, shrieking for joy, men dance and women
chant their thanksgiving prayers in the shelter of the verandas.

Water. Life. The sky is rendering the earth fruitful. This is
rebirth, the triumph of the elements. In a few hours vegetation
bursts forth from all directions, insects multiply, frogs come out in
their multitudes, reptiles are found in profusion, and birds warble
as they build their nests. Above all, the fields are covered, as if by
magic, with a blanket of the most beautiful green that grows ever
sturdier and ever taller. Dream and reality intermingle until after
one or two weeks, in a sky at last more peaceful, appears the bow of
Indra, king of all the gods, lord of the elements and of the firma-
ment. To humble peasants this rainbow signifies that the gods have
made their peace with mankind. The harvest will be good.

A good harvest would mean that this year the Pals's field,

which measured only half an acre, might perhaps produce one thousand pounds of rice—enough to feed the entire family for more than three months. While they waited for the next harvest the men would have to hire out their services to the *zamindar*, a very aleatory employment, which provided at best four or five days of work per month, but most of the time only a few hours. Such labor then earned only three rupees (about thirty U.S. cents) a day plus a portion of puffed rice and six *bidis*—these very slim cigarettes made out of a pinch of tobacco rolled up in a *kendu* leaf.

Friday June 12 came and went, however, without the slightest cloud. Throughout the days that followed, the sky remained steely white. Fortunately Hasari had taken the precaution of reserving the irrigation pump. Unable to afford this luxury, Ajit, the Pals's neighbor, had already begun to lament his lot. After a few weeks the young shoots in his small rice field began to turn yellow. The village elders delved deep into their memories in an attempt to remember when the monsoon had ever in the past kept them waiting like this. One of them recalled that in the year Mahatma Gandhi died, it had not arrived until July 2. In the year of the war with China it hardly came at all, and at other times, such as the year when the prize bull died, it had poured down so hard around about June 15 that all the seedlings had been flooded out. That was no better.

Even the most optimistic began to worry. Was Bhagavan, the great god, angry? The Pals went with their neighbors to the village priest to ask him to celebrate a *puja* to induce the rain to come. In return for his services the Brahmin asked for two *dhotis* for himself, a sari for his wife, and twenty rupees (two U.S. dollars). Everyone went rushing to the *mahajan* to borrow more money. In old times a *puja* involved the sacrifice of an animal, a he-goat for example, but these days people hardly ever sacrificed animals anymore. It was too expensive. The priest contented himself with lighting a wick impregnated with *ghee*, the ritual clarified butter, in front of the statue of Ganesh, the god who brings good fortune. Then he burned sticks of incense and intoned *mantras** while the peasants listened respectfully.

Yet neither Ganesh nor any of the other gods heard their

* Sacred formula in Sanskrit.

prayers and Hasari was compelled to hire the irrigation pump. For six hours the pulsating of its engine brought the lifeblood essential for their growth to the shoots in the Pals's field. During that time the shoots took on their beautiful emerald color and grew four inches which meant that they were now in urgent need of planting out. On the huge, cultivated plain beyond the green square of his field Hasari could see dozens of squares that were already quite yellow. Those peasants who had not been able to give their rice plants enough water were appraising the extent of the disaster. For them there would be no harvest. The specter of famine was rising on the horizon.

Now no one scrutinized the sky any longer. The *mahajan*'s radio announced that this year the monsoon would be very late arriving. It had not yet reached the Andaman Islands, which lay a long way out in the Bay of Bengal, almost off the coast of Burma. In any case the radio could no longer teach the Bankuli peasants anything. "It could bring nothing but the evil eye," reflected Hasari. "So long as we hadn't seen the cuckoo jay, we knew there would be no rain for us."

At the beginning of July a group of Bauls in ocher robes— wandering monks who sing the glory of the god Krishna—passed through the village. They stopped near the Gauri sanctuary under the banyan at the entrance to the fields and began to sing, punctuating their verses with the plucking of a single stringed lute, and with handbells and tiny cymbals. "Bird of my heart, don't keep on roving," they chanted. "Don't you know that your wanderings cause us great suffering? Oh come to us, bird, and bring our water with you."

All the Pals's attention was concentrated thenceforth on the pond that served as a communal water reserve. Its level was going down fast. The villagers speculated endlessly, trying to work out how long it would take the irrigation pumps to empty it, allowing for considerable evaporation in such torrid heat. The fateful moment came on July 23. That was the day they had to take out the fishes, which were floundering in the mud, and divide them among themselves. In such times of anguish, it was an occasion for unexpected rejoicing. To be able to eat fish was a real treat. Yet, in many a home, mothers renounced these treats with selfless foresight and dried the fish instead.

In the Pals's field the luminous emerald green soon changed first to gray green and then to a yellowish color. The rice drooped, then wilted and finally died—the very rice that they had nursed, caressed, and loved. The rice they had suffered with, bowed their heads with, and grown old with. "I couldn't bring myself to abandon it," Hasari was to confide. "Totally overwhelmed by the magnitude of the calamity, I stood motionless at the edge of our field." Before each strip of ground, other despairing peasants remained right through the night, their heads bowed in dejection. Perhaps they were thinking of the lament of the fakir, enraptured with God: "There was a treasure in my field but today someone else holds its key and the treasure is no longer mine."

It took Hasari the whole night to accept this tragic fact. At dawn he went home to sit under the veranda with his father and brothers. It was the old man, Prodip, who summed up their predicament: "We shall not go back to the field again this season." Moments later Hasari heard his mother lifting the lids of the storage jars lined up in the outhouse. The jars contained the rice that the Pals had set aside to await the next harvest. The poor woman began to evaluate how long the family could hold out on such meager reserves. Hasari already knew the answer. "If we rationed ourselves, allowing for a few handfuls of rice to be offered to the gods, we had only two months' food left." His wife, sisters-in-law, and children joined them. They all sensed that something was wrong but the old woman put the lids back on the jars and announced with apparent serenity: "We have enough rice for a good four months. Afterward, we'll have the vegetables." Reassured, old and young went back to their chores. Only Hasari remained behind. He saw tears on his mother's cheeks. His father came and put an arm round his wife's shoulders. "Mother of my sons," he said, "we shall both go without food for ourselves so that the rice lasts longer. The children must not suffer." With a nod of her head she approved the idea.

Many of the villagers were already left with nothing. The first indication of this harsh reality was the disappearance from the village of the very poorest families—the Untouchables. They had realized that this year there would be not a single head of rice to be gleaned from the fields. No one actually said anything but people knew that the Untouchables had left for the great city of Calcutta, about sixty miles away. Next it was the turn of the fathers and the eldest sons, in homes where the earthenware jars were empty. Then whole families began to take to the road that led to the city.

Their neighbors' departure was a source of great grief to the Pals. The families had known each other for so long. Before leaving his house the aging Ajit broke his clay pots and extinguished the oil lamp, the flame that burns constantly in every home; some of them had been alight for generations. With a hand that trembled slightly, he took down the pictures of the gods that had stood enthroned upon the small family altar and rolled them up in his knapsack. The gods wore great expansive smiles—smiles that seemed quite incongruous that morning. Prem, the eldest son, placed flowers and a few grains of rice outside the hole next to the doorway. This was the cobra's home. Prem recited a prayer to the snake, asking it to "guard this house and keep it safe until we return." Unfortunately, at that precise moment a black cat stalked past the hut. This did not augur well and so to thwart the evil spirits old Ajit had to draw them off on the wrong track. Thus he set off alone, heading north before gradually branching off to the South where he would rejoin his family. Before he left, the eldest son opened the parrot's cage. The parrot, at least, would be free. Instead of making straight for the sky, however, the bird seemed strangely at a loss. After some hesitation, it began to flutter from bush to bush behind its masters who were vanishing into the dust.

The summer passed almost without a single downpour and once again it was time for the winter sowing. Without water, however, there would be no winter sowing: no lentils, no sweet potatoes, no winter rice. By this time Bhaga, the Pals's one remaining cow, was nothing but skin and bone. It was a long time since they had had any straw to give her, not to mention bran. She was fed on the heart of the three banana trees which provided a little shade for the hut. One morning Hasari found her lying on her flank with her tongue hanging out. It was then that he realized that all the livestock was going to perish.

Cattle merchants closed in like vultures from the surrounding towns. They offered to buy any animals that were still alive and went off with truckloads of cows picked up for fifty rupees (five U.S. dollars) and buffalo for scarcely a hundred more. "Don't upset yourselves," they soothed with feigned compassion. "You can always buy your cattle back next year." What they omitted to say was that their price then would be ten times as much. A few days later it was the curriers' turn to come and take away the carcasses of those animals with which the peasants had not had the heart to part. Fifteen rupees was the price! (One U.S. dollar fifty!) It was that or nothing.

November went by. The departure of the cattle had cut off the peasants' only fuel supply. There was no more dung with which to cook food and no more milk either. Gone was the sound of children's laughter. Their small stomachs swelled up like balloons and several of them died, the victims of worms, diarrhea, and fever— yet in reality victims of hunger.

At the beginning of January villagers heard that food was being given out in the district capital, about twenty miles away. At first no one wanted to go. "We were peasants, not beggars," Hasari Pal was later to say. "But for the sake of the women and children we had to resign ourselves to accepting charity." Later government officials went through the villages announcing a relief operation called "Work for Food." Work sites were opened up in the area to deepen the canals, mend the roads, increase the size of the water reservoirs, raise the dikes, clear the undergrowth, and dig holes for trees to be planted. "We were given two pounds of rice for each day worked, a handout that was supposed to feed an entire family, and all the while the radio was saying that in the rest of the country the silos were full of grain."

Toward January 20 a terrible piece of news began to spread: the well near the little altar to god Gauri had run dry. Men went down to the bottom to sound it, only to find that, sure enough, the underground streams had dried up. The municipal authorities had to set up a rota system for the three other wells in the village that were still providing a little water. The water was rationed. At first there was a bucketful per family per day, then half a bucket. Eventually there was only one cup per person which had to be drunk on the spot at the mayor's house. Day and night long lines stretched out in front of the mayor's door. Eventually sentries armed with clubs had to be placed next to the only well that was not yet dry. A few miles to the North, wild elephants dying of thirst had surrounded a pool and were charging any person rash enough to come in search of water.

By now the fields were nothing but vast colorless expanses covered with a deep-cracked crust. The trees were in no better condition. Many of them were already dead and the bushes had long since been scorched.

The Pals's resistance was coming to an end. One day the old man gathered his family around him. From a knotted corner of his *dhoti* he took out five tightly rolled ten-rupee notes and two one-rupee coins and handed them to Hasari.

"You, my eldest son, take this money and go with your wife and children to Calcutta. In the big city you will find work. You will send us whatever you can. You are our only hope of not dying of starvation."

Hasari stooped down and touched his father's feet. The small man laid his palm on his son's head, then on his shoulder, and gripped him tightly until Hasari stood up again. The women wept in silence.

Next morning, as the first rays of Surya, the Sun god, dawned pale on the horizon, Hasari and his family set off, without venturing to look back at those who watched them go. Hasari walked in front with Amrita, his daughter. His wife, Aloka, dressed in a green cotton sari, followed behind with their two sons, Manooj and Shambu. Over his shoulder Hasari carried a cloth knapsack in which his wife had packed a little linen and the sandals he had received from her parents as part of her dowry. It was the first time these peasants had left their village for so distant a destination. The two boys pranced for joy at the prospect of adventure. "As for me, I was frightened," Hasari was to admit, "frightened of what laid in store for us."

4

AFTER A MORNING of walking, several hours in a swaying bus, and a night in a packed third-class train compartment, Hasari Pal and his family arrived at Howrah Station, one of Calcutta's two railway terminals. They were so stunned at the spectacle that confronted them that for several seconds they were unable to move. They were suddenly engulfed into a tide of people coming and going in all directions, of coolies bearing mountains of cases and packages, of vendors offering every conceivable sort of merchandise. Never before had they seen such riches: pyramids of oranges, sandals, combs, scissors, padlocks, glasses, bags; piles of shawls, saris, *dhotis*, newspapers, and of all kinds of food and drink. Wandering monks called Saddhus mingled among the travelers and for a twenty-*paisas* coin (two U.S. cents) would lay hands on them or pour a few drops of holy water from the Ganges into their mouths. Shoe shiners, ear cleaners, cobblers, public writers, and astrologers were all there, offering their services. Hasari and his family were dazed, dumbfounded, lost. Many of the other travelers around them seemed equally confused.

"What are we going to do?" the peasant asked himself. "Where are we going to sleep tonight?"

For a while the Pals wandered about in the midst of the throng. They gazed curiously at a family who appeared to have made their home in a corner of the main hall. They were peasants from the State of Bihar, driven there like the Pals by the drought, and they understood a little Bengali. They had been living here now for several weeks. Beside their carefully tied bundles they had set out their cooking utensils and a *chula*, a small portable stove. They were quick to put the newcomers on their guard against the police who often raided the station to turn out anyone camping there. Hasari questioned them about the possibility of finding work, but they had found nothing themselves yet. To avoid dying of starvation they admitted to having been reduced to putting their children out on the streets to beg. The shame of it was written on their faces. Hasari explained that a young man from his village was working as a coolie in the market of the Bara Bazar and that he was going to try and make contact with him. The Biharis suggested that Hasari leave his wife and children with them while he went off to make inquiries. Comforted by the goodwill of these strangers, Hasari went to buy some *samosas,* triangular-shaped fritters filled with vegetables or minced meat, which he shared with his new friends, his wife, and his children; they had eaten nothing since the previous day. Then he plunged resolutely into the flood of travelers emerging from the railway station.

The sight of this newly arrived peasant provoked an immediate tidal wave. A horde of pedlars surrounded Hasari with offers of ballpoint pens, sweetmeats, lottery tickets, and a thousand other wares. Beggars assaulted him. Lepers clung to his shirt. Outside the station a cyclone of trucks, buses, taxis, handcarts, scooters, cycle rickshaws, horse carriages, motorbikes, and bicycles swirled in a kind of collective madness. They crawled forward at a walking pace, amid a terrifying, chaotic racket. The honking of carrier tricycles, the tooting of horns, the throbbing of engines, buses' horns, cart bells, carriage bells, the clammering of loudspeakers, it was like a competition to see who could make the most noise. "It was worse than the thunder that heralds the first drops of the monsoon," Hasari would say. "I thought my head was going to burst."

In the middle of all this commotion, he spotted an impassive policeman who was trying to direct the traffic. He fought his way over to him to inquire where the bazaar was where his acquaintance was working. The policeman waved his club in the direction of an entanglement of metal girders which soared heavenward at the far end of the square. "On the other side of the bridge!" he growled.

This bridge was the only link between the twin cities of Calcutta and Howrah. It stretched across the Hooghly River, a tributary of the Ganges, and was undoubtedly the most congested bridge in the world.

Over a million people and hundreds of thousands of vehicles crossed it every day in a hallucinating maelstrom. Hasari Pal was swept up at once in a stream of people who were pushing their way in different directions between two unbroken lines of vendors squatting on the ground behind displayed wares. In the six lanes of traffic, hundreds of vehicles were completely stuck in one gigantic bottleneck that stretched as far as the eye could see. Trucks roared in an attempt to overtake the line of streetcars. Red double-decker buses were overloaded with people, who clung in clusters to their sides. Some of the buses leaned over at such extreme angles that they looked as if at any moment they would tip over altogether. There were handcarts too, crawling along beneath piles of crates, pipes, and machinery and propelled by poor fellows whose muscles looked as if they were about to burst. Coolies, their faces distorted with the strain, trotted along with baskets and packages piled up on their heads. Others transported drums affixed to either end of a long pole lying on their shoulders. Herds of buffalo, cows, and goats, driven along with sticks, attempted to wend their way through the labyrinth of vehicles. Often the panic-stricken animals escaped in all directions. "How those poor beasts must be suffering," Hasari commented to himself, recalling with nostalgia the tranquil beauty of his countryside.

On the other side of the bridge the traffic seemed even more congested. Suddenly Hasari noticed a small cart on two wheels, transporting two passengers. Between the shafts there was a man. "Good God," he thought, "there are even human horses in Calcutta!" Hasari had just discovered his first rickshaw.

The nearer he drew to the bazaar, the more there were of these curious little vehicles lugging people about, or merchandise, or both. As his gaze followed their progress he began dreaming. "Would I have the strength to earn a living for my family by pulling such a machine?"

The Bara Bazar was an area swarming with crowds, and where the houses rose several floors high, so high in fact that Hasari was amazed that they managed to keep standing. The network of small streets, covered alleys, and narrow passageways lined with hundreds of stalls, workshops, and shops was like a beehive humming with activity. Entire streets were taken up with vendors selling ornaments and garlands of flowers. Squatting behind mountains of Bengal roses, jasmine, Indian pinks, and marigolds, children threaded buds and petals like strings of pearls to make up garlands as thick as pythons. Their pendants too were made out of flowers and interlaced with gold thread. Savoring the fragrance of these flowers, Hasari bought for ten *paisas* a handful of rose petals to put on the *lingam* of Shiva, the benevolent and terrible god of the Hindu religion, that he encountered in a niche on a street corner. He paused for a moment before the black, cylindrical stone that symbolized the forces of life and asked the god who knew the whereabouts of truth to help him to find the person he sought.

Farther on Hasari passed through an arcade where dozens of stalls sold nothing but perfume contained in a multitude of vials and colored bottles. Then he entered a covered alleyway where, amid the glitter of gold and small glassware, all he could see were jewelers. He could hardly believe his eyes. There were hundreds of them, lined up like prisoners behind the bars of the cages containing their treasures. Women decked out in costly saris pressed themselves against the bars; the merchants seemed never to stop unlocking and locking the safes behind them. They handled their minute scales with surprising agility. Hasari also saw several poorer women, wearing darned veils, jostling to get near the grills. Here, as in the villages, the jewelers were also usurers.

Beyond this street of the *mahajans* lay the saris market. Women lingered over sumptuous displays, particularly in the stores that specialized in wedding attire, saris that dripped with gold and spangles.

The sun that day was overpowering and the water vendors, ringing their small bells, were doing good business. Hasari gave five *paisas* (one half of a U.S. cent) to one of them to quench his thirst. Ever watchful, he scrutinized every coolie and tradesman and questioned all the bearers, but only a miracle could help him to find his friend in such a seething mass. Nonetheless he pursued his search until nightfall. "Working a ten-acre rice field was less tiring than that endless trek through the bazaar," he would later recall. Exhausted, he bought five bananas and asked the way back to the great bridge.

His children swooped on the bananas, like starving sparrows

and the whole family went to sleep on the railway station floor. Fortunately, the police did not raid the place that night.

Next morning Hasari took his eldest son, Manooj, with him and together they explored another section of the Bara Bazar: first the metalworkers' and tinsmiths' corner, then the workshops where dozens of men and children with bare torsos spent their day rolling *bidis,* the thin Indian cigarettes. So dim was the light inside the rooms that the faces were hardly distinguishable. Hasari gave the name and description of his friend to anyone who was prepared to listen but it was like looking for a grain of rice in a bundle of straw. There were probably hundreds of coolies also called Prem Kumar and answering to his description. That second evening Hasari again took some bananas back with him. The Pals shared them with the neighboring family who had nothing to eat.

After the third day of searching, with no more money to buy bananas, Hasari was reduced to an act of supreme humiliation for a proud peasant. Before making his way back to the railway station, he picked up all the peelings and scraps he could find. "That evening my wife suggested that our daughter, Amrita, go to beg at the entrance to the station. Overwhelmed with shame and despair, she wept as she spoke. We were peasants, not beggars." The Pals could not reconcile themselves to so abhorrent an idea. For one more day and night they waited but, as dawn broke on the following day, they sent their little girl and her two brothers to take up their positions where the rich travelers got out of their taxis and private cars.

Then, dejected, Hasari returned to the Bara Bazar. As he was passing a workshop where some coolies were loading iron bars onto a *telagarhi,* a long handcart, one of the coolies suddenly began to vomit blood. His companions laid him out on the ground. He was so pale that Hasari thought the man was dead. When the workshop owner came out, shouting because the *telagarhi* had not yet gone, Hasari rushed forward and offered to replace the ailing coolie. The man hesitated but his delivery could not wait any longer and he offered three rupees for the run, payable on arrival.

Without really realizing what was happening to him, Hasari braced himself with the others to shift the heavy load. Their employer had carefully avoided to mention that their destination was a factory situated on the other side of the great bridge, well beyond

the railway station. The coolies fought like beasts to pull the heavy
load across, but to no avail. Halfway up the slope their vehicle
came to a standstill. Hasari thought the blood vessels in his neck
were going to burst. A policeman came and threatened the men
with his stick because they were holding up traffic. "Get out of the
way!" he yelled, covering the tooting horns. In response the eldest
of the coolies bent down to put all his weight against one wheel and
shouted to the others to drive them forward.

Exhausted but proud at the prospect of surprising his family
with his first earnings, Hasari returned to the railway station late
that evening. It was he, however, for whom the real surprise lay in
store. His wife and children had disappeared. So too had the other
family. After a long search he eventually found them on an embankment behind the bus terminal. "The police chased us out,"
explained Aloka, through her tears. "They said if they ever saw us
in the station again, they'd throw us into prison."

The Pals had no idea where to go next. They crossed the great
bridge and simply kept on walking. It was dark but, despite the late
hour, the streets were still full of people. Bewildered by the
throngs that milled about like ants, jostling each other and shouting, they reached a place in the very heart of the city. Pitiful in her
poor peasant sari, Aloka had taken her youngest son in her arms
and held her daughter by the hand. Manooj, the eldest boy, walked
in front with his father. They were so afraid of losing each other
that they called out constantly to one another in the darkness. The
pavement was littered with sleeping people, wrapped from head to
toe in bits of *khadi* cloth. They looked like corpses. As soon as they
found an empty space, the Pals stopped to rest a while. A family
was camping nearby. The mother was roasting *chapatis* on a portable stove. She and her family came from Madras. Fortunately, they
spoke a few words of Hindi, a language Hasari could vaguely
understand. They too had left the countryside for the mirage of
Calcutta. They offered the Pals a hot griddle cake and swept a
corner of the pavement so that the newcomers could settle themselves next to them. The strangers' hospitality brought new
warmth to the peasant's heart. At least his family would be safe in
their company until he found work. That afternoon he had learned
a harsh lesson: "Since men in this inhuman city die on the job, I'll
be damned if I can't manage one day to replace one of these dead."

5

THE CITY THAT Hasari had not hesitated to describe as "inhuman" was in fact a mirage city, to which in the course of one generation six million starving people had come in the hope of feeding their families. In the nineteen sixties, Calcutta was still, despite its decline over the previous half century, one of the most active and prosperous cities in Asia. Thanks to its harbor and its numerous industries, its metal foundries and chemical and pharmaceutical works, its flour mills and its lines, jute, and cotton factories, Calcutta boasted the third highest average wages per inhabitant of any Indian city, immediately after Delhi and Bombay. One third of the imports and nearly half of India's exports passed along the waters of the Hooghly, the branch of the Ganges on the banks of which the city had been founded three centuries earlier. Here, 30 percent of the entire country's bank transactions were undertaken and a third of its income tax was levied. Nicknamed the "Ruhr of India," its hinterland produced twice as much coal as France and as much steel as the combines of North Korea. Calcutta drained into its factories and warehouses all the material resources of this vast territory: copper, manganese, chromium, asbestos, bauxite, graphite, and mica as well as precious timber from the Himalayas, tea from Assam and Darjeeling, and almost 50 percent of the world's jute.

From this hinterland also converged each day on the city's bazaars and markets an uninterrupted flow of foodstuffs: cereals and sugar from Bengal, vegetables from Bihar, fruit from Kashmir, eggs and poultry from Bangladesh, meat from Andra, fish from Orissa, shellfish and honey from the Sundarbans, tobacco and betel from Patna, cheeses from Nepal. Vast quantities of other items and materials also fed one of the most diversified and lively trading centers in Asia. No fewer than two hundred and fifty different varieties of cloth were to be counted in the bazaars of Calcutta and more than five thousand colors and shades of saris. Before reaching this mecca of industry and commerce, these goods had often to cross vast areas that were extremely poor, areas where millions of small peasants like the Pals scratched a desperate living out of infertile patches of land. How could those poor not dream, each time disaster struck, to take the same road as those goods?

The metropolis was situated at the heart of one of the world's richest yet at the same time most ill-fated regions, an area of failing or devastating monsoons causing either drought or biblical floods. This was an area of cyclones and apocalyptic earthquakes, an area of political exoduses and religious wars such as no other country's climate or history has perhaps ever engendered. The earthquake that shook Bihar on January 15, 1937, caused hundreds of thousands of deaths and catapulted entire villages in the direction of Calcutta. Six years later a famine killed three and a half million people in Bengal alone and ousted millions of refugees. India's independence and the Partition in 1947 cast upon Calcutta some four million Muslims and Hindus fleeing from Bihar and East Pakistan. The conflict with China in 1962, and subsequently the war against Pakistan, washed up a further several hundred thousand refugees; and in the same year, 1965, a cyclone as forceful as ten three-megaton H-bombs capable of razing to the ground a city like New York, together with a dreadful drought in Bihar, once more sent to Calcutta entire communities.

Now, it was yet another drought that was driving thousands of starving peasants like the Pals to the city.

The arrival of these successive waves of destitute people had transformed Calcutta into an enormous concentration of humanity. In a few years the city was to condemn its ten million inhabitants to living on less than twelve square feet of space per person, while the four or five million of them who squeezed into its slums had sometimes to make do with barely three square feet each. Consequently Calcutta had become one of the biggest urban disasters in the world—a city consumed with decay in which thousands of houses and many new buildings, sometimes ten floors high or even higher, threatened at any moment to crack and collapse. With their crumbling façades, tottering roofs, and walls eaten up with tropical vegetation, some neighborhoods looked as if they had just been bombed. A rash of posters, publicity and political slogans, and advertisement billboards painted on the walls, defied all efforts at renovation. In the absence of an adequate garbage collection service, eighteen hundred tons of refuse accumulated daily in the streets, attracting a host of flies, mosquitoes, rats, cockroaches, and other creatures.

In summer the proliferation of filth brought with it the risk of epidemics. Not so very long ago it was still a common occurrence for people to die of cholera, hepatitis, encephalitis, typhoid, and rabies. Articles and reports in the local press never ceased denouncing the city as a refuse dump poisoned with fumes, nauseating gases, and discharges—a devastated landscape of broken roads, leaking sewers, burst water pipes, and torn down telephone wires. In short, Calcutta was "a dying city."

And yet, thousands, hundreds of thousands, even millions of people swarmed night and day over its squares, its avenues and the narrowest of its alleyways. The smallest fragment of pavement was occupied, squatted upon, covered with salesmen and pedlars, with homeless families camping out, with piles of building materials or refuse, with stalls and a multitude of altars and small temples. The result of all this was an indescribable chaos on the roads, a record accident rate, nightmarish traffic jams. Furthermore, in the absence of public toilets, hundreds of thousands of the city's inhabitants were forced to attend to their bodily needs in the street.

In those years seven out of ten families had to survive on no more than one or two rupees a day, a sum that was not even sufficient to buy a pound of rice. Calcutta was indeed that "inhuman city" where the Pals had just discovered people could die on the pavements surrounded by apparent indifference. It was also a powder flask of violence and anarchy, where the masses were to turn one day to the saving myth of communism. To hunger and communal conflicts must also be added one of the world's most unbearable climates. Torrid for eight months of the year, the heat melted the asphalt on the roads and expanded the metal structure of the great Howrah Bridge to such an extent that it measured four feet more by day than by night. In many respects the city resembled the goddess Kali whom many of its inhabitants worship—Kali the Terrible, the image of fear and death, depicted with a terrifying expression in her eyes and a necklace of snakes and skulls around her neck. Even slogans on the walls proclaimed the disastrous state of this city. "Here there is no more hope," said one of them. "All that is left is anger."

Yet on what a prestigious past this metropolis, now judged inhuman by many of its inhabitants, could pride itself! From the date of its foundation in 1690 by a handful of British merchants until the departure of its last British governor on August 15, 1947, Calcutta, more than any other city in the world, had epitomized the imperial dream of the white man's domination of the globe. For nearly two and a half centuries it had been the capital of the British Indian Empire. It was from here that until 1912 its governor generals and its viceroys had imposed their authority on a country with a population greater than that of the United States of America today. Calcutta's avenues had witnessed the passing of just as many parading troops and as many high society ladies in palanquins or barouches as the Champs-Élysées of Paris or the London Mall. Even now, dilapidated by decades of monsoons, its public buildings, its monuments, its business center, its beautiful residences with their balusters and colonnades still bore witness to that heritage. At the far end of the avenue along which, in 1911, George V and Queen Mary had processed in a gold-studded carriage between two rows of Highlanders in Scottish kilts and white spats, there rose from the heart of a thirty-acre park, the imposing 137-room building in which the Empire had lodged its viceroys. Raj Bhavan, the royal palace, was a replica of Kedleston Hall, one of the most beautiful castles in England. The viceroy, Lord Wellesley, had decorated its great marble drawing room with busts of the twelve Caesars. Before becoming, after Independence, the residence of the Indian governor of Bengal, Raj Bhavan had hosted festivities and celebrations of a sumptuousness beyond the wildest imagination. On gala evenings, the representative of Her Most Gracious Majesty took place on a throne of purple velvet highlighted with gold, surrounded by a whole retinue of aides-de-camp and officers in dress uniform. Two beturbaned Indian servants gently wafted fans of scarlet silk to refresh him while soldiers armed with silver-encrusted lances provided him with a guard of honor.

Many other no less glorious vestiges, often engulfed by the chaos of construction and contemporary slums, bore witness to the past majesty of this former jewel in the crown: buildings, such as the stadium where on January 2, 1804, the Calcutta team, led by the grandson of British Prime Minister Walpole, had opened the batting against a team of old Etonians in the first cricket match ever played in the Orient. Then there was that proud, eight-hundred-acre enclave beside the sacred waters of the Hooghly River, which harbored one of the most impressive citadels ever constructed by man. Built to protect the first three warehouses—one of which, Kalikata, so-called because it was situated near a village dedicated to Kali, was to give its name to the city—Fort William had served as a cradle for Calcutta and for the British conquest of its enormous empire in Asia.

Of all these symbols of former glory, however, none was more striking than the huge set piece in white marble which rose from the far extremity of the Maidan park. Erected with funds given by the Indian people themselves to commemorate the sixty-three-year reign of the Empress who believed she incarnated best the vocation of the white man to look after the well-being of people of the earth, the Victoria Memorial conserved, at the very heart of the modern urban jungle, the most fabulous collection of treasures ever assembled within the confines of a colonial epic. All the mementos were there, piously preserved for the incredulous scrutiny of present generations: statues of the Empress at all the various stages of her splendor, together with all the royal envoys who succeeded each other here; a portrait of Kipling; sabers with pommels inlaid with gold and precious stones, worn by British generals during the battles which gave India to Britain; parchments confirming these conquests; manuscript messages from Victoria conveying her affection to her "peoples beyond the seas."

Despite the heat, the tropical diseases, the snakes, the jackals, and even the tigers that sometimes, at night, prowled around the residences on Chowringhee Road, Calcutta had offered its creators a supremely easy and pleasurable life-style. For two and a half centuries, generations of Britishers had begun their day with a drive in a horse-drawn carriage or a limousine under the shade of the banyan trees, magnolia bushes, and palm clusters of the Maidan park. Every year, before Christmas, a glittering season of polo, horse racing, and social receptions drew the entire élite of Asia to Calcutta. In the city's heyday, the primary occupation of its ladies had been to try on in their boudoirs the very latest outfits from Paris and London, made up by local dressmakers out of sumptuous fabrics and brocades woven in Madras or Benares. For nearly half a century the most sought-after rendezvous among these same privileged ladies was with Messieurs Malvaist and Siret, two famous French hairstylists whom an astute financier had brought over from Paris.

It was because of its wealth of entertainment that the Calcutta of these times had earned the nickname of "Paris of the East." Not one of its parties began without a delightful serpentine excursion on the Hooghly, on one of those long gondolas propelled by forty or so boatmen in red-and-green turbans and white tunics girded with golden sashes. Alternatively there was always a promenade along the riverside pathways of the Garden of Eden, to which one viceroy, in love with Oriental architecture, had had a pagoda transported plank by plank, from the lofty plateaus of Burma. At the end of every afternoon the garrison's brass band provided, on this spot overlooking the river, a concert of romantic music for the delectation of expatriates in crinolines, frock coats, and top hats. Later in the evening, there were always a few rounds of whist or ombre in one of the innumerable clubs "prohibited to dogs and Indians," which constituted the pride of British Calcutta. Then there was perhaps a dinner and dance under the ornamental ceilings of the luxurious ballrooms of the Chowringhee houses or on the teak dance floor of the London Tavern. Those with a predilection for dramatic art were spoiled with choices. Calcutta prided itself on being the artistic and intellectual capital of Asia. Every evening there was a Shakespeare performance at the New Play House and all the latest London West End productions were staged in a host of other theaters. Geoffrey Moorhouse, a noted historian of Calcutta, tells us that at the beginning of the century one of the city's great society ladies, a Mrs. Bristow, had even converted one of the reception rooms in her residence into an opera stage and hosted there the best tenors and divas from Europe.* The boards of the Old Empire Theatre had borne the ballet shoes of the great Anna Pavlova in an unforgettable recital that shortly preceded her retirement. The Calcutta Symphony Orchestra gave a concert every Sunday conducted by the baton of its founder, a Bengali merchant named Shosbree. Shortly after the First World War, flourished on Chowringhee Road the most famous three-star restaurant in Asia. Firpo was to remain, until the 1960s, the Maxim's of the Orient, Calcutta's temple of gastronomic and social delectation. Like having a reserved pew in St. Paul's Cathedral, every self-respecting family had a table reserved in Firpo's large L-shaped dining room. The Italian restaurateur received people like an Oriental potentate, or perhaps even turned them away if their faces or attire did not appeal to him. Enlivened by the musicians of Francisco Casanovas, a Spanish nobleman who had switched to the art of playing the clarinet, Firpo's dance floor had formed the cradle of romance for the last generation of white men in Asia.

Those who preferred the treasures of the rich Bengali culture to the Occidental delights were no less spoiled. Since the eighteenth century, Calcutta had been the homeland of philosophers, poets, storytellers, and musicians. In the person of Tagore, Calcutta had even given to India a Nobel Prize for literature and in J. C. Bose a Nobel Prize for sciences. It was also the home of Ramakrishna and Vivekananda, two of the most venerated modern saints; of Satyajit Ray, one of the most celebrated prizewinners of world cinema; of Sri Aurobindo, one of the giants of universal spirituality; of Satyen Bose, one of the great scholars of the theory of relativity.

The vicissitudes of destiny had not completely obliterated so prestigious a heritage. Calcutta was still India's artistic and intellectual beacon and its culture continued to be as alive and creative as ever. The hundreds of book stalls in College Street were still laden with books—original editions, pamphlets, great literary works, publications of every kind, in English as well as in the numerous Indian languages. Though the Bengalis now constituted barely half of the city's working population, there was no doubt that Calcutta produced more writers than Paris and Rome com-

* *Calcutta,* by Geoffrey Moorhouse (Weidenfeld and Nicolson, London).

bined, more literary reviews than London and New York, more cinemas than New Delhi, and more publishers than all the rest of the country. Every evening its theaters put on several theatrical productions, classical concerts, and countless recitals at which everyone, from a universally renowned sitarist like Ravi Shankar to the humblest of flute or tabla players, was united with the popular audiences before whom they performed in the same love of music. Half of India's theater groups stemmed from here. The Bengalis even claimed that one of their scholars had translated the great French playwright Molière into their language, long before the British had even heard of him.

For Hasari Pal and the millions of exiles who crowded into its slums, however, Calcutta represented neither culture nor history. For them it meant only the faint hope of finding some crumbs to survive until the next day. In a metropolis of such magnitude there were always a few crumbs to be gathered, whereas in a village flooded with water or parched by drought, even that possibility didn't exist anymore.

6

AFTER ANOTHER DAY spent running about the Bara Bazar, Hasari Pal returned one evening with a triumphant smile that was altogether unexpected.

"May Bhagavan be blessed!" exclaimed Aloka when she caught sight of her husband. "Look, children, your father seems pleased. He must have found the coolie from our village. Or even better, perhaps he has found work. We're saved!"

Hasari had found neither his friend nor work. He was simply bringing his family two newspaper cones full of *muri,* this rice roasted in hot sand that the poor eat in last resort to stem their hunger. The dried grains were hard and had to be masticated for a long time, a process that prolonged the illusion of actually getting one's teeth into something.

Parents and children chewed for a while in silence. "There you are. That's for you," said Hasari, happily giving the remainder of his own share to his youngest son who was looking at him with an expression of entreaty.

Aloka watched her husband's gesture with an aching heart. Among India's poor, food was always reserved in priority to those who could work and provide for the family's needs. Hasari had lost a lot of weight since their arrival in Calcutta. His bones were protruding. Two deep cracks had carved themselves beneath his mustache, his dark, shining hair had turned gray above his ears, a phenomenon that was rare in so young an Indian. "Good God, how he has aged," thought his young wife as she looked at him stretching out for the night on the bare asphalt of their piece of pavement. She thought of the first time she had seen him, so handsome, so sturdy under the ornamental canopy erected for their marriage in front of her family hut. He had come from his village, borne on a palanquin and escorted by his relatives and friends. The Brahmin priest had anointed his forehead with rice paste and small basil leaves. He had been wearing a brand-new white tunic and a very bright saffron-colored turban. Aloka remembered her terror when her mother and aunts had left her alone with him after the ceremony. She was only fifteen and he was barely three years older. Their union had been arranged by their parents and they had never met before. He had gazed at her insistently and asked her name. She recalled too that he had added, "You are a very beautiful girl and I am wondering whether you will find me as appealing." She merely smiled in response because it was not decent for a new bride to speak freely to her husband on their wedding day. She had blushed then and, encouraged by his gentleness, she in her turn had ventured a question: did he know how to read and write? "No," he had replied simply before adding with pride, "But I know how to do many other things."

"That day the father of my children looked as strong and solid as the trunk of the great banyan tree at the entrance to our village," reflected Aloka. And now he seemed so fragile, curled up on his patch of pavement. It was hard for her to appreciate that this was the same man whose powerful arms had clasped her as a pair of pliers on their wedding night. Although her eldest aunt had given her some words of advice, she had been so timid and ignorant then that she had struggled to escape from his grasp. "Don't be frightened," he had said, "I am your husband and you will be the mother of my children."

Aloka was pondering on these memories in the darkness when an uproar broke out nearby. The neighbors, those good people who had so generously welcomed the distressed Pals, had just noticed that their daughter was missing. She was a pretty girl of thirteen, sweet and gentle, with a large braid down her back and green eyes. Her name was Maya, which meant "illusion." Every morning she used to go off to beg outside the entrance to the big hotels on Chowringhee Road and Park Street, where business men and rich tourists from all over the world stayed. No one, however, had the right to hold out his hand in such a gold mine of a district unless he was directly controlled by the syndicate of racketeers.

Each evening Maya handed over her entire day's earnings to the gang leader who, in return, paid her a daily wage of five rupees (fifty U.S. cents). Maya was lucky to have been accepted at all because, in order to incite their "clients" to greater generosity, the racketeers preferred to exploit deformed or disabled youngsters, legless men on planks with wheels, or mothers in rags with emaciated babies in their arms. It was even said that children were mutilated at birth to be sold to these torturers.

Young Maya was deeply pained by the obligation to beg. On several occasions as she was about to leave for "work," she had thrown herself, sobbing, into her mother's arms. Such scenes were frequent on the streets of Calcutta where so many people were condemned to suffer the very worst degradations in order simply to survive. Yet, Maya had never shirked her task. She knew that for her family the five rupees she brought back each night meant the difference between life and death.

That evening she had not come home. As the hours went by, her mother and father grew sick with worry. They got up, sat down again, walked around in circles uttering incomprehensible imprecations. In the three months since they had found themselves stranded on that pavement they had learned enough to know that their anguish was justified. Just as elsewhere in the world, abduction of children was a frequent crime in Calcutta. The villains responsible generally went for young girls between ten and fifteen, but small boys were not entirely exempt. The children were usually sold to a ring of pleasure house suppliers who dispatched them to Madras, Bombay, or New Delhi, or even exported them to certain Arab capitals in the Persian Gulf countries. They were never seen or heard of again. The lucky ones were locked in prostitution houses in Calcutta itself.

Shaken by their neighbors' distress, Aloka woke her husband. Hasari immediately suggested to Maya's father that they should go out and look for the girl. Accordingly, the two men plunged into the dark alleyways packed with people sleeping in doorways and on the pavements. Avoiding getting lost in such a labyrinth, where all the buildings looked alike, was no mean achievement for peasants used to finding their way in the familiar simplicity of their countryside.

After the two men had gone, Aloka sat down beside the neighbor's wife. The poor woman's cheeks, pockmarked from smallpox, were bathed in tears. She was holding a sleeping baby in the folds of her sari and two other small boys muffled in rags were asleep beside her. Nothing, it seemed, could disturb children's slumbers, not even, as here, the noisy exhausts of trucks or the harrowing grind of the streetcars passing along their heads on the avenue, not even the cramps of a hungry stomach. During the time that these peasants had been living on their piece of pavement, they had marked out their territory as if they meant to remain there forever. Their plot was a proper little campsite with one corner for sleeping, and another corner for cooking, with a *chula* and few utensils. It was winter and these shelterless people had no need to fear the torrential downpour of the monsoon. But when the December wind blew down from the Himalayas and swept through the avenues, it was as cold as death on the pavements. From every direction there rose the same haunting noises. The sound of coughing fits, of throats being cleared, the whistle of spitting. The worst for Aloka was to have to "sleep on the bare ground. You woke up in the morning with limbs as painful as if they'd been beaten." By some cruel stroke of irony, an advertisement on a billboard seemed to flout them from the opposite pavement. It showed a maharajah sleeping snugly on a thick mattress. From his dreamland he inquired solicitously, "Have you ever thought of a Simmons mattress as a present?"

Maya's father and Hasari Pal did not return for several hours and when they did it was without the little girl. Instantly something about her husband's behavior surprised Aloka. The same man who had seemed so exhausted before he left was now full of life. Maya's father was in the same state. Without uttering a word, they sat down on the pavement and began to laugh. Aloka realized her husband had been drinking. "I was indignant," She would remember. "And my husband must have sensed my anger because he slunk back to the spot where he had been sleeping a few hours earlier like a penitent dog. Our neighbor did the same and I could tell by his wife's silence that the poor woman was used to this kind of situation." It was not really all that surprising. Like all overpopulated cities, Calcutta was packed with seedy drinking and gambling dens where for a few *paisas* the poor could procure some foul concoction in which to drown their sorrows for a while.

Aloka spent the night trying to console the neighbor's wife. The woman's grief tore at her heart all the more acutely because she had just discovered that her eldest son, a boy of fifteen, was in prison. He had been going off every evening but coming back regularly each morning with about ten rupees. He belonged to an organized gang that looted railway cars. Two months earlier the police had come and arrested him. Since then the three youngest children had never stopped moaning that they were hungry. "Poor woman! A daughter lost God knows where, a drunken husband, a thief of a son behind bars. What a dreadful fate!" Aloka lamented, terrified at the thought that the same plight awaited her own family if her husband did not soon find work.

The dawn had just broken after a night of anxiety, when young Maya reappeared. Her mother reared up like a cobra. "Maya," she cried, clasping her child in her arms, "Maya, where have you been?"

The adolescent girl's face was shuttered, hostile. There were traces of red on her lips and she smelled of perfume. Freeing herself from her mother's grasp and gesturing to her two small brothers, she handed her a ten-rupee note.

"Today they will not cry."

7

THREE HUNDRED THOUSAND people stranded in this mirage city lived like those two families in the streets. Others crowded into the jumble of planks and daub that were its three thousand slums.

A slum was not exactly a shantytown. It was more like a sort of poverty-stricken industrial suburb inhabited exclusively by refugees from rural areas. Everything in these slums combined to drive their inhabitants to abjection and despair: shortage of work and chronic unemployment, appallingly low wages, the inevitable child labor, the impossibility of saving, debts that could never be redeemed, the mortgaging of personal possessions and their ultimate loss sooner or later. There was also the total nonexistence of any reserve food stocks and the necessity to buy in minute quantities—one cent's worth of salt, two or three cents' worth of wood, one match, a spoonful of sugar—and the total absence of privacy with ten or twelve people sharing a single room. Yet the miracle of these concentration camps, was that the accumulation of disastrous elements was counterbalanced by other factors that allowed their inhabitants not merely to remain fully human but even to transcend their condition and become models of humanity.

In these slums people actually put love and mutual support into practice. They knew how to be tolerant of all creeds and castes, how to give respect to a stranger, how to show charity toward beggars, cripples, lepers, and even the insane. Here the weak were helped, not trampled upon. Orphans were instantly adopted by their neighbors and old people were cared for and revered by their children.

Unlike the occupants of shantytowns in other parts of the world, in these slums the former peasants who took refuge there were not marginals. They had reconstructed the life of their villages in their urban exile. An adapted and disfigured life perhaps—but nonetheless so real that their poverty itself had become a form of culture. The poor of Calcutta were not uprooted. They shared in a communal world and respected its social and religious values, maintaining their ancestral traditions and beliefs. Ultimately—and this was of primary importance—they knew that if they were poor it was not their fault, but the fault of the cyclical or permanent maledictions that beset the places where they came from.

One of the principal and oldest of Calcutta's slums was situated in the suburbs, a fifteen minutes' walk from the railway station where the Pal family first alighted. It was wedged between a railway embankment, the Calcutta-Delhi highway, and two factories. Either out of ignorance or defiance, the jute factory owner who, at the beginning of the century, had lodged his workers on this land which he had reclaimed from a fever-infested marsh, had christened the place Anand Nagar, "City of Joy." Since then the jute factory had closed its doors, but the original workers' estate had expanded to become a veritable city within a city. By now more than seventy thousand inhabitants had congregated on an expanse of ground hardly three times the size of a football field. That included some ten thousand families divided up geographically according to their various religious creeds. Sixty-three percent of them were Muslims, 37 percent Hindus, with here and there little islands of Sikhs, Jains, Christians, and Buddhists.

With its compounds of low houses constructed around minute courtyards, its red-tiled roofs, and its rectilinear alleyways, the City of Joy did indeed look more like an industrial suburb than a shantytown. Nevertheless it boasted a sad record—it had the densest concentration of humanity on this planet, two hundred thousand people per square mile. It was a place where there was not even one tree for three thousand inhabitants, without a single flower, a butterfly, or a bird, apart from vultures and crows—it was a place where children did not even know what a bush, a forest, or a pond was, where the air was so ladened with carbon dioxide and sulphur that pollution killed at least one member in every family; a place where men and beasts baked in a furnace for the eight months of

summer until the monsoon transformed their alleyways and shacks
into lakes of mud and excrement; a place where leprosy, tuberculosis, dysentery and all the malnutrition diseases, until recently, reduced the average life expectancy to one of the lowest in the world;
a place where eighty-five hundred cows and buffalo tied up to dung
heaps provided milk infected with germs. Above all, however, the
City of Joy was a place where the most extreme economic poverty
ran rife. Nine out of ten of its inhabitants did not have a single
rupee per day with which to buy half a pound of rice. Furthermore,
like all other slums, the City of Joy was generally ignored by other
citizens of Calcutta, except in case of crime or strike. Considered a
dangerous neighborhood with a terrible reputation, the haunt of
Untouchables, pariahs, social rejects, it was a world apart, living
apart from the world.

Stranded there in the course of successive migrations, those
who occupied this slum belonged to all the races of the Indian
subcontinent. Afghans of the Turkish-Iranian type, pure Indo-
Aryans from Kashmir and the Punjab, Christian Bettiahs, negroid
Oryans, Mongoloids from Nepal, Tibeto-Burmese from Assam,
aborigines, Bengalis, Afghan moneylenders, marwaris from
Rajasthan, Sikhs proudly sporting their turbans, refugees from
distant overpopulated Kerala—they were all there. So were several
thousand Tamils from the South, who lived apart in wretched huts
with dwarf pigs, their own customs, and their own language. Hindu
sages were also to be seen there, installed in small ashrams built
out of planks; groups of Bauls, these wandering Bengali mystic
monks in ocher robes, for whom the City of Joy was a port of call;
Muslim Sufis with goatees, dressed all in white; all kinds of fakirs
decked out in the most unlikely clothes, or indeed sometimes
without any clothes at all; a few Parsee fire worshippers; and Jains
with masks over their mouths to prevent their taking any life by
accidentally swallowing an insect. There were even a number of
Chinese dentists. And the mosaic would not be quite complete
without the mention of a small colony of eunuchs. Then there were
the families of the local Mafia lords, who held a controlling hand
over the slum's activities, be it real estate speculation on the cattle
sheds, illicit distillation of alcohol, eviction for nonpayment of
rent, summary trials, punishments meted out for the slightest ver-

bal offense, the black market, smoking dens, prostitution, drugs, or the control of union and political activity.

A few Anglo-Indians, the descendants of children born of the union of casteless Indians and nonranking British soldiers, and a scattering of other ethnic groups completed the population of this Tower of Babel. Until recently only the white race of the Vikings and the Celts remained unrepresented in this ants' nest. One day, however, this gap was to be filled.

8

A FEW WEEKS after the arrival of the Pal family in Calcutta, it was the turn of a European to alight at the great glory hole of Howrah Station. With his thin mustache beneath a turned-up nose, his bare forehead, and relaxed walk and manner, he looked very much like the American actor Jack Nicholson. He was dressed in jeans and an Indian shirt, with basketball shoes on his feet, and his luggage was confined to a cloth knapsack slung over his shoulder. Only a black metal cross dangling on his chest at the end of a piece of cord denoted his status. The thirty-two-year-old Pole, Stephan Kovalski, was a Catholic priest.

For him Calcutta was the culmination of a long journey that was begun in Krasnik, a little coal mining city of Poland's Silesia, where he was born in 1933. The son and grandson of mining men, Stephan Kovalski had spent his early childhood in the gloomy environment of the pit into which his father used to descend each morning. He had just reached the age of five when his father took the whole family by train to join a group of cousins who had immigrated to the North of France; there, salaries offered to coal miners were six or seven times higher than they were in Poland. One evening in the summer of 1946, an ambulance had drawn up outside the entrance of the Kovalskis' mining home. Stephan had seen his father brought out of it. His head was wrapped up in bandages. It was the summer of the great strike which paralyzed all the pits of the Northern France coal basin. In the course of violent confrontations between the miners and the forces of law and order, Stephan Kovalski's father had suffered burns on his face and lost an eye. This traumatic experience had completely transformed this quiet and profoundly religious man. He rose up in rebellion against the suffering and the pain and took refuge in active, radical, and desperate revolt. A former militant of Catholic Workingmen's Action, he went over to join the ranks of the revolutionary Marxist League, an extreme left-wing organization. Recognizable at a distance because of the patch over his eye, he came to be nicknamed "the Pirate." He got himself mixed up in a number of serious incidents. There was talk of industrial terrorism and he was arrested. A few days later, the mayor of the locality came to inform Stephan's mother, a generous, sweet-natured Polish woman, that her husband had hanged himself in his cell.

The young Stephan had been a helpless witness to his father's metamorphosis. This suicide was a terrible shock for the adolescent boy. Stephan stopped eating, to the extent that people feared for his life. He shut himself away in his room to meditate before a picture of the Sacred Shroud of Turin which his father had given him for his First Communion. The imprint of Christ's face after his removal from the Cross, together with a photograph of France's most famous female popular singer, Edith Piaf, and a few books including a life of Charles de Foucauld, an aristocrat and officer who had become a monk in the Sahara Desert, and a Polish translation of *The Keys of the Kingdom* by Cronin, were his only companions. One morning as he kissed his mother goodbye on leaving for school, he made an announcement, "Mother, I'm going to be a missionary."

Stephan Kovalski had been mulling over his decision for a long time. "There were two factors that drove me to it," he would recount years later. "The need to get away after the death of my father but, above all, the desire to achieve by other means what he had attempted to accomplish by violence. At that time large numbers of new immigrants were working in the mines in the North of France: North Africans, Senegalese, Turks, Yugoslavs. My father, who never forgot he had been an immigrant himself, had enrolled them all in his revolutionary organization. It had become their family and he was something of a father to them. Some of them used to spend the evening at our house when they came out of the pit. There wasn't any television yet, so people talked—about everything, but especially about justice, solidarity, fraternity, about what they needed most. One day a Senegalese immigrant challenged my father: 'You're always saying you're close to us but do you really know anything about us? Why don't you go and live for a while in an African shantytown or in our poor countryside? Then you'd have a better idea of why we were forced to leave and come here to break up stones all day at the bottom of a mine.' I had never forgotten what this man had said."

The African's suggestion influenced the boy profoundly. Several years previously, during the cruel summer of 1940, Stephan had been devastated by the sight of the exodus of Belgian refugees, fleeing before the German armies on the road that ran along the back of the miners' estate. After school he had rushed off to take those wretched people something to drink. Later he witnessed the Nazi roundups of Jewish children. Together with his parents, he threw them bread and cheese from the family's own rations, underneath the barbed wire. All through the war these working-class people had shared their meager resources with others. Stephan Kovalski's vocation to serve was born out of this very revolt against injustice, and out of the life of love and sharing in which he had grown up.

On leaving the mining community, he spent three years at a small seminary in Belgium. The religious instruction he received there seemed to him far removed from everyday exigencies, but deeper study of the Gospel reinforced his desire to identify himself with the plight of the poor. Each vacation period he went home to embrace his mother before hitchhiking on to the Paris area where he sought out a kind of bearded saint. At that time the Abbé Pierre, a French priest who was also a member of Parliament, with his old béret on his head and his rag and bone disciples at his side, provided help for the most needy with the proceeds from the sale of anything they could salvage, by clearing out the cellars and attics of the more privileged.

Later, at the Louvain seminary in Belgium, Kovalski met the man who was to give a definitive direction to his journey. Padre Ignacio Fraile belonged to a Spanish order founded in the last century by a priest from the province of Asturias, now being considered for beatification by the Vatican. The Fraternity of San Vincente gathered together priests and consecrated laymen who took the vows of poverty, chastity, obedience, and charity in order to "seek out the poorest of the poor and the disinherited in the

places where they are, to share their life, and to die with them."
Small communities of priests and brothers sprung up in the industrial suburbs of numerous cities in Europe, Latin America, Africa,
Asia, everywhere in fact where people were suffering. There were
several in France itself.

Stephan Kovalski was ordained a priest on August 15, 1960,
on the Feast of the Virgin Mary. He was just twenty-seven years
old. That very evening he caught a train to spend a few hours with
his mother, who had been in the hospital for three months, suffering from cardiac problems. Before embracing her son for a last
time, she gave him a carefully wrapped box. Inside it, on a bed of
cotton wool, he found a black metal cross engraved with two dates:
that of his birth and that of his ordination. "Never be parted from
it, my boy," she said to him, clasping her son's hand in her own.
"This cross will protect you wherever you go."

Knowing that the most forsaken people were to be found not
in Europe but in the third world, Stephan Kovalski had studied
Spanish during his last year at the seminary, in the hope of being
sent to the shantytowns, or *favelas*, of South America. Instead,
however, it was to India that his fraternity required him to go.

India! A subcontinent with exceptional potential wealth—yet
where areas and social groups of overwhelming poverty survived.
A land of intense spirituality and of savage racial, political, and
religious conflicts. A land of saints like Gandhi, Aurobindo,
Ramakrishna, and Vivekananda, and of political leaders who were
sometimes odiously corrupt. A land that manufactured rockets and
satellites but where eight out of ten of its inhabitants had never
traveled faster than their oxen could pull their carts. A land of
incomparable beauty and variety, and of hideous prospects like the
slums of Bombay or Calcutta. A land where the sublime often
stood side by side with the very worst this world can offer, but
where both elements were always more vibrant, more human, and
ultimately more attracting than anywhere else.

Impatient to leave, Stephan Kovalski applied for a resident's
visa. His request marked the beginning of a prolonged purgatory.
Month after month for five years the Indian authorities promised
the delivery of the essential document. Unlike a temporary tourist
visa, a resident's permit in fact required the approval of the ministry of Foreign Affairs in New Delhi. The inclusion of his status as a

priest on Stephan Kovalski's application had given rise to difficulties. For some time India had not been permitting foreign missionaries to enter its territory. The motives for this prohibition had never been officially defined but the massive number of conversions from Hinduism to Christianity had been unequivocally denounced.

While awaiting his visa, Stephan Kovalski made his home first in a shantytown of Algerians in the Saint-Michel district of Marseilles, then in a home for Senegalese immigrants in Saint-Denis, near Paris. True to his ideal of fraternity he shared in everything: the exhausting work that was remunerated with wages below the legal rates, the punishing mattresses of immigrants' hotels, the foul stews from barrack-room-style kitchens. He became successively a machine operator, fitter, turner, metal founder, and storekeeper.

On August 15, 1965, the fifth anniversary of his ordination, Stephan Kovalski finally determined that the waiting had gone on long enough. With the agreement of his superiors, he asked for a simple tourist visa. This time, in the space left for him to fill in his profession, he wrote "skilled factory worker." On the following day, his passport was returned to him complete with the precious visa duly stamped with the seal of the three lions of the Emperor Ashoka, chosen by the founders of modern India as the emblem of their republic. Despite the fact that the permit authorized him to stay in India for only three months, now at least the great adventure of Stephan Kovalski's life could begin. Once he was actually in Calcutta, his assigned destination, he would try and obtain a permanent resident's permit.

Bombay, the "Gateway to India!" It was via this port on the West coast, which had for three centuries provided a first glimpse of the continent to hundreds of thousands of British soldiers and administrators, that Stephan Kovalski made his entrance into India. In order to familiarize himself with the country before reaching Calcutta at the other extremity of the huge peninsula, he chose to take the longest possible approach route. At Victoria Station, a prodigious caravansary bristling with neo-Gothic bell towers, he climbed into a third-class compartment of a train leaving for Trivandrum and the South.

The train stopped at every station. As it did, all passengers got

out to fulfill their bodily needs, to wash, to cook their food, in the
middle of a teeming mass of vendors, bearers, cows, dogs, and
crows. "I looked around me and did as the others did," Stephan
Kovalski was to relate in a letter to his mother. On purchasing an
orange, however, he was to discover that he wasn't quite as the
others were. He paid for the fruit with a one-rupee note but the
vendor failed to give him any change. His request for it was met
with an expression of fury and disdain: "How could a *sahib** be so
short of cash?" "I peeled the orange and had broken off a quarter
of it when a little girl planted herself in front of me, her big eyes
black with kohl. Of course I gave her the fruit and she scampered
off. I followed her. She had taken it to share with her brothers and
sisters." A moment later Stephan Kovalski had nothing but a smile
to offer a young shoe-shine boy who was circling around him; but a
smile does not fill an empty stomach. Kovalski foraged in his knapsack and offered the boy the banana he had promised himself he
would eat out of anybody's sight. "At that rate I was condemned to
die of starvation very rapidly," he would recall.

In addition to the congestion of the cars there was the sauna
heat to contend with, the dust heavy with soot that burned the
throat, and all the smells, exclamations, tears, and laughter that
made this railway journey a truly royal way to get to know a people.
It was in the restaurant of one of the stations in the South that
Kovalski experienced his first Indian meal. "I began by watching
the people around me," he recounted. "They were eating with the
fingers of only their right hands. To make up small balls of rice and
dip them into the sauce without the balls disintegrating and without burning your fingers to the bone involved a right set of gymnastics. As for your mouth, esophagus, and stomach, they're set on
fire by those murderous spices! I must have presented a somewhat
comical spectacle, because all the clients of the restaurant cracked
up. It wasn't every day that they could have a good laugh at a poor
sahib who had undertaken to master his certificate of Indianization."

Ten days later, after a short stopover in a shantytown near
Madras, Stephan Kovalski arrived in Calcutta.

* A respectful name formally reserved for the white foreigners.

9

No amount of wretchedness, not even utter destitution on a piece of pavement in Calcutta, could alter the ritual of the world's cleanest people. With the very first grind of the streetcar on the rails of the avenue, Hasari Pal would get up to respond to "the call of nature." He went to the sewer which ran along open to the heavens on the opposite side of the avenue. It was a formality that was to become progressively shorter in duration for a man deprived of nourishment. He lifted up his cotton *longhi* and squatted down over the gutter, and on the edge of the pavement dozens of other men did likewise. No one took any notice of them. It was part of the life and the surrounding scenery. Aloka and the other women had done the same, even earlier, before the men awoke. Afterward Hasari went to take his place in the line of men waiting at the fountain for their daily bath. This fountain was in reality a fire hydrant which issued a brownish liquid pumped directly out of the Hooghly River. When his turn came Hasari would squat on his heels, pour a bowl of water over his head, and scrub himself vigorously from head to toe with the poors' soap, a little ball made out of a mixture of clay and ashes. Neither the biting winter cold nor the pangs of an empty stomach would accelerate the completion of this ancestral ritual of purification, which young and old alike piously adhered to each morning.

Hasari then left with his two eldest children for the Bara Bazar. The market was always overflowing with so many goods that there was invariably some food, in a more or less rotten condition, to be gleaned from its refuse heaps. Hundreds of poor luckless families strayed like this father and his children through the same labyrinth,

hoping for the same miracle: the discovery of a compatriot from
their village, their district, their province, a relative, an acquaintance, the friend of a friend, a member of their caste, their subcaste, a branch of their subcaste; in short, someone who might be
prepared to take them under his protective wing and find them two
or three hours, perhaps a whole day, or even—miracle of all miracles—several days of work. This ceaseless quest was not quite as
unrealistic as it might appear. Every individual in India is always
linked to the rest of the social body by a network of incredibly
diversified ties, with the result that no one in this gigantic country
of seven hundred and fifty million inhabitants could ever be completely abandoned—except, perhaps, for Hasari Pal whom this
"inhuman city" seemed obstinately to reject. That morning, the
morning of the sixth day, he left his children to forage among the
refuse while he went off once more to scour the bazaar in every
possible direction. He offered his services to dozens of traders and
transporters. Several times he even followed overloaded carts in
the faint hope that one of the coolies would eventually keel over
with exhaustion and he might take his place. With his belly screaming with hunger, his head empty, and his heart heavy with despair,
the former peasant eventually collapsed against a wall. Through
his dizziness, he heard a voice. "Would you like to earn a few
rupees?"

The small man with spectacles looked more like an office
employee than a trader from the bazaar. Hasari stared at the
stranger in astonishment and motioned that he would. "All you
have to do is to follow me. I'll take you somewhere where they'll
take a little of your blood and give you thirty rupees for it. That's
fifteen for me and fifteen for you."

"Thirty rupees for my blood!" repeated Hasari, paralyzed
with amazement. "Who's going to want to take blood off a poor
bum like me and on top of that give me thirty rupees?"

"Don't be a fool! Blood is blood!" replied the man with
glasses. "Whether it comes from a pandit or a pariah, from a
marwari bursting at the seams with money or from a bum like you.
It's all still blood."

Struck by this logic, Hasari made an effort to get back on his
feet and follow the stranger.

The man belonged to a profession practiced in abundance in a city where the slightest suggestion of profit inevitably attracted a swarm of parasitical intermediaries known as "middlemen." For every transaction or service provided there were one or more intermediaries who each took their cut. The individual with the glasses was a procurer. He tracked down donors for one of the numerous private blood banks that flourished in Calcutta. His technique was always the same. He went prowling around the entrances to the work sites, factories, markets, anywhere he knew he would find men without work, ready to agree to anything for the sake of a few rupees. The taboos of Islam forbad Muslims to give their blood. He was, therefore, interested only in Hindus.

For a man at the end of his resources, the sale of his blood represented a last chance of survival, and for astute and unscrupulous businessmen this meant the opportunity to make a fortune. The need for blood in the hospitals and clinics of an immense metropolis like Calcutta amounted to several tens of thousands of bottles a year. Since the four or five official blood banks of the State of Bengal were incapable of meeting such a demand, it was only to be expected that private entrepreneurs should try and take advantage of the market. All they had to do was wangle the complicity of a doctor, lay a request before the Health Department in his name, rent premises, acquire a refrigerator, a few syringes, pipettes, and bottles, and engage a dispensary assistant. The result was a roaring trade with an annual turnover in excess of ten million rupees, one million dollars. Only the fierce competition to which these dispensaries, private or otherwise, were subjected could, it seemed, impede the flow of their profits. Hasari Pal had just put his finger on one of the best organized rackets of a city which, according to connoisseurs of such matters, practiced a multitude of rackets with a degree of art and imagination that would turn Naples, Marseilles, or New York green with envy.

Hasari followed his bespectacled "benefactor" through the streets of the business quarter, then along Chowringhee Road and at last into Park Street, the street for luxury goods, restaurants, and nightclubs. At the upper end of the block and in the adjoining streets were several blood dispensaries. That of No. 49 Randal Street had been set up in what used to be a garage. Hardly had Hasari and the procurer reached its door than they were accosted by a man with an emaciated face and a mouth reddened by a quid of betel. "Are you coming for blood?" the man asked in a low voice.

The procurer with the glasses acquiesced with that inimitable wagging of the head that is so distinctively Indian. "In that case, follow me," said the stranger with a wink. "I know another bank where they pay forty rupees. Five for me, the rest for you two. Agreed?"

This man was another cog in the wheel and was procuring for a rival blood bank two streets farther on.

A notice bore the initials of its three owners. The CRC was one of the oldest dispensaries in Calcutta. The ten additional rupees it offered had nothing whatever to do with generosity. It simply meant that it took ten liquid ounces from its donors, instead of the usual eight. It is true to say that it added to this remuneration a royal bonus for a man with an empty stomach: a banana and three glucose biscuits. Its boss was a well-known hematologist, a Doctor Rana. He too was but another cog in the wheel of the racket. As a director of one of the state official blood banks, he had no difficulty in diverting donors and purchasers to his own private dispensary. Nothing could be easier. All you had to do was to tell the donors who turned up at the official blood bank that the CRC paid better rates. As for the clients who came to buy blood for an emergency or for a future operation, the doctor simply had them informed that bottles of the required blood group were provisionally out of stock at the official bank but available at his CRC.

Yet such practices could pass for innocent commercial games by comparison with the lack of medical precautions which cursed the majority of dispensaries. The World Health Organization had stipulated a certain number of vital rules with regard to the analyses that must be undertaken before any blood was taken for use in transfusions. They were simple tests which cost little and which made possible the detection of, among other things, the hepatitis B virus or any venereal diseases. Yet at the CRC, as at numerous other private blood banks at that time, viruses seemed to be the very last worry. All that really mattered was profit.

Hasari was invited to sit down on a stool. While one male nurse knotted a rubber tourniquet around his biceps, another stuck a needle into the vein in the hollow of his elbow. Both of them watched the flow of red liquid with a measure of fascination that grew as the level in the bottle rose. Was it the sight of blood, the idea that he was being "emptied like the goatskin bottle of a water vendor in the Bara Bazar," or the lack of food? Hasari's strength began to fail him. His vision blurred and he started to sweat thick beads of perspiration, despite the fact that he was shivering with cold. The voices of the attendants seemed to reach him from another planet, through a strange clamoring of bells. Through a halo, he could just make out the glasses of his "benefactor." Next he felt the grip of two hands holding him on his stool. Then everything went blank. He had passed out.

So banal was the incident that the attendants did not interrupt their work. Every day they saw men exhausted by deprivation faint as they sold their blood. If it had been up to them they would have pumped the inert bodies dry. They were paid by the bottle.

When Hasari opened his eyes again, a dreamlike vision appeared above him: one of the men in white overalls was offering him a banana.

"There you are, little girl. Get this fruit down you. That'll bring you back as Bhim!"* The attendant mocked him gently.

Then he took a receipt book out of his pocket and inquired, "What's your name?" He scribbled out a few words, tore off the sheet, and directed Hasari in a peremptory tone to "Sign here." Hasari made a cross and pocketed the forty rupees under the covetous gazes of the two vultures who had brought him there. The money would be divided up outside. What the peasant did not know was that he had put his signature to a receipt for forty-five rupees, and not forty. The attendants, too, were taking their commission.

Light-headed and reeling, lost in neighborhoods that were unknown to him, Hasari would take hours to find the piece of pavement where his wife and children were waiting for him. Out of the seventeen and a half rupees that the procurers had left him, he decided to spend five on celebrating with his family the joy of actually having earned some money in the "inhuman city." He bought a pound of *barfi*, the delicious Bengali nougat richly wrapped in a thin silver film, and some *mansours*, yellow sweetmeats

* The strongest of the Pandavas, the five heroic brothers in the great epic tale of the Mahabharata.

made out of chick-pea flour and sweetened milk. Farther on he chose twenty or so paper cones full of *muri*, the puffed rice that crunched between your teeth, so that the neighbors on the pavement could share in the celebration. Finally he could not resist the desire to give himself a treat. He stopped in front of one of the innumerable niches where vendors as impassive as buddhas prepared their *pan*, those subtle quids made out of a little finely chopped betel nut, a pinch of tobacco, a suggestion of lime, chutney, and cardamom, all rolled up in a betel leaf skillfully folded and sealed with a clove. *Pan* gave energy. Above all, it curbed the appetite.

When Aloka caught sight of her husband, a lump rose to her throat. "Dear God, he's been drinking again," she thought. Then, seeing him laden with parcels, she feared that he had committed some felony. She ran to meet him but the children had already preceded her. Like a litter of lion cubs throwing themselves on the male returning with a gazelle carcass, they were already sharing out the nougat.

In the rush and tumble no one noticed the small red mark that Hasari still bore in the fold of his arm.

10

IT WAS HERE. He was sure it was. The exaltation that suddenly seized Stephan Kovalski, the feeling of plenitude at being at last "with them," could not be designed to deceive him. It was definitely here, in this gray, filthy, poor, sad, stinking, muddy place. In this wild turmoil of men, women, children, and animals. In this entanglement of huts built of beaten earth, this jumble of alleyways full of refuse and open drains, in this murderous pollution of sulphur and fumes, in this uproar of voices, shouting, weeping, tools, machinery and loudspeakers. Yes, it was definitely to this slum at the far corner of the world that his God had sent him. "How rewarding it was to discover the absolute conviction that I had at last arrived where I was supposed to be," he was later to say. "My enthusiasm and yearning to share had been right to push me into embarking on an experience considered impossible for a Westerner. I was so deliriously happy, I could have walked barefoot over hot coals."

A few days previously, as soon as he got off the train, Stephan Kovalski had paid a call on the bishop of Calcutta. The bishop dwelled in a beautiful colonial-style house surrounded by a vast garden in a residential area. He was an Anglo-Indian of about fifty, with a white cassock and a majestic manner. On his head he wore a purple skullcap, and on his finger an episcopal ring.

"I have come to live with the poor," the Polish priest said to him simply.

"You'll have no difficulty in finding them," sighed the prelate. "Alas, the poor are everywhere here."

He gave Stephan Kovalski a letter of recommendation to the

parish priest of a working-class district on the other side of the river.

With its two white painted towers, the church could be seen for some distance. It was an imposing building decorated with vividly colored stained-glass windows, and inside were a rich supply of statues of the saints, collection boxes, and fans suspended above the pews reserved for the faithful. Its name was like a challenge cast before the innumerable homeless people camping in the square and surrounding streets. It sprawled in luminous letters across the entire width of the façade: Our Lady of the Loving Heart.

The rector of the parish came from Goa—Father Alberto Cordeiro had a very dark skin and carefully combed curly hair. With his rounded cheeks and his plumpish paunch beneath an immaculate cassock, he looked more like a monsignor of the Roman Curia than a priest of the poor. In the courtyard of the church was parked his car, and several Christian servants assured him the soft comfortable existence, which befitted a rector in charge of a parish.

The sudden advent of a foreign priest in jeans and basketball shoes somewhat disconcerted the ecclesiastic.

"Don't you wear a cassock?" he asked.

"It wasn't exactly the most comfortable attire to travel about your country, especially in the heat," explained Stephan Kovalski.

"Ah," sighed the rector. "You Westerners can allow yourselves such flights of fancy. You will always be respected! Your skin is white! Whereas for us Indian priests a cassock is both a symbol and our protection. In a country that recognizes the sacred, it guarantees us a place apart."

The Indian acquainted himself with the bishop's message.

"You really want to go and live in a slum?"

"That's why I'm here."

Father Cordeiro appeared aghast. With a grave and preoccupied air, he began to pace up and down the room. "But that's not what our mission as priests is about! Here the people only think of wearing you down. You give them the tip of your finger and instantly they take the end of your arm. No, my dear fellow, you won't be doing them any service by going and sharing their existence. All you risk doing is encouraging their latent laziness and turning them into permanent dependents."

He stopped walking and planted himself in front of Kovalski. "And then, you won't be there indefinitely! When you go off home, it'll be here, in my house, that they'll come clamoring that the clergy aren't doing anything for them. But if we Indian priests were to take the plunge, they'd have no respect for us anymore."

The idea of going and living in the middle of a slum had evidently never occurred to the good Father Cordeiro. Yet Kovalski would later realize that this reluctance to mix with the slum population did not necessarily spring from a lack of charity, but rather from a desire that was common enough among the local clergy, to keep a certain distance between themselves and the masses, and one that arose out of traditional Indian respect for social hierarchy.

Despite his very natural reservations, the rector proved to be most understanding. He entrusted Stephan Kovalski to one of his assistants, an Anglo-Indian Christian who undertook to find him a room in the large nearby slum of Anand Nagar, the "City of Joy."

It was five o'clock in the evening on the following day when the Pole and his guide presented themselves at the entrance to the slum. The red of the sinking sun was veiled in a shroud of grayish vapor. A smell of burning infused the city, as everywhere *chulas* were lit to cook the evening meal. In the narrow alleyways the air was laden with an acrid density which burned the throat and lungs. One sound distinguished itself from all the others—the noise of coughing that racked innumerable chests.

Before arriving in Calcutta, Stephan Kovalski had spent a few days in a slum in the Madras area, built near a mine, in open countryside. It was a slum full of light and hope, for its occupants left it each morning to go work outside and they knew that one day they would live in a proper industrial estate. At Anand Nagar the opposite was true: everyone gave the impression of having been there forever, and of being likely to remain there forever. It was an impression that was directly reinforced by the intense activity with which the slum vibrated. Could the people he discovered as he picked his way behind his Anglo-Indian guide conceivably be described as "lazy?" "Ants more likely," he thought. Every single one of them, from the most worn-out old man to children hardly yet able to walk, was busy with some task. Everywhere, on the doorstep to each hut, at the foot of every stall, in a succession of little workshops or minifactories, Kovalski discovered people industriously selling, trading, manufacturing, tinkering, repairing, sorting, cleaning, nailing, gluing, piercing, carrying, pulling, pushing. After six hundred feet of exploration, he felt as if he were drunk.

Forty-nine Nizamudhin Lane—the address was painted across two planks nailed together which served as a door to a windowless hovel, scarcely more than one yard wide and twice as long. The floor was of beaten earth, and through the missing tiles of the roof one could see pieces of sky. There was no furniture, no electricity, no running water. "Exactly the room I need," appreciated Kovalski, "ideally suited to a life of poverty. With, as a bonus, the right environment."

Along the door ran an open drain overflowing with nauseating black slime. And just opposite rose a pile of refuse. On the left, a small platform planted over the drain sheltered a tiny tea shop under a bamboo roof. All the occupants of this area were Muslims except the old man running the tea shop who was a Hindu.

The owner of the room, a stout Bengali dressed in Western clothes, passed for one of the richest men in the slum. He owned a block of houses at the end of the alley, where the latrines and the well were. He had cups of tea with sweetened milk brought from the nearby tea shop.

"You're quite sure, Father, that this is where you want to live?" he asked, examining the visitor with incredulity.

"Quite sure," said Stephan Kovalski. "How much does the rent come to?"

"Twenty-five rupees a month [two dollars and fifty cents]. Payable in advance."

"Twenty-five rupees?" the Anglo-Indian exclaimed indignantly. "Twenty-five rupees for a miserable room without a window. That's highway robbery!"

"It'll do," interrupted Stephan Kovalski, taking his money out of his pocket. "Here's three months' rent."

"I was so happy I would have given the moon for a lifetime

lease of that hovel," he recalled later. He was soon to discover how privileged he was: ten or twelve persons were living in huts like his.

The deal concluded, Father Cordeiro's envoy lost no time in presenting the newcomer to the few Christians of the City of Joy. None of them would believe that the *sahib* in jeans who appeared suddenly in front of their slum houses was an envoy from God. "But as soon as they were convinced," he would later recount, "I might have mistaken myself for the Messiah!" In one of the compounds a young woman fell to her knees. "Father, bless my child," she said, holding out to him the baby she was clutching in her arms. "And bless us all for we are not worthy that a priest should enter under our roof." They all knelt down and Kovalski made the sign of the cross over their heads. Discovering that he was going to stay among them, they all wanted to organize his household. Some offered a bucket, others a mat, an oil lamp, a blanket. The poorer they were, the more eager they were to give. That night he returned home followed by an escort laden with gifts, "just like one of the three kings from the Nativity."

So began the first evening of his new Indian life, an evening that was to form one of the most intense memories of his existence. "It was already dark. Night falls very early in the tropics. I lit an oil lamp lent to me by one family. They had even had the delicacy to think of leaving me several matches. I unrolled the mat I had been given, then sat down on the ground with my back propped against the wall, and turned out my old knapsack bought, one day, in the Arab quarter of Marseilles. From it I took out my razor, my shaving brush, toothbrush, the small medicine box given to me by friends at the factory when I left, a change of underpants and shirt and my Jerusalem Bible, in other words, all my worldly possessions. Between the pages of the Gospels was the picture that had never left my side during my years among the destitute and suffering. I unfolded it carefully and contemplated it for a long while."

It was the photograph of the Sacred Shroud of Turin given to Stephan by his father years ago. The face of Christ imprinted on his shroud, the face of a man with downcast eyes and swollen cheeks, with punctured brow and a torn beard, that man who died upon the Cross was that evening for Stephan Kovalski the very incarnation of all the martyrs of the slum where he had just arrived. "For me, a committed believer, each one of them wore that same

face of Jesus Christ proclaiming to humanity from the heights of
Golgotha all the pain but also all the hope of man rejected. That
was the reason for my coming. I was there because of the cry of the
crucified Christ: "I thirst," in order to give a voice to the hunger
and thirst for justice of those who here mounted each day on the
Cross, and who knew how to face that death which we in the West
no longer know how to affront without despair. Nowhere else was
that icon more in its rightful place than in that slum."

Stephan Kovalski pinned up the picture with the aid of two
matches stuck in the pisé wall. After a while he tried to pray, but his
efforts were in vain. He was dazed. He needed some time to adjust
to his new incarnation. As he was pondering, a little girl appeared
on the threshold, barefoot and dressed in rags but with a flower in
the end of her pigtail. She was carrying an aluminum bowl full of
rice and vegetables. She set it down in front of Kovalski, joined her
hands in the Indian gesture of greeting, bowed her head, smiled,
and ran away. "I gave thanks to God for this apparition and for this
meal provided by brothers unknown to me. Then I ate, as they do,
with my fingers. In the depths of this hovel, I felt everything was
assuming a very distinctive dimension. So it was that my fingers'
contact with the rice made me understand that first night how
much the food was not a dead thing, not something neutral, but
rather a gift of life."

Toward nine o'clock, as the noise of the streets died away,
Kovalski began to be aware of the echoes of the life that was going
on around him: conversations in the nearby rooms, arguments,
tears, fits of coughing. Then the searing call of a muezzin surged
out of a loudspeaker, followed immediately by the voices of women
reciting verses of the Koran. A little later, the Muslims' prayer was
succeeded by another litany. Coming from the tea shop opposite, it
consisted of one simple syllable indefinitely repeated. "*Om* . . .
Om . . . *Om* . . ." chanted the elderly Hindu who kept the shop.
A mystic invocation which for thousands of years had assisted
Hindus to enter into contact with God, this *om* diffused an ineffable
inner peace. Stephan Kovalski had heard it for the first time in the
villages in the South and the vibrations of this simple syllable had
seemed to him to be charged with such power, such profundity of
prayer, that he had adopted it to open his own invocations to the
Lord. Pronouncing the *Om* required no conscious effort. "The *Om*

came all by itself and prolonged itself, vibrating like a prayer in the heart," he would say. "That night, as I repeated the *Oms* that came from the other side of the street, I experienced the sensation not only of speaking to God but also of taking a step forward into the inner mystery of Hinduism, something which was very important in helping me to grasp the real reasons for my presence in that slum."

Shortly after midnight silence enveloped the City of Joy. The prayer and the palavers were stilled, along with the coughs and the children's tears. Sleep had come to Anand Nagar. Numb with fatigue and emotion, Stephan Kovalski too felt the need to close his eyes. Folding up his shirt and jeans to form a pillow, he stretched out on the narrow mat. He discovered then that his room was exactly as long as he was tall: six feet. After a last look at the Sacred Shroud of Christ, he blew out the lamp and closed his eyes with an inner felicity such as he had not experienced since the day of his ordination five years earlier.

It was then that a frenzied chorus struck up right above his head. Striking a match, he discovered a team of rats chasing one another about on the bamboo framing and rushing down the walls to the accompaniment of a cacophony of shrill cries. He leaped to his feet and, despite his desire not to wake his neighbors, undertook to chase the intruders, hitting them with his shoe. But as fast as one group made off, others arrived through the holes in the roofing. The magnitude of the invasion forced him to give up. However disagreeable cohabitation of this sort might be, he realized that it was an inevitable part of his new life. With determined resignation he lay down again, but almost immediately he felt something stirring in his hair. Lighting the lamp once more, he shook his head and saw an enormous hairy centipede fall out of it. Fervent admirer of Mahatma Gandhi and his principles of nonviolence that he was, he nevertheless crushed it. Later he was to learn the identity of the creature: a scolopendra whose sting could be as venomous as a scorpion's. For the second time he lay down again and recited a chaplet of *Oms* in the hope of regaining some serenity. The City of Joy had further surprises in store, however, for the Pole's first night within its confines. Indian mosquitoes have as a distinguished characteristic the fact that they are minute, make very little noise, and tease you endlessly before making up their minds to bite. The effect is a torture of anticipation which, if it were not Indian, would almost certainly be Chinese.

A few hours later, it was the sound of something resembling a bombardment that woke up Kovalski from a brief interval of sleep. On opening his door, he discovered a delivery van in the alleyway, unloading coal outside the shop of the man who sold fuel. He was just about to lie down again when he discerned in the darkness two small silhouettes creeping under the vehicle. The coal merchant, a man with wader's legs, had spotted the young sneak thieves too. He rained down such a shower of curses upon them that they scampered off. There was the sound of galloping, then a great splash and cries. Certain that one of the fugitives had just fallen in the large sewer that cut across the alleyway a little farther down, Kovalski rushed to the rescue, but he had hardly taken three strides before a firm grasp arrested his progress.

Without ever being able to recognize the face of the man who had grabbed him, he understood the message. "I was being invited not to get mixed up with the private affairs of the City of Joy."

11

THE SALE OF BLOOD enabled the five members of the Pal family to hold out for four days. During that period they fed themselves mainly on bananas. Found in abundance and sold cheaply, this fruit was a gift of providence for the poor of India. In Calcutta its nutritive and curative qualities had made it the object of a veritable cult. At the time of the great festivities in honor of the goddess Durga, patroness of the city, banana trees appeared on the altars, draped in white saris with a red border and venerated as the wife of Ganesh, god of good fortune.

The Pals also lived on what the two eldest children gleaned from the Bara Bazar, while their father was out looking for work. The last few *paisas* of the last rupee were devoted to the purchase of four cow dung cakes to use to boil up a last stew of scraps and peelings on the neighbors' *chula*. When, finally, there was nothing left, Hasari made a heroic decision. He would go back and sell some more of his blood.

From a physiological point of view, it was a mad idea; but then this "inhuman city" was a city where madness prevailed. A medical report revealed that many men at the depths of despair did not hesitate to turn up at the doors of the blood banks every week. They did not generally live to old age: they would be found dead of anemia in some street, or on a bed in Mother Teresa's home for the dying, snuffed out like the flame of a candle deprived of oxygen. The same report also revealed that in the case of one donor in four, the hemoglobin level of the blood was less than half the minimum acceptable level. How many dispensaries, however, were actually concerned with the hemoglobin content of the blood that they collected? In any case, as Hasari was to learn, there was a way of faking the requisite content.

That day the rates of the CRC blood bank were so alluring that crowds were waiting at the door. All the procurers for rival establishments had assembled there to attempt to divert some of the clientele toward their own employers. Hasari was immediately accosted by an individual with two gold front teeth. "Forty rupees," whispered the man with the air of a prostitute lowering her price. "Thirty for you, ten for me."

"Thirty rupees! That's almost double what I got last time," thought Hasari, not yet knowing that in Calcutta the price of blood varied from day to day just like the rates for jute or mustard oil at the stock exchange in Dalhousie Square. The difference in fee stemmed in fact mainly from the capacity of the middlemen to assess the naïveté of their preys and hence to fleece them with greater or less rapacity. With his very first glance, the man with the gold teeth had registered the stigmata on Hasari's arm, which marked him as a professional.

The Paradise Blood Bank was aptly named. Painted in pink and furnished with comfortable seats, it had been set up in an outbuilding of one of the most modern and expensive clinics in Calcutta, exclusively frequented by rich *marwari* businessmen and their families. The nurse in immaculate white overalls and cap, who was in charge of admitting the donors, grimaced at the sight of the candidate's pathetic appearance. She made him sit down on a chair with a reclining back. Unlike the attendants at the CRC, however, she did not plunge a needle into his arm. Much to the amazement of the peasant, she confined herself to pricking his index finger and making a drop of blood fall onto a glass plate. As for the man with the gold teeth, he realized all too well what was happening. "The bitch is sabotaging me," he grumbled.

He had guessed correctly. An instant later the young woman informed him politely that his client's blood did not meet with the requirements of the dispensary. The reason given would have precluded the majority of the inhabitants of Calcutta's slums: inadequate hemoglobin level.

The blow was a harsh one for Hasari.

"Don't you know anywhere else?" he pleaded with the procurer as soon as they were back in the street. "I don't even have a coin to buy a banana for my children."

The man laid a friendly arm around his shoulder. "You shouldn't fool around with things like that, friend. For the moment, what you've got in your veins is water. And if you don't watch out, your family'll soon be seeing your ashes floating on the Hooghly."

Hasari felt so hounded by poverty that this prospect seemed inevitable anyway.

"This time we're done for," he sighed. "We shall all die." Hardened as he was by his extraordinary profession, the procurer was nevertheless moved by Hasari's distress. "Don't cry, my friend. Come on, I'll give you a present." He dragged the peasant over to the nearest drugstore where he bought a bottle of tablets. The chemists of the Swiss laboratory that manufactured them had most likely never foreseen the use the desperate people of the third world would make of these tablets.

"There you are, friend," said the procurer, handing Hasari a packet of ferrous sulphate tablets. "Take three a day and come back here in a week's time. Remember, in seven days exactly. But just you mind!" he added, suddenly menacing, "Don't you fail to turn up or that junk in your veins could well flow free of charge." Then softening again, he concluded, "I'll take you to a place where they'll think your blood's just fine, so fine that they'll want to drain it out to the very last drop."

12

THE EVENTS THAT marked the life of Stephan Kovalski the
day after his first night in the "City of Joy" might well seem insignificant. Yet in a place where seventy thousand people live together
in a state of promiscuity and deplorable conditions of hygiene,
even the ordinary necessities of everyday living present particular
problems. The performance of natural bodily functions was just
one example. The envoy of the rector from the neighboring parish
had urged Kovalski to go to the latrines in a Hindu quarter which
was also occupied by a number of Christians.

For a Hindu, the response to "the call of nature" is an act that
must be undertaken according to a very precise ritual. The place
chosen must not be situated within the proximity of a temple, a
banyan tree, a riverbank, a pond, a well, or a crossroad frequented
by people. The ground must not be light in color or plowed, but
flat and open and, above all, set apart from all habitation. Before
executing the act, a Hindu must remove his sandals—that is, if he
has any—squat down as low as possible, and never get up in
midperformance. He must take care, on pain of committing a grave
offense, not to look at the sun, the moon, the stars, a fire, a Brahmin, or a religious image. He must observe silence and refrain
from the sacrilege of turning around to examine his handiwork.
Finally there are rules that prescribe the means by which he must
go on to complete his ablutions with a mixture of earth and water.

The authors of these sacred instructions had obviously never
envisaged that millions of people would one day be crammed into
urban jungles, devoid of any open space set apart from places of
habitation. For Hindus in the City of Joy, therefore, "the call of

nature" could only be attended to in public, over an open sewer in the alleyways, or in one of the rare cabins recently distributed by local town planners and christened "latrines."

What an adventure his first visit to one such public convenience was for Stephan Kovalski! At four o'clock in the morning, access to it was already obstructed by a line of several dozen people. The first had already been there for nearly two hours. The arrival of the *sahib* in jeans and basketball shoes provoked a lively upsurge of curiosity and amusement, and all the more so because, in his ignorance of the customs of the country, the Pole had already committed an unforgivable blunder: he had brought with him a few sheets of toilet paper. Was it conceivable that anyone should want to preserve in paper a defilement expelled from the body and then leave it for other people? Showing him a tinful of water he was holding in his hand, a young lad tried to make Stephan understand that he should wash himself, then clean the bowl. Looking around him, Kovalski established that indeed everyone had brought a similar receptacle full of water. Some people even had several that they shuttled forward with their feet as the line gradually advanced. "I understood that they were keeping places for others who were absent," the priest later said.

A toothless old man came over to offer the Pole his pitcher. "I took the object with a smile of gratitude, not realizing that I had just committed a second act of sacrilege that would unleash a further explosion of hilarity. I had grasped the receptacle with my left hand, which was reserved for impure contacts. Before reaching the public conveniences, I had to cross a veritable lake of excrement. This additional trial was a courtesy of the cesspool emptiers, who had been on strike for five months. The stench was so foul that I no longer knew which was the more unbearable: the smell or the sight. That people could actually remain good humored in the middle of so much abjection, seemed quite sublime to me. They laughed and joked—especially the children who somehow brought the freshness and gaiety of their games into that cesspool. I came back from that escapade as groggy as a boxer knocked out in the first round. Nowhere else had I ever been subjected to such an onslaught."

On the way back, the Pole noticed a number of hostile gazes upon him. It was hardly surprising. The rumor had spread that the *sahib* was a Catholic priest. Right in the heart of the Muslim quarter this intrusion might well be interpreted as an act of provocation. "God only knows how alone I felt that first morning!" he was to say. "Not being able to breathe a single word of the languages spoken in the slum, it was like being deaf and dumb. And not being able to lay my hands on a little wine, I was deprived even of the comfort of being able to celebrate the Eucharist in the darkness of my den. Fortunately, there was still prayer!"

Prayer! For years Stephan Kovalski had begun each day with an hour's contemplation. Whether he was in a plane, a train, or a roomful of immigrant workmen, he emptied himself, turned to God, gave himself up to him to receive his word, or simply to say to his Creator, "Here I am, at your disposal." He also liked to open the Gospels at random and pick out a sentence such as, "Save me; or I perish," or "Salvation is of the Lord," or "In Thy presence is fullness of joy." He would study every word and every syllable turning them over in every possible direction. "It's a spiritual exercise that helps me to achieve silence," he would explain, "to find emptiness in God. If God has time to listen to me, then inevitably he has time to love me."

That day, however, Kovalski felt himself incapable of real silence, real emptiness. He had been bombarded with too many impressions since the previous evening. Somehow he could not manage to pray as he did on other mornings. "Sitting in front of the picture of the Sacred Shroud, I began to recite *Oms*—aloud. Then I intercalated the name of Jesus. '*Om* . . . Jesus, *om* . . . Jesus.' For me it was a way of joining in the prayer of the slum people who were so close to God and lived with him constantly, while at the same time discovering a way of communicating with my revealed God whom they did not know. After a moment I was once more in his presence. I could speak to him.

"Lord, here I am. It's me, Stephan. Jesus, you know that I am but a poor man, so have mercy on me. You know that I haven't come here to earn favor. Nor have I come here for other people. I am here for you, to love You unconditionally. Jesus, my brother, Jesus, my savior, I have arrived here in the depths of this slum with hands so empty that I cannot even celebrate the Eucharist in remembrance of your sacrifice. But then don't all these men with lowered eyes and swollen faces, don't all these innocent people martyred in this place of suffering commemorate your sacrifice every day? Have mercy on them, Jesus of Anand Nagar.

"Jesus of the City of Joy, you who are eternally crucified, you who are the voice of the voiceless ones, you who suffer within each one of these people, you who endure their anguish, their distress and their sadness, but you who know how to express yourself through their hearts, their tears, their laughter, and their love. Jesus of Anand Nagar, you know that I am here simply to share—so that together they and I can show you that we love you—you and your Father, the Father of mercy, the Father who sent you, the Father who forgives. And to tell you, too, you who are the light and the salvation of the world that here, in the City of Joy, we are living in darkness. So Jesus, our light, we need you, for without you we are lost.

"Jesus of Anand Nagar, let this slum deserve its name, let it be truly a City of Joy."

13

"HOLY MACKEREL! That bum can't even count up to seven!" stormed the procurer for the blood bank when he saw Hasari Pal walking resolutely in his direction. A full twenty-four hours had not yet passed since their fiasco of the previous day.

"Hullo, old friend!" Hasari called out to him cheerily. The peasant's cheerfulness took the man with the gold teeth by surprise.

"What's got into you, my friend? Have you won first prize in a lottery?"

"I think I've found a job, so I've come to give you back your tablets for turning blood red. Here, you can let someone else benefit from them." '

Fortune did indeed seem to be smiling at last on the Bengali peasant. Once more, he had gone to take up his stand near one of the numerous workshops on the outskirts of the Bara Bazar, one which made mechanical parts for railway carriages. It was the same place where he had once earned five rupees by standing in for the coolie who had passed out. This time two men were in the process of loading flat springs onto a handcart, when one of them tripped over a stone and dropped what he was carrying. The wretched man cried out with pain—the heavy metal part had crushed his foot as it fell. Hasari rushed to his rescue. Tearing a strip off his own cotton loincloth, he knotted it around the leg to stop the bleeding. In Calcutta, police assistance or an ambulance were rarely available in case of accident. All the owner of the workshop, a fat man in a buttoned vest, could do was to call a rickshaw. Obviously furious at the incident, he took several five-rupee notes out of his belt. He put one in the hand of the injured man and gave a second to the rickshaw puller. Seeing Hasari lifting the coolie into the carriage, he entrusted two more to him. "Keep one for yourself. The other's to grease the palm of the attendant at the hospital entrance so he lets you in." Then turning to the puller waiting between the shafts of the carriage, he ordered harshly, "All right, you bunch of lazy good-for-nothings, scram!"

Hasari Pal's hesitation in climbing into the carriage intrigued the man pulling it.

"Haven't you ever sat in a rickshaw before?"

"No," acknowledged the peasant, perching himself timidly next to the coolie with the injured foot.

The human horse braced himself against the shafts and they set off with a jolt. The man's graying hair and wizened shoulders indicated that he was no longer young. But with rickshaw pullers, physical appearance bore little relationship to age. People grew old very rapidly pulling such machines.

"You don't look as if you're from around here?" the puller questioned Hasari after having picked up a little speed.

"No, I'm from Bankuli."

"Bankuli!" repeated the rickshaw puller, slowing up sharply. "But that's only twenty miles from my home! I'm from . . ."

Although he didn't actually catch the name of the village, lost as it was in the clamor of horns, Hasari would have liked to leap out and hug the man. At last he had found in this "inhuman city" someone from his homeland. Still he made an effort to conceal his joy, for the sake of the coolie who was groaning more and more with every bump. The puller was now charging toward the hospital as fast as his bandy legs would carry him. At unpredictable intervals, however, his body would throw itself backward in a desperate movement, trying to stop sharply in front of some bus or truck cutting across his path.

Calcutta's general hospital was a city in itself, made up of a collection of somewhat dilapidated buildings, linked by endless corridors, with courtyards in which entire families were squatting. A plaque at the main entrance revealed that "In 1878, in a laboratory seventy yards southeast of this door, Surgeon Major Ronald Ross of the Indian army discovered the manner in which malaria is transmitted by mosquitoes." The rickshaw puller made directly for emergency admissions. He had often brought the sick and wounded to this hospital. Indeed, it was one of the special functions of rickshaws, to serve as ambulances in Calcutta.

"A whole string of people was waiting at the door in front of us and there was a lot of shouting and arguing going on," Hasari would recount. "There were women carrying babies so weak they didn't even cry anymore. From time to time, we saw a stretcher go past with a corpse covered in flowers that bearers chanting prayers were taking to a funeral pyre. When it came to our turn, I slipped the five-rupee note given to me by the workshop owner into the attendant's hand. The bribe paid off. Instead of sending us away with most of the other people, he told us to carry our friend into a room inside."

The two men laid the coolie down on a stretcher still besmirched with the blood of the previous patient. A penetrating smell of disinfectant prevailed in the room, but what was undoubtedly most striking was the jumble of political inscriptions that adorned the walls. Every shade of opinion was mingled there in a kind of pictorial delirium: red flags, hammers and sickles, portraits of Indira Gandhi, and slogans. The astonishment of the Bengali peasant brought a smile to the lips of the rickshaw puller. "Here, my friend, they remind you to vote for them, even when they're just about to carve you up."

"I don't remember how long they kept our coolie in their operating room," Hasari was to say. "I kept asking myself what they could possibly be doing to him for all that time. Then an idea came to me. What if he were dead? Perhaps they'd killed him without meaning to and didn't dare let his corpse be brought out in case we demanded an explanation. But that was absurd because there were bodies coming out of the room next door all the time and it was impossible to tell whether they were dead or alive. They all looked as if they were asleep. In any case I had already realized that in this inhuman city poor fellows like us were not in the habit of asking for explanations. Otherwise, the rickshaw pullers, just to mention them, would have smashed in the faces of all those SOB bus and truck drivers.

"At last some employees came out carrying a shape curled up on a stretcher. A nurse was holding a bottle with a tube that went into the patient's arm. He was asleep. I took a closer look. It was

our friend. He had a fat dressing on the end of his leg. It was only
then that I understood what they had done. Those bastards had cut
his foot off!"

"There's no point in your waiting. He'll be asleep for several
hours yet," the nurse said. "Come to pick him up in two days."

The two men retrieved the rickshaw from the courtyard and
left the hospital. For a moment they walked in silence. Hasari was
visibly shocked.

"You're still green," said the rickshaw puller. "There's no
point in getting worked up. You'll see plenty more like that."

Hasari nodded. "And yet I already feel as if I've had all I can
take."

"All you can take!" laughed his companion, jangling the bell
on the shaft of his rickshaw. "When you've had ten years of cruising about this slag heap like I have, then you can say you think
you've had all you can take!"

They had arrived at a crossroad where a policeman was directing traffic. The puller took a coin out of his shirt and put it in
the policeman's hand as he passed.

"It's a custom here," he explained with a grin. "It saves you
from all sort of troubles. Especially when you don't have a license
to operate your rickshaw." Then, sliding his palms along the
shafts, he asked, "How would you like to pull one of these machines?"

The question took Hasari by surprise. How could a bum like
him ever have the chance to become a rickshaw puller? The idea
seemed as ridiculous as if he had been asked if he would like to fly a
plane.

"Any kind of job would suit me," he replied, touched by the
fact that the rickshaw puller was showing so much interest in him.

"Try it," said his companion, pulling up sharply. He pointed
to the shafts. "Get between them and off you go! Jerk your back to
get the wheels rolling."

Hasari did as he was told. "But if you think it's easy to get one
of these jalopies moving, you've got another think coming," he was
later to say. "It takes the strength of a buffalo! And once it's
moving, it's even worse. Once started, there's no stopping the
thing. It runs all by itself, as if it has a life of its own. It's really a
very strange sensation. To pull up suddenly in an emergency takes

a special knack. With passengers on board, you might be pulling a good three hundred pounds."

The rickshaw puller showed him some marks on the shafts, where the paint had worn off.

"Look here, son, the main thing is to find the point of equilibrium for the weight you're lugging about. You have to put your hands on exactly the place where the balance is established."

Hasari simply could not get over the fact that someone could show so much patience and kindness toward him. "This city isn't all that inhuman," he thought as he handed the shafts of the rickshaw back to its owner. He mopped his forehead with a tail of his *longhi*. The effort had exhausted him.

"We should celebrate your initiation!" exclaimed the rickshaw puller. "This is a big day for you. Let's go and have a glass of *bangla!** I know a place behind Sealdah Railway Station that isn't too expensive."

The rickshaw puller was somewhat astonished at his companion's lack of enthusiasm. Hasari pulled out the five-rupee note given to him by the workshop owner.

"My children and their mother haven't had anything to eat," he said. "I must take something back."

"No problem! It's on me."

They turned right and plunged into an area of low houses and narrow alleyways packed with people at the windows and in the streets. Music blared out from loudspeakers. Washing was drying on the edge of the roofs and green streamers dangled from the ends of bamboo poles. They went past a mosque, then a school where under a porch roof a mullah was teaching a class of little girls in trousers and tunics and veils over their heads. This was a Muslim sector. Next they entered into one of Calcutta's red-light districts. Women with provocatively colored skirts, low-cut bodices, and outrageously made-up faces were talking and laughing. Hasari was struck dumb with astonishment. He had never seen such creatures in his life before, for where he came from the women wore only saris. "Several of them called out to me. There was one I found very attractive. She must have been very rich because her arms were covered in bracelets right up to her elbows.

* Clandestinely distilled alcohol.

But my companion went straight past her without stopping. He
was a serious-minded man."

Numerous rickshaws cluttered the street. They were all occupied by men who had come here in search of amusement. A lot of
poor fellows, coolies, workmen, men without work, were wandering about on the pavements. Calcutta is a city of men, where
hundreds of thousands of refugees live without their families.

A woman grabbed Hasari by the wrist. "Come with me, baby,"
she said, giving him a meaningful look. "I'll make you happy. For
four rupees. That's all." Hasari felt himself blushing to the tips of
his toes. The rickshaw puller came to his rescue. "Leave him
alone!" he ordered the girl, pointing one of his shafts at her stomach. The prostitute replied with a torrent of invective that attracted
the attention of the entire street and made the two friends roar
with laughter. The puller took advantage of the incident to give his
companion a warning: "If ever you're pulling a rickshaw and you
happen to get a girl like that for a fare, don't forget to make her pay
in advance. Otherwise, mind you, she'll slip through your fingers
just like an eel."

After the street with the girls, the two men crossed a square,
passed under an archway, and entered an enclosed area lined with
old buildings with decaying façades and balustrades, from which
there hung an array of motley laundry. Buffalo, cows, dogs, chickens, and pigs roamed about among children playing there with
paper kites. Dots of every conceivable color flew throughout the
sky on the ends of pieces of string. In Calcutta kites were favorite
toys, as if somehow those scraps of paper climbing high above the
rooftops carried the children's ambition to escape their lot, all
their need to flee their prison of mud, fumes, noise, and poverty.

In a corner behind a palisade of planks, a man in a dirty vest
sat beneath a tiled porch roof. He was the owner of the bar. The
rickshaw puller directed Hasari to a bench at one end of the only
table. The place reeked of alcohol. The owner clapped his hands.
Instantly a hirsute little boy appeared with two glasses and a bottle
that had neither label nor cork. It was full of a grayish liquid in
which little white flakes were floating about. The rickshaw puller
carefully counted out fourteen one-rupee notes, then folded them
into a nice neat bundle and handed them to the proprietor. Having
done so, he filled Hasari's glass. The peasant was struck by the acid

smell given off by the concoction, but his companion seemed so delighted with it that he did not dare say anything. In silence, they clinked glasses and swallowed a mouthful.

It was then that Ram Chander—for that was the name of the rickshaw puller—began to speak.

*

"I had to leave my village after the death of my father. The poor man had never succeeded in wiping out the family debts that went back to his father and his grandfather. He had mortgaged our land to pay off the interest, but even that hadn't been enough, and when he died I had to borrow even more to give him a proper funeral. Two thousand rupees! (two hundred U.S. dollars). First there were the four *dhotis* and no less than one hundred and twenty feet of cotton for the *pujari* to get him to recite the prayers. Then there were two hundred pounds of rice, as much flour, quantities of oil, sugar, spices, and vegetables to feed the guests. Finally, we had to have one hundred pounds of wood for the pyre and baksheesh in cash for those in charge of the cremation. I very quickly realized that I would never be able to pay back all that money by staying where I was, especially since, to procure the loan, I had lost our only source of income by mortgaging the next harvest.

"It was at that time, during the Festival of Durga, that an old friend from my younger days came back to the village. He was a rickshaw puller in Calcutta. 'Come with me,' he said, 'and I'll find you a cart to pull. You'll earn ten to twelve rupees a day.' So I decided to go with him. I can still see my wife holding my son's hand in the doorway of our hut and weeping. We had so often spoken of my leaving and now the day had come. She had prepared a knapsack for me with a *longhi* and a change of shirt and a towel too. She had even made me some *chapatis* and vegetable cutlets for the journey. To my dying day I shall still see them in front of our hut. Actually it was the memory of them that helped me to survive, because it was only after four months that, thanks to my childhood friend, I found work.

"In this damned city, the fight to forage out a job is so hard that you could very well wait for years and die twenty times of starvation in the meantime. And if you haven't anyone to help you, then you've not a chance in hell. Even at the very lowest level it's all a matter of connections, and of cash too, of course. You've got to be ready to pay out at every instant. This city is an ogress. She creates people whose only aim is to strip you of everything you have. How naïve I was when I arrived here from the countryside at home! I was quite convinced that my friend was going to lead me straight to the owner of his rickshaw and ask him to take me on. The individual in question is a Bihari who owns more than three hundred carriages, at least two hundred of which operate without a license. He simply slips a percentage to the cops and that settles it. But as for the idea of getting myself employed right away, I soon got over that. The Bihari was never anywhere to be seen. No one even knew where he lived. He is a real boss. He couldn't give a damn whether it was you or Indira Gandhi who pulled his rickshaws, provided he got his dues every evening. He had a special employee to collect them and only through him could you get a rickshaw to pull. Now, don't imagine this guy is any more approachable than his boss. You had to be introduced to him by someone he appreciated, someone who could tell him who you were, what caste you belonged to, what clan, what line of descendants. And you better salute him with your most respectful 'namaskar,'* address him as a 'sardarji,'† invoke the blessing of Shiva and all the gods upon his person and not forget the customary baksheesh, because, for a guy like him, baksheesh are almost as important as the dues. You've got nothing, you're just a poor bum, you work your guts out to earn a few rupees and feed your family, but you have to spend your entire time getting out a coin for the cop at the crossroads because you have no legal right to operate in that street, another coin for another cop because you're transporting goods when you're only supposed to carry people, a note for the proprietor so he'll let you sleep in his cow shed, another for the guy in the workshop to have him repair a spoke in your wheel, another for the former holder of the rickshaw who palmed his ramshackle vehicle off on you. It comes down to your being sucked dry all day long and then, if you don't watch out, you could well find yourself back without a rickshaw in any case, because the

---

* Namaskar: hello, greeting.
† Sardar: chief/boss: term of respect.

police have confiscated it or the person who hires it to you has fired you.

"As for me, I waited more than four months for the gods to decide to give me a break, and yet every morning I used to go and put a little rice, marigold buds, a banana, or some other delicacy in front of the statue of Ganesh in the temple near the hut where I was staying. Three rickshaw pullers lived in the same hovel in the courtyard of a tumbledown old building behind Park Circus. They too had left their families behind them in their villages. An old carpenter carved spokes and repaired cart wheels there. As they were all Hindus, they took their meals together. The old carpenter prepared the food. He cooked it over a *chula* which he fed with wood shavings from his work.

"It was there that my friend had given me shelter when I first arrived in Calcutta. Between two bamboo joists in the framework, he set up a plank for me to sleep on, just under the tiles of the roofing. In the pisé wall, a niche had been hollowed in which there presided a papier-mâché statuette of a Ganesh with a pink elephant head. I remember thinking that with a god like that present under our roof it must surely all turn out okay for me in the end. I was right. One morning as I was coming back from the temple, I recognized the representative of the rickshaw owner on his bike. I had seen him several times before when he came to collect the dues, and my friend had spoken to him about me. He was quite a small man with shrewd eyes so piercing they might have been throwing out sparks. As soon as he put a foot on the ground, I launched myself at him.

" '*Namaskar Sardarji!* To what honor do we owe the visit of a person of your importance? You, the son of the god Shiva!' He could not suppress a smile of satisfaction.

" 'I've a fellow with a broken leg. Would you like to replace him? If you would, you can give me twenty-five rupees immediately and you'll have to pay the disabled puller two rupees a day. That's on top of the regular six rupees' daily rental, of course.'

"He warned me, just in passing, that the carriage did not have a license to operate, which meant that in the event of my being caught by the police, I would be the one to have to pay the usual bribe. It was highway robbery. And yet I positively dissolved into expressions of thanks. 'I shall be eternally grateful to you,' I promised him. 'From now on I shall be as the very youngest of your brothers.'*

"The dream for which I had left my village had at last come true. I was going to earn a living for my family between the shafts of a rickshaw."

---

* Given the power and authority with which the eldest son is endowed in the traditional Indian family, this is a special mark of respect and submission.

14

AT THAT TIME the City of Joy had only about ten wells and fountains for seventy thousand inhabitants. The nearest fountain to Stephan Kovalski's room was near a buffalo shed at the end of his alleyway. By the time he got to it, the neighborhood was just waking up. Every dawn there was the same explosion of life. People who had spent the night, ten or twelve to a single rat-and-vermin-infested hovel, were born again with the daylight as if at the world's first dawning. Their daily resurrection began with a general process of purification. There, in alleyways awash with slime, beside the disease-ridden stream of a sewer, the occupants of the City of Joy banished the miasma of the night with all the ritual of a meticulous toilet. Without revealing so much as a patch of their nudity, the women managed to wash themselves all over, from their long hair to the soles of their feet, not forgetting their saris. After that, they would take the greatest care to oil, comb, and braid their hair, before decorating it with a fresh flower picked from God only knew where. At every water point, men were showering themselves with tins. Young boys cleaned their teeth with acacia twigs coated with ashes, old men polished their tongues with strands of jute, mothers deloused their children before soaping their little naked bodies with a vigor undiminished even by the biting cold of winter mornings.

Stephan Kovalski continued on his way, observing everything about him. Before reaching the fountain, his eyes were suddenly attracted by the beauty of one young mother swathed in a red sari, sitting in the alleyway, her back firmly upright, with a baby placed on her outstretched legs. The infant was naked, with only an amulet on a thin cord around his waist. He was a chubby child who did not appear to be suffering from malnutrition. There was a strange flame in the way mother and child looked at each other, as if they were talking to each other with their eyes. Captivated, Kovalski put down his bucket. The young woman had just poured a few drops of mustard oil into her palms and was beginning to massage the little body in her lap. Skillful, intelligent, attentive, her hands moved up and down, actuated by a rhythm as discreet as it was inflexible. Working in turn like waves, they set out from the baby's flanks, crossed its chest, and climbed back up to the opposite shoulder. At the end of the movement, her little finger slid under the child's neck. Then she pivoted him onto his side. Stretching out his arms, she massaged them delicately one after another, singing to him as she did so ancient songs about the loves of the god Krishna or some legend that stemmed from the depths of epic ages. Then she took hold of his little hands and kneaded them with her thumb as if to stimulate the blood flow from the palms to their extremities. Thus his stomach, legs, heels, the soles of his feet, his head, the nape of his neck, his face, nostrils, back, and buttocks were all successively caressed and vitalized by those supple, dancing fingers. The massage was concluded with a series of yogic exercises. The mother crossed her son's arms over his chest several times in succession to free his back, his rib cage, his breathing. Eventually it was the legs' turn to be raised, opened, and closed over his stomach to induce the opening and complete relaxation of the pelvis. The child gurgled in sheer bliss.

"What I was witnessing was a real ritual," Kovalski was to say, enthralled by so much love, beauty, and intelligence. He could well imagine how much intangible sustenance the massage could bring to a little body threatened by so many vital deficiencies.

After this glimmer of light amid so much ugliness, the drudgery of collecting water seemed a very banal formality. Several dozen women and children were standing in a line and the fountain's output was so feeble that it took an age to fill a bucket. Still, what did it matter? Time didn't count in Anand Nagar and the fountain was a focal point of news. For Kovalski it was a marvelous observation ground. A little girl came up to him, gave him a big smile, and with great authority took charge of his bucket. Placing a finger on his wrist, she said to him in English: "*Daddah,* * you must be in a great hurry."

"Why do you think that?" asked Kovalski.

"Because you have a watch."

*

When he got back to his house, the priest found several people outside his door. He recognized them as the occupants of the Christian compound to which, on his first evening, the envoy of the rector in charge of the neighboring parish had taken him. The young woman who had asked him to bless her child was now offering him a *chapati* and a small bottle.

"*Namaskar,* Father," she said warmly. "My name is Margareta. My neighbors and I thought that you might not have anything with which to celebrate Mass. Here is some bread and wine."

Stephan Kovalski surveyed his visitors, quite overwhelmed. "They may not have anything to eat, but they've managed to get hold of bread and wine for the Eucharist." He thought of the first Christians of Rome's catacombs.

"Thank you," he said, concealing his emotion.

"We have set up a table in our courtyard," added the young woman with a smile of complicity.

"Let's go," said Kovalski, this time showing his joy.

These people belonged to the few families—there were about fifty of them—who together formed a tiny islet of Christians in the midst of the seventy thousand Muslims and Hindus in the City of Joy. Although they too were poor, they were slightly less destitute than the rest of the population. There were several reasons for this advantage. Firstly and paradoxically, it was due to the fact that they were in such a minority: the smaller the number of people, the easier it is to provide aid for the least fortunate. Whereas the Hindu priests and Muslim mullahs in the area had to deal with more than three million faithful, the Catholic priest at the local church had less than a thousand parishioners. Secondly, to distinguish themselves from the majority of other sections of the community and improve their chances of securing white-collar work,

* Big Brother.

many Christians made the effort to conquer that key instrument to social ascent—the English language. Finally, if they managed to elude the clutches of extreme poverty a little more successfully than most, it was also because their religion did not teach them to resign themselves to their fate. For Hindus, misfortune was the result of the burden of acts carried out in previous lives; this *karma* must be accepted in order that one might be reborn under more auspicious circumstances. Exempt from such taboos, Christians were free to haul themselves out of their lot as best they could. That is why India is sprinkled with institutions and small groups of élite that endow the Christian minority with a degree of national influence which far outweighs the number of its members. The same was also true in the City of Joy.

The Christians in the slum came from the Bettiah region, an agricultural area of Bihar, which until the nineteen forties had harbored one of the most important Christian communities in Northern India. The origins of that community form an outstanding chapter in the great saga of the world's religious migrations. It was initiated toward the beginning of the eighteenth century when, persecuted by a bloodthirsty sovereign, thirty-five Nepalese converts fled from their homeland together with their chaplain, an Italian Capucin. They found refuge in a princely state where the Capucin Father "miraculously" healed the wife of the local rajah. By way of thanks the latter gave them land. This tradition of making Christians welcome was perpetuated by the rajahs who succeeded him and so the small community prospered and increased. A century later, it numbered two thousand souls. With its whitewashed houses, its narrow streets, its patios, its squares adorned with flowers, and its large church; with its men in wide-brimmed hats and its young girls in skirts and mantillas, the Christian quarter of the town of Bettiah looked a little like a Mediterranean village. One day a strange calamity was to strike the area. The British called it blue gold; the peasants called it indigo. The intensive monoculture of the indigo plant to be used for dye was to provoke, in 1920, Gandhi's first great action. It was here, in the region of Bettiah, that the Mahatma began his campaign of nonviolent action for the liberation of India. Indigo was eventually defeated in 1942 by a synthetic substitute. Blue gold did not, however, die without first taking its revenge: it had drained all the goodness out of the land and condemned thousands of peasants to exile.

The small number of families about to assist Kovalski's first Mass in Anand Nagar all came from those massacred lands. There were about twenty people in all, mainly women with babies in their arms and a few old men. Nearly all the heads of the families were absent, an indication that this compound was privileged, for others were full of men without work. In the congregation there was also an individual dressed in rags, whose wretched appearance was instantly forgotten because of his compelling radiant expression. He was known as "Gunga," the Mute. He was simpleminded and deaf and dumb, and nobody knew where he came from or how he had come to land in the City of Joy. One day Margareta had picked him up in an alleyway flooded out by the monsoon. He was on the point of drowning. Despite the fact that she was a widow and there were already eight people in her household, she had taken him in. One morning, he had vanished. For two years nobody had seen him. Then he had appeared again. He used to sleep on a few rags under the porch roof and seemed always quite content. One month ago, however, a neighbor had found him lying lifeless in an alleyway. Margareta had diagnosed cholera, loaded him onto a rickshaw, and taken him to the nearest hospital. With the help of a ten-rupee note, she had persuaded the duty nurse to find him a place on an emergency pallet. On the way home, she had visited the church of Our Lady of the Loving Heart and lit a candle. Three days later Gunga was back. When he saw Kovalski, he rushed up to him and stooped down to brush the dust from his basketball shoes, then put his hands on his head as a mark of respect.

What the priest encountered on entering the Christian compound would remain forever engraved upon his memory. "They had covered a plank supported on two crates with a square of spotless cotton material and placed a candle at each corner. A bowl and cup served as paten and ciborium. A wooden crucifix and a garland of yellow marigolds completed the decoration of this improvised altar erected next to the well in the center of the courtyard."

For a while Stephan Kovalski stood and gathered his thoughts, meditating upon the miracle that he was about to accomplish against a backdrop of smoking *chulas*, pieces of rag drying on rooftops, and children in tatters chasing each other about in the gutters, amid all the uproar of horns, singing, shouting, and life in general. With a piece of *chapati*—so like the unleavened bread Christ himself had broken at his last supper—he was about to "create" the very Creator of this matter. In his hands a piece of bread was about to become God, the God who was at the origin of all things. To Kovalski this process was the most prodigious revolution that man might ever be called upon to bring about.

He had often celebrated Mass in a hut in a shantytown, in the communal living room of a house for immigrant workers, or in some corner of a factory workroom. But today, in the midst of these suffering, despised, and broken people, he sensed all that would be unique about this offering, this sharing of bread.

"The will of God to share the plight of the most humble had always seemed an extraordinary phenomenon to me," he was to say. "As if taking upon himself the form of a man were not in itself enough to satiate his thirst for abasement, as if he wanted to draw closer still to the very poorest, the humblest, the most handicapped and rejected of this world. What an extraordinary source of happiness it is to have the power to enable God to express through the Eucharist the infinite quality of his love."

Kovalski was celebrating his Mass in a monasterylike silence when three pariah dogs, with tails cocked, scampered across the courtyard in hot pursuit of a rat that was almost as big as they were. The scene was so commonplace that no one paid any attention to it. A balloon seller passing during the reading of the Gospel did, on the other hand, attract a few glances. Flying at the tip of their bamboo canes, the colorful gold-beaters' skins stood out like stars against the expanse of gray sky. As the multicolored clusters disappeared into the distance, Kovalski's voice rose resonantly above the assembled heads. The priest had carefully chosen the message of good news it conveyed. Looking with love upon the emaciated faces that confronted him, he repeated the words of Jesus Christ.

Blessed are the poor in spirit, for theirs is the Kingdom of Heaven.
Blessed are the sorrowful, for they shall find consolation.
Blessed are those who hunger and thirst for what is right, for they shall be satisfied.

As he uttered these words, Stephan Kovalski felt a certain uneasiness. "Do these people really need words?" he wondered. "Aren't they already Christ, the vehicle, the Sacrament? Aren't they the poor of the Scriptures, Yahweh's poor, the ones in whom Jesus became incarnate when he said that where the poor were, there he was also?"

After a silence, he held out his arms as if to embrace the handful of suffering men and women. Wanting to imbue them with the Gospel message of that very first morning, he gazed intently at each of his new brothers and sisters. Then, letting Christ speak through his voice, he proclaimed, "Peace be with you for you are the light of the world."

15

STEPHAN KOVALSKI'S FIRST wash in the slum began with yet another sacrilege. He had undressed down to his underpants, as he had seen the men on the way to the water pipe do. He had then gone out into the alleyway outside his room, duly armed with his bucket of water. He had squatted on his heels in that distinctive Indian position so difficult for a Westerner to maintain, tipped some water over his feet, and was in the process of vigorously scrubbing his toes when the elderly Hindu from the tea shop opposite called out to him in horror.

"Father, that's not how you're supposed to wash yourself. It's your head you should wash first, and your feet last, after you've cleaned everything else."

The Pole was about to stammer some excuse when the little girl appeared who had brought him the plate of food the evening before. The vision of a half-naked *sahib* sprinkling himself with water amused her so much that she burst out laughing.

"Why are you washing yourself anyway, *Daddah?*" she asked. "Your skin's already so white!"

A few moments later, Kovalski committed a fourth blunder by rolling up his bedding mat the wrong way. Instead of starting with the head end, he did the opposite. As his Muslim neighbor explained him with a mimic, it meant that on the following night he risked placing his head where his feet had been the night before. "I knew that it would take time for me to grasp all the subtleties of slum life and not shock people anymore," the Polish priest acknowledged later. On the way back from the fountain he had felt his neighbors' reserve even more distinctly. Women had rapidly pulled the veil of their saris over their faces. Children playing marbles had scurried away like rabbits. The vermin were the only ones who did not ostracize him. Like the rats, the centipedes, and the mosquitoes of the night, the flies now danced sympathetic attendance on him. "There were hundreds of them. Green ones, gray ones, big ones, tiny ones—they moved about in whole squadrons, ever ready to latch on to the slightest patch of skin. They had no reservations about getting into my ears, my nostrils, my eyes, right down my throat with each small ball of food. Nothing curbed their audacity. They didn't even deign to fly away when I pursued them. All they did was move on a few inches to inflict their torture on some more distant piece of me. I was completely at their mercy. In an attempt to escape their tortures, I tried to concentrate on happier memories, on my mother beating up the egg whites for a floating island, my favorite dessert, or on my father's face, as black as coal, when he came home at night from the mine."

On that first morning, Stephan Kovalski sought help too from the picture of Christ. With his eyes fixed on the tortured face pinned to the wall, he chanted a litany of *Oms*. After a moment the invocation became completely unconscious, as he brought its rhythm into unison with the beating of his heart. This method of using his body rhythm to communicate with God freed him gradually from all exterior contingencies. The flies could attack him as they wished; he was no longer aware of them.

It was then that the smiling face of the parish priest's envoy appeared in the recess of the door. The man had come because he was concerned about how the Pole had survived his first hours in the slum. The account of his adventures at the latrines and his entanglements with rats and flies were a source of great consternation.

"Father Cordeiro has charged me to tell you that there is a comfortable room for you at the presbytery," he insisted. "That wouldn't prevent you from coming and spending as much time here as you liked. I beg you to accept it. This is no place for a priest."

The Anglo-Indian shook his head sadly, then took out of an imitation leather bag two large volumes that Father Cordeiro had asked him to pass on to Kovalski. One was a Bengali grammar; the other was an edition of the Gospel in Hindi. The Pole received the gifts with enthusiasm. He knew that they would be indispensable in helping him to break down the wall of silence that isolated him in his new existence.

Far from disheartening him, his inability to express himself and understand had at first delighted Kovalski. "For a foreigner like me arriving among such poor people, it provided a unique opportunity to place myself in the position of an inferior," he was to explain. "It was I who needed others and not others who needed me"—a consideration of fundamental importance for a man who felt himself so privileged by comparison with those around him that he wondered whether he would ever really be integrated with them. "Indeed, how could I seriously believe it possible mentally and physically to share the plight of those who lived in the slums, when I enjoyed the health of a football player, didn't have a family to feed, house, and care for, and didn't have to look for work or be obsessed with keeping my job; when I knew that at any given moment I could leave." As he had hoped, the language handicap helped his first contacts with people around him by giving them a sense of importance, of superiority. How did one say "water" in Urdu? "Tea" or "bucket" in Hindi? By repeating the words in their language the wrong way, by pronouncing them incorrectly, he provoked their laughter and gradually won their sympathy until the day came when, realizing that he wasn't just a passing visitor but one of them, they gave him the most affectionate nickname in their vocabulary, that of "*Daddah* Stephan," Big Brother Stephan.

Hindi, the great *lingua franca* of modern India, now spoken by nearly a quarter of a billion people, was understood by the majority of the occupants of the City of Joy. It was one of twenty or thirty languages used in the slum; others were Bengali, Urdu, Tamil, Malayalam, Punjabi, and numerous dialects. In the absence of a teacher, Kovalski began his learning process in a somewhat original fashion. Every morning after his hour of meditation, he gave himself a lesson in Hindi based on the Gospel texts that he knew better than the lines on his hand. He would sit down on his mat, his back straight up against the wall, his legs folded in the lotus position, his French version of the Jerusalem Bible on one thigh and on the other, the fat volume of the Gospels in Hindi sent him by Father Cordeiro. The stylish, mysterious calligraphy of the work reminded him of Egyptian hieroglyphics. Like the illustrious

French scholar Champollion who had deciphered these hieroglyphics, Kovalski realized that he had first to find a key. Patiently
he searched for it, scrutinizing the verses of the Hindi text one by
one, in the hope of discovering the name of a person or a place that
had not been translated. After several days of looking, his eye fell
at last on a nine-letter word printed in Roman capitals. Instantly he
identified the chapter from which it came and, with no difficulty at
all, inscribed against each Hindi word the French equivalent. All he
then had to do was decorticate each letter one at a time to discover
its transcription and reconstruct an alphabet. The key word
seemed to him doubly symbolic. It was the name of a town in the
image of the one where he was, a town where crowds of poor
people had gathered to turn to God. It was also a symbol of an
inextricable entanglement of people and things comparable to the
slum of the City of Joy. The magic word was Capernium.

16

ALL THE CITIES of the former colonial world have banished
them from their roads, as one of the most degrading aspects of
man's exploitation of his fellow man. All, except Calcutta, where
even today some hundred thousand slave horses harnessed to their
rickshaws run up more miles per day than the thirty Boeings and
Airbuses of the Indian Airlines, India's domestic airline. Each day
they transport more than one million passengers and no one, apart
from a few visionary town planners, has thought of relegating
these anachronistic carriages to a historical museum, for here human sweat provides the world's cheapest energy.

With their two large wheels with wooden spokes, their slender
bodies and uncurved shafts, rickshaws look like the carriages of our
grandmother's day. Invented in Japan at the end of the eighteenth
century by a European missionary, their name derives from the
Japanese expression *ji riki shaw* which means literally "vehicle propelled by man." The first rickshaws appeared in India around
1880, on the imperial avenues of Simla, the summer capital of the
British Indian Empire. Some twenty years later a few of these
vehicles arrived in Calcutta, imported by Chinese traders who used
them to transport goods. In 1914 these same Chinese applied for
permission to use them also to carry people. Faster than the palanquins of olden times and more manageable than hackney carriages,
it was not long before rickshaws imposed their presence on the
foremost port in Asia. The fashion was to reach numerous metrop-
olises in Southeast Asia. For many farmer peasants among the
millions of men who had sought refuge in Calcutta since Independence, their shafts provided a providential means of earning a

living. It is not known how many rickshaws now plow their way
through the streets and alleys of the last city in the world to retain
them. In 1939 the British limited their number to six thousand,
and since no other license to operate them has been issued since
1949, there are still officially fewer than ten thousand of them.
Unofficial statistics suggest a figure five times larger, however,
since four out of five operate illegally, with baked plates. Each one
of those fifty thousand rickshaws provides a living for two pullers,
who take turns between the shafts from one sunrise to the next.
The sweat of those hundred thousand drudges feeds as many
families. It is, therefore, estimated that a total of over one million
individuals look to the rickshaw for their daily bowl of rice. Economists have even calculated the financial implications of this unique
activity in the catalogue of professions: four million dollars, one
fourth the budget of the whole urban transport system of a city like
Paris. A sizable part of this amount—about a hundred thousand
dollars a year—represents the bribes paid by the pullers to the
police and other authorities, to be able to exercise their trade in a
city which has become so congested that more and more streets
have been banned to them.

"There's nothing like a large glass of *bangla* for putting a tiger
in your tank!" exclaimed Ram Chander, paraphrasing an old advertisement that had covered the walls of Calcutta. He steered his
newfound friend outside.

"Hell, yes!" said Hasari Pal, "it's like absorbing six *chapatis* in a
row and a bowl full of fish curry." He grimaced and rubbed his
stomach. "Except that this particular gasoline rumbles a bit inside
you."

The fact that it "rumbled" inside him was not surprising—the
concoction the two companions had just imbibed was one of the
most lethal mixtures ever brewed in stills by man. It was called
"country liquor" and came from a village situated on the fringes of
Calcutta's garbage dump. There, throughout the year, all kinds of
refuse, animal innards, and cane juice were fermented for a month
in large jars at the bottom of a putrid pool. The news item pages in
the newspapers never ceased recording the havoc worked by this
poisonous alcohol which in India claimed as many victims every

year as malaria. It had only one advantage and that was its price. Evading tax levies, it cost only seven rupees a bottle, four or five times less than a bottle of the most mediocre governmental rum.

The two friends began walking together. Soon, however, Ram Chander was hailed by an elderly but very hefty woman, dressed in the white sari of a widow. Hasari helped her to climb into the rickshaw and Ram set off at a trot. As he watched the carriage pulling away, the peasant couldn't help remarking to himself how lucky his friend was. "At least he can look other people in the eye. He has a job. He has his dignity. Whereas I'm just like the mangy dogs that roam about the streets. I don't exist."

Before parting, the two men had arranged to meet the next day at the Park Circus esplanade, at the point where the streetcar lines crossed. Ram Chander had promised to try and introduce his friend to the rickshaw owner's representative. "With a little bit of luck and a generous baksheesh, he might just find you an old heap to pull." "I should have refused to believe in anything quite so wonderful," Hasari would say, "but the *bangla* had given me wings. I felt like a paper kite." The two men had also decided to go to the hospital to visit the injured coolie.

The peasant wandered about for a long time before finding his family. "Everywhere there were uninterrupted rows of shops, stores, stalls, and thousands of people on the pavements and in the roadways. It was as if one half of the population spent its entire time selling things to the other half. There was an abundance of objects that I had never seen before, like instruments to peel vegetables with, or squeeze the juice out of fruits. There were piles of cooking utensils too, and tools and mechanical parts, sandals, shirts, belts, bags, combs, pens, and dark glasses for the sun. In some places it was very difficult to move at all because of all the people and goods crammed into the roadway. On one street corner I bought several *alu-bhurta* from a pedlar. My children loved those potato fritters dusted with sugar, but with five rupees I couldn't buy many of them and perhaps I'd have done better to buy several portions of puffed rice for the whole family instead. But when your stomach and head are full of *bangla*, you're not responsible for your madness."

Night had long fallen by the time Hasari at last recognized the avenue where he had set up camp. Before he actually reached his family's piece of pavement, he heard shouting and saw a mob. Fearing that something dreadful had happened to his wife or one of his children, he rushed to the scene, but it was the neighbor's wife who was howling. Her face was bleeding and there were the marks of blows on her shoulders and arms. Once again her husband had come home drunk. They had quarreled and he had hit her with an iron bar. If the neighbors had not intervened he would have killed her. He had also beaten the two smallest children. Then he had picked up his ragged clothing and simply gone off, committing his family to the mercy of the devil. The poor woman found herself alone on the pavement with three young children and another on the way, not forgetting a son in prison and a prostitute daughter. "Sometimes there are good reasons for cursing your karma," thought Hasari.

By luck, that night, Hasari's two eldest children had managed to bring back some gourd and turnip scraps from their day's foraging in the rubbish of the Bara Bazar. They were enormously proud of their achievement because so many people explored the refuse heaps that good finds were few and far between. Their mother borrowed the neighboring woman's *chula* to cook a soup which the Pals shared with her and her abandoned children. They also shared the fritters. Nothing appeases grief and fear more effectively than a good meal, especially when you live on the pavement, with not even a sheet of corrugated iron or canvas over your head. That night the two families drew a little closer together before they went to sleep. Only the poor may need the help of other poor.

17

EVERY NIGHT at about eleven o'clock, it started up again. First came the tears. Gradually they increased in intensity. The rhythm became more accelerated and developed into a series of rattles which cascaded through the dividing wall. A ten-year-old Muslim boy was dying of osteotuberculosis in the hovel next door. His name was Sabia.

"Why this agony of an innocent in a place already scarred by so much suffering?" protested an indignant Kovalski.

During the first few evenings the priest had succumbed to cowardice. He had stopped up his ears with cotton so that he would not hear. "I was like Job on the brink of revolt," he was to explain. "In vain I scoured the Scriptures by the light of my oil lamp. I could not find a satisfactory explanation for the idea that God could let such a thing happen. Who could ever venture to say to a child like that, writhing in pain: 'Blessed are the poor, for theirs is the Kingdom of Heaven; blessed are the sorrowful, for they shall find consolation; blessed are those who thirst, for they shall be satisfied?' The prophet Isaiah tried hard to justify the suffering of the innocent. It was *our* suffering that the boy was enduring, Isaiah affirmed, and he would help to save us from *our* sins. The idea that the suffering of one human being could help to save the world was certainly very alluring, but how could I concede that the suffering of my little neighbor was part of that redemptive process? Everything in me rebelled against the idea."

It took several nights before Stephan Kovalski could accept the experience of listening to Sabia's cries and several more for him to listen to them not only with his ears but also with his heart.

He was torn between his religious faith and his very human feelings of revolt. Had he any right to be happy, to sing praises to God while that intolerable torment was going on right next to him? Every night when his young neighbor began to groan again, he emptied himself and prayed. Then he ceased to hear the tears, the cries, the noises; he ceased to notice the rustle of the rats in the darkness; he no longer smelled the stench of the blocked drain outside his door. He entered into what he described as a state of "weightlessness."

"In the beginning my prayer was exclusively concerned with young Sabia's agony. I begged the Lord to alleviate his suffering, to lessen his sacrifice. And if, in his judgment, this trial was really useful for the redemption of the sins of mankind, then I asked him, the Father who had not hesitated to sacrifice his own son, to let me assume a part of it, to let me suffer instead of that child." Night after night, his eyes turned in the darkness toward the picture of the Sacred Shroud, Stephan Kovalski prayed until the groans were still. Tirelessly he prayed and pleaded: "You who died on the Cross to save mankind, help me to understand the mystery of suffering. Help me to transcend it. Help me, above all, to fight against its causes, against the lack of love, against hatred and against all the injustices that give rise to it."

The illness of his young neighbor grew worse and the sounds of his agony increased. One morning the priest caught the bus to the nearest hospital.

"I need a syringe and a dose of morphine. It's very urgent," he said to the attendant in charge of the hospital pharmacy, handing him thirty rupees.

"Since his illness was incurable and my prayer had proved abortive," he would later say to justify himself, "Sabia should at least be able to die in peace."

Helped by her three daughters, aged eleven, eight, and five, Sabia's mother spent her days squatting in the alleyway, making paper bags out of old newspapers. She was a widow and this activity represented the only income with which she could support her family. A hundred times a day she had to get up and clear everything out of the way to allow a cycle-car or cart to pass. Yet Stephan Kovalski had noticed that her smile never deserted her.

Hostile gazes beset him as soon as he stopped outside Sabia's

hovel. Why did this infidel want to visit the little Muslim who was
dying? Was he going to try to convert the boy to his religion? Tell
him that Allah was not the true God? There were many in the area
who mistrusted the priest. So many stories were told about the zeal
of Christian missionaries, about their diabolical capacity to whee-
dle their way in anywhere. Wasn't it merely to reduce their vigilance that this particular one wore trousers and sneakers instead of
a cassock? Nevertheless, Sabia's mother welcomed him with her
remarkable smile. She sent her eldest daughter to fetch him a cup
of tea from the old Hindu and invited the priest to come in. The
smell of putrid flesh caused him to hesitate for a few seconds on
the threshold. Then he plunged into the half-light.

The little Muslim boy was lying on a mattress of rags, his arms
crossed, his skin pitted with sores, crawling with lice, his knees half
bent back over his fleshless torso. Stephan Kovalski drew nearer to
him and the boy opened his eyes. His gaze lit up with a spark of joy.
Kovalski was totally overwhelmed. "How could I believe my own
eyes? How could so much serenity radiate from that little martyred
frame?" His fingers tightened on the vial of morphine.

"Salaam, Sabia," he murmured, smiling.

"Salaam, *Daddah,*" responded the child cheerfully. "What
have you got in your hand? Sweets?"

Startled, Stephan Kovalski dropped the vial which shattered as
it fell. "Sabia had no need of morphine. His features were imbued
with a peace that quite disarmed me. Bruised, mutilated, crucified
as he was, he remained undefeated. He had just given me the most
precious gift of all: a secret reason never to despair, a light in the
darkness."

How many brothers and sisters of light like Sabia did Stephan
Kovalski have in this haven of suffering? Hundreds, perhaps even
thousands. Every morning after celebrating the Eucharist, he
would visit some of them with the few reserves he had at his
disposal: a little food, some medicine, or simply the comfort of his
presence.

Nothing raised his spirits more than his visits to a blind Christian leper woman who lived next to the railway lines. Incredible as
it might seem, this woman too, plunged as she was into unutterable
stages of decay, radiated serenity. She would spend entire days in
prayer, curled up in a corner of her hovel, without lighting or

ventilation. Behind her, hanging from a nail in the mud wall, was a crucifix, and in a niche above the door nestled a statue of a Virgin blackened with soot. The leper woman was so thin that her shriveled skin accentuated the angles of her bones. What age might she be? Certainly younger than she looked. Forty at the very most. As if her blindness were not enough, leprosy had reduced her hands to stumps and eaten away her face. The widow of one of the municipality's lesser employees, she had lived in the slum for twenty years. No one knew how she had come to catch leprosy, but she was so consumed by the disease that it was too late to cure her. In another corner of the room her four grandchildren, aged between two and six, slept side by side on a piece of threadbare matting.

Around this Christian woman and her family had been woven one of those networks of mutual help and friendship that transformed the City of Joy into one of those privileged places to which Jesus of Nazareth referred when he called upon his disciples to "gather in a suitable spot to await the last Judgment and the Resurrection." Such help was all the more remarkable because the neighbors were all Hindus, a fact that would normally have prevented them from touching anyone suffering from leprosy, from entering that person's house or even, so it was sometimes said, from tainting their eyes with the sight of a leper. Yet, every day, those Hindus took turns bringing the Christian woman a dish of rice and vegetables, helping her wash, doing her housework, looking after her grandchildren. The slum, so inhuman in other respects, gave her something which no hospital could have provided. This broken woman suffered from no lack of love.

Some sixth sense always alerted her to Kovalski's arrival. As soon as she sensed him approaching, she would make an attempt to tidy herself. With what was left of her hands she would smooth down her hair, a touching gesture of coquetry amid such utter degradation. Next she would tidy up the area around her, groping to rearrange a tattered cushion for her visitor. Happy then, all she had to do was wait patiently, reciting her rosary. That morning the priest was going to fill her with joy.

"Good morning, Father!" she was quick to call out to him as soon as she heard his footsteps.

"Good morning, Grandma!" replied Kovalski, taking his shoes off in the doorway. "You seem to be in good form today."

He had never heard her complain or utter words of self-pity at her predicament, and on this occasion, again, he was struck by the sight of the joyous expression on her tortured face. She signaled him to sit down beside her and as soon as he was settled, held out her arms in a gesture of maternal love. The blind leper woman caressed the priest's face as if to feel the life in it. "I was utterly bewildered," he was to say. "It was as if she were giving me the very thing that she sought in me. There was more love in the soft touch of that rotten flesh than in all the world's embraces."

"Father, I do so wish the good Lord would come and fetch me at last. Why won't you ask him to?"

"If the good Lord keeps you with us, Grandma, it's because he still needs you here."

"Father, if I have to continue suffering, I'm ready to do so," she said. "Above all I'm ready to pray for other people, to help them endure their own suffering. Father, bring me their suffering."

Stephan Kovalski told her about his visit to young Sabia. She listened with her sightless eyes fixed upon him.

"Tell him that I shall pray for him." The priest searched in his knapsack for the clean handkerchief in which he had carefully wrapped a piece of *chapati* consecrated during his morning Mass. The short silence intrigued the leper woman.

"What are you doing, Father?"

"Grandma, I've brought you communion. Receive the body of Christ."

She parted her lips and Kovalski placed the fragment of griddle cake on the tip of her tongue. "Amen," she murmured after a moment, her face radiant with joy. There was a long silence, broken only by the buzzing of flies and the outbreak of an argument outside. The four little sleeping bodies had not stirred.

When Stephan Kovalski rose to go, the leper woman lifted up her rosary in a gesture of salutation and offering.

"Be sure to tell those who are suffering that I am praying for them."

That evening Stephan Kovalski was to jot down in his diary: "That woman knows that her suffering is not useless and I affirm that God wants to use her suffering to help others to endure theirs." A few lines further on he concluded: "That is why my prayer for this poor woman must not be one of sadness. Her suffering is like that of Christ on the Cross; it is constructive and redemptive. It is full of hope. Every time I leave the hovel where my sister, the blind leper woman, lives, I come away revitalized. So how can one despair in this slum of Anand Nagar? In truth this place deserves its name, City of Joy."

18

HE RULED OVER his fleet of carriages like a pimp over his army of prostitutes. No one ever saw him, but everyone—his pullers, his stewards, and even the police—had for the last fifty years accepted the power of Bipin Narendra, the most influential rickshaw owner in Calcutta. Nobody knew just how many vehicles operated under his ensign. Rumor had it that there were at least four hundred, of which more than half functioned illegally with no official plate. Yet if you had encountered Bipin Narendra on the steps of the Kali Temple, you would almost certainly have offered him alms. With his oversized trousers, his broken down sandals, his baggy shirt spattered with stains, and his crutch that supported a slightly wasted leg, he looked more like a beggar than a captain of industry. Only the sempiternal white forage cap planted on top of his bald skull elevated the poverty-stricken appearance of his personage. No one knew his age; even he knew it only approximately, to within two or three years. It was said that he must be in his nineties; he had never drunk a drop of alcohol, smoked a cigarette, or eaten an ounce of meat in his life. Nor had he, of course, sweated between the shafts of those rickshaws which had killed hundreds of his pullers and made him a rich man.

His longest memory went back to the time when he had first left his native Bihar to come and earn his living in Calcutta. "It was at the beginning of the Great War in Europe," he used to recount. "There were many soldiers in Calcutta and every day more and more of them boarded the waiting ships. There were parades in the Maidan and regimental bands played military music. Life was very entertaining—much more so than in the province where I was born. My parents were landless peasants, agricultural laborers, in fact. My father and brothers hired themselves out to the *zamindar* but there was only work for a few months in the year. That was no life."

Bipin Narendra found his first job as an assistant to the driver of a bus that belonged to a Bihari from his village. His role consisted of opening the doors at every stop and getting the passengers on and off. Another man was employed as the conductor. It was he who collected the fares according to the distance involved. It was he, too, who rang the bell as a signal to move off. "I envied him greatly because he pocketed a percentage on every ticket and, as it was usual for the conductor to split the proceeds with the driver, all the buses raced between themselves to pick up passengers. Many say that the same system still applies today."

After three years, the owner of the bus was able to buy a second vehicle and Bipin Narendra was given the job of conductor. He was quite unable to say how many thousands of miles he had covered in the huge metropolis. "But the city was very different in those days. There weren't so many inhabitants and the streets were clean and well maintained. The British were very strict. You could earn money without resorting to subterfuge, by working honestly."

Rickshaws had been a roaring success right from the day they had first appeared, because they provided a means of transport cheaper than any horse-drawn carriage or taxicab. One day in 1930 Bipin Narendra bought himself two of these machines. They cost two hundred rupees each, new, but he had managed to unearth some secondhand ones for only fifty rupees. He hired them out immediately to two Bihari expatriates from his village. Later he was to borrow sixteen hundred rupees from his boss and buy eight more brand-new Japanese rickshaws. That was the beginning of his fortune. After a few years, the man who from that time was only referred to as "the Bihari" owned approximately thirty carriages. With the rent that he collected each day, he bought a plot of land in Ballygunge, in South Calcutta, and had a house built on it. Ballygunge was quite a poor area, occupied for the most part by Hindu and Muslim employees, where the price of land was not very expensive. In the meantime the Bihari had gotten married and thereafter, every time his wife became pregnant, he had one more room built onto his house. Now he was the owner of a four-story mansion, the highest in the area, for his wife had given him nine children, three sons and six daughters.

The Bihari had been a hard worker. For nearly half a century he had gotten up every morning at five and set off on his bicycle to do the rounds of the rickshaw pullers, to collect payment for the daily hiring. "I could neither read nor write," he was to say with pride, "but I've always known how to add and I never missed out on a single rupee that was owed to me." As each one of his sons reached working age, he gradually diversified his business affairs. He kept the eldest one with him to assist him in the management of his fleet of vehicles that now came to more than three hundred. The second son he put in charge of a bolt factory that supplied the railways. For the youngest he bought a bus which covered the route from Dalhousie Square to the suburb of Garia. To obtain the franchise for this particularly lucrative route, he had given a substantial bribe to a *babu* at the municipality. As for his daughters, he had married them all off, and married them well. A fortunate father indeed was the Bihari! The eldest was the wife of a lieutenant-colonel in the Army, the next youngest that of a naval commander. He had married the two daughters next in line to tradesmen, the fifth to a *zamindar* in Bihar, and the youngest to an engineer in the highways department, a man who worked for the Bengal government. All in all, it was a superb accomplishment for the descendants of an illiterate peasant.

Yet in the evening of his life, the Bihari had lost much of his former enthusiasm. "Business is not what it used to be," he lamented. "Nowadays you have to be furtive about earning money. Effort, success, and good fortune have become crimes. Each successive government controlling our country has tried to liquidate the rich and appropriate the fruits of their labors, as if by making the rich poorer, the poor become richer! Here in Bengal, the Communists have instituted laws to restrict private ownership. They have decreed that no one individual has the right to own more than ten rickshaws. Ten rickshaws, can you imagine! As if I could support a family on ten rickshaws when I have constantly to pay out for maintenance, repairs, accidents, and baksheesh for the police. So I had to look after my own interests. I did what all the large landowners did when they were prohibited from owning

more than forty acres of land, I transferred the title of ownership
for my carriages to the names of my nine children and twenty-two
grandchildren. And just for the record, I even put some rickshaws
in the names of a dozen of my nephews. Officially my three hundred and forty-six vehicles belong to thirty-five different owners."

In fact the one and only master of the entire fleet was the
Bihari.

Few of his rickshaw pullers knew his face. Some of them did
not even know his identity. During the last ten years, he had ceased
to be seen around the area. "Now I am nothing but an old man,
doddering with the aid of a stick to meet the God of death, whom I
await in peace and serenity," he was to say. "I have a clear conscience. I have always been kind and generous to those who pulled
my rickshaws. Whenever one of them had difficulty paying his
hiring fee, I would let him have one or two days credit. Naturally I
asked him for interest but I was reasonable. I asked for only
twenty-five percent per day. Similarly, if one of them was sick or
the victim of an accident, it was I who advanced him the hospital
fees for medicine or a doctor. Afterward I increased the man's
hiring fee to cover what I had paid out and the puller had several
weeks in which to reimburse me. Now, my factotum looks after all
such matters. Alas, nowadays the pullers don't have the same good
mentality they used to have. They are forever asking for something. They'd like some magic wand to give them the ownership of
their carriages. They have even formed a union for that goal. And
they've taken strike action. The world is upside down! So now we
owners too have had to organize ourselves. We, too, have created a
syndicate, the All Bengal Rickshaw Owners Union. And we've
taken on henchmen to assure our protection. There was simply no
alternative, with a government that spent its time turning workers
against their bosses in the name of the so-called class struggle.
Several big shots in high circles even wanted to ban rickshaws
altogether, under the pretext that they were an insult to human
dignity and that the pullers were exploited like workhorses. Rubbish! They can shoot their mouths off all they like about their so-
called respect for the human being. Nothing is going to change the
fact that there are over a million poor bastards without work in
Calcutta, and that if you eliminate the livelihoods of a hundred
thousand rickshaw pullers, you'll condemn eight or nine hundred

thousand more people to starvation. It's a matter of common sense, but then politics and common sense aren't dugs of the same cow! So you just have to get by as best you can."

As long as his steward brought him the rent money each day after sunset, the Bihari would know that nothing had fundamentally changed. For this old man in the twilight of his life, there was still the joy of seeing his factotum's shirt bulging with bundles of bills. "The wise men of our nation say that nirvana is the attainment of a state of supreme detachment. For me nirvana is to be able, at the age of ninety plus a few years, to count out each evening, one by one, the rupees earned by my three hundred and forty-six rickshaws on the asphalt of Calcutta."

19

"WHEN I WAS A CHILD," Stephan Kovalski recalled, "I used to like to go for walks in the country and it amused me to chop the heads off flowers with a stick. Later, when I went to school, I used to like to pick a flower and put it on my table. Then I told myself that flowers were beautiful right there where they grew, and so I stopped cutting them and admired them in their natural setting. It was the same with women. One day I told the Lord that I didn't want to pick any one single woman because I wanted to let them all bloom right there where they were.

"Saint John of the Cross once wrote, 'Heaven is mine. Jesus is mine. Mary is mine. Everything is mine.' As soon as you want to hold on to any one particular thing, everything else escapes you, whereas by detachment you can enjoy everything without actually possessing anything in particular. That's the key to voluntary celibacy, without which chastity would make no sense. It's a choice of love. Marriage, on the other hand, means giving yourself, body and soul, to one single human being. As far as the body and carnal love were concerned, that would not have been difficult, but it was impossible for me to give my soul to any one single person. I had already decided to give it to God and there was no one in this world with whom I could share that gift—not even my mother whom I adored. 'Whoever has renounced a wife, children, a field, in my name will have them returned a hundredfold,' said Christ; and he was right. I had never had a sister, yet there, in the City of Joy, I found plenty of them who brought me great joy. With them I shared a sense of communion and solidarity which was so essential in a slum where people have so much need of one another.

"Nevertheless, having said all that, how could I fail to dream sometimes of a certain human tenderness? How, amid so much misery, could I fail to succumb to desirable women, who were such beacons of grace and seduction in their multicolored saris? In the ugliness of the slum, they were beauty itself. They were flowers. My problem was to adjust to their presence and remain lucid. Since I had decided not to seek a lasting love, with all its associated implications, I had no right to accept passing loves either. After all, I had responded once and for all to the appeal of the Lord of the Gospels and made mine his injunction to have no other household except the one that he would show me.

"I was not in a very comfortable position, particularly as my reputation for being a sort of Santa Claus often brought the women of the slum to me. An innuendo, a hand laid on mine, a flirtatious way of adjusting a sari, or a disturbing look sometimes led me to think their intentions might be suspect. But then perhaps I was mistaken, because in India links between men and women are frequently stamped with a certain ambiguity. Like the majority of other Indian women, still untouched by feminist liberation movements, the women in the City of Joy had no way other than seduction to attract masculine attention and assert their identity.

"I had hoped that my well-known status as a religious man would protect me from such manifestations of feeling, but I was wrong, and it wasn't really all that surprising. Wasn't there always, in every work of sacred Hindu literature, a scene in which the guru was tempted? And what about the erotic sculptures in the temples, where veritable orgies sprawled right across the bas-reliefs? I noticed that it was always during periods of relaxation that temptation hit me hardest, and not during intervals of intense trial. It was always during a phase when my relationship with God was in some way impoverished that I was at my most vulnerable. If you don't find your joy in God, you seek it elsewhere.

"I was particularly aware of this kind of danger in my relationship with Margareta, the young Christian widow who had brought me the bread and wine for my first Mass in the slum. It was not that she had ever made the slightest gesture or hint that was in any way compromising, but her body, molded in a simple piece of muslin, exuded a sensuality, a fragrance, a magnetism, which I found more difficult to resist than the attractions of other women. What was more, such a capacity for love, such an abandonment of herself emanated from her look, her smile, her voice, and her bearing that this flower seemed ever open to me. Probably I was wrong. I suspected the surroundings of distorting my perception."

One evening, at the end of one of those days that the fall of the barometer had made particularly trying, one of those days when your shirt sticks to your back and your mind is devoid of energy, Kovalski was trying to pray in front of the picture of the Sacred Shroud. In the moisture of the air, the little flame of his oil lamp made the face of Christ and his shadow dance in a ghostly ballet. He felt as if he were roaming about in a drifting vessel. In vain he struggled to concentrate his heart and soul on the Lord. He felt agonizingly deserted. It was then that he sensed her presence. He had not heard her enter but that was not very surprising. She moved about with the litheness of a cat. It was her scent that gave her away, the delicate fragrance of patchouli. He pretended not to notice her. He was praying aloud but soon the words became nothing but sounds. Her presence, her soft breathing in the darkness, the thought of the woman he could not see but whom he could smell, cast a spell over him in a way that was both marvelous and terrible. It was then as if the Lord abandoned him altogether. Suddenly from the other side of the wall came a moan, then a rattle, then uninterrupted groaning. The agony of Sabia, his little Muslim brother, had just begun again.

Those cries of anguish drove the Pole and the Indian woman instantly toward each other. Like two victims of a shipwreck clinging to the same buoy, they were two people in distress wanting to proclaim on the threshold of death their irresistible desire to live.

A kind of euphoria was flooding over Stephan when a knocking at the door wrested him from the grip of temptation. The Lord had rushed to his rescue.

"Big Brother Stephan!" called the mother of Sabia. "Come quickly! Sabia is asking for you."

20

HASARI PAL TURNED up at the Park Circus esplanade but Ram Chander, his friend the rickshaw puller, was not there. The peasant decided to wait. "This guy was my only hope," he was to explain, "my only assurance that somewhere in this infernal city a small lamp was burning for me also. I was prepared to wait until evening, all through the night if necessary—and all the next day too."

Ram Chander arrived in the early afternoon. He was without his rickshaw and looked dejected.

"The bastards have pinched my rickshaw," he growled. "Last night, after I dropped off the old lady I took on when we parted, I was going home when a cop stopped me. It had just gotten dark. 'Where's your lamp?' the son of a bitch asked me. I apologized, I told him I'd forgotten to take it with me that morning. But he didn't want to know. He suggested the usual arrangement."

"The usual arrangement?" asked Hasari.

"Yes, of course! 'Give me fifteen rupees,' he says to me, 'or I'll arrest you and take you to the police station.' It didn't matter how much I protested that I didn't have that kind of money. He was totally unmoveable. He drove me off to the police station, beating me with his *lathi*.* There they confiscated my carriage and, to top it all off, they reported me officially and ordered me to appear at police court tomorrow. They're going to saddle me with a fine of at least thirty rupees."

Ram took a long puff on the cigarette he held wedged in the

* Club.

hollow of his hands. "Let's go and get something to eat," he said. "Even the worst troubles look better on a full stomach."

He led Hasari to a cheap restaurant in Durga Road which was a regular haunt of his. It consisted of a small low room with five marble-topped tables. The owner, a fat Muslim, presided bare-chested over the cooking pots. On the wall behind him hung a grimy engraving of the Kaaba, the great black sacred stone of Mecca. On each table stood a bowl of coarse salt and dried pepper, and on the ceiling an antiquated fan showed ever-increasing signs of fatigue, with every turn of its blades. There was a strong smell of frying. A young boy brought them two plates of rice and a bowl of *dal*—boiled lentils. The two friends poured the soup over the rice and stirred the mixture with their fingers, then ate in silence. This was a real feast for Hasari, his first proper meal since he arrived in Calcutta. By the time they had finished, Ram Chander's optimism had been restored.

"There's enough wealth in this city to fill everyone's stomach." Hasari smoothed his mustache and looked skeptical. "It's true, I assure you," continued the rickshaw puller. "You still think like a peasant. But soon you'll be a real Calcutta *wallah* * and know all the tricks!"

Ram Chander left three rupees on the table and they set off for the hospital. They walked along a wide avenue, which was a street-car route, until they came to the Sealdah Railway station. Next to it was a market where the rickshaw puller bought some mandarin oranges and bananas for the injured coolie they were going to visit.

"Outside the hospital there were even more people than on the previous day," Hasari was to recount. "Everyone was trying to get in. There was shouting and arguing going on all around us. An ambulance with a red cross narrowly missed running over some people who were crowding the emergency entrance where we had left our friend the day before. I thought for a moment that the angry crowd was going to tear the driver to pieces, but he managed to extricate himself and open the door at the back of the vehicle. Inside I could see several bodies covered in blood. They looked as if they had been burned, shreds of flesh were hanging off their legs. It wasn't a pretty sight but we were in a hospital, after all, not in a

* An inhabitant of Calcutta.

paddy field. In a corner of the courtyard was a collection of rusty ambulances with broken windows and flat tires. Their red crosses were hardly visible. A number of lepers had made their home in this junk yard.

"We wandered about the hospital corridors, trying to find our friend. A nurse directed us to a room. I think she must have been in charge because she was the only one with a wide belt around her waist, an enormous bunch of keys, and stripes on her shoulders. Also she seemed to frighten everyone. To our left and right were larger rooms where employees were writing, drinking, and chatting, surrounded by mountains of paper tied together with little bits of string. Some of the papers must have been there for a long time because they were crumbling to dust—at least what the rats had left. Talking of rats, we saw a number of them coming and going. They must have a marvelous time in a place like that. Ram informed me that they sometimes attacked the sick and the injured. He cited the case of an old woman who was paralyzed, whose feet and hands were gnawed away during the night.

"Ram slipped a five-rupee note to the male nurse in charge of the ward for people who'd had operations. It was a vast room with several windows and large green fans on the ceiling. There were about fifty or so beds squeezed up against each other. At most of the bed heads hung a bottle from which a tube went into the patient. Generally the liquid was clear like water but in some instances it was red. That must have been blood from some poor bum like me who had sold it to feed his children. We went around between the beds, looking for our friend. It wasn't very pleasant because there were fellows there who weren't very nice to look at. There was one poor old man imprisoned from head to toe in a plaster cast. Nurses went from bed to bed pushing a cart laden with bottles of every imaginable color, and with cotton, dressings, and instruments. Those women must have their hearts in the right place to do that kind of work. Some patients clung to their white saris; others pushed them away with insults and threats.

"Our friend was lying on a *charpoy*, a frame strung with light ropes, because there were no more iron beds available. He looked pleased to see us. He told us that his foot was very painful but, even as he said so, he must have realized that it had been cut off because his eyes filled with tears. Ram gave him the fruits. He smiled, took a mandarin orange, and pointed to the next bed on which lay a small body whose head, arms, and legs were swathed in bandages. The child had been burned in a paraffin stove explosion and was groaning weakly. I peeled the fruit the injured coolie had given me and pressed a segment between the boy's lips. He opened his mouth and, with great difficulty, swallowed. The poor child, he was the same age as my Shambu.

"Our friend seemed to be in bad shape. His beard had grown, which served to accentuate how ill he looked, and his eyes appeared to have sunk into their sockets. His expression was full of despair. Ram and I did our best to comfort and reassure him that we wouldn't just leave him in the lurch. He had no one to call his own in Calcutta. We had become his only family. I'm not speaking for Ram, but having a bum like me for family was certainly no big deal.

"We stayed with him for quite a while. He must have had a very high fever because his forehead was constantly wet. Eventually a male nurse told us to leave. Our friend took our hands in his and held on to them, but we had to go. We said a few more things to him to try and raise his spirits, and we promised to come back. Before leaving the room, I turned around for one last time. I saw his hand waving weakly, like a reed in the evening breeze."

21

A MUSLIM FAMILY of seven—four children and three adults—occupied the hovel adjoining Stephan Kovalski's room. The head of the family was called Mehboub. He was a wiry, muscular little man in his thirties with a lively, determined expression beneath his shaggy eyebrows and a forehead half-concealed by a thick shock of curly hair. His wife, Selima, wore a little inlaid stone in her nostril. Despite the fact that she was several months pregnant, she was constantly on the go, sweeping, cleaning pots and pans, preparing meals, or doing the wash. Mehboub's mother, an old woman with short-cropped white hair who could hardly see, lived with them. For hours on end she would remain squatting in the alleyway murmuring snippets from the Koran. Nasir, the eldest son aged ten, was employed in a small workshop. Two of his sisters went to the Koranic school. The youngest, who was three years old, scampered about the alleyway. The family was quite well-off. For thirteen years Mehboub had worked as a day laborer in a naval yard in East Calcutta, forging propellers for boats. He earned about three hundred rupees a month, thirty U.S. dollars, a small fortune in a slum where thousands of families were unable to lay a hand on one rupee per person per day.

For several weeks Stephan Kovalski's relations with his neighbors had been confined to the mere exchange of a polite "Salaam" each morning and evening. Evidently these Muslims (and they were not the only ones) persisted in disapproving of the intrusion of a foreign Catholic priest into their neighborhood. As always, it was thanks to the children that relations gradually thawed. A few attentions, indications of interest in their games, was all it took to win them over.

A dramatic incident was to break the ice once and for all. One evening Mehboub came home from work looking totally dejected. The naval yard had just laid off all its work force. It was a practice that had been current since the introduction of a law obliging employers to pay their workers on a monthly basis after several months of regular work. With the exception of those whose interests it served, no one wanted to see this law implemented. It was even said that government, management, and the unions had actually joined forces against it. The government, because the increase in number of workers paid on a monthly basis would fatally reinforce the strength of the unions; management, because a laborer working on precarious terms was much more readily exploited; the unions, because their membership was composed of monthly workers eager to restrict their advantages to their own minority. Furthermore, as always in India, in addition to objective reasons there were considerations of tradition, inherited from the past. If all the day laborers became monthly workers, what would become of the custom by which the eldest son of a monthly worker was accorded the privilege of being employed by the factory where his father worked? Thus everyone conspired together to get around the law. To avoid having to give employment contracts, people were laid off periodically, then rehired. So it was that thousands of men lived under the shadow of not knowing whether or not their jobs would be waiting for them on the following day. After thirteen or fourteen years of employment, when it was no longer possible to put off giving them a contract, they were laid off once and for all. This was what had just happened to Stephan Kovalski's neighbor.

This sturdy man, with the muscles of his legs, chest, and shoulders strengthened by hard labor, began to waste away, before Kovalski's very eyes, and in the space of a few weeks. He shriveled up like a dried fruit. His stomach racked with hunger, he walked miles each day around the industrial suburbs of Calcutta in search of any available means of earning a crust of bread. In the evening, worn out, he would enter the priest's room and sink down, without a word, in front of the picture of the Sacred Shroud of Christ. Sometimes he would remain there for an hour, seated in the lotus position before the face of the man he so resembled. "Poor Mehboub," Kovalski was to say. "While you were praying in front of my icon, I was revolting at the Lord, just as I had done about little Sabia's agony. I found it so difficult to accept that He could allow such injustices to occur."

The seven members of that family soon had to survive on the twenty rupees (two U.S. dollars) that Nasir, the eldest boy, earned each month in the sweat shop where for twelve hours a day, he dipped the clips for ballpoint pens into a chrome bath. Despite the fact that all day long he inhaled toxic vapors from the metal under electrosis, Nasir was a sturdy lad, which in fact, was not really surprising. In poor families the food was always kept for the one who was working. The others were left with the crumbs. Nasir supplemented his wages with the ten rupees that Kovalski gave him. Every morning at dawn he took a tin full of water and lined up for the priest at the latrines, then came running back to tell Stephan when his turn had come.

One evening, after meditating in front of the picture of Christ, Mehboub invited the priest to come into his home. The room measured barely six by four feet. Two thirds of it was taken up by a low platform made out of planks which served as a table by day and a bed by night, when it was covered over with a patchwork of rags. The last born slept between his mother and his grandmother on the "table bed," while Nasir and his two elder sisters slept underneath it. As for Mehboub, he stretched out on a mat outside, under the porch roof. The only other piece of furniture consisted of a metal trunk in which the clothes for the feast days of the Muslim calendar were religiously preserved, carefully wrapped in cinema posters taken from the walls of Calcutta. Like millions of other Indian women, Selima fed her *chula* with cakes of cow dung and cinders gleaned from the ballast of the railway track. Their hovel with no window, no water, and no electricity was nonetheless meticulously clean, so much so that the floor of beaten earth was just like marble. No one would have dreamed of treading on it without first removing his shoes.

The more extreme the destitution, the warmer was the welcome. No sooner had Kovalski entered under their roof than his neighbors eagerly offered him tea, *jelebis,* * and other sweetmeats of

* Small syrupy fritters shaped like coils.

which the Bengalis are so fond. In a matter of seconds they had used up their resources for several days, just to honor him in this way.

Naturally Stephan Kovalski wanted to help this family, but how could he do so without falling into the trap of becoming a foreign Santa Claus? A relatively minor incident provided him with a solution. One morning, as he was cooking rice on his paraffin stove, he burned his hand. He used his clumsiness as a pretext to ask his neighbor's wife if, in the future, she would prepare his meals. In payment for his board he offered her three rupees a day (thirty U.S. cents), a princely sum by slum standards. For the Pole it was actually an opportunity to try out an experience on which he had set his heart. He insisted that the young woman prepare exactly the same food for him as she did for her family.

"How could I share faithfully the living conditions of my brothers in the City of Joy without knowing their most fundamental anguish," he was to explain, "the anguish that conditioned every instant of their lives: hunger—Hunger with a capital 'H'—the hunger that for generations had gnawed away at millions of people in this country, to the point where the real gulf between the rich and the poor existed at the level of the stomach. There were the *do-belas* who ate twice a day, the *ek-belas* who ate only once, and the others who could not even be sure of one daily meal. As for me, I was a three-*bela*, the almost unique representative of a species of consumer unknown in the slums."

The neighbor's wife looked with astonishment at the Pole.

"You, a *Father Sahib!*" she protested. "You, who people say are one of the richest men in your country, you want to eat the food of the poor? Stephan *Daddah*, it's not possible. You must be out of your mind!"

"Selima, little sister, how I wanted to beg your pardon!" Stephan Kovalski was later to say. "How indeed could you understand even for one second, you who lived among the refuse, who never saw a bird or the foliage of a tree, you who sometimes had not even a scrap to offer your children, you who could feel another little innocent stirring inside you, a child who tomorrow would hang from your empty breasts screaming famine, yes, how could you understand how anyone could be mad enough to exchange a karma in paradise for this infernal slum and come to share your poverty?"

"I mean it, little sister," confirmed Kovalski. "From tomorrow onward, you'll be the one to feed me, if you'll do me the kindness."

Next day at noon, one of Selima's daughters brought him a plate with his food for the day: a ladle of rice, a little cabbage and turnip, some *dal*—the lentils which often provided the poor of India with their only protein. For the other *ek-belas* of the slum this would have been a princely portion. With his European appetite, more accustomed as it was to alimentary excesses than Indian frugality, the Pole prepared to gulp his meal down in two minutes. As he had feared, however, Selima had remained true to Indian tradition which required that all food should be inflamed with chilis and other incendiary spices. He had no alternative but to absorb each mouthful slowly and cautiously. Having one day protested in front of an Indian doctor against this custom which, he thought, took all the flavor away from the food, Kovalski was to discover the real reason for this culinary practice. Because it releases perspiration, stimulates blood circulation, and accelerates assimilation of food, chili is first and foremost a means of duping the hunger of millions of undernourished people. And it makes it possible to swallow absolutely anything, even the most rotten food!

Not having to undertake any strenuous physical activity, the Pole put up with his new diet quite valiantly for the first two days. Whenever he felt the pangs of hunger, he would go and drink a cup of sweet tea from the old Hindu's shop across the way. On the third day, however, things became different. Violent cramps accompanied by dizziness and icy sweats began to gnaw at his stomach. Hardly had he eaten his one meal, that he had to crawl onto his mat, brought down by the pain. He tried to pray but his spirit seemed as empty as his stomach. Throughout the next day and the days that followed it, his hunger gave him no respite. He was ashamed. So few people were lucky enough to have even once a day a plateful of food like the one Selima cooked for him. He noted his body's reactions. His pulse was considerably faster, and so was his breathing. "Am I going to be able to hold out?" He worried, humiliated at finding himself already reduced to a limp rag while his companions in wretchedness managed to carry on, pulling carts

or carrying loads more fit for beasts of burden, on far fewer calo-
ries. After a few days, however, his troubles disappeared and the
sensation of hunger faded as if by magic. His body had adapted
itself. Not only did he no longer suffer, but he even experienced a
certain feeling of well-being.

It was then that he made a fatal mistake. A visitor from France
having brought him a tin of quenelles from Lyon and a Camembert
cheese, he went to offer these delicacies from his former adopted
homeland to the neighbors who had so little. Mehboub would
accept them only on condition that his friend shared in the treat.
The result was disastrous. It awoke the Pole's appetite in a way that
was completely uncontrollable. The nausea, cramps, and attacks of
sweating and dizziness reappeared with increased vigor. Kovalski
felt himself becoming weaker daily. His muscles wasted visibly. His
arms, thighs, legs, and pectorals were as if emptied of all substance. He lost several pounds more. The slightest task, even going
to fill his bucket at the fountain, took immeasurable effort. He had
difficulty staying upright for half an hour. He suffered from hallucinations. Nightmares haunted his sleep. He even began to bless the
chorus of rats that woke him at the point when, in his dreams, an
endless procession of emaciated men was bearing down upon him.
He was physically living the curse of hunger in his flesh. Physically
and mentally, Stephan Kovalski had joined the ranks of the majority of the occupants of Anand Nagar—and thus he had achieved his
objective.

Yet he was no fool. He knew the exact range of his experience,
and its limitations. "I was like those volunteers in survival who
know that they will be rescued after a certain amount of time.
Whereas the real tragedy of the truly poor is despair. I knew that if
my hunger exceeded bearable limits, I had only one gesture to
make to eat as much as I wanted. I knew that if I were to be struck
by the slightest ailment, thirty-six people would rush to my rescue.

"Mehboub and all the other occupants of the City of Joy were
real castaways. To the cries of their empty stomachs was added the
anguish of those who had no hope of rescue. And so their dignity
seemed all the more admirable. Not a single complaint ever issued
from the mouth of my neighbor. He allowed his turmoil to show
only when his youngest daughter cried with hunger. Then only did
his fine face become stricken with pain. But he reacted always

quickly. He would take hold of the little girl, sweep her up onto his knee, tell her a story, and sing her a song. Soon the child would begin to laugh. Forgetting her hunger, she would tear herself from her father's arms to go and play once more in the alleyway. There were times, however, when nothing would stop her tears. Then Mehboub would take his daughter in his arms and go into the neighboring courtyard to beg a piece of *chapati*. A poor person would never close his door on him. That was the law of the slum."

22

WITH HIS GRAY polo shirt, his beige linen trousers, and his leather sandals, Musafir Prasad was quite unlike the other human horses. After twenty years of toiling between the shafts of a rickshaw, he had moved on to the side where the money was. At forty-eight, this onetime peasant immigrant from Bihar had become a boss. He was the man who held the trust of Bipin Narendra, the old rickshaw owner whom people referred to as "the Bihari." Beneath his black wavy hair, shiny with mustard oil, his brain functioned just like a computer. This man with protruding ears and a nutcracker chin ran the empire of three hundred and forty-six carriages and some seven hundred human horses who pulled them; and he did so without either pencil or paper—for the very good reason that he could neither read nor write. Yet nothing escaped the diabolical vigilance of this phenomenon who was gifted with the quality of ubiquity. No matter whether it was a hundred and ten degrees in the shade or the monsoon was raging, he would cover several dozen miles a day on his squeaking bike. Because of his slightly bandy legs and the way he waddled as he pedaled, the rickshaw pullers had nicknamed him "the Wader." And, strange as it might seem, everyone in the streets of this inhuman city liked the Wader.

"When the Old Man summoned me to hand it all over," he recounted, "I thought God was bringing the sky down on my head. For the twenty years I had been working for him he had always confined me to the subordinate tasks, such as repairing the rickshaws, palavering with the cops, accidents, odd jobs, and so on. But the sacrosanct collection of the daily hiring fees was his task

and his alone. He never missed a single day, even when he was up
to his thighs in water. He was the only one who knew all the ins and
outs, for although the majority of rickshaw pullers paid for the hire
of their vehicle by the day, there were others who settled their
accounts on a weekly or monthly basis. Some paid at a cheaper rate
than others because repairs were their responsibility, or because
their rickshaw was operating without a license. Since there were
two men to each carriage, that made about seven or eight hundred
fellows to be managed. An enormous task which only the Old
Man's fat head, it seemed, could control. But one day the Old Man
began to feel the burden of his years. 'Listen to me, Musafir,' he
said to me. 'You and I, we've known each other for many years. We
are both Biharis and I trust you. You will be my representative.
From now on you will collect the money and bring it back here each
evening. For every rupee I will give you five *paisas.*' The Old Man
was not someone with whom you discussed things. I prostrated
myself, touched his feet, then raised my hands to my head. 'You are
the son of the god Shiva. You are my master,' I replied, 'and I shall
be eternally grateful to you.'

"Next day I got up at four because I wanted to go to the
latrines and the fountain before the other people in my neighborhood. The four companions with whom I lodged in a shack near
the Old Man's big house, were still asleep. They too, worked for
the Old Man as bus driver, mechanic, rickshaw puller, and joiner.
They too were Biharis, and they too had left their families behind
in their villages to come and earn a living in Calcutta.

"At four-thirty, I straddled my bicycle and pedaled straight to
the temple of Lakshmi, our goddess of prosperity, behind the Jagu
Bazar. It was pitch dark and the Brahmin priest was still asleep
behind his grill. I rang the bell and eventually he appeared, whereupon I gave him ten rupees and asked him to celebrate a *puja* just
for me so that the day might begin under the best of auspices. I had
taken with me a coneful of rice, some flowers, and two bananas.
The priest deposited my offerings on a tray and we entered the
interior of the sanctuary. He lit several oil lamps, then recited
mantras before the divinity. I repeated some prayers. The *puja* filled
me with intense joy and the certainty that from that day onward I
was going to earn a lot of rupees. Solemnly I promised Lakshmi
that the more money I had, the more offerings I would bring her.

"After the *puja*, I cycled off in the direction of Lowdon Street, near the Bellevue clinic nursing school, where the Old Man had six rickshaws. Because of the early hour, all the pullers were still there. They were asleep on the canvas seats with their legs dangling in midair. Most of the pullers had nowhere else to live. Their vehicle was their home. Where they were two to a cart, there were quarrels which I was supposed to arbitrate. It wasn't easy to tell one that he could sleep in his old rattletrap, and not the other!

"Next I made for Theatre Road where the Old Man had a dozen carriages. Then I cut down Harrington Street, a pretty, residential road with fine mansions set in gardens and buildings where rich people and foreigners lived. Outside the gate to one of these houses there were always uniformed guards and an American flag. The Old Man had at least thirty rickshaws in that sector. Because it was a wealthy neighborhood, it was also a problem area. There were always one or two characters who'd had their carriages pinched by the cops under some pretext or other. And the cops asked for a lot of baksheesh because they knew the men earned a better living there than elsewhere. You had only to look at the sidewalk along the police station in Park Street, opposite Saint-Xavier's College. It was permanently cluttered with a column of confiscated rickshaws slotted into each other and chained together. They stretched for more than a hundred yards. That first morning I had to go and bow and scrape and grease the brutes' palms with more than sixty rupees for the release of a number of carriages, a formality which invariably complicated my accounts because I had subsequently to make sure that the dues from the pullers concerned were raised for a prescribed number of days.

"After Harrington Street I set off as fast as I could for the rickshaw stand in front of the Mallik Bazar, on the corner of the great intersection of Park Street and Lower Circular Road where, of the thirty or forty carriages parked there, a good twenty were again the property of the Old Man. Before this next call, however, I pulled up on the corner of New Park Street to drink a cup of tea— tea that was nice and hot and strong, with plenty of sugar, as only Ashu, a fat Punjabi installed on the pavement, knew how to make it. His was the best tea on the pavements of Calcutta. Ashu mingled the milk, sugar, and tea in his kettle with as much solemnity as a

Brahmin carrying out *Arati*.* I envied him the way he spent his days, seated on his ass, lording it over his utensils, being appreciated and highly thought of by his customers.

"My pedaling took me next to the fish, meat, and vegetable market on Park Circus, next to which a good fifty carriages were always parked. As I progressed through my rounds, the corner of my shirt into which I stuffed the notes swelled up to create a bulge at my waist. Sporting a fat belly in Calcutta was in itself a strange sensation but for the fat belly to be compiled of a cushion of bank notes belonged to the realms of make-believe. By this time many of the pullers were already carrying a fare or cruising the streets ringing their bells on their shafts to attract the attention of customers. That meant I had to scour half the city. At midday, however, I recouped myself outside the area's schools and colleges, where hundreds of rickshaws concentrated twice a day. Taking the children to school and back was, in fact, a speciality of the corporation and the only opportunity to earn a regular income, since each kid usually had his regular puller. This arrangement was called a "contract" and by becoming the beneficiary of one or more daily contracts a puller could double or even triple the amount of the money order he sent each month to his family. It was also a fine guarantee of his standing with the clients. But how many fellows had that sort of luck?

"I knew that to do my job properly, I needed a heart of stone like my boss. How else would I be able to claim the five-or-six-rupee hiring fee from some poor bum whose carriage hadn't budged from the spot. I knew that some days many of them would have to go without food to pay me. Poor guys! How are you supposed to pull two clients and all their parcels or two fat women from one of the rich neighborhoods with nothing in your stomach? Every day pullers collapsed in the street. And each time some fellow couldn't get back on his feet, I had to look for a replacement. Thank God there was no shortage of candidates! But the Old Man had always gone to a great deal of trouble to choose the right pullers, to find out about their background. He had good reason for doing so. He didn't want to get mixed up with politics. Claims for this or that, blackmail, threats, strikes were a nightmare to him.

* Ceremony of the offering of lights.

'Musafir, I don't want any worms in my guava,' he would say repeatedly, because rickshaw pullers now had their own unions and the government was trying to infiltrate them with phony pullers who would stir up action against the owners. Rickshaw pullers, people were saying, should be granted the ownership of their instruments of labor. Up till now it had never actually happened. I knew one or two who had become, as I had, their owner's representative. I knew even some who had managed to swap their shafts for the steering wheel of a taxi. But I didn't know of anyone who had managed to buy his own rickshaw—even an old jalopy with no operator's license.

"The goddess Lakshmi, in her goodness, was not deaf to my prayers and my offerings. By the end of my first week I had a nice bundle of a hundred and fifty rupees to take to the *munshi** outside the post office in Park Street. My family in the village would be well and truly surprised. Their last postcard asking me for money had arrived only two days before. Their cards always said the same thing. Either they asked me for money or they informed me that my last money invoice had arrived safely and that they had been able to buy the paddy or whatever else for the family field. I had left behind in my home village my father, mother, wife, three sons, two daughters, and three daughters-in-law plus their children. Altogether there were a good twenty mouths to feed off two poor acres. Without what I sent, famine would strike the dried mud hut in which, forty-eight winters previously, my mother had brought me into the world.

"At the post office in Park Street I had my regular *munshi*. His name was D'Souza and he was a Christian. He came from the other end of India, a place called Goa, below Bombay. The *munshi* always greeted me with a smile and some kindly words of welcome, for we were good friends. I had brought him business from my rickshaw pullers working in that area and he slipped me a commission on any transactions he undertook for them. It was in the usual run of things. There is nothing like money matters for cementing strong bonds between workers.

"That was what I was thinking about on the morning I saw Ram Chander, one of my pullers, rushing toward me with two ten-

* Public letter writer.

rupee notes in his hand. Ram was one of the few Bengalis who worked for the Old Man. The night before, he had had his carriage picked up by the cops for having no light. It was only a pretext for baksheesh in a city where the vast majority of trucks and cars operate without lights. Nevertheless, Ram Chander wasn't offering me twenty rupees for me to go and get his rickshaw out of the pound, but rather for me to take on the companion he had with him. '*Sardarji*, you are the most noble son of Ma-Kali,'* he exclaimed. 'I'd like to introduce a compatriot of mine to you. He comes from my district. I and my family have known his clan and his lineage for generations. He is a brave and honest worker. For the love of Our Mother Kali, give him one of your rickshaws to pull.'

"I took the two notes he was holding out to me and examined the man who seemed slightly reluctant to come forward. Although he was very thin, his shoulders and arms looked solid. I asked him to lift up his *longhi* so that I could check the condition of his legs and thighs too. The Old Man always used to do that before employing a puller. He used to say that you shouldn't entrust a rickshaw to a young goat. I weighed the pros and cons before responding to the eager expectation of the two Bengalis. 'You're in luck. There's a man who died last night near Bhowanipur market.'"

* The goddess mother Kali.

23

THE MUSLIM QUARTER of the City of Joy had burst into a celebration state. During the last two days, in all the compounds, women had unpacked the festive clothes they had so religiously preserved. The men had strung garlands of multicolored streamers across the alleyways. Electricians had installed loudspeakers and strings of colored light bulbs. On every street corner, confectioners were heaping up mountains of sweetmeats on their trays. Their poverty and anguish forgotten, the fifty thousand Muslims in the slum were preparing to celebrate one of the most important events in their calendar, the birth of the prophet Muhammad.

Resounding strains of hymns and chants transformed this stricken neighborhood into a frenzied kermis. Prostrate and facing in the direction of the distant, mystical Kaaba, thousands of the faithful filled the six mosques for a night of uninterrupted prayer.

The barbers', tailors', and jewelers' shops were packed with shoppers. The poor adorned themselves for the occasion like princes. Hindu women came running to assist their Muslim neighbors with the cooking of the traditional feasts. Others, armed with combs, brushes, flowers, and ribbons, helped with the hairdos. Yet others brought saffron, carmine, and henna powder to embellish their friends' faces, arms, and feet with skillful motifs. Children were the objects of a particularly subtle toilet. With their eyes accentuated with great rings of kohl, their skinny bodies draped in shiny silk tunics and muslin veils, and their feet tucked into Turkish slippers, they looked just as if they had stepped out of an illustration of *A Thousand and One Nights*.

For all their noises, the popular rejoicing and the loudspeakers could not drown, however, the groans Kovalski could hear. But the torture that Sabia, his little neighbor, was going through, no longer repelled the priest. Eventually he had conceded that it was indeed Jesus who was suffering on the other side of the mud wall and that his suffering was a prayer. One question, however, continued to haunt him: Was the child's sacrifice really indispensable?

> *Allah Akbar! God alone is great!*
> *Peace be with Muhammad his prophet!*
> *Allah Akbar!*
> *Peace be with Noah, Abraham, Moses, Zachariah,*
> *Jesus, and all the other prophets!*

The congregation took up in a chorus each verse as it was called into the microphone by the blind mullah with the goatee from the Jama Masjid, the City of Joy's main mosque. With its cream façade pierced by meshed windows and its four minarets tapered like candles, it was the tallest and most colorful building in the slum. It rose from a square that formed the only uncluttered space in the ants' nest, beside a pool of stagnant water in which the occupants of the neighborhood did their washing. A joyful crowd filled the square and all the surrounding streets. Above their heads fluttered a multitude of little green-and-white flags, red banners marked with the crescent of Islam, and banderoles decorated with verses from the Koran and the golden cupolas of the sacred mosques in Jerusalem, Medina, and Mecca—magic symbols that illuminated with faith and dreams their decaying surroundings.

The blind mullah, a venerable patriarch in a white silk turban, walked at the head of the procession. Two religious figures dressed in gray *abayas* guided his way. Blaring from a cyclecar equipped with a loudspeaker, a litany of canticles taken up by thousands of voices gave the signal to move off. Every two minutes the mullah stopped, took over the microphone, and chanted invocations that electrified the faithful. Soon the cortege extended for more than a mile, a prodigious stream of color and voices flowing between the walls of the hovels and irrigating the pestilential labyrinth through which it passed, with its vibrant faith and glittering finery. On this festive day Islam was infusing the slum with lights, noise, and religious fervor.

From the doorway of his hovel, Kovalski looked on with

amazement as the procession approached. How, he wondered, could so much beauty spring out of so wretched a place? The sight of the children was particularly compelling. The pinks, blues, golds, and cameos of the girls' *shalwars* and *ghaghras,* and the boys' embroidered muslin *kurtas* and braided *topis** robed the procession in an enchanting medley of color. Kovalski recognized his neighbor, Mehboub, in the third row, holding the pole of a red-and-green standard decorated with a minaret. The feast day had metamorphosed the famishing unemployed worker into a superb soldier of the prophet. Among the children, paraded his eldest son, Nasir, the one who lined up for the latrines on Kovalski's behalf, and also his two little daughters, together with Sabia's sisters, all dressed up and ornamented like princesses with sparkling glass bracelets, spangled sandals and multicolored muslin veils. "Thank you, Lord, for having given the down-trodden people of this slum so much strength to believe in you and love you," the priest murmured softly to himself, overwhelmed by the crescendo of voices, proclaiming aloud the name of Allah.

It was at that point that he heard someone calling him. "Big Brother Stephan, I would like you to bless my son before he is taken away. Sabia was very fond of you and you are truly a man of God." Sabia had just died. He had died at the very moment the procession of the prophet was passing the hovel in Nizamudhin Lane that had sheltered his agony.

Even in her pain, Sabia's mother's dignity remained exemplary. At no time throughout her great trial had this woman's face betrayed the slightest despondency. Whether she was crouched in the street making her paper bags, wading through the mud with her bucket of water, or kneeling in prayer at her son's bedside, she had held her head high and managed to maintain the serenity of her smile and the beauty of a temple statue. "I never met her without giving thanks to God for having lit such a flame of hope in this place of suffering," Kovalski was to say. "Because she never gave up. On the contrary, she fought like a lioness. In order to pay for the doctor's consultation and the expensive medicines, she took the last of her jewelry to the usurer—two bracelets, a pendant,

* Trousers drawn in at the ankles; skirts; shirts without a collar; and toques, respectively.

a pair of earrings which had survived other disasters. Often at night I heard her reciting verses from the Koran to ease her child's pain. Sometimes she would invite the neighboring women in to pray with her at his bedside, just as the holy women of the Gospels prayed at the foot of the Cross. In her there was neither fatalism nor resignation. Nor did I ever hear her utter a single word of rebellion or complaint. That woman taught me a lesson in faith and love."

Now, she cleared a way for him between the mourning women. The child was lying on a litter, swathed in a white shroud, with a garland of yellow marigolds placed upon his chest. His eyes were closed and every feature of his face had relaxed into an expression of peace. With his thumb Stephan Kovalski traced the sign of the Cross on the boy's forehead. "Goodbye, my glorious little brother," he whispered. A few moments later, borne by youths from the alleyway, Sabia left his hovel on his final journey to the Muslim cemetery at the far end of the slum. Immersed in prayer, Stephan Kovalski followed the small cortege. Because of the festivities, there were not many people along the route to mark the passing of an innocent child. In any case, death was so natural a part of everyday life in the City of Joy that no one paid particular attention to it.

PART TWO

*Human Horses and
Their Chariots of Fire*

24

HASARI PAL STOOD and gazed at the rickshaw before him, as if it were Ganesh in person—Ganesh the elephant-headed god, benefactor of the poor who brought good fortune and removed obstacles. Instead of the rickshaw's shafts, Hasari could see a trunk; in the place of wheels large ears. Eventually he approached the vehicle with respect and rubbed the moonstone in his ring on the shafts, then touched his heart and his forehead with his hand.

"That carriage, lined up against the pavement, was a gift of the gods," he was to say, "an urban plow with which to make my sweat bear fruit and provide food for my children and for all my relatives waiting expectantly in the village. And yet it was just an old jalopy, completely run-down and with no license to operate. The paint was peeling off in strips, the straw stuffing was coming out of the holes in the seat, several hoops in the hood were broken, and the rubber tires around the wheels were so worn that you could see the wood through them. Under the seat there was a locker designed to contain any essential accessories, a bottle of oil to grease the hubs every now and then, a wrench to tighten up the wheel bolts, a lamp to light at night, the linen screen that hooks onto the front of the hood when you're transporting Muslim women who wish to remain concealed from men's eyes, or to protect travelers during the monsoon downpours.

"If I mention these things, it's only because my friend, Ram Chander, had shown them to me in the locker of his rickshaw, the day we took the injured coolie to the hospital. My locker was empty. Someone must have ransacked it when the previous puller dropped dead in the street. Ram had already warned me that if it was possible to steal the air we breathe, there'd be people in Calcutta prepared to do it.

"On the back of the carriage a metal plate bore a number and some inscriptions. I didn't know what the latter meant but I engraved the number on my mind like a talisman, like the magic formula that was going to open the gateway to a new karma. Overwhelmed with happiness, I had shown my friend and benefactor, Ram, the number 1 and the three 9s that were featured on the plate. It didn't matter that the number was a phony one, it was made up exclusively of figures that in our calendar augur well.

"Having admired it at length, I finally took my place between the shafts of the rickshaw, raised them respectfully, and placed my fingers on the worn spot vacated only hours earlier by the hands of the poor fellow to whom the number 1999 had certainly not brought good fortune. I thrust my hips forward and heard the wheels creak. That creaking was like the reassuring sound of a millstone grinding the grains of rice from our land. How could I fail to believe in the benediction of the gods? What was more, that first day of my new life fell on a Friday, the best day in the week along with Monday, because that was when the most money was about. And it was the beginning of the month. From the fifteenth day onward, people were apparently as tight as the trident of Shiva. Good old Ram had already revealed plenty of secrets and taught me the tricks of the trade. 'There are all sorts of people,' he'd said to me. 'Good ones and bastards. There'll be those who make you run and others who'll tell you to take your time. Some will try and knock a few *paisas* off the cost of the journey. But if you're lucky enough to pick up a foreigner, you can ask for more money.' He had put me on my guard against *gundas** who, like some prostitutes, specialize in giving you the slip without paying when you reach their destination. 'You'd be well advised to lay in a stock of mustard oil to massage your limbs,' he had also warned me, 'because for the first few days your thighs, arms, and back will be as painful as if every cop in Calcutta had busted his *lathi* on you.'

"I found myself alone, alone with this extraordinary cart in the middle of an unknown city, teeming with people. It was terrifying. How would I ever find my way through the labyrinth of streets? Or

* Crooks.

manage to edge between the trucks, buses, and cars that bore down upon me with a deafening roar, like waves from a tidal storm? I was panic-stricken.

"As Ram had advised me, I pulled my rickshaw to Park Circus to wait for my first client. Park Circus was a very busy junction where several bus routes and streetcar lines intersected. There were lots of little workshops and schools there, as well as a large market frequented by housewives from the rich neighborhoods. A long string of rickshaws was permanently parked on this privileged junction. I can't say that the pullers waiting patiently there, sitting on their shafts, received me with shrieks of joy. There were so few crumbs to be gathered up in this inhuman city that the arrival of one more competitor was not exactly guaranteed to induce a state of joy. They were all Biharis. Most of them were very young, but the older ones had a really worn look about them. You could count their ribs beneath the threadbare cotton of their vests.

"The line shortened swiftly. Soon my turn would come. As it approached, I felt my heart pounding in my chest. Would I actually manage to pull this old heap? The prospect of plunging with it into the furious flood of traffic was already paralyzing my arms and legs. To give myself strength, I went and bought a glass of sugarcane juice for twenty-five *paisas*, from the Bihari who passed bits of cane back and forth under his grinding wheel. He did a good business. There was a constant line in front of his grinder, for a glass of cane juice was often all that a fellow could manage to get down him all day. The poorest among us sometimes had to content themselves with buying a piece of cane and chewing on it to keep hunger at bay. That cost only ten *paisas* (one U.S. cent). But drinking a whole glass was like putting a whole tank of gasoline in your engine. I felt a blast of warmth descend from my stomach to my thighs. As for the old jalopy, I could gladly have pulled it to the highest peak of the Himalayas.

"The memory of the old happy days, when I used to follow the slow progress of the buffalo through the rice field, came through my mind. Then, as if out of a dream, I heard a voice, 'Rickshaw *wallah!*' I saw a young girl with two long braids down to her waist. She was wearing the white blouse and navy blue skirt of the girls from a nearby school. Clambering into my rickshaw, she asked me to take her home. Realizing that I hadn't the faintest idea where her

street was, she gave me directions. I shall never forget those very
first moments when I suddenly found myself in the middle of
traffic. It was quite insane. I was like a man who had thrown himself
into the water to get away from wild animals, only to find himself
surrounded by a herd of crocodiles. The bus and truck drivers led
the dance. They seemed to derive a malignant satisfaction from
terrorizing rickshaws, charging them like wild bulls amid the noise
of their horns and engines. The wildest of all were the minibus
drivers and the turbaned taxi drivers. I was so terrified that I
moved forward at a walking pace, my eyes on the lookout to left
and right. I concentrated on trying to keep the vehicle in balance,
on finding the exact place to put my hands, in order to distribute
the weight most effectively. It was more easily said than done in the
middle of bumpy thoroughfares, ditches, holes, ruts, the mouths of
open drains, streetcar lines. You had to be a real acrobat! But
Ganesh's trunk was watching over my rickshaw during that first
run. It steered me through the obstacles and brought me to the
girl's house safe and sound.

"'How much do I owe you?' inquired the girl as she stepped
out of my carriage. I hadn't the faintest idea. 'Give me whatever
you think.' She looked in her purse. 'There's three rupees. That's
more than the usual price, but I hope it brings you luck.'

"I took the notes and put them next to my heart, thanking her
effusively. I was deeply touched. I kept my hand on them for a
while, as if to imprint myself with that first money earned in the
skin of a Calcutta rickshaw *wallah*. Feeling those notes between my
fingers brought me a sudden surge of hope, the conviction that by
working hard I could actually achieve what my family were expecting of me and become their feeding bird, the one who would
distribute food to all the starving fledglings in our village hut.

"In the meantime it was to my wife and children that I wanted
to present the money from that first journey. I rushed to the
nearest vendor selling fritters and started to run for the pavement
where we were camping, with a bag of fritters as my only passenger. My arrival instantly attracted a crowd. The news that a pavement dweller had actually become a rickshaw *wallah* had spread
from one end of the street to the other, like the sound of a fire-

cracker at Diwali.* It did not matter that my old heap was one of the most common vehicles to be found in Calcutta; kids crawled up its wheels to sit on the seat, men felt the weight of the shafts, and women looked at me with admiration and envy. Arjuna going off in his chariot to the great war of our Mahabarata could not have made more of an impression. To all those poor people who, like us, had left their rice fields, I was a living proof that there was always grounds for hope.

"That reception spurred me on more effectively than a whole plateful of green chilis. I set off again and had barely covered a few yards before two enormous matrons hailed me to take them to the Hind Cinema in Ganesh Avenue. They must have weighed four hundred pounds between them and I thought my ramshackle carriage was going to give out at the first turn of the wheels. The hubs squeaked heartrending creaks, and the shafts shuddered in my palms like reeds on a stormy day. In vain I strained; I simply could not manage to find the right balance. I was like a buffalo harnessed to a house.

My two passengers must have sensed my incompetence because one of them ordered me to stop. As soon as they had gotten out, they hailed another rickshaw. I don't know what chilis that puller had eaten that day but I watched him trot away with no more difficulty than if he had been carrying two statuettes of Durga to the Ganges.

"After such bitter humiliation, I felt a burning need to redeem myself. I was ready to pick up literally anyone, even free of charge, just to show what I was capable of.

"The opportunity presented itself on the corner of Park Street, a wide road in the city center flanked by arcades. A young man and a girl coming out of a pastry shop with ice-cream cones in their hands signaled to me to pick them up. The boy asked me to put up the hood and fix up the linen screen that is used during the monsoon or to protect Muslim women from indiscreet eyes. Unfortunately, I didn't possess that accessory! All I could suggest was that they used my spare loin cloth. The young man helped the girl in and directed me to go around the block. I was intrigued but without any further question I fixed the material on to the hood

* The Hindu festival of light when Lakshmi, goddess of prosperity is venerated.

and there we were, off on a journey with no destination. Hardly had I turned the corner than frantic jolts nearly made me lose my balance. Clinging onto the shafts to keep my course, I soon understood the reason for the jerking. My old jalopy was serving as a love nest.

"Calcutta, you are no longer a cursed city. Quite the opposite, let me bless you for having given me, a poor peasant exiled from Bengal, the opportunity to earn seventeen rupees on this first day. And let me bless you too, dear Ganesh, for having kept all snares and dangers from my carriage and harness, and for allowing me to complete seven runs without problem or accident. I decided to devote a part of my earnings to the purchase of one accessory that is the emblem of rickshaw pullers. The peasant's trade also has its noble tools, like the plowshare and the sickle used to harvest the rice. These instruments are fêted at the great *puja* of the god Vishwakarma.*

"The instrument I was intent on buying was the bell that the rickshaw pullers carry, slipping their right index finger into its thin strap and thus using it to attract clients by jangling it against a rickshaw shaft. Bells come in all different shapes and sizes, and at a variety of prices. They range from the most ordinary gray scrap iron ones to superb copper bells that shine as brightly as the planet Brihaspati. Some of them exude sounds like that of a crested crane fishing on the surface of a pond. Others are more like the call of a kingfisher pursuing a dragonfly. It was from a puller in Park Circus that for two rupees I bought my first bell. It had a fine leather strap which I fastened to my index finger next to my moonstone ring. With such jewels on my fingers, how could I fail to feel good energies welling up inside me? How could I not believe in the generosity of my karma?

"It would not take long for me to be disenchanted. Next morning when I awoke, my arms, legs, back, and the nape of my neck hurt so much that I had great difficulty in getting up on my feet. My friend Ram Chander had warned me—you don't turn into a human horse overnight, even if you are of good peasant stock. The prolonged effort involved in pulling, the brutal jolts, the exhausting acrobatics entailed in keeping the thing balanced, the

* The god of working tools.

violent and sometimes desperate stiffening of the whole body in order to stop in an emergency—it all gives you a brutal shock when you've hardly eaten for months and your body is already pretty worn out.

"In vain I followed Ram's advice to massage myself from head to toe in mustard oil, like the wrestlers on Howrah Bridge before a fight. I was quite incapable of taking up the shafts of my rickshaw. I could have wept. I entrusted the machine to the care of my wife and dragged myself off to the Park Circus stand. I was absolutely set on giving the five rupees for the day's rental to the owner's representative. I would have gone without food, I would have taken my moonstone to the *mahajan* just to pay off those five rupees. It was a matter of life and death; thousands of other starving peasants were waiting to get their hands on my rickshaw.

"At Park Circus I ran into Ram. He had just gotten his carriage back after his clash with the police the other evening. He thought it was a joke to see me shuffling along, bent over like an old man."

"You haven't seen anything yet!" he jeered at me. "Before three months are up you'll be coughing red too."

"That's how I discovered that my friend, who always seemed so hearty and sure of himself, had an infection of the lungs.

"Are you taking any medicine for it?

"He looked at me in surprise."

"You must be joking? You've seen for yourself the lines at the dispensary. You get there at dawn and by evening you're still there. You're better off treating yourself to a nice bit of pan every now and then."

"Pan?"

"Certainly. To camouflage the enemy. When you cough, you don't know whether it's blood or betel. That way you don't worry so much."

"Thereupon, Ram suggested that we go visit our coolie friend in the hospital. It was two days since we had been to see him. So much had happened during those two days! Taking pity on the state I was in, Ram offered to transport me in his rickshaw. It made quite an entertaining spectacle. The other pullers at the stand were hugely amused to see the pair of us going off like that. They didn't have that many opportunities for a laugh.

"It was a very strange sensation for me to find myself suddenly in the position of passenger! It was even more terrifying than being down in between the shafts. All those buses and trucks whose metal panels almost brushed your face! I was in the prime position to see everything, including the taxi bearing down on us like a stampeding elephant, which forced Ram into a pirouette at the very last second. And the heavily laden *telagarhi* emerging from the right that nothing, not even a wall, would have been able to stop. I admired the virtuosity with which Ram changed the position of his hands on the shaft so that the wheels took all the weight of the load. With his bell, you might have taken him for a Katakali dancing girl.

"The trek to the hospital was a long one. All the streets were blocked by processions with red banners, which completely obstructed the traffic. In Calcutta such processions seemed to be part of the general decor. I had already seen a number of them. Here the workers were organized and kept parading all the time for their demands. That sort of thing didn't go on in the villages. Who were we supposed to go and demand anything from in the country? You can't march in protest against the sky because it hasn't yet sent the monsoon. Here there was a government to take your dissatisfaction to.

"We stopped in a bazaar to buy fruits. This time I was the one who paid for it with the money left from the previous day. I also bought a pineapple that I had the vendor peel and cut up into wedges. That way we'd be able to eat them with the coolie.

"The hospital was still overflowing with people. We went straight to the building where we had last seen our friend. Before we did so, Ram chained a wheel of his rickshaw to a streetlamp and took with him the contents of the locker. The same attendant was still watching over the patients who'd been operated on, and he let us in without any difficulty after we'd slipped two rupees into his pocket. There was still that appalling smell that seemed to grab you by the throat. We picked our way between the rows of beds to our friend's cot at the far end, near the window, next to the burned child whom I'd fed the orange. As I was having difficulty walking with my stiffness, Ram was quite a way in front of me when he called out, 'He's not there anymore!'

"Our friend's bed was occupied by an old Muslim with a goatee, whose body was covered with bandages. He couldn't tell us anything, nor could the attendant. I should say that we didn't even know the name of the injured coolie. Perhaps he had been moved elsewhere? Or perhaps they had simply discharged him to make room for someone else? We explored several wards. We even managed to get into the room adjacent to the one where they performed operations. Our friend was nowhere to be found.

"As we were coming out of the building we saw two male nurses carrying a body on a stretcher. We recognized our friend. His eyes were open; his cheeks were sunken and gray with stubble. His lips were not closed. It was as if he were trying to say something to us. But for him it was all over. I couldn't help wondering whether there'd be more handcarts for him in his next incarnation, or whether he'd be a *sardarji* behind the wheel of a taxi.

"Ram questioned the nurses to find out where they were taking our friend. 'He's an indigent,' replied the elder of the two. 'He'll be thrown into the river.' "

25

THE DEATH OF young Sabia changed the attitude of Stephan Kovalski's neighbors. It dispelled their reticence. Even the most mistrustful now greeted the priest with "Salaam, Father!" The children squabbled over who was to carry his bucket on the way to the fountain.

Then came another event that served to complete this transformation. A few doors away from his room lived a girl of fifteen who had become blind as a result of a virus infection. Her eyes were purulent and she suffered so much that she cursed the world and everything in it. Her name was Banno and she had long braids like a princess in a Mogul miniature. One day her mother came and stood before Stephan Kovalski, her hands joined together in a gesture of supplication.

"*Daktar,** for the love of God, do something for my little girl," she implored.

How could he cure an infection of that kind when all he had in the way of drugs were a few aspirin tablets, a little paregoric, and a tube of some sort of pomade? All the same, Stephan Kovalski decided to apply a little of the pomade on the girl's eyes. Three days later the miracle had occurred; the infection had been stopped, and by the end of the week young Banno had recovered her sight. The news spread like wildfire. "There's a white wizard in the neighborhood."

This exploit earned the Pole his final certificate of acceptance and a degree of notoriety which he could well have done without.

* Doctor.

Dozens of sick people and invalids wended their way to 49 Nizamudhin Lane. He was compelled to procure other medicines. His room became a haven of refuge for those in the very direst straits. It was never empty. One morning two bearers set down a bearded man whose shaggy hair was covered with ashes. He was attached to a chair. He had no legs and no fingers on his hands. He was a leper, yet his young face radiated a joy that was astonishing in one so disinherited.

"Big Brother, my name is Anouar," he announced. "You must look after me. As you can see, I'm very sick."

His gaze alighted next on the picture of the Shroud of Christ.

"Who is that?" he asked, surprised.

"It's Jesus."

The leper looked incredulous.

"Jesus? No, it can't be. He doesn't look like he usually does. Why does your Jesus have his eyes closed and look so sad?"

Stephan Kovalski knew that Indian iconography reproduced images of Christ in abundance, but those of a Christ with blue eyes, triumphant and brightly colored, like the gods of the Hindu pantheon.

"He has suffered," said the priest.

The Pole sensed that further explanation was necessary. One of Margareta's daughters translated his words into Bengali.

"His eyes are closed, so that he can see us better," he went on. "And so that we, for our part, can look at him more readily. Perhaps if his eyes were open, we wouldn't dare to, because our eyes are not pure, nor are our hearts, and we carry a large share of the responsibility for his suffering. For if he is suffering it's because of me, you, all of us; because of our sins, because of the evil that we do. Still he loves us so much that he forgives us. He wants us to look at him. That's why he closes his eyes and those closed eyes invite me, too, to close my eyes to pray, to look at God inside me . . . and inside you too. And to love him. And to do as he does and forgive everyone and love everyone, especially those who suffer like him, they invite me to love you who are suffering like him."

A little girl in rags who had remained hidden behind the leper's chair came forward and planted a kiss on the picture, caressing it with her small hand.

"*Ki Koshto!* How he must suffer!" she murmured, after touching her forehead with three fingers.

The leper seemed to be deeply moved. His dark eyes were shining.

"He is in pain," Stephan Kovalski went on, "but he doesn't want us to weep for him, but rather for those who are suffering today, because he suffers in them, in the bodies and hearts of the lonely, the abandoned, the despised, as well as in the minds of the insane, the neurotic, and the deranged. You see, that's why I love that picture. Because it reminds me of all that."

The leper nodded his head thoughtfully. Then, raising his stump in the direction of the icon, he said, "Stephan *Daddah*, your Jesus is much more beautiful than the one in all our pictures."

"Yes, you are beautiful, Jesus of the City of Joy," Kovalski was to write that evening in the notebook he used as a diary, "as beautiful as the crippled leper you sent me today with his mutilated body, his sores, and his smile. It was you I saw in him, you who are the incarnation of all pain and anguish, you who experienced Gethsemane, who sweated blood, who knew what it was to be tempted by Satan, abandoned by the Father, brought down, discouraged, hungry, thirsty—and lonely.

"Jesus of Anand Nagar I tried to care for that leper. Every day, I try to share in the plight of the poor. I bow my head with those who are crushed and oppressed like 'grapes in a press and their juice has squirted onto my garments and my clothing has been stained.' I am not guiltless, nor am I a saint. I am just a poor fellow, a sinner like all the rest. Sometimes I am crushed or despised like my brothers in the slum but with this certainty deep in my heart— that you love me. I also have another certainty—that no one can take away the joy that fills me, because you are truly present, here in the depths of this wretched slum."

26

"WITH HIS PUDGY fingers covered with rings, his shirt bursting open over his rolls of fat, and his hair shiny with perfumed oils, my first client of the day was frankly repulsive," Hasari Pal recounted. "And so arrogant on the top of it. But I was too hard pressed to treat myself to the satisfaction of refusing to take him. He was a marwari.* No doubt he was used to rolling about in a taxi. He was in a hurry. 'Faster!' he kept calling out and, in the absence of a whip, he bombarded my ribs with kicks that were particularly painful because he was wearing slippers with hard, pointed toes.

"He hadn't actually told me where he wanted to go. When he got in, he had simply said, 'Straight on and fast!' That marwari must have been used to speaking to horses, or slaves. 'Turn right! Turn left! Faster!' He barked out his orders and I performed the appropriate acrobatics in between the buses and the trucks. Several times he ordered me to stop and then had me set off again immediately. Sharp stops like that, involving a jerk of the lower back and a pull in reverse to halt the full weight of movement, are horribly painful. It's as if all of a sudden your hamstrings are supporting the total weight of the rickshaw and the client. Setting off again was no less painful, but this time the pain came from the shoulders and forearms because it took a supreme effort to get the old machine rolling again. Poor old jalopy! With every stop and start its shafts shuddered as violently as my bones. I don't know whether it was because of the heat wave that had been scorching

* A merchant, originally from the state of Marwar in Rajasthan, with a reputation for toughness in business.

Calcutta for two or three days, but that day the bus and taxi drivers
seemed to be afflicted with an extreme attack of nervous irritation.
On the corner of one avenue a *sardarji* put his arm out of his
window to grab the shaft of my rickshaw; he pushed it away with
such violence that I lost my balance—a predicament that earned
me a fresh outburst from my passenger and a whack from the cop
directing the traffic. A little farther on, a group of kids hanging out
the doorway of a packed streetcar, rained down a shower of kicks
on my head. It was impossible to retaliate. These were humiliations
that had to be swallowed in silence."

Hasari's run finished that day outside the door to a restaurant
in Park Street. Before putting down his shafts to allow his passenger to get out, he asked for five rupees. Staring at the puller as if
the latter had just thrust a gun into his stomach to steal his wallet,
the fat marwari, scarlet with fury, exclaimed, "Five rupees! Five
rupees for a journey with a lame horse!"

At this point, however, the incident took an unexpected turn.
Alerted by the marwari's protestations, a dozen rickshaw pullers
who had been waiting outside a nearby restaurant came rushing
over to form a circle around him. Frightened by their threatening
air, the fat fellow calmed down and lost no time in foraging in his
pocket. Without a word, he handed to Hasari a crisp, green five-
rupee note. As the Bengali peasants say, "When the dogs howl, the
tiger sheaths its claws."

This city was indeed a jungle, with laws and hierarchies like
those in the forest. There were elephants, tigers, panthers, snakes,
and all kinds of other urban animals, and it was undoubtedly best
to know which were which, if you didn't want to run into trouble.
One day when Hasari was parked outside the Kit Kat, a nightclub
on the corner of Park Street, a Sikh taxi driver signaled to him to
clear out so that he could take his place. The puller pretended not
to understand. The Sikh's turban stirred angrily behind the steering wheel. He trumpeted loudly with his horn, like an elephant
preparing to stampede. Hasari really believed that he was going to
charge his rickshaw, and so he seized his shafts to move off. He had
made a mistake: he had failed to respect one of the laws of the
Calcutta jungle, one that stipulates that a rickshaw must always
give way to a taxi.

The most trying part of his existence as a human horse was

not, however, the physical hardship; in his village there were jobs that were just as exhausting as pulling two obese *poussahs* from Park Street to the Bara Bazar. But those tasks were seasonal, interspaced with long periods of inactivity when a man could take a rest. The life of the rickshaw wallah was a form of slavery that spanned every day of the week and every week of the year.

"Sometimes I would have to take people to Howrah Station on the other side of the river. Over there there weren't any rickshaws drawn by men on foot, only cycle rickshaws. I had never pedaled one of those machines but it seemed to me that there must be less effort involved. I mentioned this fact one day to Ram Chander but he merely placed the flats of his hands on his buttocks with an air of great long suffering."

"You poor fellow," he groaned, "you've no idea what it's like to spend ten or twelve hours on the saddle of a bike! To start with you get an ass full of sores. Then your balls get stuck up and after two or three years you can't screw anymore. Your bike has made your prick as soft as cotton."

"Good old Ram, there was no one quite like him for making you realize that there was always someone worse off than you."

27

"YOU'LL SEE, my dear fellow, they'll gnaw you right down to the bone. They'll expect everything of you because of your white skin. Just think of it, a European in a necropolis like the City of Joy. Such a thing is completely unheard of!"

Stephan Kovalski couldn't help thinking of the words of the Indian rector from the parish of Our Lady of the Loving Heart as he handed out aspirin tablets to a woman who had brought him her child stricken with meningitis. The recovery of the young blind girl and his compassion for all the afflicted had been enough to guarantee the realization of Father Cordeiro's prediction. The "Father" of 49 Nizamudhin Lane had become Santa Claus, a Santa Claus especially tailored for the needs of a slum, a man who was prepared to listen and could understand, onto whom the most neglected could project their dreams, in whom they found friendship and compassion. Suddenly, he found himself credited with the smallest good thing that might occur, like the municipality's decision to dig ten new wells, or the exceptional mildness of the temperature at the beginning of that winter. The constant need to relate to a person is a characteristic trait of the Indian soul. No doubt it is due to the caste system and to the fact that within each social group there was always somebody in charge. Unless you knew this "somebody," or had access to him, you had very little chance to obtain anything, whether it was from the civil administration, the police, the hospitals. For the hundreds of despised and rejected occupants of his neighborhood, Stephan Kovalski thus became the ultimate "somebody," an almighty intercessor who could do absolutely anything because of his white skin, the cross of a man of God that he wore on his chest, and his wallet which, for poor people with nothing, must have seemed as fat as that of G. D. Birla, Calcutta's celebrated multimillionaire.

This kind of notoriety exasperated the Pole. He did not want to be Santa Claus, nor Social Security, nor Divine Providence. All he wanted to be was a poor man among the poor. "My ambition was primarily to give them confidence in themselves, so that they would feel less abandoned and want to undertake actions to improve their own lot."

A few weeks before the festival of Durga, his wish was to be fulfilled. One evening some of his neighbors, led by Margareta, walked into his room.

"Stephan, Big Brother," declared the young Christian widow, "we want to discuss with you how we can do something useful for the people here."

Margareta performed the introductions. With her were a young Hindu couple, an Anglo-Indian Christian, a Muslim laborer, and an Assamese girl in her twenties—six, poors who wanted to restore their own dignity and "build something together." The Hindu couple, named the Ghoshs, were attractive, healthy, and bright. Beneath her red cotton veil, decorated with a floral pattern, the young woman with her very smooth clear skin looked like a Renaissance madonna. The intensity of her gaze struck Kovalski immediately. "That young woman was burning with an inner fire." Her name was Shanta and she was the eldest daughter of a poverty-stricken peasant from Basanti, a large isolated borough in the Ganges delta. To provide for his eight children, her father used to go off with the local fishermen on regular expeditions to the flooded jungle of the Sundarbans. There they would collect wild honey. One day, however, her father did not return. He had been carried off by a man-eating tiger, of the kind that kill more than three hundred honey collectors a year in that part of the country. It was on the puddled clay floor of the little local primary school that Shanta had gotten to know the bearded fellow with the curly hair who was her husband. He was twenty-six-year-old Ashish (which means "hope"), one of eleven children of a landless day laborer.

This couple's case was unique: they had married for love. Their defiance of all tradition had provoked such a scandal that they had been forced to flee from the village and seek refuge in

Calcutta. After starving for nearly a year, Ashish had found a job as an instructor in one of Mother Teresa's training centers for handicapped children. As for Shanta, she was a teacher in a Howrah school. After the birth of their first child they had found their El Dorado: a room in a Hindu compound in Anand Nagar. Two regular incomes of two hundred rupees (twenty U.S. dollars) a month might seem a pittance, but in Anand Nagar it was a small fortune. The Ghoshs were privileged people, which made their readiness to serve others all the more remarkable.

The Anglo-Indian bore the extravagant name of Aristotle John. He was a small man with a sad face and the worried air typical of many members of a community that has become particularly marginal in contemporary India. He worked at the railways. The fifty-two-year-old Muslim, Saladdin, had a short mustache and wore a little embroidered skullcap on his head. It was he who had been longest in the slum. Having escaped the massacres of Partition, for the last twenty years he had shared a hovel with three mullahs for whom he acted as cook and guide.

To build something together! In this "gulag" where seventy thousand men fought each day for their survival, in this ants' nest which at times looked more like a death camp where hundreds of people died each year of tuberculosis, leprosy, dysentery, and all the diseases caused by malnutrition, in this environment so polluted that thousands never reached the age of forty, there was everything to build. You needed a dispensary and a leprosy clinic, a home for rickety children, emergency milk rations for kids and pregnant women, drinking water fountains, more latrines and sewers. The urgent tasks were countless.

"I suggest we all make an individual survey," said Kovalski, "to find out what are the most immediate problems our brothers want to see given priority." The results came in three days later. They were all identical. The most pressing desires of the inhabitants of the City of Joy were not the ones that the priest had anticipated. It was not their living conditions that people wanted to change. The sustenance they sought was not directed at their children's frail bodies, but at their minds. The six surveys revealed that the primary demand was for the creation of a night school so that children employed in the workshops, stores, and tea shops in the alley, could learn to read and write.

Kovalski gave Margareta the task of inviting the families concerned to find a hut which would serve as a classroom, and he offered to share in the remuneration of two teachers. "I had achieved my main objective," he was to say, "that of encouraging my brothers in Anand Nagar to take charge of themselves."

That first step was the beginning of an enterprise based on solidarity and sharing that would one day completely revolutionize living conditions in the slum. At the very next meeting Kovalski suggested the creation of a team of volunteers to help accompany the sick to the Calcutta hospitals. To go by themselves for treatment in such caravansaries was often so nightmarish a prospect that most people didn't dare undertake the voyage.

Anyone could attend the meetings in the room at 49 Nizamudhin Lane. A new rumor soon spread: "there are actually people willing to listen to the poor." The idea was so revolutionary that the Pole christened his little team the Listening Committee for Mutual Aid. It was also a revelation: people discovered that there were others worse off than themselves. Kovalski made it a rule that each meeting should begin with the reading of a chapter from the Gospel. "No reading could have more appropriate to life in the slum," he was to say, "no example could have been more apt than that of Christ relieving the burdens of his contemporaries. Hindus, Muslims, Christians, all men of goodwill could understand the link between the message of the Gospel and their lives of suffering, between the person of Christ and those who had taken it upon themselves to continue his work."

No one seemed to feel this link with greater intensity than the young Assamese girl who had come that first evening to offer her services to Kovalski. With her braid hanging down her back, her slits for eyes, and her pink cheeks, she looked like a little Chinese doll. Her name had all the resonance of a mantra. She was called Bandona which means "praise God." Although she belonged to the Buddhist faith she had been instantly captivated by the Gospel message. By revealing that it was in the service of others that God is best found, the message spoke to her impatience. "Every time some unfortunate person explained his difficulties, her face was transformed into a mask of pain," Kovalski was to comment. "All suffering was her suffering."

Yet this girl who was so hypersensitive to others was almost unhealthily modest when it came to anything that concerned her. In response to any personal question she would veil her face with the tip of her sari and lower her head. Kovalski's curiosity was aroused by this. One day when he was teasing her she replied curtly, "Didn't your Jesus himself say that we are only here to carry out his Father's will and that our own identity does not matter? In which case, why are you so interested in me?"

Still the priest managed to glean a few bits of information that would enable him to understand how a girl from the lofty mountains of Assam had come to be washed up in the filth of a Calcutta slum. Her father was a small peasant of Assamese stock, who had settled in the region of Kalimpong, to the extreme north of Bengal, in the shadow of the first foothills of the Himalayan mountain range. Like all the other mountain people in that area, he worked a small terraced plot of agricultural land, painfully wrested from the hillside. It was enough to provide his wife and four children with a meager living. One day, however, entrepreneurs from Calcutta set about exploiting the wood from the forests. They fixed a daily quota of trees to be chopped down. Years before, the region had already been radically changed by the development of the tea gardens. With the arrival of the lumbermen, the wooded jungles shrank. Peasants were compelled to venture ever farther afield to find the necessary wood to cook their food, and new land to cultivate. The number of bushfires increased and, since the vegetation no longer had time to recover before the monsoon cataracts came, erosion ravaged the soil. Deprived of their traditional grazing land, the cattle, too, became part of the destructive process. The growing scarcity of natural products obliged families to increase the growth of crops needed for their own food. As firewood became progressively rarer, they had to use animal dung to cook their meals, thus depriving the land of its richest fertilizer. The yield dropped. Deterioration of the land became more rapid. Because of the deforestation, water was no longer retained, springs ran dry, reservoirs stood empty, the underground water dried up. Since this area was subject to one of the heaviest rainfalls in the world—up to thirty-three feet of water a year in Assam—with each monsoon the arable earth and humus was washed away to the plains, leaving only the bare rock. In a matter of years the whole region had become a desert. For those who lived there, there was no alternative but to leave, to leave for the city which had ruined them.

Bandona was four years old when her family set out for Calcutta. Thanks to a cousin who worked in a clothing shop, her family was lucky enough to find a room in Anand Nagar. Five years later her father died of tuberculosis. Her mother, a little woman who could not be daunted, had burned incense sticks before the blackened picture of the founder of the Buddhist sect of the Yellow Caps, and then, after a year, married again. Shortly afterward, however, her husband had gone off to work in the South. Alone, she had brought up her four children by retrieving metal objects from the garbage heaps and selling them to a scrap metal dealer.

At the age of twelve Bandona had started work, first in a cardboard factory and then in a workshop that turned out parts for trucks. From then on she became her family's only support, for her mother was struck down with tuberculosis. Bandona would go out at five in the morning and rarely get back before ten o'clock at night, after a two-hour bus ride and walking three miles. Often she would not come home at all: power cuts necessitated her sleeping at the foot of her machine tool so she could make up the time lost when the electricity was restored. In Calcutta, tens of thousands of workers lived like that, chained to their machines because of load shedding and electricity failures. Bandona earned four rupees a day (forty U.S. cents), which only just enabled her to pay the rent for the family hovel and guarantee her mother and brothers a bowl of rice or two chapatis once a day. On Sundays and feast days, instead of resting or indulging in the usual distractions of her age group, she would prowl the slum looking for distressed people to help. That was how she came one evening to enter the home of Stephan Kovalski.

A number of donations from Europe made it possible for the priest to help her leave her workshop and work full-time in the service of the Listening Committee for Mutual Aid. No one had a better understanding of sharing and dialogue, of respect for other people's faiths and beliefs, than Bandona. She knew how to listen to the confessions of the dying, how to pray with the families of the dead, wash the corpses, accompany the deceased on the last journey to the cemetery or the funeral pyre. No one had ever taught her, yet she knew it all through intuition, friendship, love. Her extraordinary capacity to communicate enabled her to go into any compound, any hut, and sit down among people without encountering any prejudice of caste or religion, and this ability was all the more remarkable because she was not married. Normally it would be inconceivable that a young single woman would go anywhere at random, especially into a milieu outside her own caste. Married women never took a young girl into their confidence, even one belonging to their own caste, because tradition required that young girls know nothing about life so that they could come to their marriage innocent, on pain of being accused of immorality and thereupon rejected.

Two or three times a week, the young Assamese girl would accompany groups of sick and dying people to the hospitals of Calcutta. Steering these unfortunates through terrifying traffic, then guiding them through corridors and packed waiting rooms, was quite a venture. In such institutions, a poor person without an escort would have only the remotest chance of actually reaching an examination room. Furthermore, even if given the opportunity, he would never have been able to explain what was wrong or understand the treatment he should follow because, nine times out of ten, he wouldn't speak the Bengali the doctor spoke, but only one of the twenty or thirty dialects of the enormous hinterland that exported its millions of poor to Calcutta. Demanding, storming the doors, forcing entry, Bandona fought like a wild beast to have her protégés treated like human beings and to see that the medicines prescribed were properly given to them, a benefit that rarely occurred. In a few weeks she was to become the pillar and heart of the Listening Committee for Mutual Aid. Her memory was the card index of all the miseries of the slum. Above all, however, it was the quality of her expression, her smile, her love that was to earn her a nickname. The poor soon called her *"Anand Nagar ka Swarga Dug"*—the "Angel of the City of Joy."

One evening, returning from one of her expeditions in a hospital, Bandona burst into Stephan Kovalski's room like a missile to inform him that a doctor had diagnosed a fatal skin disease on a pregnant woman from the slum. Only a serum made in England might possibly save her.

"Stephan, *Daddah,*" she pleaded, taking hold of the priest's hands," you must have that medicine sent over urgently. Otherwise that woman and her baby will die."

The next day Kovalski rushed to the post office in Howrah to send a telegram to the head of his fraternity who could contact his connections in London. With a little bit of luck, the cure could arrive within a week. Sure enough, a week later Stephan Kovalski received, via the excellent Indian postal service, a slip from customs asking him to come and pick up a parcel.

That was the beginning of an odyssey that he would not soon forget.

28

"HE'S GOING to die right here in the street," Hasari thought
with horror. His friend Ram Chander's chest had suddenly distended, desperately trying to take in air. His ribs stood out so that
his skin looked as if it would burst, his face had suddenly turned
yellow, and his mouth was gaping open like that of a drowning man
deprived of oxygen. A sudden fit of coughing made him shudder
and shake, sounding like a piston in a water pump. He began to
bring something up but as he had pan in his mouth, it was impossible to tell whether he was spitting out blood or betel juice. Hasari
helped his friend onto the seat of his rickshaw and suggested that
he take him home. Ram shook his head, and reassured his companion. "It's only this damned cold," he said. "It'll pass."

That year the Bengali winter was murderous. Winds from the
Himalayas had brought the thermometer down to fourteen degrees, a temperature that was positively frigid for a population
used to baking in an oven for eight months of the year. For the
human horses it represented a particularly harsh trial. Condemned
to switching from the sweatbaths of a run to the cold of prolonged
waiting, their undernourished bodies had little resistance. Many of
them died.

"Ram was a brother to me in the jungle of Calcutta, where
everyone preyed on somebody else," Hasari Pal would later recount. "It was he who had helped and supported me, he who had
found me my rickshaw. Every time I saw his gray hair, I would
speed up just to park my carriage next to his. How many hours we
spent, sitting side by side on the corner of Park Circus or Wellesley
Street, or when it was hot, in front of the big market on Lower

Circular Road which everyone called the 'Air Conditioned Market' because there were machines inside that blew out that marvelous substance which I used to think only the peaks of the Himalayas could provide—cool air. Ram's dream was to one day go back to his village and open a grocery shop. 'Just to sit there all day in the same spot, without moving, without having to run around,' he would say, chatting about his future paradise. And he would tell me about how he imagined his life, enthroned in his shop, all around him sacks overflowing with all kinds of dal and rice, and other sacks full of intoxicatingly aromatic spices, piles of vegetables, on the shelves all sorts of other items: bars of soap, incense sticks, biscuits, and sweetmeats. In short, he dreamed of a world of peace and prosperity, of which he would form the fixed center, like these lingam of Shiva,* those symbols of fertility standing on their yoni† in the temples."

Before this dream could be realized, however, Ram Chander had a promise to keep. He had to reimburse the *mahajan* in his village for the loan he had taken out to pay for his father's funeral rites. Otherwise the family field, which was serving as collateral, would be lost forever. A few days before the payment term expired, he had managed to negotiate another loan with a usurer from a neighboring village. For peasants, paying off one debt with the help of another loan, then paying off *that* loan with a third, and so on, was a common practice. When it came to the final reckoning they invariably lost their land.

Ram Chander's five years were due to expire in a few weeks, just before the festival of Durga. Despite the deterioration of his health, Ram went on working. One morning Hasari ran into him outside the post office in Park Street. The robust fellow looked like a shadow of his former self. He had come to have the *munshi* fill in the form for his monthly money invoice. The sheer bulk of the package of notes he pulled out of his *longhi* amazed Hasari.

"I swear you've robbed the Bank of India!" Hasari exclaimed.

"No," replied Ram with unusual gravity, "but this month I've got to send them *everything*. Otherwise our field will be lost."

Sending them everything meant that for the past month he

---

* Stone in the form of a phallus, symbolizing god Shiva.
† The feminine sexual organ.

had cut his own food down to starvation rations: two or three griddle cakes, a cup of tea or a glass of sugarcane juice a day.

"As soon as I saw the neighbor's boy running toward me, I understood," Hasari was later to say. "The news spread instantly around all the main rickshaw stations in the area and there were soon about thirty of us assembled in the little shed behind the Chittarajan Hospital, where Ram Chander lived. He was lying on the plank that had served as his bed for the five years he had spent in Calcutta. His thick shock of gray hair was like a halo around his head. His eyes were half-open and his lips were shaped into one of his mischievous grins that were so familiar. He looked as if he were enjoying the joke he had just played on us. According to the carpenter-joiner who shared his lodgings, Ram had died in his sleep, which probably explained why he looked so peaceful. The night before, he had had several very violent fits of coughing. He had spat a great deal and even vomited blood. Then he had gone to sleep, and he never woke up again.

"Now we had to carry out the funeral rites. We held a discussion among the rickshaw pullers to establish whether we were going to carry him to the cremation ghats on foot or whether we should hire a Tempo. In Calcutta you can hire little three-wheeled carts for one hour, two hours, or however long you want, for thirty rupees an hour. In view of the distance to the Nimtallah ghat, we agreed to hire a Tempo, so I suggested we organize a collection. Some gave twenty rupees, others ten, others five. I searched in Ram's waist, in the place where I knew he hid his money, and found twenty-five rupees. His neighbors also wanted to join in the collection, for Ram was much loved in the neighborhood. No one compared with him when it came to storytelling, and the children adored him. Someone brought cups of tea from the nearest tea stall and we all drank, standing around our friend. Whether it was because of his smile I don't know, but there was no sadness there. People chatted and came and went just as if he were alive and joining in the conversation. I went to the market next to Sealdah Station with three colleagues, to buy the items necessary to complete the funeral rites, beginning with the litter needed to transport the body to the ghat. We also bought incense sticks, a pot of *ghee,* * fifteen feet of white linen, and a long cord to tie the linen around the body; also garlands of white jasmine and a clay pot with which to pour water from the Ganges into the mouth and over the head of the deceased.

"We regarded ourselves as his family, so we performed his last toilet ourselves. It didn't take very long. Ram had died in his pants, *longhi,* and working vest. We washed him and wrapped him in the shroud we had bought, so that only his face and the tips of his feet were visible. Then we lifted him onto the litter. Poor Ram! He really didn't weigh very much. No rickshaw puller is very heavy but he really broke all records for being a featherweight. He must have lost forty pounds since the winter. Recently he had been obliged to turn down passengers who were too fat. After all, you can't ask a goat to pull an elephant! Next we decorated the litter with the garlands of white jasmine and lit incense sticks at the four corners of it. One after another, we walked around the body in a final *namaskar* of farewell.

"Before leaving the shed, I gathered up his things. He didn't have much—a few cooking utensils, a change of *longhi,* a shirt and trousers for the festival of Durga, and an old umbrella. These were all his worldly possessions.

"Six of us climbed into the Tempo with Ram, and the others caught a bus to the cremation ghat by the river. It was just like the festival of Durga except that we were taking the body of our friend instead of a statue of the divinity to the sacred river. It took us over an hour to cross the city from east to west and we sang hymns throughout the journey. They were verses from the Gita, the sacred book of our religion. Every Hindu learns these verses when he is a child. They proclaim the glory of eternity.

"We met up with the others again at the ghat. There were always pyres burning there and several corpses were already waiting on litters. I made contact with the man in charge of cremations. He was an employee belonging to the Dom caste, who specialize in the cremation of the dead. They live with their families next to the funeral pyres. The man in charge asked me for a hundred and twenty rupees for wood. Wood for a cremation is very expensive. That's why indigents and people without families are thrown into

* Melted butter, purified five times.

the river without being burned. All together it would cost a hundred and fifty rupees to have the body of our friend vanish into smoke. When our turn came, I went down to the river to fill the clay pot with water and each one of us let a few drops fall onto Ram's lips. The Brahmin attendant poured the *ghee* we had brought onto his forehead and recited the ritual mantras. Then we placed the body on the pyre. The employee covered it with other fagots until the body was completely imprisoned in a cage of sticks. The Brahmin poured more *ghee* over the fagots until we could see only a patch of white shroud.

"As the final moment drew nearer, I felt my throat tighten with emotion and tears well up in my eyes. No matter how hardened you were, it was a terrible thing to see your brother encased on a funeral pyre, ready for burning. Images flooded through my memory: our meeting outside the Bara Bazar warehouse when we took the injured coolie to the hospital, that first bottle of *bangla* we drank together afterward, Sundays spent playing cards in the Park Circus restaurant, our visit to the rickshaw owner's representative to beg him to entrust a rickshaw to me. Yes, in this inhuman city, Ram had been a father to me and now, without him, I felt like an orphan. One of the other pullers must have noticed my grief because he came over to me, put a hand on my shoulder, and said, 'Don't cry, Hasari. Everyone has to die some day.' It wasn't perhaps the most comforting of remarks, but it did help me to get a grip on myself. I drew nearer to the pyre.

"Since Ram had no family in Calcutta, the Brahmin asked me to plunge the lighted torch into the pile of wood. As ritual required, I walked five times around the pyre, then thrust the torch into the place where the head was. Instantly the pyre flared up amid a shower of sparks. We were forced to draw back because of the heat. When the flames reached the body, I wished Ram a good journey. Above all, I wished that he might be reborn with a better karma, in the body of a zamindar, for example, or in that of a rickshaw owner!

"The cremation lasted several hours. When there was nothing left but a pile of ashes, one of the officials in charge of cremations sprinkled the ashes with water from the Ganges, then put them in a baked clay pot. And then we all went down to the river and scattered the ashes on the current so that they would be borne away to the eternity of the oceans. Then we all immersed ourselves in the waters for a purifying bath and left the ghats.

"There remained just one last rite for us to carry out. Actually it was more a tradition than a rite. To conclude that sad day we invaded one of the numerous dives that were open day and night in the vicinity of the cremation ghats and ordered up plenty of bottles of *bangla.* Then, drunk out of our minds, we all went off for a meal together, a real feast of curd, rice, dal, and sweetmeats—a rich man's feast in honor of a poor man's death."

29

A CRUMBLING OLD BUILDING, with a staircase that stank of urine and filled with a confusion of silhouettes in *dhotis* wandering about, the Calcutta customs office was a classic shrine to bureaucracy. Brandishing like a talisman the notice for his parcel of medicine, Stephan Kovalski swept into the first office. Once inside, however, he had no sooner taken a step before his commendable enthusiasm deserted him. Seized by the spectacle before him, he stopped in his tracks, transfixed. Before him extended a battlefield of old tables and shelves, sagging beneath mountains of dog-eared files, spewing out yellowing paperwork tied vaguely together with bits of string. There were piles of ledgers all of which appeared to be chewed by rats and termites, and some of which looked as if they dated back to the previous century. The cracked cement of the floor was likewise strewn with paper. From drawers that were coming apart bulged an infinite variety of printed forms. On the wall Kovalski noticed a calendar for some year long past, which sported a dusty effigy of the goddess Durga slaying the demon-buffalo, the incarnation of evil.

A dozen *babus** in *dhotis* were seated in the middle of this chaos, beneath a battery of fans which throbbed out a veritable sirocco of moist air and sent the papers into a whirl of confusion. While some scrambled to catch documents as if they were chasing butterflies, others jabbed a single finger at antique typewriters, pausing after each letter to verify that they had actually managed to

---

* Originally a term of respect, now used to designate lesser officials in the civil service.

hit the right key. Others were talking on telephones that didn't appear to be connected to any line. Many of them seemed to be engrossed in activities that were not, strictly speaking, professional. Some were reading newspapers or sipping tea. Others were asleep, with their heads propped up on the papers that covered their desks, looking like Egyptian mummies on a bed of papyrus. Yet others, seated in their chairs in the hieratic position of yogis, looked as if they had attained the ultimate stages of nirvana.

On a pedestal near the entrance, three divinities from the Hindu pantheon, bound together by a tangle of cobwebs, watched over the enormous office, while a dust-covered portrait of Gandhi contemplated the chaos with supreme resignation. On the opposite wall, a yellowing poster proclaimed the glorious virtues of teamwork.

The entry of a foreigner had not aroused the slightest bit of interest. Eventually Kovalski's eye fell on a little man with bare feet who happened to be passing with a teapot. The employee stabbed his chin in the direction of one of the officials who was typing with one finger. Stepping gingerly over stacks of files, the priest reached the man in question and handed him the slip he had received in the mail. The *babu* in glasses examined the document at length, then, taking stock of his visitor, he inquired, "Do you like your tea with or without milk?"

"With," replied Kovalski, somewhat taken aback.

The man rang a bell several times, until a shadow emerged from among the pyramids of files.

He ordered a tea. Then, fiddling with the document, he consulted his watch.

"It's nearly lunchtime, Mr. Kovalski. Afterward, it'll be a bit late to find your file before the offices close. Please, come back tomorrow morning."

"But it's a question of a very urgent consignment of medicines," protested the priest. "For someone who could die."

The official assumed a compassionate air. Then, pointing to the mountain of paperwork that surrounded him, he said, "Wait for your tea. We'll do everything we can to find your parcel as quickly as possible."

With these words, enunciated with the utmost affability, the *babu* got up and withdrew.

Next morning at precisely ten o'clock, the time when all the administrative offices in India open, Kovalski was back. A line of some thirty people preceded him. A few minutes before his turn came up he saw the same official with the glasses get up and leave, just as he had done on the previous day. It was lunchtime. Kovalski rushed after him. Still with the same courtesy, the *babu* merely pointed to his watch with a grave expression. He made his apologies: it was midday. In vain Kovalski pleaded with him; the man remained inflexible. The Pole decided to remain where he was and await the *babu*'s return. But on that particular afternoon the official did not reappear in his office.

As luck would have it, the next day was one of the two holiday Saturdays in the month. Kovalski had to wait until Monday. After three more hours of lining up on the steps of the betel-stained staircase, he found himself once more before the *babu* with the glasses.

"Good morning, Father!" cried the latter amicably, before the inevitable, "Do you like your tea with or without milk?"

This time Kovalski was full of hope. The *babu* began by popping into his mouth a wad of betel that he had just made up for himself. After several efforts at mastication, he got up and headed for a metal cabinet. Straining at the handle, he had to make a number of attempts at opening it before he actually succeeded. When the door finally did turn on its hinges, the cabinet expelled an avalanche of files, ledgers, notebooks, and different documents, almost burying the unfortunate official altogether. Had there not been a human life at stake, Kovalski would have burst out laughing, but the urgency of the issue preserved his calm. He rushed to the victim's rescue, bent on extracting him forcefully from his ocean of papers and procuring the immediate surrender of the parcel of medicines. He was not quite familiar with the sometimes subtle ploys of local bureaucracy. In his haste, he tripped over a coconut that another *babu* had deposited on the floor next to his chair, to quench his thirst during the course of the morning. Fortunately there was no shortage of papers to soften the Pole's fall.

As it happened, the incident had a positive effect. The official with the glasses began to thumb through the pages of several ledgers that had spilled out of the cabinet. Kovalski watched him for a while, fascinated. The man was running his fingers down a confusion of boxes and columns in search of some cabalistic *mantra* scrawled in almost illegible ink. Suddenly he saw the *babu*'s finger stop on a particular page. He leaned forward and could hardly believe his eyes. In the midst of all this geological subsidence of paperwork and records, one single entry brought all the chaos back into touch with a living, palpable, indisputable reality. What he read was his name. This bureaucracy was not quite as ineffective as even the Indians themselves claimed.

The discovery propelled the official in the direction of another section of the sea of papers that looked as if it might totally engulf him at any second. With all the dexterity of a pearl fisher, he fished out a yellow-covered file on which Kovalski deciphered his name for a second time. Victory! A few more moments of patience and Bandona's protégée could have her first injection of the saving serum. However, as if exhausted by the effort of his find, the *babu* straightened himself up, consulted his watch, and sighed, "Father, we'll continue after lunch."

That afternoon the *babu* looked more forbidding. "The information on the ledger does not correspond to that on the slip you were sent," he announced. "It'll have to be verified in other ledgers."

"Only the expression of sincere regret on the official's face prevented me from bursting into a rage," Kovalski was to say.

The sixth and seventh days passed without their being able to find the correct ledger. On the eighth day, the *babu* claimed forty rupees from the priest to assign two additional employees to the search for the right references. Another whole week went by. Bureaucratic disaster was systematically swallowing up even the very best of intentions. Stephan Kovalski had given up all hope when, after six weeks, he received by post a further notice inviting him urgently to come and clear his parcel. By some miracle Bandona's protégée was still alive.

The *babu* received his visitor with all the transports of affection befitting an old friend. His joy at seeing Kovalski again was very real. He asked for another thirty rupees for the purchase of revenue stamps and took charge of a pot of glue and a brush with four remaining bristles. Liberally he brushed the place reserved for the stamps, but in the meantime the stamps, caught up in the whirlwind from the fans, fluttered away. Kovalski was compelled to

produce another thirty rupees for three new stamps. Then he was
invited to fill in a series of forms to establish how much duty he was
to pay. Working this out, and also computing the amount owed for
the various taxes took nearly all day. The final sum was exorbitant:
three hundred and sixty-five rupees, three or four times the declared value of the medicines. But then there was no price to be put
on a human life.

"Even then my difficulties weren't altogether over," the Pole
would sigh. "The customs office wasn't permitted to receive direct
payment of the duty it proscribed. The duty money had to be
cleared by the central bank which would then issue a receipt. This
meant one more day wandering from counter to counter in that
tentacular establishment."

At last, clasping the precious receipt to his chest, Kovalski ran
back to the customs office. By this time he had become such a
familiar figure that everyone welcomed him with a cheery "Good
morning, Father!" His *babu*, however, displayed an unaccustomed
reserve. He refrained from even examining the document and
instead asked the priest to accompany him. Together they went
down two floors and entered a storeroom where mountains of
parcels and crates from all over the world were piled high on
shelves. The *babu* asked one of the uniformed customs officers to
go and fetch the package of medicines. Moments later, Stephan
Kovalski at last confronted the precious dispatch, a box hardly
bigger than two packs of cigarettes. "It was like a mirage, a vision
of life and hope, the promise of a miracle. The long wait, all that
time spent in fruitless activity, all that desperate effort was at last
going to result in the saving of a life."

He held out his hand to take possession of the parcel.

"I'm sorry, Father," apologized the uniformed customs official. "But I can't let you have it."

He pointed to a door behind him on which hung a sign with
the words, "Goods incinerator."

"The date for your medicines expired three days ago," he
explained, making for the door. "We're obliged to destroy them.
It's an international regulation."

The *babu* who until now had remained silent, intervened
swiftly, grabbing hold of the tail of the man's shirt.

"This Father is a holy man," he protested. "He works for the poor. He needs that medicine to save the life of an Indian woman. Even if the date has run out, you must give it to him."

The uniformed customs officer surveyed Kovalski's patched shirt.

"You work for the poor?" he repeated respectfully. Kovalski nodded. Then he watched as the customs officer crossed out the word, "perished."

"Father, don't say anything to anybody, and may God bless you."

Despite the medicine, Bandona's protégée died four weeks later. She was twenty-eight years old, a widow, and she left four orphans. In an Indian slum, such a qualification didn't really apply to any children. When parents died, and God knows that happened often enough, they didn't leave orphans behind; other members of the family—an elder brother, an uncle, an aunt—or in the absence of any relatives, neighbors would adopt them at once.

The young woman's death was very quickly forgotten. That was another characteristic of the slum. No matter what happened, life went on with an energy and vigor that was constantly renewed.

30

SCINTILLATING SERPENTS SUDDENLY spattered the sky, as a burst of fireworks exploded over the slum. Diwali, the Hindu festival of light, was celebrated on the darkest night of the year and marked the official arrival of winter. In a country where all is myth and symbol, it represented the victory of light over darkness. Illuminations commemorated one of the greatest epic stories of the legend of Ramayana, the return of the goddess Sita, brought back by her divine consort Rama, after her abduction to Ceylon by the demon Ravana. In Bengal, it is also thought that the souls of the departed begin their journey on this date in the year, and lamps are lit to light their way. It is also the festival of the goddess Lakshmi, who never enters a dark house, but only the houses that are brightly lit. And, since she is the goddess of wealth and beauty, she is venerated in the hope that she will bring happiness and prosperity. Finally, for many Bengalis this is also the festival of Kali, the somber divinity who symbolizes the dark trials through which man must pass in order to attain the light. For the inhabitants of the City of Joy, Diwali is, above all, the hope at the end of the night.

Like other households in Hindu India, the hovels in the slum were the setting that night for frenzied card games. The festival perpetuated a custom born of another legend, that of the famous dice game in which god Shiva wins back the fortune he has lost during a previous game against Parvati, his faithless wife. To achieve this victory the god enlisted help from his divine colleague Vishnu, who conveniently materialized as a pair of dice. Thus the festival of Diwali was also a form of homage to gambling.

Every Hindu gambled that night, be it at cards, dice, or roulette. They played with ten-, five-, or one-rupee notes, or even with just a few *paisas*. When they had no money, they played with a banana, a handful of almonds, a few sweetmeats. It mattered not what they played with, just that they played. Even Kovalski could not escape the ritual. For, despite the fact that it was occupied by Muslims, even Nizamudhin Lane had its wild spark.

The old Hindu from the tea shop invited his foreign neighbor to join in a heated game of poker that went on until dawn. As in the legend, Shiva's devotee was allowed to win back the twenty rupees his opponent had taken from him, in the very last round.

It was as he was returning home that morning that Stephan Kovalski heard the news. Selima, the wife of his neighbor Mehboub, who was seven months pregnant, had disappeared.

The young Muslim woman had been discreetly approached by one of her neighbors three days earlier at the fountain. With her face pockmarked from smallpox, the portly Mumtaz Bibi was something of a mystery figure in this world where promiscuity rendered everybody transparent. Although her husband was only a simple factory worker, she enjoyed a certain opulence. She lived in the alley's only brick house and it was not exactly a hovel. From her ceiling hung a rare and wondrous ornament: an electric light bulb. It was said, too, that a number of rooms in the surrounding compounds were her property, yet no one was able to specify precisely where her money came from. Malicious tongues had it that outside the neighborhood Mumtaz exercised occult powers. The local Mafia godfather had been seen going into her house. There was talk of traffic in *bhang*, Indian marijuana, of the clandestine distillation of alcohol, of prostitution, and even of a network for buying up little girls for brothels in Delhi and Bombay. No one, however, had ever managed to support such slander with any proof.

"Stop off at my house on the way back from the fountain," she said to Selima. "I have an interesting proposition for you."

Despite her surprise, Selima did as she was asked. The poor woman had become little more than a shadow since her husband had lost his job. Her beautiful smooth face now looked haggard, and the small stone in her nostril had long since tumbled into the usurer's coffer. She, who had always carried herself with such dignity in her worn sari, now walked like an old woman. Only her belly remained unaffected, a belly that was swollen, taut, superb.

She carried it with pride, for it was all she had. Two months later she would give birth to the tiny being that stirred inside her—her fourth child. Mumtaz Bibi had prepared a plateful of tidbits and two small cups of tea with milk. She motioned her visitor to sit down on the low platform she used as a bed.

"Are you set on keeping that child?" she asked, pointing at Selima's belly. "If you'd agree to sell it to me, I could make you a good deal."

"Sell you my child," stammered Selima, flabbergasted.

"Not exactly your child," the fat woman corrected her, "only what you've got inside you at the moment. And for a good price: two thousand rupees (two hundred U.S. dollars)."

The opulent dowager of Nizamudhin Lane was carrying on the very latest of Calcutta's clandestine professions: the sale of human embryos and fetuses. The mainsprings of the industry were a network of foreign buyers who scoured the third world on behalf of international laboratories and institutes for genetic research. The majority of these buyers were Swiss or American. They used the embryos and fetuses either for scientific work or in the manufacture of rejuvenating products for a clientele of privileged people in specialized establishments in Europe and America. The demand had provoked a fruitful trade for which Calcutta was one of the central sources. One of the recognized providers of this unusual merchandise was an ex-pharmacist named Sushil Vohra. He obtained his supplies from several clinics that specialized in abortions, and he looked after the packaging of the consignments which left for Europe or the U.S.A., via Moscow on the Soviet airline, Aeroflot's, regular flight.

The most sought-after fetuses were the most developed ones, but these were also the most difficult to come by, a fact which accounted for the high sum offered to Selima, compared with the less than two hundred rupees paid for an embryo that was only two months old. In fact, it was very rare indeed for a woman who had reached her sixth or seventh month of pregnancy to part with her child. Even in the poorest of families the birth of children is always greeted with joy. They are the only riches of those who have nothing.

Mumtaz assumed a maternal tone.

"Think good and hard about it, little one. You already have

three children. Your husband's out of work and I've heard it said
that your family doesn't eat every day. This is not perhaps the time
to add another mouth to your household. Whereas, you know, with
two thousand rupees you can fill plenty of plates of rice."

Poor Selima knew that only too well. Finding a few peelings
and scraps to put on her family's plates was her daily torture.

"What's my husband going to say when I come home with two
thousand rupees and nothing in my . . . ?"

The dowager gave her a smile of complicity.

"That doesn't have to be a problem. I'll give you the two
thousand rupees in small installments. Your husband won't think
anything of it and you'll be able to buy something to feed your
family every day."

The two women parted on these words, but just as Selima was
leaving, Mumtaz called her back.

"There's just one thing I'd forgotten," she added. "If you
agree, you needn't have any fears about yourself. The operation is
always carried out under the very best conditions. What's more, it
only takes a few minutes. You'll only be away from home for three
hours at the most."

Strangely enough the idea of danger had not even crossed
Mehboub's wife's mind; to a poor woman from the slums death was
of no real concern.

All day and all night the wretched woman was haunted by that
visit. Every movement she felt inside her seemed like a protest
against the horrible exchange that had just been suggested to her.
She could never agree to what amounted to murder, not even for
two thousand rupees; but then there were other voices too that
haunted Selima in the night, the familiar voices of her three other
children crying out with hunger. At dawn she made her decision.

It was all fixed for two days later. As soon as he got the news,
the trafficker Sushil Vohra prepared a large jar of antiseptic fluid. A
seven-month-old embryo was almost the same size and shape as a
newborn baby. He took the container to a small clinic where the
operation was to take place. The festival of light posed a few
problems. The usual Hindu surgeons had all gone off to play cards
or dice, but Sushil Vohra was not one to allow such obstacles to
stop him. Undaunted, he sent for a Muslim surgeon.

The medical establishment into which Mumtaz directed Se-

lima had few pretensions to the title of clinic. It was a kind of
dispensary made up of a single room divided in two by a curtain.
One half served as a reception and treatment area, the other as an
operating room. The surgical equipment was of the most basic
kind: a metal table, a fluorescent light, one bottle of alcohol and
another of ether standing on a shelf. There was no sterilizer, no
oxygen, and no reserve supply of blood. There weren't even any
instruments. Each surgeon had to bring his own personal case.

Disturbed by the smell of ether that had impregnated the floor
and walls, Selima sank down on a stool that constituted the only
piece of furniture. The act that she was bracing herself to have
performed seemed to her progressively more monstrous, yet she
approached it with resignation. "This evening my husband and
children will be able to eat," she kept telling herself. Between her
blouse and her skin she could already feel the friction of the first
bills Mumtaz had given her: thirty rupees, enough to buy almost
twenty-five pounds of rice.

The surgeon called for the operation was a man in his fifties
with a receding hairline and large hairy ears. He asked Selima to lie
down on the table and examined her attentively. Behind him, the
trafficker was growing impatient. The Aeroflot plane was due to
take off in four hours. He would only just have time to take the jar
to Dum Dum Airport. He had alerted his contact in New York. The
transaction would earn him about a thousand U.S. dollars net.

"What are you waiting for, Doctor?"

The surgeon took out his instrument case, slipped on a gown,
asked for some soap and a basin to wash his hands, then steeped a
large piece of cotton in ether and placed it over Selima's nose and
mouth. He toyed nervously with his mustache while the young
woman lost consciousness, then took up his lancet. Twenty minutes later, mopping up with gauze compresses the blood flowing
from the uterus, he placed the fetus with the placenta in the hands
of the trafficker. The child would have been a boy.

It was after he had cut the umbilical cord that disaster struck.
A reddish bubbling issued from Selima's womb, followed by black
dots, and then a veritable torrent of blood spurted forth in a single
gush. In a matter of seconds the floor of the room was covered in it.
The surgeon tried to compress the lower abdomen with a very
tight bandage, but the red tide continued to escape. He undid the

dressings and tried to feel out the position of the abdominal aorta. Applying his fist to the vessel, he pressed with all his might in an attempt to stem the hemorrhage. Without the assistance of a massive dose of coagulants, however, all his efforts were in vain. He tried to find her pulse, but Selima's wrist was already showing only the most imperceptible and irregular beat. At that point, he heard a door bang behind him and turned round. The trafficker had left with the jar. Mumtaz Bibi, the dowager, did likewise, having first swiftly recovered her thirty rupees from her victim's bodice. The surgeon spread the old sari over the dying woman. Then he took off his blouse soaked in blood and carefully folded it up. He arranged his instruments in their box and put everything into his canvas attaché case. And he too left.

Selima remained alone with the employee of the "clinic." Above the grinding of the fan the sounds of voices could be heard coming from outside. The piece of cotton impregnated with ether still concealed her face. The employee was a stunted little man with bushy eyebrows and a hooked nose, like an eagle's beak. To him the bloodless body on the table was worth more than all the Diwali card parties put together. He knew a useful address where they cut up unidentified corpses to recover the skeletons for export.

31

FIFTY THOUSAND BOMBS dropped on each of the fifty thousand rickshaws in Calcutta could not have caused more of an uproar. The rickshaw owners had just announced that they were increasing the daily rent paid by the pullers. It was going up from five rupees to seven, starting the very next day.

For the pullers it was the worst blow inflicted by the rickshaw owners since the confrontations of 1948, when the owners had demanded that every vehicle should bring in two sets of fees, one for daytime and the other for nighttime use. This claim had been the cause of their first strike, an eighteen-day *hartal** which had ended with victory for the human horses and with a major achievement on their part: the formation of a union. The person primarily responsible for this initiative was a former Bihari peasant with bushy gray hair, now aged fifty-four, a record age in a corporation where the average life expectancy was barely more than thirty. In some thirteen thousand days, Golam Rassoul had covered, between the shafts of his rickshaw, more than four times the distance between the earth and the moon. This survivor of more than a third of a century of monsoons, incidents, and humiliations had realized that a powerful union was the only means by which the population of rickshaw *wallahs* could make its voice heard. Unlike the factory workers, however, the pullers worked individually and their limited ambitions made it extremely difficult to get them together for collective action.

Rassoul learned to read and write, compiled tracts, and con-

* Total stoppage of all activity; strike.

tacted in the trade union movement an expert in mass meetings, a Communist member of Bengal Parliament named Abdul Rahman. "Lead a crusade," he exhorted him, "so that the Calcutta rickshaw pullers will stop being treated like animals!"

Thus was born the Rickshaw Workers Union, one of the most unusual unions in the world, an organization of human horses determined to raise their heads and group themselves together to defend their rights. Affiliated with the Communist Federation of Indian Trade Unions, the syndicate chose as its president Abdul Rahman, and as its general secretary its instigator, the gray-haired veteran rickshaw puller, Golam Rassoul. Two rooms on the fourth floor of the Trade Unions' dilapidated building became the new organization's headquarters. Every morning at six, before harnessing himself to his shafts outside Sealdah Station, Rassoul stood there to listen to the grievances of his comrades and to offer them the support of the union in their confrontations with the rickshaw proprietors or the police.

In the beginning the meetings attracted only very small numbers. Soon, however, pullers began to come from all over the city. In the afternoons, Rassoul would exchange his shafts for an object that was hardly part of a rickshaw puller's general equipment. Armed with a ballpoint pen, he would install himself behind the piles of dusty ledgers in the municipal department for "hackneys and carriages," to oversee formalities for the renewal of rickshaw licenses. The ceremony took place beneath cobwebs waving in the exhalations of an expiring fan, and overlooked by yellowing pictures of Kali, the bloodthirsty, four-armed goddess, dressed in a great floral robe. In theory the renewal cost twelve *paisas* (a little more than one U.S. cent). The price had not changed since 1911. In practice, however, it was said that a puller would have to pay about thirty rupees in baksheesh to the police officials to procure the precious document. When their protector Rassoul was not there, the sum could well be three times greater.

Protector was the right word. In thirty years of union action, the indefatigable Rassoul had fought relentlessly. With protest meetings, hunger marches, and strikes, he had inspired and organized the resistance of the human horses of Calcutta against the voracity of their employers and the interference of the police. He had fought against what he referred to as the arbitrariness of the

municipal authorities who were forever banning rickshaw pullers
from new streets under the pretext of relieving the traffic congestion which grew worse every day. The urban disaster of Calcutta
constituted a fatal threat to those trying to earn a living among its
bottlenecks. Even the most acrobatic pullers found themselves
caught like fishes in a net. To escape the net and avoid the forbidden streets, the men were obliged to embark on exhausting de-
tours.

Now the exorbitant rise in rent was hitting them with a further
blow. So it was that from street to street, from square to square,
from the banks of the Hooghly to the skyscrapers of Chowringhee,
from the slums of Howrah to the gracious portals of the residences
on Wood Street, the city began to resound with a strange concert.
Tap, tap, tap—the haunting sound of bells struck against the wood
of rickshaw shafts. The time for anger had come.

"Some men have knives to defend themselves, or guns, or
even worse weapons," Hasari Pal would recount. "All we had was a
little ball of copper about the size of a betel nut. But that poor little
bell, which made a sharpish sound when struck against the shafts
or the base of a streetlamp, was mightier than any weapon. It was
the voice of the rickshaws of Calcutta—our voice. And our voice
must have made a real din that morning, to get the owners' representatives to rush and explain why their bosses had decided to
raise the rent. Normally they gave us bad news without making any
bones about it. Who has to provide slaves with explanations? But
on this occasion, because of the uproar that was reverberating
throughout the city, they must have realized we weren't going to
swallow their decision like the dutiful little goats in the zoo at
Alipore. The increase was far too high. Shouting as loudly as he
could to make himself heard above the bells, Musafir, my owner's
representative, challenged me publicly. 'Do you know, Hasari, how
much it costs nowadays to change the spoke in a wheel?' 'Or a new
hood?' cried another factotum. 'Or how much the baksheesh for
the cops comes to?' said a third.

"They were men in positions of confidence who had done
their homework well. But we didn't give a damn about the cost of
wheel spokes or baksheesh for the cops. We hadn't been breaking
our backs between the shafts of our rickshaws in order to weep for
the owners' predicament. To a puller the only thing that really

mattered was the bundle of rupees he took to the *munshi* each month to feed the family he had left behind in his village.

"A discussion started up, but as everyone was shouting at the same time, it was impossible to make yourself heard. The arrival of Golam Rassoul, the secretary of our union, put a stop to the noise. Despite his slight build—he looked like a sparrow that had fallen out of its nest—he had an enormous amount of authority. He confronted the line of representatives. 'Go and tell your employers to give up their rent increase. Otherwise there won't be one single rickshaw left on the streets of Calcutta.'

"Rassoul opened the cardboard box he had brought with him and handed out leaflets. None of us knew how to read or write, but we all guessed the contents. It was a call to strike. The representatives disappeared to report to their owners. They also had a syndicate.

"Pullers came running with their carts from every corner of the city. There were even cycle rickshaws from a long way away on the other side of the river, from Barrackpore and the distant suburbs. The cyclists were poor fellows just like us, except that they made more journeys in the course of a day.

"The Park Circus esplanade was soon so packed with people that the streetcars and buses couldn't get through. Police vans appeared to try and get the traffic moving again, but what could thirty cops do against a crowd like that? They dealt out a few random blows, then gave up. One union member unrolled a red banner affixed to two long bamboo poles. It bore the symbol of the hammer and sickle with the name of our union. Raised above our heads, it formed a victory arch.

"The noise of the bells increased with every minute, as new rickshaw *wallahs* appeared on the scene. It became quite deafening, just as if billions of cicadas were rubbing their wings together all at the same time. The owners must have heard that concert from their hiding places. Provided, of course, they hadn't all put balls of cotton in their ears.

"The dejected look of the stewards when they came back was more eloquent than any words: their bosses were sticking to the increase they'd announced. Rassoul got up on a *telagarhi* with a loudspeaker. I couldn't help wondering how so powerful a voice could come out of so puny a chest. 'Comrades!' he shouted, 'the owners of your rickshaws want to increase their profits even more. Their voracity knows no limits. Yesterday they demanded the payment of two lots of rental, one for the day shift and the other for the night. Today they're increasing your fees by fifty percent! Tomorrow, God knows what new demands they'll impose on you.'

"Rassoul spoke for some time. His face disappeared behind his loudspeaker. He talked about our children and said that this increase would condemn them to starvation. He said that we had no way out of our position as slaves, that most of us had lost our land, and that if the hope of earning a living by pulling our rickshaws was taken away from us, there would be nothing left for us to do but die. He said that we had to get rid of this menace at all costs, that we were numerous and strong enough to impose our wishes and make the owners back off. And he ended up by asking us all to vote for an unlimited strike.

" 'Inkalabad zindabad! Long live the revolution!' he then proclaimed. 'Rickshaw Workers Union zindabad!'

"We all took up the slogans in a chorus and repeated them several times. It made me think of my friend Ram Chander. How pleased he would have been to see all his companions gathered shoulder to shoulder in defense of their family's bowl of rice. He had so often fought alone. We were carried away, as if by the wind that blows before the monsoon. Long live the revolution! The revolution? Like all the others, I let the word roll off my tongue, but I didn't know exactly what it meant. All I wanted was to be able to take a few more rupees to the munshi each month and to be able to knock off a bottle of bangla with my friends now and then.

"Rassoul asked all those in favor of the strike to put up their hands. We looked at one another in silence. Who among us could face without apprehension a single day without the means of earning his living? Does a bird saw through the branch he's sitting on? The owners would be all right—they had their jars full of rice and dal. We could be reduced to skeletons before they lost a single roll off their paunches. And yet we had no real choice.

"A fellow next to me put up his hand. He was a Bihari; I knew him by sight. He was called 'Scarface' because a blow from a cop had smashed his cheek in. He coughed like Ram, but he didn't chew pan. When he spat there was no mistaking what the red stuff was. No doubt he'd said to himself that, strike or no strike, it would make very little difference to him.

"Other hands went up. Then more. Finally, one by one, all the hands went up, including mine. It was odd to see all those hands in the air. Not one of them was closed in a fist. There was no hatred, rather, there was a kind of resignation. There was no use in Rassoul repeating that striking was our only weapon, you could sense that the pullers had put their hands up reluctantly. How could you hold it against them? The rickshaw union wasn't the workers union at Dunlop or GKW or any other big factory. There, when the workers went out on strike, the union gave them funds. They could hold out for months.

"Rassoul took up his loudspeaker again to announce that the motion to strike had been carried unanimously. Then he called out, 'Comrades, our revered president, Abdul Rahman, calls upon us all to meet at the Maidan esplanade this afternoon at three o'clock. United, we will make our anger felt. United, we'll break the owners.' And he started up again with slogans about the revolution that we all repeated as a chorus. It was as if we were drunk. We shouted without thinking. We shouted because we were all poor men who had come together to shout together.

"The most tremendous thing about it was the feeling of revenge that suddenly came over us. The great city of Calcutta belonged to us, to us the pullers of men, the ones whom taxi, bus, and truck drivers insulted and despised, the ones whom the cops tormented and beat, the ones whom passengers were always trying to cheat out of a few *paisas*. We, the sweating, suffering slaves of the *sardarjis* and the owners, we the population of rickshaw wallahs, were suddenly the masters. Not a single vehicle could pass through the city center anymore, blocked as it was by thousands of rickshaws. It was like a flood, except that the monsoon had poured down empty carriages. I don't know how many of us there were—perhaps fifty thousand or more. Like the many arms of the Ganges, our various processions all converged on Chowringhee, along the Maidan, the great avenue that those gentlemen of the police force had closed to our old rattletraps three months previously, under the pretext that we took up too much room and caused traffic jams. Today they watched us pass with heads bowed beneath their white helmets, their guns in their highly polished belts, and their *lathis* ready to batter the poor on the skull or the back.

"The union leaders had distributed red posters all along the route. They announced that we were the rickshaw pullers of Calcutta and that we were rejecting the new increase in rent. They also said that we'd had enough of police harassment and that we claimed the right to earn our rice like anybody else. Passers-by watched us with astonishment. Never before had they seen so many rickshaws at once. They were used to the city officials demonstrating or the railway employees or the streetcar conductors—in short, those who were fortunate enough to have a proper job and be well paid. That bums whom they regarded as beasts of burden, whom they never saw other than with their backs bent, should dare to demonstrate too seemed to be quite beyond them.

"As we walked, we chanted slogans rounded off with three jangles of our bells. It made an impressive noise. On the corner of Lindsay Street, a coconut vendor cut the tops off his fruits and handed them out to us to keep us going. It was a shame that the procession forced us to go on walking because I would have very much liked to go and tell that fellow that he could get into my rickshaw and go wherever he wanted free of charge. It wasn't every day that we were offered something to drink in this city. Farther on, in front of the arcades of the Grand Hotel, where I'd been to forage in the garbage cans with my children, there were foreign tourists who couldn't get back to their cars because of our march. They seemed to find us interesting, because they were taking photographs. Some of them even came right into the middle of our procession to have their pictures taken with us. The rickshaw wallahs of Calcutta angry must be as exciting a sight as the white tigers in the zoo at Alipore. I don't know whether rickshaw people go on strike in other countries, but they could probably show those pictures to their friends and relatives when they got home and tell them that there are some very strange experiences to be lived in the streets of Calcutta.

"Our procession reached the rallying point on the edge of Chowringhee. As we joined up with one another, the march swelled to become a river wider than the Ganges. Our final destination was the Sahid Minar, the column on the Maidan that soars up so high, it seems to pierce the clouds. High up on the balcony you could see the cops. Just think, all the thousands of rickshaws in Calcutta gathered together—that must have given the police a few headaches. At the base of the column was a platform decorated with red flags. It looked really splendid. As we arrived, union men invited us to leave our carts along the edge of the Maidan and go and sit in front of the platform. I couldn't help wondering how we were all going to find our own vehicles again among such a pileup of carriages.

"Golam Rassoul climbed onto the platform. For this occasion he had changed into a clean *dhoti* and *kurta*. For all his fine clothes, however, he still looked just as puny. There were several other people on the platform with him, but we didn't know who they were. After a moment Rassoul took hold of a microphone and called out something in Hindi. Nearly all the pullers got to their feet and yelled, 'Abdul Rahman *zindabad!*' Rassoul repeated his words, this time in Bengali, which was how I learned of the arrival of the president of our union. He was a plump little man who looked like a *babu* from a political party. He can't have pulled many rickshaws, unless of course it was during some other life. He was surrounded by a dozen men who cleared his way through the people in front of him. They only just stopped short of sweeping the dust from under his feet. He waved his hand as he passed among them, and what he had on his finger was no mere moonstone, but several gold rings with enormous precious stones that glinted in the sunlight. He climbed onto the platform and sat down with his entourage in the front row.

"Rassoul announced that he was going to present to us the representatives of the other unions who had come to bring us the support of their members. There were representatives from the jute mills, from Hindustan Motors, from the shipyards, and goodness knows where else. Each time the signal was given we sent up a torrent of 'Zindabads' for each one, and each time we did so the crows dispersed in all directions. We had a warm feeling in the pits of our stomachs at the thought that there were people prepared to take an interest in poor fellows like us. Rassoul had us acclaim our president once more. Thrilled by the applause, the man with the rings got up to speak.

"He must have been very used to this kind of meeting, because his every movement seemed to be specially calculated. To start

with there was his silence. For a full moment he stood and looked
at us without saying anything, nodding his head slightly like a
peasant content to contemplate the shoots in his rice field undulat-
ing far away to the horizon. Then he decided to speak, mixing
sentences in Bengali and Hindi. I couldn't follow exactly what he
was saying because he spoke mainly in Hindi, which most of the
Bihari pullers could understand. But he spoke damn well, that *babu*
Abdul. I managed to make out that he was telling us that the bosses
were inflicting starvation on us, that they were making their futures
out of our sweat and blood, and that all this would go on just as
long as the capitalist government would not make up its mind to
expropriate our carriages and give them to us, the people who
actually had to pull them. It was really a very good idea and we
applauded heartily. There were even men who shouted that we
should demand expropriation immediately. That way there would
never be any increase in rent.

"Abdul Rahman went on with his speech, talking progressively faster and more loudly. You'd have thought he was reciting
the Ramayana, for all the passion he put into his words. His finger
pointed out imaginary owners and seemed to pierce them through
with a knife. The effect was so spellbinding that some of my colleagues began to clap their hands, or shout, shaking their fists. The
youngsters picking their way through the ranks to sell sweetmeats
and tea, and even the fellows who were collecting the money,
stopped to brandish their fists and shout along with the others. I
don't know whether the owners and their factotums were watching
this scene from afar and listening to our shouting, but if they were,
they must have been making some very strange faces. If, at that
moment, Abdul had asked us to go and set fire to their houses, I
can well believe we would have followed him to a man. Instead,
however, he took advantage of the assembly of poor fellows listening to him as if he were a guru straight out of Ganesh's trunk, to
score political points and attack the government over the increase
in police harassment and brutality. This was a chapter so close to
our own hearts that a tremendous ovation interrupted his speech.
Voices began to chant, 'Everyone to the Writers' Building!'

"The Writers' Building is the enormous building in Dalhousie
Square, in which the government offices are housed. Abdul
Rahman raised his arms to try and still the shouting, but a wind of

rage had suddenly blown up among his audience, like a tornado that announces a cyclone.

"Something strange happened next. One of the pullers emerged from the crowd and, pushing aside everyone who got in his way, ran to the platform, mounted the steps, and grabbed the microphone before Abdul or anyone else could intervene.

" 'Comrades!' he cried, 'what the *babu* is doing is lulling us off to sleep! He is trying to drown our anger in beautiful phrases! So that we remain lambs. So that all the *sardarji* can go on devouring us without our protest!'

"We were in such a stupor that we got to our feet. That's when I recognized Scarface. The people on the platform hadn't dared to snatch the microphone from him. He spoke with difficulty because of his chest disease.

" 'Comrades! It's by our actions that we should demonstrate our anger!' He raised his arm in the direction of Chowringhee. 'We have no business standing here on this esplanade. Under the windows of the owners of our rickshaws is where we should be demonstrating. I know where one of them lives! Did you know that more than three hundred rickshaws belong to him alone—to Mr. Narendra Singh, the man you call the Bihari? Comrades, it's to him and his associates that we should be demonstrating our strength. Let's go right now to Ballygunge!'

"Scarface was just catching his breath when a dozen men in khaki uniforms burst onto the platform. They surrounded him and dragged him to the foot of the steps, whereupon Abdul took the microphone again.

" 'Provocation!' he cried. 'That man is an agitator!'

"There were a few moments of confusion as Scarface was taken away. Several pullers rushed to his rescue but they were pushed brutally aside. It was not the evening appointed for the revolution.

"Abdul Rahman went on talking, then it was the turn of the representatives from other unions. You could sense that they were trying to warm us up a bit, but after the incident with Scarface our hearts were no longer in it. All we could see was the fact that all those speeches had prevented us from earning our living that day and that the next day would be the same. We were asking ourselves just how long we were going to be able to hold out with the strike.

At the end of all the talking, the president of the syndicate took the microphone and asked us to sing the workers' song with him. I knew nothing about any such song but the older ones among us, those who had been to meetings on the Maidan before, knew it. Abdul Rahman and the people on the platform struck up the song and thousands of voices on the esplanade joined in. My friends told me that it was the song of workers all over the world. It was called 'The Internationale.'"

32

IT HAD ALL BEGUN with the simple matter of redistributing the land. As soon as a leftist government had come to power in Bengal, the Communist party had invited those peasants who had no land to take possession of the properties of the *zamindars* and to reorganize themselves to farm them collectively. Aside from the murder of a number of landowners who tried to resist, the process was completed without much violence. It was then, however, that the Naxalbari incidents broke out, and immediately the question ceased to be that of a simple confrontation between landowners and peasants and became one of the most serious political crises to threaten India since Independence.

Naxalbari is a region at the heart of a narrow strip of land formed by the North of Bengal between the borders of Nepal and Bangladesh. Tibet and China are only a hundred miles away. It is an area scattered with tea plantations and jungles ideally suited to infiltration and guerrilla activity. There is not one single town, only a few villages and camps inhabited by peasants of tribal origin who scratch a miserable subsistence from plots of ground so poor that the planters did not want them.

A long tradition of Red activism fired these people, who had already risen up against the authorities on several previous occasions. Nowhere was the new policy of land redistribution implemented with so much vigor—nor with so much violence. Urged on by Maoist students from Calcutta, possibly trained in Peking, the Naxalites murdered, waited in ambush, and attacked the forces of order. Soon the word "Naxalite" had found its place beside those of Bolshevik and Red Guard in the lexicon of Indian Communism.

Drawing their inspiration from the revolutionary teachings of Mao Zedong, the guerrillas mixed terrorism with popular warfare. In the village squares they lit bonfires to burn the title deeds and proof of debts before beheading, after the Chinese fashion, some of the moneylenders and the large landowners in front of enthusiastic crowds.

The contagion spread as far as Calcutta. Bomb attempts, assassinations, violent demonstrations, the sequestration of political leaders and factory owners increased. Not even the slums escaped. Molotov cocktails were thrown in the streets of the City of Joy, claiming a number of victims. The Naxalites had even gone so far as to desecrate the statue of Gandhi at the entrance to Park Street, by daubing it with tar. Completely overwhelmed, the government had found itself divided over what course of action to take. The Communists in power accused both Peking of seeking to destabilize the power of the left in Bengal, and the CIA of infiltrating the Naxalite commandos to pave the way for the return of conservative forces.

The accusations against the CIA were part of a traditional argument. Since the departure of the British, the American organization had become the habitual scapegoat whenever it was convenient to implicate foreigners in India's internal affairs. Such attacks would have been of no great consequence if they had not eventually resulted in a kind of psychosis of espionage, which meant that a certain number of foreign residents were subjected to police interference. Stephan Kovalski was to be one of these victims.

The fact that he was a Polish Catholic priest was in itself suspect. To make matters worse, however, his circumstances were somewhat irregular. His tourist visa had expired ages ago and all efforts to obtain a permanent resident's visa had remained fruitless. Still, in India, bureaucracy can never be rushed. For as long as it had not officially rejected his request, Kovalski could hope that he would not be deported. What really ran the risk of weighing most heavily against him was the place where he lived. No official could seriously believe that a European would willingly and purely for his own satisfaction share in the misery and poverty of those who lived in the slums. His presence in the City of Joy must be for other motives.

So it was that one morning, at about eight o'clock, four inspectors in Western attire and belonging to the District Intelligence Branch of the Calcutta Police (DIB), showed up at the entrance to Nizamudhin Lane. The police intrusion provoked a lively reaction. Instantly the entire neighborhood was alerted. Dozens of people came running to the scene. Some of them had armed themselves with sticks to prevent anyone taking away their "Father." The Polish priest himself would have been surprised to find out about the upheaval around his person. This morning hour was the time when he had his daily dialogue with his Lord. Seated in the lotus position, his eyes closed, his breath slowed to a minimum rate, he was praying before the picture of the Shroud of Christ.

"I didn't hear the police banging on my door," Kovalski was to recount. "How could I have heard them? That morning, as on every other, I was deaf to any noise, deaf in order to be alone with my God, in order to hear nothing but his voice in the very depths of myself, the voice of the Jesus of Anand Nagar."

As custom dictated, the policeman who appeared to be in charge took off his sandals before entering the room. He was a chubby man and his teeth were reddened with betel. From the pocket of his shirt protruded three ballpoint pens.

"This is where you live?" he asked in an arrogant tone, casting a look around.

"Yes, this is it."

The picture of the Sacred Shroud attracted the policeman's attention. He closed in on it with a look of deep suspicion.

"Who is that?"

"My Lord."

"Your boss?"

"If you like," agreed Stephan Kovalski with a smile.

The policeman was obviously in no mood for pleasantries. He scrutinized the picture closely. Doubtless he had found a piece of evidence. He summoned one of his subordinates and ordered him to take it off the wall.

"Where are your personal effects?" he asked.

Stephan Kovalski indicated the small metal trunk that a Christian family had lent him to protect his Gospels, a few medicines, and the small amount of linen he possessed.

The inspector examined each item, as he searched methodically through the contents of the trunk. A horde of beetles made off in all directions.

"Is this all?" he marveled.

"That's all I have."

The man's incredulous expression wrung a certain pity from Stephan Kovalski, who found himself wanting to apologize for having so few possessions.

"Do you have a radio?" he asked.

"No."

The policeman looked up to inspect the framework of the hovel and established that there was not even an electric light bulb. He took out a notebook and began to draw a floor plan of the room. This took quite a while because none of his three ballpoint pens would work properly.

It was then that an unexpected diversion occurred. Alerted by some of the neighbors, Bandona burst into the room, fire in her eyes. She grabbed the inspector and pushed him toward the door. "Get out of here!" cried the young Assamese girl. "That is a poor man sent by God. God will punish you if you torment him."

The policeman was so astonished that he raised not the slightest resistance. Outside the mob had grown—the street was full of people.

"She's right!" a voice cried. "Leave our 'Big Brother' alone."

The policeman in charge appeared perplexed. Then turning to the priest, he joined his hands in front of his forehead and said courteously, "I would be very grateful if you would accompany me to the general police headquarters. I would like to furnish my superiors with the opportunity of a short conversation with you."

Then addressing himself to Bandona and the assembled crowd, he added, "Don't worry. I promise to return your 'Big Brother' to you by the end of the morning."

Kovalski waved goodbye to the friends who had come to his rescue and accompanied the inspectors to the police van parked at the entrance to the slum. Ten minutes later he got out in front of a dilapidated building not far from Howrah Hospital. Four flights up a dark staircase stained with red spittle of betel chewers led to a large room cluttered with worm-eaten cupboards full of piles of official papers protected from the circling of the fans by scraps of old metal. Apparently it was teatime because the inspectors in the room seemed far more preoccupied with emptying their cups and chatting than studying files concerned with state security. The entry of this sahib in basketball shoes disrupted their various conversations.

"This is the Polish priest who lives in Anand Nagar," announced the policeman with as much pride as if he had been bringing in the murderer of Mahatma Gandhi.

The one who seemed to be the senior officer present, a small man with carefully sleeked gray hair, dressed in an immaculate *dhoti,* invited Kovalski to sit down in front of him. After fetching Kovalski a cup of tea, he lit a cigarette and asked, "Do you like it in our country?"

"Enormously."

The police officer looked thoughtful. He had a strange way of smoking. He held his cigarette between his index and his middle finger and inhaled the smoke from the cavity formed by his thumb and bent index finger. He looked as if he were "drinking" it.

"But don't you think that our country has more beautiful things to offer a foreign guest than its slums?"

"Certainly," agreed Kovalski, "but it all depends on what one is looking for."

The chief inspector inhaled another puff. "And what might you be looking for in a slum?" he asked.

Kovalski tried to explain. Listening to himself talk, he found himself so unconvincing that he was sure he was only increasing the suspicions of his interviewers. He was wrong. In India there is so much respect for compassion for others that his explanations aroused sympathy.

"But why aren't you married?" asked an inspector with a mustache.

"I *am* married," the Pole said. Confronted with their skeptical expressions, he elaborated, "I am married to God."

The policeman who had searched his room proceeded to unfold the picture of the Sacred Shroud and put it on the gray-haired senior officer's desk.

"Sir, this is what we found in his place. He claims it's a picture of his 'Lord.' "

The chief inspector examined the picture carefully.

"It's Jesus Christ," explained Kovalski. "Just after his death on the Cross."

The man nodded respectfully.

"And this is who you're married to?"

"I am his servant," the priest replied, not wishing to complicate the discussion.

So great is the impact of the sacred in India that Stephan saw a light of sympathy on the faces surrounding him. This time he was sure he had dispelled their suspicions.

It was then that the chief inspector sat down in his chair again. His face had hardened.

"All the same I would like to know what your connections with the CIA are," he asked.

Kovalski was so stunned by the question that he was at a loss for words. "I have no links at all with the CIA," he eventually managed to articulate.

There was so little conviction in his voice that the senior officer persisted.

"And you are not in contact with anyone connected with the CIA?"

Kovalski shook his head.

"And yet the majority of foreigners who purport to be social workers are CIA agents," added an assistant with a shiny skin. "Why should you be an exception?"

Kovalski made a supreme effort to remain calm.

"I wouldn't know whether the majority of 'social workers' are CIA agents," he said steadily. "But I read enough spy novels when I was young to be able to assure you that it would be very difficult for a poor fellow living twenty-four hours a day in a slum to be an effective agent. And your policing is quite efficient enough for you to know that the only visits I have are from people who live in the slums. So please be good enough not to waste your time and mine with such nonsense."

The gray-haired senior officer had listened without stirring. By now all his colleagues had formed a circle around him and the Pole.

"Shri Kovalski, forgive me for causing all this unpleasantness," the chief inspector apologized, "but I have my duty to perform. So tell me a little about your connections with the Naxalites."

"The Naxalites?" repeated Kovalski, flabbergasted.

"The question isn't quite as absurd as you appear to think," the chief inspector added curtly. Then, more gently, he went on, "After all, don't your Jesus Christ and the Naxalites have a number of factors in common? Don't they claim to be rebelling against the same thing? Against the injustices that repress the poor and the weak, for example?"

"Yes, indeed," agreed Kovalski. "But with the important distinction that Jesus Christ conducts his rebellion with love; the Naxalites murder and kill."

"So you're against the activities of the Naxalites?" intervened the assistant with the shiny skin.

"Resolutely. Even if at the beginning their cause was a just one."

"Does that mean you're equally opposed to the Maoists?" inquired the senior officer.

"I'm opposed to anyone who wants to achieve happiness for some by cutting off other people's heads," said Kovalski firmly.

At this point in the cross-examination there was a little light relief. The chief inspector lit up a fresh cigarette and the office boy refilled the teacups with boiling milk. Several of the policemen made themselves up a wad of betel which turned their teeth and gums an unattractive sanguinolent color. Then the questioning continued.

"If you're not a member of the CIA, nor of the Naxalite commandos, nor of the Maoist action groups," recapitulated the chief inspector, "then you must be a Jesuit?"

For a few seconds Kovalski was silent, torn between anger and the desire to burst out laughing.

"If you're now trying to get me to admit that I'm a missionary," he said eventually, "you're wasting your time again. I'm no more a missionary than a CIA agent."

"But you know what the missionaries did in Nagaland," insisted the chief inspector.

"No."

"Come, come, Shri Kovalski, you really don't know that the

missionaries joined forces with the separatist movements to spur the local people into rising up and reclaiming their autonomy?"

"I can assure you that the work of the vast majority of missionaries in this country—Jesuit or otherwise—has been an action to better the lot of the people," replied Kovalski sharply, indignant at the turn taken by the interrogation. "What's more, you know for a fact that when people here talk about the 'missionary spirit,' it is often to draw attention to the work of someone who has in truth devoted himself to others, who has given only love to his Indian brothers."

There was silence and then, suddenly, the chief inspector stood up and offered his hands to his interlocutor, in a gesture marked with respect. His assistant with the shiny skin did likewise and so did the others, one after another. At last they had come to an understanding.

Before accompanying the visitor back, the chief inspector pointed to the picture of the Sacred Shroud spread out on his table.

"I am a Hindu," he said. "But I would like to ask your permission to keep this picture as a souvenir of our meeting."

Stephan Kovalski could hardly believe his ears. That's fantastic, he thought. The chief of the police asking me for a picture of Christ! "It was a present and I'm very attached to it," replied the priest, "but I could have a photographer make up a copy for you."

The man seemed delighted at the idea. The chief inspector then put down in front of Kovalski a sheet of paper bearing several administrative seals.

"In exchange, here is a document that will no doubt please you. This is your resident's permit. My country is proud to welcome authentic holy men like you."

33

SHE IS THE TRIUMPHANT GODDESS, the destructor of the demons of evil and ignorance, wife of the god Shiva, daughter of the Himalayas, a queen of manifold incarnations, the feminine force of the gods, alternately the symbol of gentleness and of cruelty. The Puranas, the golden legends of Hinduism, devote thousands of verses to the legendary exploits she accomplishes under a score of names, guises, and attributes.

In her tender guise, she is called Ouma, light and grace; Gauri, the goddess with the light skin; Parvati, queen of the mountains; or Jagan Mata, mother of the universe. In her destructive form she takes the names of Kali the Black one, Bhairavi the Terrible, Chandi the Furious, or Durga the unattainable. It is under this latter name and in the guise of the divine conqueror of evil that she is specially worshipped in Bengal. Every child knows her fabulous story.

Hundreds of thousands of years ago a terrible demon ravaged the earth, throwing the seasons into confusion. He was the demon of evil, in other words, of ignorance, and the gods themselves could not get rid of him. Brahma, the Creator, had declared that only a son born to the god Shiva could conquer him, but Shiva's wife was dead and he, in his grief, could give no thought to bringing a son into the world. He lived the life of an ascetic, begging in the villages for his food, like so many others seen in the India of today, with their long hair and their bodies covered with ashes.

Meanwhile the situation on earth grew worse and in the heavens the gods lamented the fact that Shiva could not consider marrying again. The gods themselves appealed to Kama, god of love and desire, to cause love to be born in the heart of Shiva. Kama set out, accompanied by his wife, Voluptuousness, and their friend, Spring. They came to the foot of the mountain where Shiva was meditating and, at a moment when the ascetic seemed to relax his concentration, Kama released from his floral bow the jasmine arrow that no one can resist. From that moment onward, Shiva began to think of Ouma, daughter of the Himalayas, in whose body his first wife had been reincarnated. After various trials, they were married and she took the name of Parvati, "daughter of the mountain."

Yet the demon of evil continued to lay waste to the earth and by the time a son of Shiva was available to tackle him, it might be too late. So it was that the gods united their diverse energies in a single breath of fire and concentrated it upon Parvati who was thereby transfigured. She became the great goddess, Durga, "she whom nothing can attain." In order to combat the demon in the ten directions of space, she had ten arms which the gods equipped with their own weapons. Her father, Himalaya, King of the Mountains, provided her with a lion as a mount, then the moon gave her a rounded face and death her long black hair. She was the color of the dawn.

The demon then appeared in the form of a huge buffalo accompanied by the multitudes of his army. Battle commenced. Axes, arrows, and javelins hurtled through space and the roaring lion on which the goddess was mounted pounced upon the army of demons like flames upon a forest. She herself, with her armored hands, smote her enemy, their horses, elephants, and chariots so that they crashed into a heap of chaos. The furious bellowing of the giant buffalo made the worlds tremble; with his horns he uprooted the mountains and hurled them at the goddess, who pulverized them with her arrows. Thus the battle raged for three days. Several times Durga was on the point of defeat. At one point, on the evening of the third day, she interrupted her onslaught to raise to her lips a cup filled with the liquid of the gods. Then, with a terrible blow, she sank her trident into the monster's chest. Mortally wounded, the monster immediately tried to abandon his body. From his mouth there issued the figure of a hero, brandishing a scimitar. At once, however, the triumphant goddess decapitated him.

It was then that she turned completely black and became known as Kali, "the Black one," as black as time which consumes everything. Then earth and heaven resounded with cheers of joy and songs of victory.

Once a year, at the end of the monsoon, the eight million Hindus in Calcutta commemorate this victory by celebrating a four-day festival, the splendor and fervor of which are probably without equal in the rest of the world. For four festive days the city becomes a city of light, joy, and hope. Preparation for the festival begins several months beforehand, in the old quarter occupied by the potters' caste, where hundreds of artisans create a collection of the most magnificent statues ever consecrated to a deity or his saints. For one whole year the craftsmen compete between themselves to produce the most colossal and most sumptuous representation of the goddess Durga. Having constructed a framework out of braided straw, the potters coat their models with clay before sculpturing them to produce the desired shape and expression. Finally they complete their handiwork by painting and clothing them. Ordered in advance by families, communities, neighborhoods, factories, or workshops, these thousands of Durgas are all destined to take their places, on the first day of the festival, under one of the thousand canopies, known as *pandals*, erected in the streets, avenues, and crossroads of the city. The construction of these canopies, and especially their decoration, is the subject of great rivalry.

Some weeks before the festival, Stephan Kovalski received a visit from two gentlemen who introduced themselves as representatives of the Neighborhood Committee for the Construction of Canopied Shrines in Anand Nagar. Courteous in the extreme and far too well-dressed to be actual occupants of the slum, the visitors showed him a notebook full of subscriptions and invited the priest to pay them the sum allocated to him, namely, fifty rupees. In one morning alone, they had already collected more than a thousand rupees by racketting one after another the hovels in the alleyway, including those occupied by Muslims and Christians.

Kovalski was outraged that so much money should be squandered on a festival, while so much poverty prevailed. He was wrong. His rational Western reaction failed to take into account the most essential point of all: that these people lived in a state of osmosis with their deities. And he forgot too the role these gods played in everyday life. Any intervention of fortune, good or bad: work, rain, hunger, a birth, a death—in fact *everything* was ascribed to the gods. And that is why the country's most important festivals never commemorate historic anniversaries, not even the glorious day of Indian Independence, but always some religious event. No other people honors its gods and its prophets as fervently as does the population of Calcutta—despite the fact that the heavens often seem to have completely abandoned the city to its tragic destiny. Every day, or almost every day, the slum and other areas of the city resounded with the noise of some procession bearing witness to, the mystical marriage of a people and its creator.

The previous week, Kovalski had run into a brass band on the corner of Chitpore Road. Blocking traffic, dancers performed their contortions, calling out the name of the prophet Hussain and swirling in the sunlight curved swords above their heads. It was Moharram, the great Muslim festival that marked the beginning of the Islamic holy year. In the slum, as elsewhere in the city, all the Shi'ite Muslims changed into their festival clothes. It was a municipal holiday, one of fourteen or fifteen such holidays in the calendar of this city that was a veritable mosaic of peoples and beliefs.

Two days previously, a thunderous burst of fireworks had woken the tenant of 49 Nizamudhin Lane with a start. The several Sikh families in the slum were celebrating the birth of the guru Nanak, the revered founder of their community, born in the Punjab at the other end of India. A procession of beturbaned men, armed with their traditional *kirpans,* * went through the slums to the triumphant sound of a brass band and made for the small local *gurdwara.* † Meanwhile, from every corner of the city, other processions, accompanied by carts richly decorated with garlands of flowers, made their way to other *gurdwaras*. Inside these sanctuaries priests took turns participating in an uninterrupted reading of the Granth, their sacred book. A huge blue-and-white tent had been erected on the grass of the Maidan for a colossal feast. One of the leaders of the Sikh community in Anand Nagar, Govind Singh, a likable giant in a scarlet turban and a taxi driver by profession, had

---

* Small dagger/sword, one of the five attributes of the Sikhs.
† Sikh temple.

invited the Pole to be present at the celebrations. Hundreds of the faithful came to sit on the ground in long rows, with the women in tight trousers and Punjabi tunics on one side, and the men in their pointed turbans on the other. Generous people carrying caldrons of rice and curried vegetables passed along the rows and ladled curry onto banana leaves placed before each guest. Little girls with dark eyes made up with kohl poured tea into small baked clay bowls which would be broken after use. All day long hundreds of loudspeakers proclaimed the joy of the Sikhs from one bank of the Hooghly to the other.

On the previous day the Bara Bazar, the huge market on the other side of the bridge, had been the scene of effervescent rejoicing. Followers of the Digambara Jains sect, a reformed branch of Hinduism born about the time of the Buddha, had been celebrating the return of their pilgrimage season, marked by the official end of the monsoon. Preceded by two life-sized horses made out of white cardboard and affixed to the chassis of a Jeep, the procession carved its way through trucks, handcarts, rickshaws, indeed vehicles of every kind, inextricably entangled with a seething multitude of pedestrians. In the middle of the cortege, on a flower-bedecked float pulled by men curiously dressed in the costumes of Elizabethan lackeys, the sect's pope sat enthroned, half-naked in a golden shrine, waving to the multitudes who acclaimed him with the clash of cymbals and drums.

Of all these celebrations, however, surely none bore witness to the presence of God in Calcutta with more intensity than the Hindu *pujas* in honor of the goddess Durga. Even though with the passing of the years the festival had changed somewhat to become more of a commercial fair, it still contributed to making this city a place of faith. Nowhere was this characteristic so clearly in evidence as in the slums, at the heart of those disinherited people to whom the experts of the Ford Foundation predicted no improvement of their condition before the year 2020. In the depths of their poverty, they had managed to preserve the heritage of their traditions, and none of these traditions was more visibly expressed than the taste for celebration.

Deep in their veins flowed dedication to festivities that for the space of a day or a week removed them from reality. Festivities for which people went into debt or without food in order to buy their families new clothes in honor of the gods. Festivities that were a more effective vehicle for religion than any catechism. Festivities that embraced the heart and the senses with the magic of song and the ritual of long and sumptuous liturgical ceremonies.

What did it matter, therefore, that swindlers made their cut out of the sweat and hunger of the poor? In the final reckoning it was the poor who were the richer. In Anand Nagar racketeers had no qualms about obliging rickshaw cyclists and *telagarhi* pullers to pay their bit toward the shrines, or stopping trucks and buses on the Great Trunk Road to racket drivers and passengers. Even the leper quarter at the far end of the slum did not escape the fund-raising. No one knew exactly what percentage of the manna went straight into the pockets of the collectors, but what was left for the festival was enough to create magic.

As the day approached, a kind of vibration washed through the slums. Large bamboo frames shaped like Roman triumphal arches began to pop up everywhere. Artists dressed these struc-tures in multicolored materials. They decorated the supports and capitals with splendid patterns, in the form of mosaics or check-ered squares, giving the drapes a geometry of exemplary refine-ment. The shrine destined to receive the statue of the goddess was itself a sumptuous floral creation, a veritable scaffold of roses, marigolds, and jasmine that embalmed the surrounding stench. Most surprising of all was the improbable panoply of accessories that came with the decorations. No *pandal* was complete without an abundance of floodlights, garlands of bulbs, lamps, and even Vic-torian chandeliers. Small islands of light suddenly brought to the roofs and façades a supernatural halo. Discharged by loudspeak-ers, songs and music poured out over the slum, day and night, endorsing the fact that everywhere in India celebrations are ac-companied by excessive noise. This concert was the signal for a ritual of purification which, in the space of a few days, would completely transform a universe of squalor.

All Hindu families and a substantial number of Muslim and Christian households set about whitewashing their hovels inside and out—their verandas, the curbstones of the wells, and their shop fronts. The pious old Hindu who kept the tea shop opposite Kovalski's hovel took advantage of the priest's absence to repaint the façade of his room in a beautiful white that filled the entrance with light. Then followed the people's special toilet. On this unique occasion in the year, thousands of poor people exchanged their worn clothes for the carefully preserved festival attire, or perhaps even bought for the occasion by going into debt with the neighborhood usurer. All the Calcutta traders encouraged such purchases by offering special reductions in honor of the goddess. Like film stars, the Durgas passed through the hands of an army of dressers and makeup artists, who adorned them with sumptuous clothes and jewels, before they were turned out as food for the hungry gazes of their public. The installation of statues in their shrines was the occasion for a meticulous ritual undertaken under the watchful eye of the police.

On the appointed day, at six o'clock in the evening, the plaintive sound of conches and the haunting roll of thousands of *daks*,* which down through the centuries had beaten out the *pujas* to Durga, announced the official beginning of the festival. For four intoxicating days of *kermis*, the slum people, like millions of others in the city, would proceed with their families in a blaze of floodlights past the four *pandals* erected in the City of Joy. Hindus, Sikhs, Muslims, Buddhists, Christians were all brothers, united in a dream. The men wore woolen *sherwanis* over their trousers and their wives were dressed in green silk *kurtas*, with gold earrings which gave them the air of Oriental princesses. Mehboub's eldest son, Nasir, who made ballpoint pens in a workshop, and his sisters, even the last little one with her stomach swollen with worms, were also made up and attired like little princes, despite the fact that, tragically scarred by their mother's disappearance, the family had sunk into wretchedness. Next to Mehboub and his children, Kovalski recognized the old Hindu from the tea shop. His forehead was decorated with the three streaks of ashes of the worshippers of Shiva. Visibly moved by his *darshan†* with the deity, oblivious to the lights and the din of the loudspeakers, he was immersed, eyes closed, in a state of bliss. The sight of this holy man at prayer reminded Stephan Kovalski of the words of the prophet Isaiah, "The prayer of the poor and the orphaned never rises to the Lord without response."

* Large double drum, hung horizontally round the neck.
† Visual encounter with a deity or great soul.

On the fourth day at dusk, all the statues in the City of Joy were hoisted onto illuminated carts, draped in material and flowers, to be conducted solemnly in procession, accompanied by brass bands, bagpipes, drums, and conches as far as the banks of the Hooghly. At the same time, all over the city, similar corteges were heading for the same destination. Borne on trucks, handcarts, taxis, private cars, and even cycles and hand-pulled rickshaws, thousands of Durgas descended to the river, escorted by their devout owners. One of the rickshaws caught up in this tide bore the number 1999. At every stop along the way Hasari Pal turned around to gaze at the marvelous spectacle of the goddess he was transporting on the seat of his old carriage, a Durga almost as large as life, with ten arms and magnificent black hair crowned with a golden diadem, and with the eyes of a conqueror. "Oh dear God," he said to himself, "even my rickshaw has become a shrine."

That evening hundreds of thousands of the city's inhabitants squeezed themselves onto the banks of the river; it took Hasari hours to reach the water's edge. When at last he did manage it, the members of the family who owned the statue, who had followed it in a second rickshaw, garlanded the goddess with flowers and lowered her slowly and respectfully into the water. Hasari watched with emotion as she moved away, carried along by the current. Like all the other Durgas she was bearing away, to the immense expanse of the ocean, all the joys and the hardships of the people of Calcutta.

34

IT WAS NO easy venture! After the Hindi and Urdu he had so painfully deciphered by means of a comparative study of the Gospels, Stephan Kovalski had resolved to break through his linguistic isolation once and for all. Armed with a grammar book, every morning and evening he applied himself to conquering the Bengali language. By a stroke of good fortune, at the very beginning of the work there were a number of sentences translated from Bengali into English. Assuming that the names of towns and other proper nouns would be written the same way in both languages, he identified the corresponding words and broke them down to work out a Bengali alphabet for himself. In the chapter on pronunciation, diagrams showed the position of the tongue in relation to the palate, teeth, and lips for each letter. Thus the *O* was pronounced with the extremity of the lips slightly open but with the mouth closed. To make the *U* sound, you had to wedge the tongue against the upper teeth. It was so complicated that he had to go to the bazaar in Howrah to buy a mirror, a piece of equipment which greatly aroused the curiosity of his neighbors. Thus equipped, he was able gradually to master the gymnastics of the innumerable aspirated letters which made people appear permanently breathless when speaking the Bengali language. These efforts also provided him with the opportunity to make a discovery. "The image that the glass threw back at me was far from cheering. My hairline had receded badly and my cheeks were hollow. They had taken on the gray tinge of the slum."

His sad appearance was an indication that Kovalski's Indianization was well under way. One day his neighbors recognized that

the process was almost complete. It was at the conclusion of a
marriage ceremony. Some Hindu friends had just married their
last daughter to the son of one of his neighbors. Kovalski knelt
down in front of the father and mother to do what possibly no
other foreigner had done before him. He wiped the dust from their
sandals and raised his hands to his forehead. This gesture was a
way of saying to them, "Since my little sister has married my little
brother, you are my parents. I have become a member of your
family."

That evening Kovalski went to the jeweler-usurer in the alleyway. He showed his metal cross with the two dates—the ones of his
birth and his ordination—and asked him to engrave underneath
them the word "Premanand" he had chosen to be his Indian name.
In Bengali, Premanand meant "Blessed is he who is loved by
God." He asked the jeweler to leave a space next to the inscription,
so that he could engrave, when the time came, the third most
important date in his life. For that very day Kovalski had taken an
extraordinary step, a step that was quite incomprehensible to Indians convinced that nothing could change the condition given to
them at birth, except death and another life.

He had been to an office in the Home Ministry to fill in the
forms, asking the government of India for the honor of becoming
officially one of the race of the poor in the City of Joy. He had
applied for Indian citizenship.

*

Ashish and Shanta Ghosh, the young Hindu couple on the
Committee for Mutual Aid, interrupted Kovalski one evening
when he was engaged in one of his linguistic miming sessions in
front of his mirror.

"Father, we've got some news for you," said the boy, fretfully
rubbing his beard. "You'll be the first to know."

Kovalski invited the visitors to sit down.

"We've decided to leave the slum soon and go back to our
village."

From beneath her red veil, Shanta watched for the priest's
reaction.

"Dear God," thought Kovalski, "this is the greatest thing I've

heard since I arrived in the City of Joy. If people actually start
making their way back to their villages, we're saved!" He could not
actually conceal his joy.

"What's made you . . . ?"

"For three years now we've been saving up *paisa* after *paisa*,"
Shanta went on. "And we've been able to buy two acres of good
land near the village from a Hindu who was marrying off his daughter."

"We're going to have a big pool dug out in the middle, to
breed fish," her husband explained.

"And the water will provide us with a second harvest in the dry
season," added Shanta.

Kovalski sensed that he was witnessing a kind of miracle, the
miracle of which thousands of starving people compelled to take
refuge in Calcutta dreamed.

"Shanta will go first with the children," said Ashish. "She will
sow and pick the first crop of rice. I shall stay here to earn a little
more money. If the first harvest is adequate, I shall leave too."

The young woman's beautiful dark eyes glowed like embers.

"But, above all," she said, "we want our return to bring something for the people of our village, something that will be like a
breath . . ."

"Of fresh air," said her husband. "The Bengal earth could
yield three harvests if it were properly irrigated. I shall try and
form a cooperative."

"And I shall start up a craft workshop for the women."

His eyes half-closed, his mirror on his knees, Kovalski listened
in wonder. "May God bless you," he said at last. "For once light
and hope will spring forth from out of a slum."

35

THE RECEPTIONIST burst into the room without knocking. "Monsieur le Consul, there is an Indian lady outside who insists that she wants to speak to you urgently. She says that in the slum where she lives a Polish missionary is dying of cholera. She says this missionary holds a French passport. This is why she has come to our consulate. He's refusing to allow himself to be taken to a clinic. He wants to be treated like all the others . . ."

Sixty-two-year-old Antoine Dumont, complete with his bow tie and rosette of the Legion d'Honneur, was the representative of the French Republic in Calcutta. Ever since Louis XV's filibusters had come to these latitudes to tickle British supremacy and set up their warehouses, France had maintained a consulate in one of the old blocks in the neighborhood of Park Street.

The diplomat scratched his mustache and stepped out into the corridor that served as a waiting room. Thirty years of postings in Asia had accustomed him to putting up with many an annoyance occasioned by his compatriots or holders of French passports. Hippies, drug addicts, easy riders, deserters, tourists who'd been robbed: he had never begrudged any of them assistance and support. Nevertheless, this was undoubtedly the first time he had received an SOS concerning an ecclesiastic who was dying "voluntarily" of cholera in the depths of an Indian slum.

The previous evening Shanta and Margareta had discovered Kovalski lifeless in his room. He was lying, completely drained, in the middle of his own vomit and excreta. It was just as if his insides had been eaten up by some invading parasite. His muscles had collapsed and his skin, stretched over his bones, looked more like parchment. He was conscious, but so weak that any effort to talk risked extinguishing the little life still burning in him.

The two Indian women had instantly diagnosed his illness: a lightning form of cholera which, oddly enough, showed a predilection for more robust consitutions.

Kovalski had felt the first symptoms of it during the previous night, when painful stomach cramps had sent him rushing to the latrines several times. Despite the heat, he had begun to shiver. Next he had felt a tingling sensation in the tips of his hands and feet, followed shortly afterward by a general twitching of his muscles. His feet and legs turned a curious bluish color. The skin of his hands dried up, before wrinkling and hardening. Although sweating profusely, he grew colder and colder. He felt the flesh of his face shrink over his cheekbones, then across his nose, his forehead, as far as his skull. It was more and more difficult for him to close his mouth and eyes. His body was racked with spasms. He began to vomit. His breathing became jerky and painful. He made an effort to drink but nothing, not even a few drops of water, would clear his throat that was as if paralyzed. At about four or five in the morning, he could no longer feel his pulse. That was when he sank into a kind of torpor.

When he awoke, he wanted to get up to go back to the latrine, but he had not the strength to stand up, or even to kneel. He had to let himself go right there where he was. Soon he told himself he was going to die. The idea brought with it no fear. On the contrary, in his extreme weakness he experienced a kind of euphoria.

The two Indian women interrupted what he would later call "a delicious sensation of tiptoeing towards nirvana." Neither Shanta nor Margareta, however, felt disposed to let their "Father" die without a fight. Margareta seized the bowl and sprinkled the sick man's face and torso to moisten his skin. Her first concern was to check dehydration, but the Indian woman knew that only an immediate infusion with plasma had any chance of stopping the disease. They must get the priest to an intensive care unit without delay.

"Hang on, Stephan *Daddah*," she begged, as she moistened his face with a corner of her veil. "We're going to take you to Bellevue."

Every inhabitant of Calcutta, even the poorest of the poor, knew the name of the luxurious private clinic set among palm trees in the Park Street neighborhood. There Bengal's medical élite operated on and nursed rich *marwaris*, senior government dignitaries, and members of the colony of foreigners, in conditions of hygiene and comfort comparable to those of a Western establishment. Margareta knew that the Bellevue clinic would not refuse to take in her "Father." He was a *sahib*.

A grimace contorted Kovalski's face. He wanted to speak but had no strength to do so. The Indian woman bent over him. She realized then that he was refusing to leave his room. He wanted "to be cared for like the poor here." Stephan Kovalski had known dozens of men struck down by cholera in the City of Joy. They stayed where they were. The toughest survived; the others died. During the monsoon the number of cases increased. Because of lack of space, medicines, and doctors, the hospitals almost invariably turned them away. For him there was no question of being given privileged treatment.

Confronted by this unexpected resistance, the two women went to confer with their neighbors. It was decided that the rector of the church should be alerted. He was the only one, they thought, who might be able to persuade his fellow priest to allow himself to be transported to the Bellevue clinic. Father Cordeiro gave them a somewhat reserved reception and immediately dismissed any idea of his intervening personally with Kovalski.

"I can see only one solution," he said. "And that's to inform the Polish consul. Or better, the French consul, since Kovalski holds a French passport. After all, the person concerned is one of those for whom he's responsible. Only he can oblige that stubborn foreigner to let himself be cared for in the normal fashion. Or at least he can try."

Margareta was designated as emissary. So effectively did she convince the diplomat of the urgent need for his intervention, that a gray Peugeot 504 decorated with a tricolor pennant pulled up at the entrance to Anand Nagar that very afternoon. The appearance of the car caused such a sensation that Antoine Dumont had difficulty squeezing his way through the crowd. Turning up his trouser bottoms, he ventured into the muddy alleyway. On two or three occasions, discomforted by the smells, he was compelled to stop and wipe his face and neck. Despite his long experience, he had never before penetrated into quite such a setting. "This priest must be completely mad," he repeated to himself, as he tried to avoid the puddles. On reaching the shriveled body in the depths of the hut, he volunteered with an enthusiasm that was slightly forced.

"Good day, Reverend! I bring you the respectful greetings of the French Republic. I am the French consul in Calcutta."

Stephan Kovalski opened his eyes with difficulty.

"To what do I owe the honor?" he inquired feebly.

"Didn't you know that a consul's primary duty is to look after the citizens under his jurisdiction?"

"I'm very grateful to you, Monsieur le Consul, but I have no need of your concern. I have enough friends here."

"It is precisely those friends who alerted me. Because your state of health requires . . ."

"Repatriation?" interrupted Kovalski, suddenly discovering a little energy. "Is that what you came here to suggest to me? Repatriation for medical reason? You really shouldn't have gone to so much trouble, Monsieur le Consul. I thank you for your kindness but beg you to save yourself unnecessary expense. The poor of the slums are not eligible for "repatriation."

He let his head sink back and closed his eyes. The sharpness of his tone had not eluded the diplomat. "This priest is a tough nut," he thought to himself.

"At least agree to let yourself be cared for in a good clinic." He sought after words that would convince. "Think of all that your life can give your friends. And of the vacuum your death would undoubtedly leave behind you."

"My life is in God's hands, Monsieur le Consul. It is for him to decide."

"I'm quite sure that it is because he has decided that you should be cured that I find myself here," argued the diplomat.

"Perhaps," agreed Kovalski, touched by the logic of this argument.

"In that case, I beg you to allow your friends to transport you to . . ."

"To a hospital for everyone, Monsieur le Consul, not to a clinic for the rich."

Dumont sensed that he was halfway there. A little patience and Kovalski would allow himself to be convinced altogether.

"The better the treatment you have, the sooner you'll be able to continue your activities."

"My desire is not to continue my activities, Monsieur le Consul, but to be sure of being able to look at the people around me without shame."

"I understand. But let me reassure you that not a single rupee will be taken from the poor to pay for your hospitalization. The consulate will cover any expenses."

Kovalski sighed; the conversation had exhausted him.

"Thank you, Monsieur le Consul, but it isn't a question of money. For me it's a matter of respecting a commitment freely undertaken. This illness is providential. I implore you not to insist."

A spasm shook the sick man. Antoine Dumont considered the inanimate body and wondered for a moment if he were dead. Then he noticed the irregular wheeze of the priest's breathing.

Outside in the alleyway, Ashish and Shanta, Bandona, Margareta, Aristotle John, Saladdin, old Surya, Mehboub, and numerous other neighbors were waiting anxiously. When the diplomat emerged, they all closed in.

"Well?" asked Margareta.

The Consul adjusted his bow tie.

"Only half a victory! A clinic is out of the question, but he's agreed to go to 'a hospital for everybody.' That's his expression. I think we should respect his wishes."

As soon as the diplomat had left, Margareta loaded Kovalski onto a rickshaw and took him to the City Hospital, one of Bengal's capital's main medical centers. With its carefully manicured lawn, pool, fountain, and bougainvillea walk, the establishment offered rather fine surroundings. A red sign in the emergency wing pointed to a vast building, the doors and windows of which were nearly all broken. Margareta was tempted to ask the rickshaw puller to turn back. Even the most painful visions of the City of Joy had not prepared her for the shock of the sights that awaited her: bloodstained dressings strewn about the corridors, broken beds serving as trash cans, mattresses bursting open and crawling with bugs. Wherever you went you found yourself treading on some form of debris. Worst of all, however, were the people who haunted the place. The severely ill—suffering from encephalitis, coronary thrombosis, tetanus, typhoid, typhus, cholera, infected abscesses, people who had been injured, undergone amputations, or been burned—were lying all over, often on the bare floor.

Margareta eventually managed to dig out a bamboo stretcher on which she installed the unconscious Kovalski. Since no one came to examine him, she slipped a note into the hand of a male nurse to procure a bottle of serum and a syringe which she, herself, inserted into the patient's arm. Then she asked for anticholera drugs. Like so many other establishments, however, the City Hospital was short of medicines. The press frequently denounced the pilfering that went on in hospitals and kept flourishing numerous little pharmacies outside its walls.

"I'm thirsty . . ."

Kovalski opened his eyes to the nightmare world of this "hospital for everybody." There was neither a jug nor water at the patient's bedside. From time to time a boy came around with a waterskin. He charged fifty *paisas* a cup (five U.S. cents). At the end of the corridor were the latrines. The door had been torn off and the drain was blocked. Excrement had spilled over and spread into the corridor, much to the delight of the flies.

Hundreds of sick people jostled with each other daily outside the doors to establishments such as this, in the hope of receiving some form of treatment, of obtaining a place in a bed—or on the floor—in order at least to be able to eat for a few days. There was the same crush almost everywhere. In some maternity wings it was perfectly possible to find three mothers and their babies bedded down on a single mattress, a situation which sometimes caused the asphyxia of newborn babies. Regular press campaigns condemned the negligence, corruption and theft that paralysed certain hospitals.

In the hospital where Stephan Kovalski was, a costly cobalt bomb had remained out of use for months because no one would take the responsibility for spending the sixty-eight hundred rupees necessary to have it repaired. Elsewhere a cardiac resuscitation unit was closed because of the lack of air-conditioning. In yet another hospital the two defibrillators and ten out of the twelve electrocardiograph machines had broken down, as had half the bedside monitors. Oxygen and gas cylinders for sterilization were lacking nearly everywhere. "The only piece of equipment that seems to function properly, but then again, only when there are no power cuts, is the apparatus for electric shock treatment in Gobra Mental Hospital," one newspaper reported. It had not been possible to open the new surgical wing at one large hospital simply because the Health Service had not yet approved the nomination of an elevator attendant. The lack of technicians and plates nearly everywhere meant that most patients had to wait four months for an X ray and weeks for any analysis. At a hospital near the Sealdah Station, eleven out of twelve ambulances were broken down or abandoned, with their roofs smashed in, their engines stolen, and their wheels stripped. In many operating units, the containers of forceps, scalpels, clips, and catgut were nearly empty, their contents having been stolen by staff members. The few instruments that actually remained were rarely sharp. The catgut was frequently of such poor quality that stitches burst. In many places reserve blood supplies were virtually nonexistent. In order to procure the precious liquid before an operation, patients or their families sometimes had to resort to those specialist racketeers with whom Hasari Pal had already been dealing. Such parasites found in the hospitals idyllic opportunities for self-enrichment. Some of them sandbagged the sick (especially poor people who had come up from the country) and, when they arrived, promised them immediate hospitalization or a medical examination in exchange for some money. Others passed themselves off as bona fide doctors, luring their victims into consultation rooms manned by nurses who were partners in complicity. They then asked the women to hand over their jewels in preparation for an X ray and vanished.

In some hospitals the pilfering of food intended for patients had assumed such proportions that meals had to be transported in padlocked carts. In spite of these precautions, large quantities of food and milk were regularly diverted to the innumerable tea shops that had set themselves up in the vicinity of the hospital. Sugar and eggs were systematically spirited away to be resold on the spot at prices twice as low as in the market. The newspapers revealed that such pilfering was not confined to food. Some establishments had no more doors or windows. At night, treatment had to be given by candlelight: all the electric light bulbs had disappeared.

As is often the case in India, however, the best fortunately mixed with the worst. In all these establishments there was also a network of people who bonded together to dispel isolation, anonymity, horror. A few mattresses away from Kovalski lay a poor fellow who, following an accident, had undergone one of the most delicate and daring operations of modern surgery, a spinal fusion of the rachis involving the grafting of the vertebral column. Day by day, Kovalski followed his progress. In a communal ward that was sordid in so many other aspects, that man was the object of admirable care and attention. Each morning the nurses got him up and helped him gradually regain the use of his legs. Every time he did his rounds, the heavily overburdened surgeon would find the time to examine and to talk with him, demonstrating as much solicitous concern as competence. A few beds farther on, a mother squatted on the floor beside her baby's cradle. The child was suffering from meningitis. No one would have thought of preventing the poor woman from remaining with her infant, and the people in charge of the food never went past without offering her also a bowl of rice.

Highly surprised to discover that they had a *sahib* as a companion in their hardship, several patients dragged themselves over to ask Stephan to decipher the bits of scrap paper used for prescriptions. This was an occasion for Kovalski to marvel at the conscientiousness and precision with which some of the overburdened doctors prescribed their treatment for even the most anonymous of their patients.

Nothing was ever totally rotten in this inhuman city.

The priest would no doubt have been most indignant at what Margareta had done. She had just slipped twenty rupees into the nurse's hand to get him a bed underneath a fan. There was nothing unusual about this: patients were constantly being turned out of their pallets to be replaced by the purveyors of baksheesh.

Without the bottles of serum, medicines, and food that the indomitable Indian woman brought him each day, the Pole might well have died. She had organized a collection in the slum and all the poor people had contributed to the saving of their "Big

Brother." Mehboub's children had gone along the railway lines picking up cinders. Surya, the old Hindu from the tea shop, had donated several bags of sweetmeats. The mother of Sabia, the child who had died of tuberculosis in the room next door, had cut out and stitched a shirt for *Daddah* Stephan. Even the lepers had given up the proceeds of several days' begging. Stephan Kovalski had failed: in his affliction he had not been able to be a poor man like his brothers of the slum.

36

CALCUTTA HAD NEVER seen such a spectacle: thousands of rickshaws abandoned all over the city. The strike—the first great strike of the last human horses in the world—paralyzed the town's most popular means of transport. "But striking is a rich man's weapon," Hasari acknowledged regretfully. "Fine resolutions don't last long when your belly's gripped with the cramps of hunger and your head's as empty as a skin discarded by a cobra. Those brutes, the owners, knew that only too well. They knew we would crack. After only two days some of our comrades picked up their shafts again. Others followed. Soon we were all back on the road chasing after clients, even doing bargain-rate runs just to get something to eat right away. And we were forced to pay the new rent. It was very hard. But fortunately something always crops up in this city to stop you from crying too much over your lot.

"When I first made the acquaintance of my colleague Atul Gupta, I rubbed my eyes several times. I couldn't help wondering whether, instead of waiting for a client on the corner of Russell Street, I wasn't actually watching a film, for Atul Gupta looked like a hero straight out of a Hindu film. He was a handsome fellow, with well-groomed black mustache, carefully combed hair, full cheeks, and the look of a conqueror. He was dressed in a colorful shirt and proper *sahib*'s trousers, and—what was even more incredible—he was wearing socks and shoes, real shoes that enclosed the foot, not junk plastic sandals. Yet there was something even more surprising about him: he was sporting a gold watch on his wrist. Can you imagine, a rickshaw puller wearing a gold watch?

"I had seen films where heroes disguised themselves as rick-

shaw *wallahs,* but that was in the movies. Gupta was real. No one
knew where he came from. It's true that in Calcutta you lived
alongside people about whom you knew nothing, whereas in our
village, everyone had known each other for generations. Only one
thing was certain about Gupta: he must have been to school a lot
because he was more knowledgeable than all the Brahmins in
Calcutta put together. No one could recite the Ramayana quite as
he could. He was a real actor. He would sit down anywhere and
start to recite poetry. Instantly a little group would form around
him and in a few seconds he would make us forget the cuts on our
feet, the cramps in our stomachs, the heat—everything. He used to
cast a spell over us. He had an amazing way of personifying Rama,
then Sita, then the terrible Ravana, all in turn. We could have
listened to him for hours, days, nights, while he transported us
over the mountains, across the seas and the sky. Afterward the
rickshaw weighed less heavily. In a matter of months Gupta became a hero among the pullers of Calcutta. How had he come to
finish up in the skin of a poor fellow like me? The answer remained
a mystery.

"Some people claimed he was a spy, others that he was a
political agitator. He lived in a boardinghouse in Free School
Street frequented by peculiar people, foreigners who went barefoot and wore necklaces and bangles around their ankles. Word
had it that those people injected themselves with drugs and
smoked, not *bidis* but the *bhang* that transports you to nirvana. In
any case, Gupta himself didn't go barefoot and I never saw him
with a cigarette between his lips. He worked as hard as any of us. At
dawn he was always the first to arrive at the stand on Park Circus
and he was still trotting around long after nightfall. It must be said
that he didn't have years of working with an empty stomach behind
him like the other pullers. His engine was still running nicely. But
like the rest of us, he had no license for his rattletrap. In Calcutta a
good baksheesh would buy you the keys to paradise.

"In any case, license or no license, Gupta must have had some
good days because women used to fight with one another to get
into his rickshaw. No doubt they thought they were being pulled
along by Manooj Kumar.* But then in our line of business it's

* A famous Indian film star.

better to be taken for the poorest of poor devils than to look like a film star. The more you stood out from the crowd, the more people kept tabs on you."

One day when he was taking two young girls back to their house in Harrington Street, the handsome Atul Gupta was to experience the truth of these words for himself. A trash cart had broken down in the middle of the carriageway and the whole street was blocked. Gupta tried to bypass the obstruction by going onto the sidewalk, but a policeman intervened. There followed a violent altercation between Gupta and the cop, who made no bones about hitting Gupta several times with his *lathi*. Furious, Gupta put down his shafts and hurled himself at the policeman. The two men rolled on the ground in a savage scrum. Eventually the policeman ran to get reinforcements and a crew of cops rushed to capture the puller and seize his rickshaw.

When the police finally released him at noon the next day, Atul Gupta was a mass of flesh and blood. They had beaten him all night and burned his chest with cigarettes. They had hung him from a hook, first by his arms, then by his feet, and whipped his body with a bamboo cane. It wasn't only because he had fought with one of their men that they punished him, but also because of his clean trousers, his shirt, his *sahib*'s shoes, and his gold watch. A slave had no right to be different from all the other beasts of burden.

Not content with having beaten him, the police registered a complaint against Atul Gupta before the judges at the Bonsal Court, Calcutta's municipal court. On the day of the trial, the rickshaw pullers gave their comrade a proper guard of honor. Since he could hardly walk, they put him in one of their carriages decorated with flowers. "He was just like a maharajah or a statue of Durga, our friend," Hasari Pal was to recall, "except that he had bandages on his arms and legs, and his eyes and face looked as if they had been painted with kohl, his features were so marked with ecchymosis."

The Bonsal Court was an old brick building on the other side of Dalhousie Square, in the center of town. In the courtyard, at the foot of a great banyan tree, stood a small temple. The pullers helped Gupta get down in front of the altar decorated with portraits of Shiva, Kali, and the Monkey god Hanuman because he was very religious and wanted to have a *darshan* with the deities before facing his judges. Hasari took hold of his hand to help him strike the clapper of the bell suspended above the altar. Gupta recited a few *mantras*, then placed a garland of flowers around the trident of Shiva.

On the pavement all along the railings, a crowd was squeezed in between a double row of vendors. The warm air intensified the smell of hot oil and frying. Farther away, in the entrance to the courtyard, people were lining up for public writers, who squatted behind typewriters. Inside the courtyard, others were having coconuts cut open or drinking tea or bottled drinks. There were even beggars on the steps up to the audience chambers. What was most striking of all, however, was the constant coming and going. People went in, came out, stopped to talk. Accused men went past chained to policemen. Legal men in black tailored jackets and striped trousers talked among themselves and to the prisoners' families.

Gupta and his friends went into a vestibule that smelled of mildew. Women were breast-feeding their babies on benches. Some people were in the middle of eating, others were asleep on the bare floor, wrapped up in a piece of *kadhi*.

Someone informed Gupta that he must go and find himself a lawyer. At the end of a long dark corridor, there was a room full of them. They were seated behind small tables under fans that scattered their papers about. Gupta chose a middle-aged man who inspired confidence. He was wearing a shirt and tie under a black jacket as shiny as the surface of a pool in moonlight. The defending counsel led his client and escort to a staircase that stank of urine. At the turn of every floor, judges were dictating their opinions to clerks who typed them out with one finger.

The small troop at last arrived in a great chamber. A faded photograph of Gandhi decorated one wall. The back of the room was furnished with a pyramid of old metal trunks, which contained thousands of pieces of evidence used in the course of countless trials: knives, pistols, all kinds of weapons, and stolen goods. In the middle of the chamber, benches were arranged in rows in front of a platform. On the platform were two tables and a cage linked to a tunnel of iron railings which ran right across the room. "I had seen

a tunnel like that once before in a circus," Hasari Pal was to recount. "It was used to convey tigers and panthers into the ring."
Here it was used to bring prisoners before their judges. Atul Gupta
did not have to use it because he was appearing before the court as
a free man.

The room was soon completely full of rickshaw pullers drinking tea and smoking *bidis* as they awaited the arrival of the court.
Gupta sat before the platform on a bench beside his counsel.
Eventually two men in rather grimy *dhotis* made their entrance.
They were carrying under their arms files bulging with papers, and
they moved with an air of boredom. They were the clerks. One of
them clapped his hands, ordering that the two great fans suspended from the ceiling be set in motion. The machines were so
worn that their blades took a while to start up, like two vultures
who, having just devoured a carcass, couldn't quite manage to take
off.

A door opened at the back of the room and the judge entered.
A very thin man with a sad expression behind his glasses, he was
wearing a black robe trimmed with fur. Everyone stood up, even
Gupta, who had great difficulty in remaining upright. The judge
sat down in the ceremonial chair in the middle of the platform. The
accused and his friends could hardly make out his face behind the
volumes of the Indian penal code and the files that covered the
table. He had hardly settled himself when a pigeon perched itself
on one of his books and attended to its own particular needs. A
clerk mounted the platform to wipe away the droppings with a
corner of his *dhoti.* Several families of pigeons had built their nests
in the heaps of files and the trunks at the back of the chamber.

A small figure, likewise dressed in a black robe, had entered
behind the judge. He was so cross-eyed that it was impossible to
tell whether he was looking to his right or left. He was the P.P.—
the public prosecutor. Below, to the left of the platform, stood a
police officer. As Hasari Pal was to say, "It was just as if they were
getting ready to play a scene from the Ramayana with lots of
characters."

One of the clerks began to read out the charge accusing Atul
Gupta of having assaulted the policeman in Harrington Street. The
judge had taken off his glasses, closed his eyes, and sunk back in his

chair. All that could now be seen of him was his bald head, which gleamed above the heaps of files. When the clerk had finished, the judge's voice was heard asking Gupta's defense counsel what he had to say. Then Hasari saw the rickshaw puller place his hand on his lawyer's shoulder, to prevent him from standing up. Gupta wanted to conduct his own defense.

In the space of a few minutes he gave such a detailed account of the brutality to which he had been subjected that the entire room began to sniff and weep. The P.P. and counsel for the prosecution then intervened, but there was no real point. The judge too was sniffing behind his mounds of books and papers. Gupta was found not guilty and acquitted. Furthermore, the judge ordered that his rickshaw be restored to him.

The hearing had lasted less than ten minutes. "The longest part of it was our applause," Hasari was to say. "We were proud and happy for our friend."

News of Gupta's acquittal spread like wildfire among the city's rickshaw pullers. Scarface and Golam Rassoul, the pillars of the rickshaw pullers' union, suggested that an enormous demonstration be organized immediately outside the Writers' Building, the seat of the Bengal government, to protest against police violence. Rassoul alerted the leaders of the *telagarhi wallahs*, the handcart pullers' union. They jumped at the chance: rickshaws and *telagarhis* were the scapegoats of the Calcutta police.

The procession set off from Park Circus in the early afternoon. Left-wing party leaders had provided streamers, banners, and red flags, so that it looked like a field of red marigolds on the move. In front, seated in a rickshaw decorated with flowers and red streamers, rode the hero of the day, pulled by men who took turns doing a hundred yards between the shafts. It was carriage number 1999 that had the honor of transporting him, the jalopy between the shafts of which Hasari Pal had sweated, suffered, and hoped for four years.

Along the route hundreds of handcart pullers came to join the procession. Traffic was brought to a standstill and soon the paralysis stretched as far as the suburbs. This time the inhabitants watched the demonstrators pass without astonishment. Never before had a cortege marched past with so many flags and streamers. The Communists had sent their team, armed with loudspeakers.

The leaders shouted and chanted slogans which the pullers repeated at the tops of their voices. It took more than three hours to
reach Dalhousie Square. The police had barricaded the approaches to the government building with vans, trucks, and hundreds of men in khaki, armed with guns. The long red brick façade
studded with statues was protected by more policemen.

The column had to stop at the barricade. A police officer in a
flat cap stepped forward and asked the men at the head of the
procession if they wished to convey a message to the Prime Minister's secretariat. Atul Gupta replied that the organizers of the
demonstration demanded to be received by the Prime Minister in
person. The officer said that he would pass on the request. The
party leaders took advantage of the ensuing wait to give voice to
fiery speeches against the police; they shouted revolutionary slogans.

After a few minutes the officer returned to announce that the
Prime Minister agreed to receive a delegation of four rickshaw
pullers. Rassoul and Gupta together with two other union members were authorized to cross the barrier. When they came back
half an hour later, they harbored an air of satisfaction, especially
Gupta. He announced through a loudspeaker that the Prime Minister and the chief of police had given their assurance that there
would be no recurrence of police brutality. Applause and cheers
greeted the news. Gupta added that he had personally received a
solemn promise that the policemen who had ill-treated him would
be punished.

There was a fresh round of acclamations. Gupta, Rassoul, and
the two other delegates were then decorated with garlands of
flowers. "We felt as if something that was of great significance for
us had just occurred," Hasari Pal was to say. "We could take leave
of each other happily and in peace. Tomorrow would mark the
beginning of better days."

The procession broke up without incident. Rickshaw *wallahs*
and *telagarhi wallahs* returned to their homes. Gupta climbed back
into Hasari's rickshaw. They and a few friends went to a drinking
place in Ganguli Street to celebrate their victory with some bottles
of *bangla.* It was just as they were leaving the bar that Hasari heard
a dull sound like that of a bursting bicycle tire. Gupta uttered a cry,
his head flopped onto his chest, then his whole body crumpled

against the shafts. Hasari saw that he had a hole in his head, just above his ear from which the blood had begun to flow. Gupta tried to say something, then his eyes turned completely white.

"Our enemies had avenged themselves. They had robbed us of our hero."

37

A LITTLE COLONY had installed itself in the far reaches of the slum, in an area bounded by the railway tracks. From the outside nothing distinguished it from other quarters in the slum. The same compounds in the form of a square around a courtyard were to be found there, with the same sort of laundry drying on the roofs and the same open drains. Yet this was a ghetto of a very particular kind. No other occupants of the slum ever ventured there, for it was in this place that the City of Joy's six hundred lepers lived, squeezed ten or twelve together to each room.

India numbers about five million lepers among its population. The horror and fear inspired by disfigured faces, hands and feet reduced to stumps, and wounds at times infested with vermin, condemned the lepers of Anand Nagar to total segregation. Although they were free to go about the slum, an unspoken code forbade them to enter the houses or compounds of the healthy. By having gone to Stephan Kovalski's room, the cripple Anouar had transgressed the rule, and the infraction could have cost him his life. There had already been several lynchings, although more out of fear of the evil eye than out of fear of contagion. Though they would give alms to lepers to improve their own karma, most Indians looked upon leprosy as a malediction of the gods.

In the heart of the leper colony, a hut made out of bamboo and dried mud provided shelter for a few mattresses. In this hovel laid a number of refugees from the pavements of Calcutta, who had come to the end of their Calvary. One of these was Anouar.

"That man too had a smile that was difficult to understand in the light of his suffering," Stephan Kovalski was to say. "He never uttered the slightest complaint. If ever I ran into him by chance in an alleyway, he would always greet me in a voice resonant with joy.

" 'Well, Stephan *Daddah,* are you well today?'

"Coming from a human wreck groveling in the mud, the question seemed so incongruous that I hesitated before replying. I had formed the habit of stooping down to him and grasping the stump of his right hand with my hands. The first time I did it the gesture took him so much by surprise that he surveyed the people around him with an expression of triumph, as if to say, 'You see, I'm a man just like you. The *Daddah* is shaking my hand.' "

Stephan Kovalski knew that Anouar had reached the advanced stages of his illness and was going through utter torment. There was nothing more that could be done for him since the disease had reached his nerves. When the pain became too intolerable, he used to have himself carried to 49 Nizamudhin Lane where the priest gave him a shot of morphine. Kovalski had managed to procure some vials of it from the hospital in Howrah. He kept them for desperate cases.

The day after one of these injections Kovalski encountered Anouar in one of the alleyways. He looked unusally preoccupied.

"What's wrong with you, Anouar?" asked the Pole, concerned.

"Oh nothing, Stephan *Daddah,* I'm fine. But my neighbor, Saïd, is not too good. You ought to come and see him. He's so ill he can't eat or sleep."

The cripple creeping along in the filth asked nothing for himself. Worried only about his neighbor, he was the living message of the Indian proverb, "The hell with misery as long as we are miserable together."

Stephan Kovalski promised to come that afternoon.

It was a journey into sheer horror. What the priest discovered was not so much a leper colony as a kind of ossuary. Were those skeletons consumed with gangrene, whose closed eyes were covered with white mushrooms, really human beings? Those breathing corpses whose crackled skin oozed out a yellowish liquid? Even so the sight was nothing by comparison with the stench. "I had never smelled anything like it. A mixture of decay, alcohol, and incense. You needed to have Hope with a big *H* well anchored in the bottom of your heart to withstand it." Squatting among the rubbish and excreta, children played marbles, with great shrieks of laughter. Kovalski had no difficulty in identifying Anouar's friend. Saïd was a man of barely forty, left with no hands and no feet. Leprosy had also eroded his nose and eaten away his eyebrows. Anouar performed the introductions. Saïd turned his blind face toward the priest and Kovalski thought he detected a smile on it.

"Stephan Big Brother, I'm fine," he assured him. "You shouldn't have taken the trouble to visit me."

"It's not true," corrected Anouar, shaking his mop of hair, "you're in a lot of pain."

Kovalski took hold of his arm and examined the stump. The wound was greenish in color and maggots were crawling over the bone. Saïd too was beyond all treatment. Kovalski filled a syringe with morphine and looked for a vein beneath the hard, crackled skin. He could do nothing more.

Nearby, a woman was stretched out on a rough bed with a baby lying next to her. The child was a bouncing boy. An allergic reaction to her medicines had covered the mother's face with swellings and pustules. It was a common phenomenon and one that was so traumatic that many lepers refused any kind of treatment. The poor woman's body was concealed by a piece of cloth pulled up to her chin. Kovalski bent over and picked the child up in his arms. He was amazed at the force with which the boy's little hand gripped his finger.

"He's going to be a big fellow," he promised the mother. The leper woman turned away. Kovalski thought he had hurt her.

"Here, you take him. He's yours and shouldn't be away from you."

An interminable moment passed. The mother made no move to take her son. She was crying. Eventually she pushed back the sheet and held out her arms. She had no fingers.

Kovalski placed the child carefully at her side. Then, joining his hands in the Indian gesture of salutation, he left without a word. Outside, a host of cripples, blind men, and limbless people awaited him. They had all come running to receive a *darshan* from the "Big Brother," who had dared to enter their lair. "They too were smiling," the priest was to say. "And their smiles were neither forced nor suppliant. They had the smiles of men, the bearing of men, the dignity of men. Some of them clapped their maimed hands to applaud me. Others jostled with each other to get near to me, to escort me, to touch me."

Anouar led the visitor to a compound where four lepers were playing cards, squatting on a mat. His arrival interrupted them but he begged them to continue their game. This proved to be an opportunity for him to witness a juggling act worthy of the most celebrated circus. The cards flew about between the palms of their hands before tumbling to the ground in a ballet punctuated with laughter and exclamations.

In a neighboring compound, beggar musicians performed a concert for him on flutes and drums. Everywhere he went in the leper colony, people came out of their hovels. His visit was turning into a fête. "Outside the door to one shack, a grandfather who was almost blind thrust in my direction a three-year-old boy he had just adopted. The old man used to beg in front of Howrah Station. One morning this child sought refuge with him, like a dog lost without a collar. That same old man who didn't have enough to feed himself every day, and who would never be cured, had taken the boy under his wing." A little farther on, Stephan was awestruck by the sight of a small girl massaging, with fingers that were still intact, the chubby body of her little brother as he lay in her lap. Anouar led the way, propelling himself along on his plank on wheels, with a fervor that was redoubled by his pride at acting as guide for his "Big Brother Stephan."

"Stephan *Daddah,* come and sit over here," he ordered, gesturing to a mat made out of jute sacks sewn together that a woman had just unrolled for him in one of the courtyards. Several lepers scrambled to settle themselves next to him. That was when he realized that he was being invited for a meal.

"I thought I had come to terms with everything about poverty, yet I felt revolted by the idea of sharing food with the most bruised of all my brothers," Stephan was to admit. "What a failure! What lack of love! What a long way I still had to go!" He hid his uneasiness as best he could and very soon the warmth of the lepers' hospitality dispelled it. Women brought metal bowls full of steaming rice and vegetable curry, and the meal began. Kovalski did his utmost to forget the fingerless hands battling with balls of rice and pieces of marrow. His hosts seemed overwhelmed with joy, wild with gratitude. Never before had a foreigner shared their food. "Despite my heaving stomach, I wanted to show my friendship for them," he would explain, "show them that I wasn't afraid of them. If I wasn't frightened of them it was because I loved them. And if I loved them it was because the God with whom I lived and for whom I lived, loved them also. These people needed more love than anyone else. They were pariahs among the pariahs."

His generosity of heart did not, however, prevent Kovalski from feeling a certain indignation that men could allow themselves to be reduced to such a state of physical decline. He was well aware that leprosy was not a fatal disease. Provided it was treated in time, it was even quite easily cured and left no aftereffects. It was that day, confronted by the horrible sight of so much mutilation, that he made his decision. He would set up a leprosy dispensary in the City of Joy, a proper place with specialists who knew how to cure the disease.

Next day Stephan Kovalski climbed aboard the bus that went across the Hooghly. He was going to the south of Calcutta to lay his plans before the only person in the city who could help him to implement them.

38

LIKE A FLOWER straining toward the sun, the sugarloaf-shaped
dome of the temple of Kali surfaced from the imbroglio of alleyways, residences, hovels, stores, and pilgrims' rest houses. This
high place of militant Hinduism, built near a branch of the Ganges,
on the banks of which the dead were burned, was the most frequented shrine in Calcutta. Day and night crowds of the faithful
swarmed inside and around its gray walls. Rich families, their arms
laden with offerings of fruit and food wrapped in gold paper;
penitents dressed in white cotton, leading goats to the sacrifice;
yogis in saffron robes, their hair tied up and knotted on the crowns
of their heads, the sign of their sect painted in vermilion on their
foreheads; troubadours singing canticles as plaintive as sighs; musicians, tradesmen, tourists; the motley throng milled about in an
atmosphere of festivity.

This is also one of the most congested places in the overpopulated city. Hundreds of shops surround the temple with a string of
multicolored stalls. There is something of everything sold here:
fruit, flowers, powders, imitation jewels, perfumes, devotional objects, gilded copper utensils, toys, and even fresh fish and caged
birds. Above the antlike activity hovers the bluish mist of the funeral pyres and the smell of incense mingled with burning flesh.
Numerous funeral corteges wend their way between the cows, the
dogs, the children playing in the street, and the flock of faithful
worshippers. At the temple of Kali, the most vibrant life goes hand
in hand with death.

Around the corner from this sanctuary stands a long, low
structure with windows obstructed by plaster latticework. There is

no door in the imposing sculpted porchway. Anyone can enter at any time. A wooden board announces in English and Bengali: "Municipality of Calcutta, Nirmal Hriday—The Place of the Pure Heart—Home for Dying Destitutes."

Stephan Kovalski had reached his destination. He mounted the few steps and went into the building. An indefinable smell which even disinfectants could not obscure floated around. Once his eyes had grown accustomed to the dimness, he made out three rows of litters with thin green mattresses, squeezed in tightly side by side. Each one had a number painted in front of it. Shadowy shapes moved silently between the rows. On the beds lay fleshless bodies stretched out in various postures of agony. In a second room, rows of similar beds were provided for women.

What struck Kovalski immediately was the serenity of the place. There was no horror here. No longer were the wretched people who had come together in this place tormented with anguish, solitude, destitution, or neglect. They had found love and peace.

The one hundred and ten occupants of the Place of the Pure Heart owed that peace to the staunch little woman in a white cotton sari with a blue border, whom Stephan Kovalski spotted leaning over a dying man at the far end of the room. India and the world were beginning to recognize the name of this saint who for some years now had been revolutionizing the practice of charity. Newspapers and magazines had popularized the nun who picked up abandoned children and dying destitutes from the streets of Calcutta. Her work had already spread beyond the frontiers of India, and nations had awarded her their highest distinctions. Her name was Mother Teresa and she had just turned fifty-four years of age when Stephan Kovalski walked in to meet her.

Despite her sturdiness, she looked older. Her face was already furrowed with deep wrinkles, her bent form bore witness to years of self-sacrifice and sleepless nights.

Agnes Bojaxhiu was born in Skopje, Yugoslavia, of Albanian parents. Her father was a prosperous merchant. She was attracted to the life of a missionary in India at a very early age. At eighteen, taking the name of Teresa in memory of the little Flower of Lisieux, she entered the Missionary Order of the Loreto Sisters and, on January 20, 1931, she stepped off a steamship onto the quay at Calcutta, then the largest city in the Empire after London. For sixteen years she taught geography to the daughters of well-to-do British and Bengali society in one of the most prestigious convents in Calcutta. One day in 1946, however, during a train journey to Darjeeling, a town on the slopes of the Himalayas, she heard a voice. God was asking her to leave the comfort of her convent, to go and live among the poorest of the poor in the vast city beyond. Having first obtained permission from the Pope, she changed into a plain white cotton sari and founded a new religious order whose vocation was to relieve the misery of the most neglected of men. In 1950, the order of the Missionaries of Charity was born, a congregation which thirty-five years later would have two hundred and eighty-five houses and several thousand charitable foundations throughout India and all the other continents, including countries behind the Iron Curtain. The home for the dying which Kovalski had just entered was born out of a particularly moving encounter experienced one evening by Mother Teresa.

It was in June 1952. The monsoon cataracts were beating down upon Calcutta with a noise that seemed to herald the destruction of the world. A white figure, stooping under the deluge, was skirting the walls of the Medical College Hospital. Suddenly she stumbled upon something stretched out on the ground. She stopped and discovered an old woman lying in the middle of a pool of water. The woman was hardly breathing. Her toes had been gnawed to the bone by rats. Mother Teresa scooped her into her arms and ran to the door of the hospital. She found the emergency entrance, went into a reception room, and deposited the dying woman on a stretcher. Instantly an attendant intervened.

"Take that woman away immediately!" he ordered. "There's nothing we can do for her."

Mother Teresa took the dying woman in her arms and set off again at a run. She knew another hospital, not far away. Suddenly, however, she heard a rattle. The body stiffened in her arms and she realized that it was too late.

Putting down her burden, she closed the poor creature's eyes and made the sign of the cross as she prayed beside her in the rain.

"In this city, even the dogs are treated better than human beings," she sighed as she turned away.

The next day, she rushed to the municipal building and besieged its offices. The persistence of this European nun in a white cotton sari was a source of considerable astonishment. One of the mayor's deputies finally received her. "It's a disgrace that people in this city are forced to die in the streets," she declared. "Give me a house where we can help the dying to appear before God in dignity and love."

One week later the municipality placed at her disposal a former rest house for Hindu pilgrims, next to the great Kali temple. Mother Teresa was overjoyed. "This is God's doing. The place is ideally situated. It is to the precincts of this sacred spot that the destitute come to die, in the hope of being cremated on the temple pyres." At first the intrusion of a nun dressed in a white sari and adorned with a crucifix, in a neighborhood wholly consecrated to the worship of Kali, provoked curiosity. Gradually, however, orthodox Hindus became indignant. The word spread that Mother Teresa and her Sisters were there to convert the dying to Christianity. Incidents broke out. One day a shower of stones and bricks rained down upon an ambulance bringing the dying to the home. The Sisters were insulted and threatened. Eventually Mother Teresa dropped to her knees before the demonstrators.

"Kill me!" she cried in Bengali, her arms outstretched in a gesture of crucifixion. "And I'll be in heaven all the sooner!"

Impressed, the rabble withdrew, but the harassment continued. Neighborhood delegations presented themselves at the town hall and the general police headquarters to demand that the "foreign nun" be expelled. The chief of police promised to satisfy their demands but insisted upon first making his own inquiries. He made his way to the home for the dying and there found Mother Teresa kneeling at the bedside of a man who had just been picked up off the street, a skeleton figure lying there in a state of indescribable filth, with his legs swollen with purulent sores. "Dear God," he wondered, "how ever can she put up with that?" Mother Teresa cleansed the horrible wound, applied antibiotic dressings, and promised the unfortunate man that he would get better. Her face was bathed in an extraordinary serenity and the chief of police found himself strangely moved.

"Would you like me to show you around?" she asked him. "No, Mother," he excused himself. "That won't be necessary."

As he emerged from the building, the neighborhood's young fanatics were waiting for him on the steps.

"I promised you that I would expel this foreign woman," he told them. "And I will do so on the day that you persuade your mothers and sisters to come here and do what she is doing."

The battle was not won yet. During the days that followed, troublemakers continued to throw stones. One morning Mother Teresa noticed a gathering of people outside the Kali temple. As she drew near to them she saw a man stretched out on the ground with turned-up eyes and a face apparently drained of blood. A triple braid denoted that he was a Brahmin, one of the priests from the temple. No one dared to touch him. They knew he was suffering from cholera.

She bent over, took the body of the Brahmin in her arms, and carried him to the home for the dying. Day and night she nursed him, and eventually he recovered. One day he was to exclaim, "For thirty years I have worshipped a Kali of stone. But here is the real Kali, a Kali of flesh and blood." Never again were stones thrown at the little Sisters in the white saris.

News of this incident spread throughout the whole city. Every day, ambulances and police vans brought the suffering to Mother Teresa. "Nirmal Hriday is the jewel of Calcutta," the nun was to remark one day. The jewel was granted the protection of the city itself. The mayor, journalists, and many eminent people rushed to visit it. High-caste ladies came to offer their services and tend the dying with the Sisters. One of these was to become a great friend of Mother Teresa.

Amrita Roy, at thirty-five, was rich, beautiful, and powerful. Her uncle, Dr. B. C. Roy, a man of the heart, was none other than the chief minister of Bengal, an associate who would smooth out many an obstacle in a city where every aspect of life was an ordeal: the climate, pollution, overpopulation and, above all, bureaucracy. Like Stephan Kovalski, Mother Teresa sometimes had to spend days in customs warehouses retrieving from petty officials crates of medicines and boxes of powered milk sent by friends around the world.

Taking in dying destitutes, however, was only a first step for

Mother Teresa. The living too needed care, and among the most neglected of the living were the newborn babies that might be found one morning on a rubbish heap, in a gutter, or in the doorway of a church.

One day "the hand of God" directed Mother Teresa to the portal of a large unoccupied house on a road very near the place where her congregation had made its home. On February 15, 1953, "Shishu Bhavan," the Children's Home, welcomed its first guest, a premature baby wrapped in a piece of newspaper, picked up from the pavement. He weighed less than three pounds and had not even the strength to suck at the bottle Mother Teresa gave him. He had to be fed with a nasal tube. The nun persisted and won her first victory in this new haven of love and compassion. Soon several dozen babies were bundled together in cots and playpens. Five or six more arrived every day. Her Sisters and good Father Van Exem, her confessor, were worried. How was she going to provide for so many people? Together with the occupants of the home for the dying, there were now several hundred mouths to feed.

Her response to this question was an all-illuminating smile. "The Lord will provide!"

Sure enough, the Lord did provide. Gifts poured in. Rich families sent their chauffeurs with cars full of rice, vegetables, fish. One evening Mother Teresa encountered the man who had given her a room in his house in the very earliest days.

"It's wonderful," she announced to him jubilantly, "I've just obtained from the government a monthly grant of thirty-three rupees for a hundred of our children."

"From the government!" repeated the man with compassion. "I really feel sorry for you. Because you've no idea what bureaucratic mess you'll be forced into."

True to this prediction, six months had not gone by before a meeting was held in the government building. A dozen bureaucrats in *dhotis* examined the nun's account books. They asked questions, quibbled over details, and criticized. Exasperated, Mother Teresa stood up. "You think you can demand that I spend thirty-three rupees on the children you sponsor," she exclaimed indignantly, "when I can spend only seventeen on our other children who are by far the more numerous. How can I spend thirty-three rupees on some and seventeen on others? Who could do a thing like that? Thank you, gentlemen, but I will do without your money." And she left the room.

In a city already overwhelmed by too high a birthrate, she declared war on abortion. She had her Sisters draw and put up posters announcing that she would take in every child that was sent to her. Under the cover of night, pregnant girls came to ask her for a place for their prospective babies.

The angel of mercy was constantly flying to the rescue of some new group of needy people. After the dying and the abandoned children, it was the turn of those most wretched of all creatures, the lepers. At Titagarh, a shantytown in an industrial suburb of Calcutta, she constructed, on land lent by the railway company, a building of rough bricks and corrugated iron, in which she harbored the worst cases, bringing them dressings each day, medicines, and words of comfort. Soon hundreds of patients stormed the gate to this oasis of love.

Titagarh was only a beginning. Next she dispatched commandos of Indian Sisters out into the city, their mission being to open seven more dispensaries. One of them set herself up in the slum where Mother Teresa had first tended the poor. Lepers flocked there in hordes. An employee at the town hall who lived in the vicinity protested against such unpleasant neighbors and threatened to alert the authorities. Eventually Mother Teresa was compelled to give in. But as always, she knew how to make the best of her defeats.

"What we need," she announced to her Sisters, "are mobile clinics."

Several small white vans bearing the emblem of the Missionaries of Charity would one day patrol the enormous city to bring treatment into the most neglected areas.

It was one of these vehicles that Stephan Kovalski wanted to bring into Anand Nagar. Even better, he hoped two or three of Mother Teresa's Sisters would come to assist him in the running of the little leper clinic he planned to set up in the former Muslim school next to the buffalo sheds in the City of Joy. That was why he had come to see Mother Teresa.

He made his way between the rows of bodies and approached

the kneeling figure. The nun was bathing the wounds of a man who was still young but who was so thin that he looked like one of the living dead discovered by the Allies in the Nazi concentration camps. All his flesh had melted away. Only his skin remained, stretched taut over his bones. The woman was speaking softly to him in Bengali.

"I shall never forget that man's expression," Kovalski was to say. "His suffering was transformed into surprise, then peace, the peace that comes from being loved." Sensing a presence behind her, Mother Teresa stood up. She did not fail to notice the metal cross the visitor was wearing on his chest.

"Oh Father," she excused herself humbly, "what can I do for you?"

Stephan Kovalski felt awkward. He had just interrupted a conversation in which he identified something unique. The eyes of the dying man seemed to be imploring Mother Teresa to bend over him once more. It was deeply touching. The priest introduced himself.

"I think I've heard people talk about you!" she said warmly.

"Mother, I've come to ask for your help."

"My help?" She pointed a large hand toward the ceiling. "It's God's help you want to ask for, Father. I am nothing at all."

At that point a young American in jeans came along carrying a bowl. Mother Teresa called him over and drew his attention to the dying man.

"Love him," she ordered. "Love him with all your might." She handed the young man her tweezers and cloth and left him, steering Stephan Kovalski toward an empty area with a table and bench between the room for men and the one for women. On the wall was a board bearing a framed text of a Hindu poem which the priest read aloud.

> If you have two pieces of bread,
> Give one to the poor,
> Sell the other,
> And buy hyacinths
> To feed your soul.

The Pole outlined his plan for a leper clinic in the City of Joy. "Very good, Father, very good," commented Mother Teresa in her picturesque accent, a mixture of Slavonic and Bengali. "You are doing God's work. All right, Father, I'll send you three Sisters who are used to caring for lepers."

Her gaze strayed over the room full of prostrate bodies and she added, "They give us so much more than we give them."

A young Sister came over and spoke to her in a low voice. Her presence was needed elsewhere.

"Goodbye, Father," she said. "Come and say Mass for us one of these mornings."

Stephan Kovalski was overwhelmed. "Bless you, Calcutta, for in your wretchedness you have given birth to saints."

39

THE SITUATION WAS growing steadily worse. Terrifying bottlenecks immobilized the flow of traffic more and more frequently. At certain times, advancing just one step was quite a feat. The roads in the city center were frequently jammed with streetcars deprived of electricity, broken-down trucks with radiators steaming, double-decker buses with broken axles or even turned over on their sides. Hordes of yellow taxis with their paintwork in shreds forced their way to the clamor of horns. Buffalo carts and hand-pulled carriages creaking beneath enormous loads, and hosts of coolies carrying mountains of merchandise on their heads tried to move across the engulfing tide. Everywhere swarms of pedestrians competed with rickshaws for a share of asphalt in streets disrupted by frequent water pipe or drain bursts. Everything seemed to crack and crumble a little more with each passing day.

"There were clients too, who pricked you in the stomach with the point of a knife and demanded the day's takings," Hasari Pal was to recount. "Drunkards who paid you with their fists, *goondas* and prostitutes who vanished without settling up for the ride, elegant *memsahibs* who cheated you out of a few *paisas*."

One day Hasari asked the *munshi* to add to his money invoice a short message for his father in the space reserved for correspondence: "We are well. I am earning my living as a rickshaw puller." His chest swollen with pride at having been able to make this gesture for those who expected everything of him, he hurried back to the pavement where he was camping with his wife and three children. He had an important piece of news to announce to them.

"Wife!" he called out as soon as he saw Aloka, crouched

down, cleaning out the neighboring woman's tin can. "I've found us a place in a slum!"

A slum! For peasants used to a daily bath in a pool, the cleanliness of a hut and the healthy food of the countryside, the prospect of living in a slum, with no water, no drains, and sometimes no latrines, offered little to be joyful about. Still, anything was better than the pavement. There at least, a few bits of cloth and sheet iron placed on four crates would furnish them with something resembling a lodging place, a precarious shelter to ward off the next winter and, a few months later, the excesses of the monsoon.

The shantytown, where Hasari had foraged out their thirty square feet of space, was situated right in the middle of the city on an extension of the great Chowringhee Road which skirted the Maidan park. Its foundation dated back to the time of the war with China, when thousands of refugees from the North descended upon Calcutta. One day a few families had stopped on the ground between two roads, put down their miserable bundles, set up a few stakes, and stretched out some bits of cloth between them as a shield against the sun. Other families had joined this initial nucleus, and so the small encampment had become a shantytown, right in the heart of a residential area. No one raised any objections to it—neither the municipal authorities, nor the police, nor the owners of the land. The city was already pockmarked throughout with similar patches of misery, places where several hundred uprooted people lived, sometimes without so much as a drinking water point. Some of these little islands had existed for a whole generation. Not everyone, however, was quite so disinterested in the squatters. No sooner had a newcomer installed himself on his square of mud or concrete than someone set about fleecing him. That was one of the stupefying things about the extortion business conducted by the Mafia, with the cooperation of certain authorities. It was a strictly indigenous "Mafia" which had no reason to envy its famous Italo-American model.

Even before he had moved in, Hasari received a visit from a small, shady-looking man who claimed to represent the "owner" of the colony—in other words, the local godfather. Every time a handful of refugees stopped somewhere to set up some kind of shanty, the Mafia representative would turn up armed with a *bona fide* demolition order issued by the city's authorities. The squatters then found themselves confronted with a choice between paying regular rent or purchasing the plot. For his thirty square feet Hasari Pal was forced to pay out fifty rupees in "key money" and a monthly rent of twenty rupees payable in advance. The bloodsuckers did not, however, confine their racket merely to collecting rents and other "residential taxes." Their control extended, in fact, to all aspects of life in the slum. Being the only local authority, the Mafia set itself up as the "protector" of the population. In a way its claim was true. The Mafia intervened whenever a conflict required arbitration, or at election times by distributing a host of favors in exchange for votes: ration cards, a lead off the water pipes, the building of a temple, the admission of a child into a government-run school.

Anyone who dared to question the legitimacy of this underground power was punished without mercy. Every now and then shanties caught fire. Sometimes a whole neighborhood went up in flames. At other times a body was recovered, riddled with stab wounds. This omnipresent dictatorship manifested itself in many and various ways. Sometimes directly, as was the case in Hasari's slum, where several Mafia representatives lived right there. In other tenements planted in the vicinity of a construction site, a distillery, a garbage dump, or a quarry, the Mafia ruled via the manager or the owner of the enterprise. These intermediaries exercised absolute power over the inhabitants because the latter depended on them for their daily bowl of rice. Elsewhere, it was through committees and associations that it imposed its law. These organizations were little more than cover-ups. Whether they were religious in nature or represented a caste or a place of origin, they all provided the Mafia and its political connections with the ideal means by which to infiltrate the very depths of the slum population. Thus it was no longer a simple matter of rent and taxes. The Mafia meted out justice even within the family unit. It fixed the level of fines, collected donations for religious festivals, negotiated marriages, divorces, adoptions, inheritances, levied out excommunications—in short it managed everyone's rites and practices from birth to death inclusively: no Muslim would ever find a place in a cemetery, no Hindu have himself cremated, without paying a cut to the Mafia.

The Pals's departure from their pavement occurred discreetly under the cover of night. No sooner had they piled their meager possessions into the rickshaw and turned the corner of the avenue, than a new refugee family moved in to take their place.

40

THE DRAMA ERUPTED just as Stephan Kovalski was coming out of the latrines. He heard shouts and saw a mob of children and adults charging toward him. At once a deluge of stones and missiles rained down all around the little public convenience, only narrowly missing the priest. He leaped backward only to discover the target of all the fury: a wretched woman in rags, with disheveled hair and a face stained with blood and grime. Her eyes were full of hatred, her mouth was foaming, and she was emitting animal sounds as she flailed her fleshless hands and arms about her. The more insults she uttered, the more the mob set upon her. It was as if all the latent violence in the slum was exploding at once: the City of Joy wanted to claim a lynching! The Pole tried to rush to the rescue of the unfortunate woman but someone grabbed him by the shoulders and pushed him backward. They were about to close in for the kill. Men were getting their knives out. Women urged them on with their clamoring. It was dreadful to see.

Suddenly, however, the priest saw a little gray-haired man brandishing a stick surface from the crowd. He recognized the old Hindu who kept the tea shop opposite him. Swinging his stick about, he rushed to the woman's side and, shielding her with his frail figure, turned on her aggressors.

"Leave this woman alone!" he shouted to them. "God is visiting us."

The rabble came to a halt, transfixed. The yelling stopped abruptly. All eyes were turned upon the frail figure of the elderly Hindu.

After a few seconds that seemed more like an eternity to

Kovalski, he saw one of the assailants, armed with a knife, approach the old man. Having reached him, he prostrated himself, placed the weapon at his feet, and went through the motions of wiping the dust from his sandals and touching his forehead with it as a mark of respect. Then he stood up, turned on his heels, and walked away. Others followed his example. In a few minutes the mob had disappeared.

The old Hindu went over to the mad woman who was looking at him like an animal run to earth. Slowly, delicately, with the tail of his shirt, he wiped the excreta and blood from her face. Then he helped her up and, supporting her around the waist, led her away down the alleyway toward his tea shop.

It was quite some time before Kovalski came to know the history of that lover of justice and bearer of the luminous name of Surya, or Sun. Three years previously the hands that now handled bowls of tea and kettles had fashioned balls of clay thrown on a stone wheel. In the course of their circuits those balls would be transformed, between the fingers of the old Hindu, into goblets, pots, cups, dishes, religious lamps, vases, and even the gigantic six-foot-high vases used at weddings. Surya had been the potter for Biliguri, a large borough with about a thousand inhabitants, one hundred and twenty miles north of Calcutta. His ancestors had been village potters since time immemorial. The role of the potter formed as intimate a part of community life as that of the Brahmin priest or the moneylender. Every year, in every Hindu family, the pots were ceremonially broken; also they were broken every time there was a birth, as a mark of welcome to the new life, and every time there was a death, to allow the deceased to leave for the afterlife complete with his plates and dishes. They were also broken on the occasion of a marriage; in the bride's family because by leaving, the young woman died to the eyes of her family, and in the groom's family because the arrival of the young wife meant the birth of a new household. Again, they were broken to mark numerous festivals because the gods wanted everything on earth to be new. In short, a potter was never in danger of being out of work.

Apart from Surya and his two sons who worked with him, there were only seven other artisans in the village. Their workshops all opened out on to the main square. There was a blacksmith, a carpenter, a basket maker who also made traps and snares, and a jeweler who had his own design for what were called "savings necklaces." Whenever a family had saved up a little money, the women would rush to have one or two silver links added to their necklaces. There was also a weaver, a cobbler, and a barber whose particular talents lay less in his skill in looking after his fellow villagers' hair than in ensuring the happiness of their offspring, for it was he who was the official matchmaker. Finally, on either side of Surya's workshop were two stores: that of the grocer and that of the confectioner. Without the latter's *mishtis*, sweetmeats that were sweeter than sugar, no religious or social ceremony could ever be properly observed.

Toward the end of the monsoon that year, there occurred in Biliguri one of those incidents that appear quite insignificant. Nobody, therefore, took much notice of it at the time. Ashok, the weaver's eldest son who worked in Calcutta, came back to the village with a present for his wife—a pail made out of plastic as red as hibiscus. Cut off as they were in the countryside, people had never seen a utensil like that before. The light supple material out of which it was made provoked general admiration. It was passed from hand to hand with wonder and envy. The first person to really understand the usefulness of this new object was the grocer. Less than three months later, his store was decorated with similar buckets in several different colors. Goblets, dishes, and gourds subsequently arrived to further enrich his collection. Plastic had conquered a new market. At the same time it had mortally afflicted another craftsman in the village.

Surya watched his clientele rapidly diminish, and in less than a year he and his sons had foundered into destitution. The two boys and their families set out on the path to exile and the city. Surya, himself, tried to resist. Thanks to the solidarity of his caste, he found work about thirty miles away in a village not yet caught up in the plastic fever. The virus was on the rampage, however, and soon all the villages in the area were contaminated.

Then the provincial government gave a manufacturer from Calcutta a grant so that he could construct a factory. One year later every potter in the region was ruined.

Surya had no recourse but to embark also upon the road to

Calcutta. With him he took his wife, but the poor woman suffered from asthma and could not cope with the shock of urban pollution. She died after only a few months, on the corner of pavement where they had made their home.

After his wife's cremation on one of the pyres on the banks of the Hooghly, the potter wandered for some time beside the river, completely at a loss. About one mile from Howrah Bridge he noticed a man on the riverbank, filling a basket with clay. Surya started up a conversation with him. The man worked in a potters' workship on the edge of the City of Joy, where they made the handleless cups used as teacups that were broken after use. Thanks to this miraculous encounter, the very next day Surya found himself squatting behind a wheel making hundreds of the small receptacles. The workshop supplied numerous tea shops scattered throughout the alleyways of the City of Joy.

One day the old Muslim who kept the tea shop in Nizamudhin Lane was found hanging from a piece of bamboo in the framework. He had committed suicide. Surya, who no longer felt physically able to do prolonged manual work, went to see the proprietor of the shop and obtained the concession for it. Ever since then he had been intoning his "Oms" and heating his kettles of milky tea on a *chula* that filled the alleyway with smoke from one end of the day to the other. The old Hindu was such a good and holy man, however, that the residents of Nizamudhin Lane forgave him for the smoke.

Shortly after his arrival, Stephan Kovalski had received a visit from his neighbor. The old man had entered the priest's room with his hands pressed together at the level of his heart. Despite the fact that the Hindu's mouth was almost devoid of teeth, his smile warmed the Pole's heart and he invited him to sit down. For a while they remained there, surveying each other in silence. "In the West," Kovalski was to note, "people's gazes barely brush over you. That man's eyes revealed his entire soul." After about ten minutes, the Hindu stood up, joined his hands together, bowed his head, and left. He came back the next day and observed the same respectful silence. On the third day, at the risk of shattering a delicate mystery, the priest inquired as to the motive for his silence.

"Stephan *Daddah,*" he replied, "you are a Great Soul and in the presence of a Great Soul, words are not necessary."

Thus it was that they became friends. In the midst of the Muslim families that surrounded the Pole, the Hindu became a kind of life raft to which Stephan could cling whenever he lost his footing. Establishing a bond with Hindus was indeed easier. For them God was everywhere: in a door, a fly, a piece of bamboo, and in the millions of incarnations of a pantheon of deities, in which Surya considered Jesus Christ naturally had his place in the same way that Buddha, Mahavira, and even Muhammad. For them, these prophets were all avatars of the Great God who transcended everything.

41

THE CITY OF Miami, Florida, lies approximately eight thousand miles west of Calcutta. In reality, however, the immensity of the gulf separating these two cities would be better measured in light-years. Certainly, Miami possesses slums almost as poverty-stricken as those of Calcutta: its black ghetto and its miserable shantytowns built by refugees from Cuba and Haiti on its southwestern fringes. During the 1970s, burglaries, armed robberies, muggings, rapes, a whole array of violent crimes engendered by drug addiction, a dismal poverty and a bleakness born of despair became such commonplace events in Miami that only the most outrageous among them inspired the city's headlines writers. So great was the psychosis of fear gripping parts of the city that many residents preferred to move to safer suburbs or even immigrate to less troubled parts of the United States.

For all the poverty of its slums, no such psychosis of physical insecurity has ever overwhelmed the citizens of Calcutta. With the exception of the brief period of Naxalite terrorism, the people of Calcutta have never had to go out in fear for their physical safety or their property. Fewer violent crimes are committed each year in the vastly overpopulated capital of Bengal than are committed in downtown Miami alone. Fear is by and large a stranger to Calcutta's streets. A young girl can walk along Chowringhee Road or any of the city's other main thoroughfares in the middle of the night without the slightest fear of being attacked. An elderly woman can carry home a day's shopping down any of the main Calcutta streets without listening in fear for a mugger's thread.

Side by side with its slums and its shantytowns, Miami the city that proudly describes itself as the gateway to the American South, also harbors islands of wealth and luxury far beyond the wildest imagining of any inhabitants of Calcutta, even its most privileged residents whose feet have never ventured inside a slum. One of them was called King Estates. It was a vast marina nestling among elegant palm trees and clusters of jacaranda, a heaven for multimillionaires and their sumptuous villas. Most houses had swimming pools, tennis courts, and private docks from which cabin cruisers and yachts, some almost the size of ocean liners, rode the bright blue sea. Several properties had heliports, others a polo field with stables to accommodate several dozen horses. A high iron grille sealed off this little island of privilege. Armed private guards, their patrol car equipped with searchlights and sirens, prowled the enclave night and day. No one entered King Estates, even on foot, unless he or she possessed a magnetic pass whose code was changed weekly, or was personally inspected and cleared by one of the estate's guards.

It was a prison for the wealthy and one of its most distinguished inmates was a highly reputable Jewish surgeon called Arthur Loeb. His Mexican hacienda with its luminescent white walls, its patios, its fountains, and its colonnade cloisters, was among the estate's showpieces. Loeb was a giant of a man, his red hair barely flecked by gray, who was given over to four passions: police novels, deep-sea fishing, ornithology, and his luxurious one-hundred-and-forty-bed Bel Air Clinic where he treated diseases of the respiratory system with techniques that were at the cutting edge of medical science.

Married for twenty-nine years to Gloria Lazar, the blond and gentle daughter of one of the pioneers of talking movies, Loeb had two children: Gaby, twenty, a sparkling brunette studying architecture at the Miami College of Fine Arts, and Max, twenty-five, like his father a red-headed giant wrapped in freckles. Max was about to receive his diploma from the Tulane University Medical School in New Orleans. In two years, after he had completed his internship, he intended to specialize in thoracic surgery. He was a source of enormous pride and happiness to his father. Not only was he following in the elder Loeb's professional footsteps, his decision to specialize in chest surgery seemed to promise that the direction of Loeb's Bel Air Clinic would one day pass into his hands.

"Professor, I'm leaving the country."

There was no mockery in the title "professor." His children had given Arthur Loeb that affectionate nickname the day he had stepped onto the podium at Columbia University to receive an honorary degree of Professor of Medicine.

Arthur Loeb reined in his horse and turned to face his son.

"What do you mean, you're leaving the country?"

"I'm going to India for a year."

"To India? And what about your internship?"

"I've asked for a deferment."

"A deferment?"

"Yes, Professor, a deferment," repeated Max, trying with difficulty to remain calm.

His father freed off the reins. The horses set off at a slow trot.

"And to what do we owe this surprise?" his father asked after their horses had advanced several paces.

Max pretended not to notice the irritation lurking behind the question.

"I need a change of air . . . and I want to be of service to someone."

"What do you mean 'you want to be of service'?"

"Just that. To help people who need help." Max knew he couldn't go on beating around the bush much longer. "I've been invited to fill in for someone in a dispensary," he said.

"Where in India? After all, India is a large place!"

"Calcutta, Professor."

The word stunned Arthur Loeb so much that he lost his stirrups. "Calcutta! Of all places, Calcutta!" he repeated, shaking his head.

Like many other Americans, Loeb felt very little sympathy for India. His dislike turned into downright revulsion when it came to Calcutta, a city synonymous for him with misery, beggars, and people dying on the city's pavements. How many television programs had he seen, how many magazine articles had he read, in which all the tragedies of Calcutta had been set before him in lurid details! Even more, however, than the specter of famine, overpopulation, and poverty, it was the image of a man in particular that provoked the surgeon's special aversion to the world's largest democracy. It was the face of a man with arrogance and hatred giving the world lessons in morality from the rostrum of the United Nations. Like so many Americans, Loeb recalled the diatribes of Krishna Menon, India's envoy to the United Nations in the 1950s, with an uncontrolled rage. A dangerous visionary he had seemed, a kind of high priest spitting out his venom all over the West in the name of the values of the third world, values which he claimed were being strangled by the white man.

"Is that the best place you can find to exercise your talents?" asked a bewildered Arthur Loeb. "And do you really think, you poor naïve creature, that your friends are going to keep a place warm for you? By the time you get back, they'll all have their diplomas and you'll find yourself in with a new group who won't do you any favors, believe me."

Max made no reply.

"Does your mother know?"

"Yes."

"And she approves?"

"Not exactly . . . but in the end, she seemed to understand."

"And Sylvia?"

Sylvia Paine was Max's fiancée, a beautiful, tall blond girl of twenty-three, a healthy, athletic American girl. Her parents owned the property next to the Loebs in King Estates. Her father was the owner of the *Tribune,* one of Miami's daily newspapers. She and Max had known each other since they were children. They were due to marry in June after his exams.

"Yes, Professor. She knows," replied Max.

"And what does she think of the idea?"

"She suggested she come with me!"

Six weeks after their conversation, Max Loeb flew off to Calcutta. Like the good sports they were, his parents had given a farewell party in his honor. The invitation cards stipulated that Max Loeb was going to spend a sabbatical year of study and reflection in Asia. Asia was a vast place and Max had agreed not to reveal his exact destination to anyone, so as not to invite any disagreeable comments from the small colony of multimillionaires of King Estates. Naturally he spent his last evening in America with his fiancée. He took her to dinner at The Versailles, a fashionable French restaurant in Boca Raton. There, he ordered a bottle of Bollinger, his favorite champagne, and she proposed a toast to the success of his mission and his earliest possible return. Sylvia was wearing a very low-cut pink linen dress with a simple string of pearls around her neck. Her hair, caught up in a chignon and pinned with a shell comb, revealed the nape of her neck and the superb bearing of her head. Max could not take his eyes off her.

"You're so beautiful," he said, "how am I going to manage without you?"

"Oh, you'll find plenty of beautiful Indian girls. People say they are the best lovers in the world. They say they even know how to prepare special drinks that make you fall madly in love with them."

Max thought of the slum Stephan Kovalski had described in his letter, but the idea of arousing Sylvia's jealousy was not altogether unpleasant.

"I'll do my best to master their techniques so that I can make you even happier," he said with a wink.

He was joking. Max knew too well that beneath Sylvia's beautiful exterior there lay a private and modest nature. Poetry was her great passion. She knew thousands of verses by heart and could recite works of Longfellow, long extracts from Shelley, Keats, Byron, and even Baudelaire and Goethe. Although they had been lovers ever since their high school days (it had first happened on Max's father's cabin cruiser during an expedition to catch swordfish between Cuba and Key Largo), the course of their love had been more intellectual than physical. Apart from horseback riding and tennis, they had not really taken part in the usual pursuits of young people their age. "We hardly ever went to parties," Max would recount, "and we detested dancing. Instead we preferred to spend hours lying on the sand beside the sea, discussing life, love, and death. And Sylvia would recite to me the latest poems she had memorized since our last meeting."

Sylvia had come to visit him in New Orleans on several occasions. Together they had explored the historical treasures of Louisiana. One night when a tropical storm confined them to a plantation on the banks of the Mississippi, they had made love in a bed in which Mademoiselle de Granville and the Marquis de Lafayette had slept. "There was no doubting the fact that our marriage was written in the stars," Max was to say. "Despite the fact that Sylvia's family were Presbyterians and mine were practicing Jews, we knew that no event could please our parents more."

Then, suddenly, exactly seven months before the date fixed for the wedding, Max had decided to go off for a year. He had said nothing to his fiancée of the deeper reasons for his decisions. There were some actions in a man's life, he thought, that did not call for explanation. Yet on that last evening, carried away by the euphoria of the champagne and the mild smell of a contraband Havana Montecristo cigar, he decided to admit the truth. "Just in case anything should happen to me, I wanted everyone to know that I hadn't just gone off on a whim." He told the story of how one day, in the university library, his gaze had fallen on the photograph of a child on the illustrated cover of a magazine published in Canada by a humanitarian organization. The child was a little Indian boy of five or six sitting in front of the crumbling wall of a house in Calcutta. A black shock of hair concealed his forehead and part of his eyes, but in between the locks of hair there shone two little flames—his eyes. What struck Max most of all was the boy's smile, a tranquil, luminous smile which dug two deep ditches around his mouth and revealed four shining teeth. He didn't appear to be starving but he was surely very poor because he was completely naked. In his arms he was clutching a baby, only a few days old and wrapped in pieces of rag.

"He was holding it with so much pride," Max recalled for his fiancée, "with so much gravity behind his smile and with such an obvious sense of his responsibilities, that for several minutes I was unable to take my eyes off him.

"The child was an inhabitant of the City of Joy and the baby in his arms was his little brother. The journalist who took the photograph wrote in his article about his visit to the slum and his encounter with a 'white apostle who had come from the West to live among the world's most disinherited people.' The white apostle in question was Stephan Kovalski. In answer to one of the journalist's questions, Stephan had expressed the wish that someone with advanced medical training, preferably a young doctor, should come to Anand Nagar for a year to work with him and help him to organize proper medical help in a place deprived of aid.

"I wrote to him," concluded Max. "And he replied that he

would expect me as soon as possible. Apparently the winter is coming to an end there and soon it'll be the scorching heat of the summer and the monsoon."

Mention of the monsoon brought a quickening to the blue eyes of the American girl.

"The monsoon!" she echoed pensively. She was thinking of a poem by Paul Verlaine for which she had a special affection. *"Il pleut dans mon coeur,"* she recited in French tenderly caressing Max's hand, *"comme il pleut sur la ville. Quelle est cette langueur qui pénètre mon coeur?"**

---

* "There is weeping in my heart, like the rain falling on the city. What is this languor that pierces my heart?"

42

THE PICTURE IN its gold frame decorated with a garland of flowers was an expression of strength and beauty. On his elephant, caparisoned with carpets and encrusted with precious stones, the figure portrayed looked like a conquering maharajah. He was wearing a tunic embroidered with gold thread and studded with jewels. The only features that distinguished him from a man were his wings and his four arms brandishing an ax, a hammer, a bow, and the arm of a set of scales.

His name was Viswakarma and he was not a man, nor indeed was he a prince, but rather a god belonging to the Hindu pantheon. One of the mightiest gods in Indian mythology, Viswakarma was the personification of creative power. The hymns of the Vedas, the sacred books of Hinduism, glorified him as "the architect of the universe, the all-seeing god who fashioned the heavens and the earth, the creator, father, distributor of all the worlds, the one who gives the deities their names and who resides outside the realms of mortal comprehension." According to the Mahabharata, the epic legend of Hinduism, Viswakarma was not only the supreme architect. He was also the artificer of the gods and the maker of their tools, lord of the arts and carpenter of the cosmos, constructor of the celestial chariots and creator of all adornments. It followed, therefore, that he was the protector of all the manual trades that enabled man to subsist, a fact that gave him a particular following among the laborers and artisans of India.

In the same way that Christians glorify "the god of the universe, who gives bread, the fruit of man's labor," during the Offertory of the Mass, the Indians venerated Viswakarma, the source of labor and life. Each year after the September moon, in all the myriad workshops of the Calcutta slums, as in all the large modern factories of the suburbs, his triumphant effigy presided over man's places of work, richly decorated for a fervent two-day *puja*. It was a marvelous moment of communion between owners and workers, a wild rejoicing of rich and poor, united in the same adoration and the same prayer.

Like all the other slums, the City of Joy celebrated the festival of Viswakarma with special fervor for the god who provided their rice. After all, was it not true that the entanglement of huts that made up the slum harbored the most amazing ants' nest of workmen imaginable? Every day a hovel sighted behind an open door, the grinding of a machine, a pile of new objects outside a hut, would reveal to Stephan Kovalski the presence of some tiny new workshop or small factory. Here, he might discover half a dozen half-naked children engaged in cutting off sheets of tin to make pannikins; there, other urchins like Nasir, Mehboub's son, would be dipping objects into tanks exuding noxious vapors. Elsewhere, children made matches and Bengal firecrackers, gradually poisoning themselves as they handled phosphorus, zinc oxide, asbestos powder, and gum arabic.

Almost opposite the Pole's hut, in the darkness of a workshop, blackened figures laminated, soldered, and adjusted pieces of scrap iron, amid the smell of burning oil and hot metal. Next door, in a kind of windowless shed, a dozen shadows made up *bidis*. They were nearly all victims of tuberculosis who no longer had the strength to maneuver a press or pull a rickshaw. Provided they didn't stop for a single minute, they could roll up to thirteen hundred cigarettes a day. For a thousand *bidis*, they received eleven rupees, a little more than one dollar. A little farther on, in a tiny room, Stephan Kovalski noticed one day an enormous ship's propeller next to a forge. The door was so narrow that the entrance of beaten earth had to be enlarged with a pickax to get the mastodon out. Eventually five men succeeded in shifting the propeller and levering it on to a *telagarhi*. The owner then harnessed three coolies to the cart and ordered them to proceed. Backs and hamstrings braced themselves in a desperate effort. The wheels turned, and the employer sighed with satisfaction. He would not need to take on a fourth coolie. But what would happen, Kovalski wondered,

when the three unfortunates reached the bottom of the slope leading up to the Howrah Bridge?

How many years would it take him to discover all the places
where men and children spent their lives making springs, truck
parts, spindles for weaving looms, bolts, aircraft tanks, and even
turbine meshing to a sixth of a micromillimeter. With surprising
dexterity, inventiveness, and resourcefulness a whole work force
was to copy, repair, renovate any part and any machine. Here the
slightest scrap of metal, the tiniest piece of debris was used again,
transformed, adapted. "Nothing was ever destroyed," Kovalski
was to say, "because by some miracle everything was always born
again."

Amid the shadows, the dust, and the clutter of their sweatshops, the workmen of Anand Nagar were the pride of the God
who gives rice to man. Alas, they often gave him cause for remorse
too.

Article 24 of the Indian constitution stipulated that "no child
must work in a factory or mine, nor be employed in any other
dangerous place." For reasons of profit and docility, however, a
large proportion of the work force was extremely young. In fact, a
child was almost always hired in preference to an adult. His little
fingers were more adept and he was content with a pittance as a
salary. Yet these pittances earned by children with so much pride
meant so often the difference between their family's starvation and
survival!

The workers in the slum were among the worst protected in
the world. They were not eligible for any social security; they were
often shamelessly exploited, working up to twelve or fourteen
hours at a stretch in premises in which no zoo in the world would
dare to keep its animals. Many of them ate and slept on the spot,
without light or ventilation. For them there were no weekends or
vacations. One day's absence and they could find themselves laid
off. A misplaced remark, a claim, a dispute, being one hour late,
could mean instant dismissal and without compensation. Only
those who managed to acquire some form of qualification (as a
turner, a laminator, expert press operator) had any real hope of
keeping their jobs.

In the City of Joy alone there were thousands of them—perhaps fifteen or twenty thousand—and naturally several hundred

thousand in Calcutta and millions throughout India. "How was it that they had never used the weight of such numbers to change their lot?" Kovalski was one day to remark. "That was a question that had always intrigued me and one to which I had never really found a satisfactory answer. Certainly, their rural origins had not prepared them for making collective demands. Their poverty was such that any kind of work, even in a sweatshop, was a blessing of a kind. When so many were unemployed, how could they protest against work that at least enabled them to take home to their families the bowl of rice they needed each day? And when a family is reduced to the most extreme poverty because of a father's sickness or death, wasn't it understandable that one of the children should be prepared to work anywhere? No doubt morality would dictate otherwise, but who can talk about morality and what is right, when it all comes down to a question of survival?

"And what did the unions do to protect them? Along with three powerful central federations incorporating several million members, there are in India nearly sixteen thousand unions, of which seventy-four hundred and fifty belong exclusively to Bengal. And there is no lack of strikes on their list of achievements. In Bengal alone more than ten million working days are lost each year. But in a slum like the City of Joy who would dare to instigate a strike? There are too many people waiting to step into your shoes.

"With all due deference to Viswakarma, the giver of rice, these people were the real damned of the world, the slaves of hunger. And yet with what ardor and faith they fêted their god each year and called down his blessing upon the machines and tools to which they were chained."

Work had stopped in all the slum workshops since the previous evening. While all the workers hastened to clean, repaint, and decorate their machines and their tools with foliage and garlands of flowers, their employers had gone to Howrah to purchase the traditional icons of the god with four arms, perched on his elephant, and the statues of him in painted clay, sculpted by potters from the *kumar's* district.* The size and splendor of the images depended on the magnitude of the business concern. In large

* Potters.

factories, statues of Viswakarma were two or three times as large as life and were worth thousands of rupees.

In the space of one night all the dungeons of suffering had been transformed into places of worship, adorned with ornamented temporary altars bedecked with flowers. Next morning the entire slum resounded anew with the joyous din of the festival.

The slaves of the previous day now wore multicolored shirts and new *longhis;* their wives draped themselves in ceremonial saris, so carefully conserved throughout the year in the family coffers. Children were resplendent in the garb of little princes. The joyous saraband of the wind instruments and drums of a brass band replaced the thud of machines, around which the Brahmin priest now circled, ringing a bell with one hand and bearing the purificatory fire in the other, so that every instrument of labor might be blessed.

That day a number of workmen sought out Kovalski to ask him to bless also the means of their survival in the name of his god. "Praise be to you, O God of the universe who gives bread to man, for your children in Anand Nagar love and believe in you," the priest repeated in each workshop. "And rejoice with them for this day of light in their lives of sorrow."

After the blessings, the festivities began. The employers and foremen served the workmen and their families a banquet of curry, meat, vegetables, yoghurt, *puris,** and *laddous.†* The *bangla* and *todi‡* flowed freely. People drank, laughed, danced and, above all, they forgot. Viswakarma could smile from his thousand beds of flowers. He had united men through their labor.

The revelry went on into the middle of the night, in the beams of the floodlights. A populace deprived of television, movies, and virtually all other entertainments surrendered itself once more to the magic of festival. Workers and their families ran from workshop to workshop, pausing to marvel at the most beautiful statues and congratulate the creators, while loudspeakers poured popular tunes over the roofs, and fireworks illuminated the libations.

The next day, the workmen from each workshop loaded the

* Puffed corn griddle cake fried in *ghee.*
† Small ball of curdled milk, sweetened, condensed, and fried.
‡ Palm wine.

statues onto a *telagarhi* or a rickshaw and accompanied them, to the sound of drums and cymbals, as far as the Banda *ghat* on the banks of the Hooghly. There they hoisted them onto boats and rowed out to the middle of the river. Then they threw the images overboard so that their clay bodies could dissolve in the sacred water, mother of the world. *"Viswakarma-ki jai!* Long live Viswakarma!" cried millions of voices at that special moment. Then each one returned to his machine and the curtain fell for another year upon the slaves of the Lord, the giver of rice.

43

"WE CALLED THE festival of Viswakarma 'the rickshaw *puja*,'"
Hasari Pal was to explain. "Our factory, our workroom, our machines were all made up of two wheels, a chassis, and two shafts.
One wheel had only to break in a hole, or a truck tear off a shaft, or
a bus flatten the bodywork like a *chapati*, and it would be goodbye
to Hasari! There would be no use going crying in the owner's
gamsha. * All you could hope to get from him was a good beating.
More than anyone else, we had a great need for the god's protection, not only for our carriages but also for ourselves. A nail in your
foot, an accident, or the red fever that got Ram or Scarface, and
you were done for."

Like their pullers, the rickshaw owners were fervent worshippers of the god Viswakarma. Not for anything in the world would
they have failed to take out insurance with him by organizing a *puja*
in his honor that was as vibrant and generous as those held in all
the other workplaces in Calcutta.

The celebrations were generally held in their homes. Only the
old man, Narendra Singh, known as the Bihari, persisted in concealing his address. "Perhaps in case one day we got angry and
decided to pay him a visit," joked Hasari. So Narendra Singh's
eldest son rented a large house surrounded by gardens behind
Park Circus and set up there a magnificent *pandal* decorated with
garlands of flowers and hundreds of light bulbs fed by a generator
rented for the occasion.

On the day before the festival, every puller set about giving his

* A kind of large handkerchief.

rickshaw a meticulous cleaning. Hasari had even bought the remains of a tin of black paint to camouflage the scratches on the woodwork. He carefully greased the hubs of the wheels with a few drops of mustard oil so that there would be no disagreeable noise to irritate the god's ears. Then he went to fetch his wife and children.

Aloka had prepared his festival clothes for him: a *longhi* with little maroon checks on it and a blue-and-white striped shirt. She herself was dressed in a ceremonial sari of red and gold, which they had brought with them from their village. It was her wedding sari and, despite the rats, the cockroaches, the humidity, and the overflowing drains she had managed somehow to preserve its original freshness. The children too were splendidly dressed; they looked so clean and smart in fact that people came to admire them. The god could rest contented. The whole family might well live in a shanty made out of crates and bits of cloth but for today at least the people who issued from that hovel were princes.

Aloka, her daughter, and youngest son climbed into the rickshaw. The old jalopy had never before transported such proud, elegant passengers. Together the three of them were like a bouquet of orchids. Manooj, the eldest son, harnessed himself to the shafts because his father did not want to perspire in his beautiful shirt.

The house rented by the Bihari's son was not far away. One of the city's distinguishing features was that the rich people's quarters and the slums for the poor were close to one another.

Few rickshaw pullers had the good fortune to be able to celebrate the *puja* as a family. Most of them lived alone in Calcutta, having left their families in the villages. "It was a shame for them," Hasari said. "There is nothing more enjoyable than celebrating a festival with the whole family together. It's as if the god becomes your uncle or cousin."

The owner had done things well. His *pandal* was decorated just like a proper shrine. Interwoven red-and-white flowers and palm leaf trimmings formed a triumphal arch over the entrance. In the middle, on a carpet of marigolds and jasmine, was enthroned an enormous statue of Viswakarma, magnificently made up with rouge on his lips and kohl on his eyes.

"How imposing our god is! What power he exudes!" Hasari

enthused. "The statue's arms reached the tip of the tent, brandishing an ax and a hammer as if to force gifts from the heavens.
His chest looked as if it could blow the winds of a storm, his biceps
as if they could raise mountains, his feet stamp out all the wild
beasts of creation. With such a god for protector how could the
sorry-looking old carts fail to become celestial chariots? And the
poor devils that pulled them winged horses?"

Hasari and his family prostrated themselves before the divinity. Aloka, who was very devout, had brought offerings—a banana,
a handful of rice, jasmine, and marigold petals—which she placed
at his feet. Her husband went to park his rickshaw next to the
others in the garden. One of the owner's sons busied himself
decorating it with garlands of flowers and foliage. "What a pity he
can't speak to thank you," Hasari remarked. All those carts with
their flower-covered shafts pointing like spears toward the heavens, made a splendid spectacle. The former peasant barely recognized the shabby, creaking carriages that he and his colleagues
pulled so breathlessly each day. "It was just as if the stroke of a
magic wand had given them a new incarnation."

When all the rickshaws were in their places, there was a roll of
drums, then a clash of cymbals. An elderly priest made his entry at
this point, preceding a band of some fifty musicians in red jackets
and trousers trimmed with gold. A young Brahmin whose bare
torso was girded with a small cord began frenetically to bang the
clapper of a bell to inform the god of their presence, then the priest
passed slowly between the rows of carriages, sprinkling each one
with a few drops of water from the Ganges and a little *ghee*. Every
rickshaw *wallah*'s heart was constricted with emotion. For once it
was not sweat or tears of pain that were flowing over their poor old
carts, but the life-giving water of the god who would protect them
and give their children food.

When the priest had blessed all the rickshaws, he returned to
the deity to place upon his lips a little rice and *ghee* and to cense him
with the burning *arati* the Brahmin carried in a little cup. One of
the employer's sons then called out: "*Viswakarma-ki jai!* Long live
Viswakarma!" The six hundred or so pullers present repeated the
invocation three times. It was a sincere and triumphant roar that
charmed the ears of the owners infinitely more than the hostile
slogans shouted on the occasion of the recent strike.

"But why didn't we cry out at the same time, 'Long live Viswakarma and long live the solidarity of rickshaw workers?' " wondered Hasari. "And why not also, 'Long live the revolution!' Wasn't Viswakarma god of the workers first and foremost, before he was god of the owners? Even if sometimes he did give us the impression that he had forgotten to oil the wheel of our karma."

After the ceremony the Bihari's eldest son invited the pullers and their families to sit down on the grass. Pullers originating from the same regions grouped themselves together as did those who had come with their families. The Bihari's other sons then placed before each person a banana leaf on which they put several ladles of rice and mutton curry with some *chapatis*, pastries, and a mandarin orange. It was a real banquet, one which stomachs contracted by deprivation could not absorb in its entirety. "In any case," Hasari was to say, "what satisfied my stomach most was the sight of our bosses bending over to serve us. It was like seeing a family of tigers offering grass to a herd of antelopes."

44

SOMEONE WAS KNOCKING at the door of 49 Nizamudhin Lane. It was Anouar. Stephan Kovalski helped the cripple over the threshold and settled him on the mat made out of rice straw that served as a bed. The leper looked embarrassed.

"Stephan, Big Brother, I have a big favor to ask of you," he eventually said, joining his wasted palms together in a gesture of supplication.

"I am your brother. You can ask me anything."

"Well, in that case, could you go and tell Puli that I would like to marry Meeta."

"Meeta?" repeated Kovalski, surprised. "But she's his wife!"

"Exactly, Stephan *Daddah*, that's why I would like it to be you who asks him. He'll listen to you. Everyone respects you."

Puli was a lean little man of about fifty, with a very dark skin. Originally from the South, he had visited Calcutta one day and had never left. He must have contracted leprosy when he was young, during the long peregrinations of his nomadic life. At one time he had been an exhibitor of monkeys. Having changed to begging, for years he had haunted the steps of the Kali Temple until a clash with the local gang leader of the begging racketeers forced him into exile on the steps of Howrah Railway station on the other side of the river. His gifts as a comedian earned him an appreciable income. No traveler could resist the drollery of his mimicry or the horror of his wounds. He had been relatively spared by his illness and so he made up false dressings and painted them with red iodine. Puli lived in one of the most wretched compounds in the leper colony of Anand Nagar, together with his wife, Meeta, a sweet young woman of twenty-seven, and three lovely children aged four years to six months.

Meeta was the youngest daughter of a refugee potter from East Pakistan. At the age of sixteen, when her parents were about to marry her to a potter of her caste, the girl discovered a small whitish patch on her right cheek that was insensitive to touch. After weeks of hesitation, she went to join the line for consultation at Howrah Hospital. The medical verdict was instantaneous. It was a patch of leprosy. As far as her parents were concerned, God had cursed their daughter. They banished her immediately from the family hut. Had they not done so, the whole family would have been in danger of being expelled. Reduced to begging around the station, Meeta was picked up by a Bengali who sold her to a brothel in Calcutta. When the proprietor discovered that his new lodger was a leper, however, he beat her black and blue and threw her out. She was salvaged by some ragpickers, taken to Mother Teresa's home for the dying, and saved just in time. Afterward she went back to begging near the station and it was there that the onetime exhibitor of monkeys found her. He immediately took her under his wing and one year later, married her.

Anouar's request left Kovalski dumbfounded. He still did not fully appreciate to what extent the leper world was a universe apart, with its own distinctive laws. Leprosy, particularly in its advanced stages, exacerbates sexuality. This is why lepers have occasionally more than one wife and usually many children. Knowing that in any case they are cursed by God and excluded from the rest of the human race, lepers feel they have no taboos to respect. They are free. No representative of the law would ever come and poke his nose into their affairs. In Anand Nagar, these disfigured, crippled, fallen men did not go without women. The revenue they made from begging invariably enabled them to buy them. The last recourse of a very poor family who had not managed to marry off one of its daughters because of physical disgrace or some infirmity was often to sell her to a leper. One spouse was rarely, however, enough for the appetites of these disease-ridden men. Women, also, had sometimes more than one husband. Such polygamous transactions were set up by an intermediary and then solemnized with a ceremony that was as ostentatious and expensive as any other marriage.

"Big Brother Stephan," insisted Anouar eagerly, "I assure you that you won't have any difficulty convincing Puli. I've got enough to keep him happy."

With these words, the leper thrust his stumps into the top of his loincloth and brought out a bundle of notes tied up with a piece of string. "Three hundred rupees isn't to be sneezed at!"

"Have you asked Meeta what she thinks?" inquired the priest with concern. This question was primordial to him.

Anouar seemed surprised.

"Meeta will do as her husband orders," he replied.

Naturally Kovalski refused. He was prepared to play virtually any other role in the service of his brothers, but not that of procurer. Anouar would have to address himself directly to his "rival."

After laborious negotiations, the transaction was finally concluded for five hundred rupees, two hundred more than the sum contained in the bundle Anouar carried at his waist. The cripple borrowed the difference (and more besides, to cover the cost of the marriage) from the colony's usurer, a fat Punjabi who had several beggars working for him.

In a community where each member believed himself to be unclean and condemned by God, religion had no role to play. No Brahmin or mullah ever came to celebrate a ceremony here. Hindus, Muslims, and Christians lived together in relative indifference to the beliefs and rites of the religion of their origins. All the same, one or two odd customs such as the choice of an auspicious date for a wedding had been preserved. The colony even had its own astrologer, an old man with a white beard called Joga, who for forty years had exercised his profession as a fortune-teller on the esplanade of the Maidan. His work was not always easy, especially when, like Anouar and Meeta, the prospective marriage partners did not know their dates of birth. Old Joga contented himself with suggesting a month that was under the benign influence of the planet Venus and a day of the week that was not Tuesday, Saturday, or Sunday, the three ill-omened days in the Indian weekly calendar.

The ghetto of the damned was in a state of full bacchanalian revelry. On the day appointed, dazzled by the glare of the floodlights and bewildered by the bellowing of a sound system gone wild, Stephan Kovalski entered the neighborhood of the cursed. Although in his heart of hearts he disapproved of the nature of the alliance about to be formed, he had not been able to bring himself to turn down his friends' invitation. It was so rare, after all, for anyone in good health to provide these pariahs with the reassurance of their presence. Leper women draped in bedizened muslin saris were waiting at the door to adorn the bride and groom's guest of honor with garlands of marigolds and jasmine and to place upon his forehead the *tilak* of welcome, the patch of scarlet powder symbolizing the third eye of knowledge. That evening Kovalski would have plenty of need of that additional eye to discover all the refinements of the unwonted festivities of which he was to be the prince. He had swapped his sneakers and his old black shirt for gondola-shaped mules and a magnificent embroidered white cotton *kurta,* gifts from the prospective husband and wife to their partner in poverty.

The spectacle around him was beyond belief. In their new shirts and colored waistcoats, their cheeks clean-shaven and their dressings immaculate, the lepers had almost reassumed human form. Their gaiety was heartening. The master of ceremonies was none other than Puli, the bride's first husband. He had managed to dig out from somewhere a morning coat and a top hat.

"Welcome to our gathering, Big Brother Stephan," he cried in his falsetto voice, clasping the priest to him.

His breath betrayed the fact that he had already paid a few visits to the stock of *bangla* procured for the reception. He steered his guest of honor in the direction of the groom's hut. Kovalski hardly recognized the vile shed. The lepers had repainted everything in honor of Anouar's marriage. Garlands of flowers hung from the bamboo framework and the beaten earth of the floor sparkled with a *rangoli* carpet. Expressions of popular joy on occasions of celebration and great solemnity, *rangolis* are marvelous geometric compositions outlined in rice flour and colored powders and are designed to bring good fortune.

In the middle of the hut stood a solitary *charpoy,* it too decorated with garlands of flowers and covered with a superb Madras patchwork quilt made out of dozens of little striped squares. Seated on this regal bed was Anouar. Next to him was the throne

on which he would soon have himself carried to the site of the
ceremony. He received his best man with effusive tenderness.
Then, quite abruptly, his expression became one of gravity.

"Stephan, Big Brother, have you got a bit of medicine for
me?" he asked in a low voice. "I'm in terrible pain this evening."

Stephan Kovalski had learned from experience never to go
visiting the lepers without taking a dose of morphine in the bottom
of his pocket. That evening, however, he could not help but wonder what effect the powerful sedative might have on his friend
during the ceremony and particularly afterward when he found
himself alone with his young bride. As a precaution he injected
only half the vial. Hardly had he restored the syringe to his pocket
than half a dozen married women garbed in long dresses of many
colors, their hair adorned with diadems, and their necks and arms
covered with costume jewelry, entered singing *bhajans*, religious
hymns. Beneath all their makeup and finery their infirmities were
forgotten. Despite the fact that Anouar was Muslim by origin, they
had come to carry out one of the rites that was essential to all
Hindu marriages, the *holud-nath*, a purification of the groom.

They took charge of Anouar's body and rubbed it with all
kinds of unctions and yellow pastes which exuded a strong smell of
musk and saffron. The scene would have been comic, had not the
object of all these attentions been a body that was half destroyed.
Their anointing completed, the matrons went on to the groom's
toilet, sprinkling him with water. Then they undertook to dress
him. Anouar let himself be treated like a child. They slipped on a
long *kurta*, a superb shirt in green silk with gold buttons. How
could a man who dragged himself through the mud on a plank on
wheels ever have dreamed of such a garment?

"That crippled leper all dressed up in so festive a setting
suddenly brought a knot to my stomach," the Pole was to admit.

In the absence of any religious authority, it fell to the master of
ceremonies to direct the evening. No theologian of any religious
creed would ever have found his way through the ritual imbroglio
of the lepers of the City of Joy. Puli, however, was a star and, in any
case, the marriage closely concerned him. There was nothing,
therefore, that he left out, least of all the sacrosanct custom of
which he would be the indirect beneficiary: the fiancé's sending of
presents to his betrothed.

"Stephan, Big Brother, you are the best man, so you'll be the one to take the presents from Anouar to Meeta," he announced. The invitation was accompanied by a wink which was to say, "With you at least, I can be sure that nothing will disappear en route."

Anouar proceeded to take out of his mattress a collection of small packages wrapped up in newspaper and secured with elastic bands. Each packet contained some article of finery or ornament. Apart from three real silver rings, the remainder were cheap trinkets from the bazaar, a toe ring, earrings, a stone for her nose, an amber necklace, and a *matika*, the diadem worn by married women. In any event, the choice of these presents had been negotiated between Puli and Anouar. In addition to the jewels there were two saris, a few tubes of cosmetics, and a box of cinnamon sweetmeats. Puli deposited everything in a basket which he handed to Kovalski. Then he summoned the escort.

Eight lepers crowned with red cardboard shakos and dressed in yellow jackets and white trousers entered the hut. They were the musicians. Two of them held drumsticks between their consumed fingers, two others cymbals, and the two last dented trumpets. Puli raised his top hat and the small procession moved off amid the hubbub of a carnival. As majestic as King Belshazzar proceeding to Jerusalem, Stephan Kovalski stepped out with his basket of gifts balanced upon his head, taking care not to slip into a drain with his gondola-shaped mules.

Puli was so proud to be able to show off his guest of honor to the colony that he had the procession do the tour of the neighborhood before entering Meeta's compound. The spectacle that awaited the Pole in this wretched hole of a colony where he had spent so many hours comforting the condemned of the slum was so extraordinary that he found himself wondering whether he was not in fact the victim of some hallucination. The entire courtyard was covered with muslin veils and strung with garlands of marigolds, roses, and jasmine blossoms. Powered by an electricity generator especially hired for the occasion, dozens of light bulbs illuminated the courtyard with a clarity that it had never known before.

Kovalski surrendered his basket of offerings to one of the matrons standing guard at Meeta's door. Then, led by Puli and the band, who did their utmost to compete with the bellowing of the sound system, he returned to Anouar's hut. By this time it was almost midnight, that auspicious hour when in the heavens "the day straddles the night." The ceremony could commence.

There were no white mares caparisoned with gold and velvet to conduct the crippled man to the muslin-draped courtyard where his fiancée Meeta awaited him, her face veiled with a square of red cotton. Nevertheless, his chair decorated with flowers and borne like a palanquin by four other lepers, was equal to the most glorious of mounts. Crowned with a golden turban and preceded by the indescribable Puli, who greeted the crowd with waves of his top hat, Anouar traversed the neighborhood like a Mogul emperor processing to his coronation. Behind him, Kovalski carried the piece of folded cloth which in a moment would veil the face of the leper, before he entered the courtyard appointed for the marriage. Amid all those noises, all that laughter, all the smells, among the disfigured and the crippled, the Pole experienced a "fantastic lesson in hope" and marveled once more that "so much life and joy could spring from such abjection."

Puli raised his hat and the music stopped. They had reached the entrance to the courtyard and the bridegroom's face had to be concealed. Two matrons took the piece of cloth from Kovalski's hands and pinned it to the dome of Anouar's turban. The groom's fine bearded face disappeared from the gazes of the onlookers. Puli's top hat rose then above the surrounding heads and the procession set off again to the sound of trumpets and cymbals. "In the kingdom of heaven their faces will be the most beautiful of all," reflected the priest as his gaze encountered the range of distorted humanity waiting all around the little courtyard.

In a cupful of oil placed in the center of the *rangoli* flooring burned a flame. This was the traditional sacrificial fire offered up to the gods, so they might bless the union about to take place. The frail Meeta was seated on a cushion, her head inclined forward, completely hidden by her veil. She looked as if she was meditating. On her hair shone the gilded diadem which Anouar had sent her in his basket of presents. The smell of incense impregnated the air already heavy with smoke.

When the procession had made its way around the courtyard three times, Puli made a sign to Kovalski for him to take his place to the left of the bride. Then he directed the bearers to place Anouar on her right. With his top hat planted firmly on his skull, his chest thrust out under a morning coat that was too large for him, he then began to officiate.

Dear Puli! No one could imitate a Brahmin the way he could. Assuming an attitude of inspiration, he began to pronounce in his rasping voice an interminable series of formulas. The assembly appeared to be spellbound by the monotonous chant, punctuated at regular intervals by the clash of cymbals. After this preamble he finally came to the main body of the ceremony. The *Panigrahan* was the essential rite of Brahmin marriage. Puli pulled a small violet cord out of his pocket and, taking the right palms of the bride and groom, tied them together, repeating their names aloud. Thus was celebrated the first physical contact of man and wife. While Puli recited further prayers, Kovalski gazed at those two mutilated limbs bound together, and what he saw made him think of a sentence he had read one day in a book by a French writer named Léon Bloy: "We do not enter paradise either tomorrow or in ten years time. We enter today if we are poor and crucified."

Next came the most intense moment of the ceremony. The band and congregation fell silent as Puli invited the newlyweds officially to make each other's acquaintance. Slowly and timidly, with their free palms, they each removed the other's veil. The joyous bearded face appeared before Meeta's large eyes, slightly sad and blackened with kohl. Stephan Kovalski leaned forward to capture all the emotion of that moment, to try and guess too the thoughts of the young leper woman whose husband had sold her for five hundred rupees. Meeta's eyes were bright with tears.

An authentic Hindu wedding would have included a whole host of other rites, variable according to province and caste. One of them, however, was universal. Without it no ceremony was complete. Puli invited the couple to walk seven times around the sacrificial fire, their palms still joined by the piece of cord. In his excitement he had forgotten Anouar's infirmity. Again he had to call for the bearers. The leper saw his big brother rise from his cushion and approach him with open arms.

"Old friend, let me help you to accompany Meeta round the flame," said the priest with affection.

Kovalski picked up the fragile little body, and the three of them walked slowly, seven times round the cosmic fire. The residents of the courtyard and dozens of neighbors who had scaled the roofs watched the scene with emotion. When Kovalski had restored him to his place, Anouar asked:

"What about you? When are you going to get married?"

Puli, who had overheard, burst out laughing. Waving his hat about in something resembling a waltz, he interjected, "And I'll be the Brahmin again!"

They all laughed. Only poor Meeta seemed ill at ease in her new role.

Now it was time for the feast. At a signal from Puli, children brought piles of banana leaves which they distributed to everyone present. Immediately women came out of various houses, laden with steaming bowls of rice, vegetables, and fish. Little girls began to serve the food. People talked, laughed, sang, and cracked jokes. To keep a child amused, an old leper without a nose pretended to be wearing a mask. The fragrance of spices filled the courtyard, as the banana leaves were gradually filled. Even the neighbors on the roof tops were served. The sound system made the tiles vibrate. Resplendent on their cushions, the newlyweds and Kovalski received the homage of the community, under the delighted eye of Puli whose buffoonery increased by the minute. Every now and then he would disappear only to reappear an instant later in a state of even greater excitement. It did not take Kovalski long to guess what he was up to.

Alcohol! The celebration was on the point of degenerating into a monumental drinking bout. Concealed up to now at the back of the hovels, bottles of *bangla* began now to circulate among the guests. The effect of the drink was instantaneous and totally unexpected. Instead of flattening such sick and undernourished constitutions, the abrupt ingestion of alcohol electrified them. Those lepers who still had limbs leaped to their feet and began to dance. Stumps joined stumps in a frenzied farandole that snaked its way about the courtyard to the laughter and cheers of all the others present. Children ran about after each other. Women, too, freed from their inhibitions by large glasses of *bangla*, hurled themselves into dizzy circles that spun like tops about the courtyard. They had so much energy! So much vitality! So much zest for living! Once again Kovalski marveled. Let no one ever again say to him that lepers were just apathetic people, a bundle of rags and tatters, a collection of derelicts resigned to their lot. These men and women were life itself, LIFE in capital letters, the life that throbbed, the life that vibrated in them as it vibrated everywhere else in this most blessed of cities, Calcutta.

It was then that something amazing happened. At a signal from Puli's top hat, the dancing abruptly ceased, the singing and shouting faded, then stopped completely. The garlands of lights went out all at once. After one last hiccup, the generator came to a halt. Darkness fell and a cloak of silence enveloped the assembly. There was not a sound, not a word. Even the children were quiet.

On his cushion of honor Stephan Kovalski held his breath. Why this sudden obscurity? Why the stillness? Bemused, he could just make out shadows slipping away in the darkness and entering the different lodgings that opened onto the courtyard. Others felt their way across the roofs. Yet others melted into the blackness of the ground. The newlyweds next to him had vanished. Straining his ears, he detected the faint sound of voices that sounded like groans. He even heard a number of quickly stifled cries. Then he understood.

The celebration was not over. It was still going on. It was reaching its climax in the ultimate ritual, a last act of homage to all-powerful Life. The lepers of the City of Joy were making love.

45

"IT BEGAN WITH a feeling of utter fatigue and a strange aching in my bones, as if dozens of cops had been beating me with their *lathis*," Hasari Pal was to recount. "I told myself that it was probably old age creeping up a bit early, as it did with many rickshaw pullers. In Calcutta even the leaves on the trees in the squares fell earlier than those in the countryside. Then I felt a strange warmth in my chest. Even when I was standing still, waiting for a fare, I felt the heat of it, bathing me in perspiration from head to toe. It seemed all the stranger for the fact that it was winter and, God knows, in Calcutta it can be as cold in winter as it's hot in summer. The fact that I never took off the old sweater given to me by a customer from Wood Street made no difference; I was still cold. Perhaps I'd caught the mosquito disease.* According to Chomotkar, a friend of mine who was a taxi driver, that illness gives you the same sort of shivers. He'd had it himself and had been cured with small white tablets. He brought me a whole load wrapped up in a piece of newspaper and told me to swallow two or three a day. We began the treatment with a bottle of *bangla*. Chomotkar claimed that *bangla* was a universal medicine, but I think he was wrong because I went on sweating like a pig. The heat in my chest began to burn so much that every breath was painful. Every time I took on a customer, even a lightweight like a schoolboy, I had to stop every two or three minutes to get my breath back. One day I was really frightened. It happened in Park Street. I had parked my rickshaw to go and buy some *bidis* under the arcades

* Malaria.

when suddenly, as I was going past Flury's pastry store, I saw myself in the shop window. For a second I asked myself who the old man in front of the display of cakes might be, with his hollow, stubbled cheeks, and his head of white hair. Suddenly I saw the image of my old man on the morning he blessed me before I left for Calcutta. I shall never forget that sight.

"By the way she'd been looking at me for some time, I knew that my wife too was alarmed about my health. She had become particularly attentive to my every word and gesture. It was as if she was desperate for the slightest indication to reassure her, to prove to her that I was well. No doubt that was why she responded with such unusual enthusiasm whenever I expressed the desire to make love. The strange thing about it was that the more worn out with fatigue I felt, the more I desired my wife. It was as if all the vitality in my shattered body had taken refuge in my reproductive organ. What was more, it was not long before my wife announced that she was expecting a child. This news filled me with such joy that for several days I was oblivious to the fatigue, the cold, and my sweating.

"Then afterward things got very much worse. One day when I had just picked up a *marwari* with a pile of packages, I was forced to stop and put down my shafts. Something had wedged itself in my chest. I couldn't breathe anymore. I collapsed onto my knees. The *marwari* was a kind man. Instead of abusing me and calling another rickshaw, he tried to help me get my breath back by striking me sharply on the back. When he did so, I felt something hot gurgle into my mouth. I spat it out. The *marwari* surveyed the spittle and grimaced. Handing me a five-rupee note, he transferred his packages to another rickshaw. As he drew away he gave me a slight wave of his hand.

"I remained there for quite a while before getting up. But the act of spitting had brought me some relief. Little by little I got my breath back and found enough strength to move on. That wasn't the day the god was coming for me. My wife burst into sobs when I told her about the incident. Women are like animals. They sense the oncoming storm long before men do. She ordered me to go and see a quack immediately and buy some drugs. A quack was a street doctor. He would ask only one or two rupees whereas a real doctor who had completed his studies would expect five or ten times more. But before I went to find the quack, my wife suggested that we take offerings to the temple to ward off the ogress Suparnaka, who was responsible for so many sick people. On a plate she placed a banana, jasmine petals, and the equivalent of a handful of rice and off we went to the temple, where I slipped the Brahmin the five-rupee note that the *marwari* had given me. He recited some *mantras*. We laid our offerings at the foot of the statue of Ganesh and lit several sticks of incense. When the elephant-headed god had disappeared behind a veil of smoke, we withdrew to leave him to crush the ogress with his trunk. Next day I had recovered enough strength to pick up the shafts of my rickshaw again.

"At that time a spell of icy cold had hit the North of the country. The tar on the Calcutta streets burned the bare soles of our feet just as acutely with the cold as it did with the heat during the worst dog days before the monsoon. The nights were terrible. It was no use our huddling together like dried fish in a packing case. The cold bit into our skin and bones with teeth more pointed than a crocodile's.

"The potions from the quack in Wellesley Street must have contained some miraculous substance, because two bottles were enough to appease the pain in my bones and the heat in my chest within a matter of days. I was quite convinced that soon I would be able to go back to Flury's pastry shop and look at myself in the window without fear. That was when I began to feel strange scratchings at the base of my throat that provoked a series of uncontrollable coughing fits. It was a dry, painful cough which became progressively more violent until it shook me like a coconut tree in a tornado, then left me completely exhausted. It's true that such coughing fits are a music as familiar to rickshaw pullers as the ringing of their bells. All the same it was a terrifying experience. It proved that the god had not heard my prayer."

46

WITH ITS HANDLEBARS bristling with headlights and horns,
its thick wheels painted green and red, its tank gleaming like a
streak of silver, and a seat covered with panther skin, the motorcycle looked just like one of those flashy machines you see in films.
Strapped into leather trousers with wide elephant thongs, topped
with a silk shirt, its rider drove through the muddy alleyways of the
City of Joy, spitting an exhaust inferno with obvious delight. Everyone knew the strapping fellow in the dark glasses who dispensed
waves and smiles like a campaigning politician. He was as familiar a
character as the blind mullah from the great mosque and the old
Brahmin from the little temple next to the railway lines. His name
was Ashoka, like the famous emperor in Indian history. He was the
eldest son and first lieutenant of the local Mafia boss.

Despite a population of more than seventy thousand, the City
of Joy had no mayor, no police force, no legal authority of any kind.
As in the Pals's slum, this gap had however been promptly filled by
the Mafia who reigned supreme over the City of Joy. It was they
who directed affairs, extorted, arbitrated; no one disputed their
power. There were several rival families among them but the most
powerful godfather was a Hindu with thick-lensed glasses, who
lived with his sons, his wives, and his clan in a modern four-story
house built on the edge of the slum on the other side of the Grand
Trunk Road, the main Calcutta-Delhi highway. He was about sixty
and known as Kartik Baba, a name given to him by his father as a
tribute to the son of Shiva, god of war.

Practically all the clandestine drinking dens in the slum were
his property. Similarly, it was he who controlled the drug traffic

and local prostitution. He could also pride himself on being one of the largest real estate owners in Anand Nagar. He had exercised great dexterity in choosing his tenants. Instead of refugee families, he preferred cows and buffalo. Most of the cattle sheds that harbored the approximately eighty-five hundred head of cattle living in the slum belonged to him. This animal invasion, with its stench, its entourage of millions of flies, and the river of liquid manure it discharged into the drains each day, went back to the days when for reasons of hygiene the municipality had banished the cattle sheds from the center of Calcutta. There had been a great uproar about the creation of municipal dairies on the outskirts of the town but, as always, nothing had actually been done, and the animals had simply been rehoused in the City of Joy and other similar slums. The godfather had been one of the principal beneficiaries of this operation. It was more advantageous to house a cow than a family of nine people. As he himself said, "For the same rent and the same amount of space, there is no risk of the least complaint or demands of any kind."

Everyone knew that the godfather had plenty of other sources of revenue at his disposal. In particular, he managed a network of fences who bought and resold goods stolen from the railways. The profits from this racket came to millions of rupees. Above all, however, he derived considerable benefit from a particularly odious form of exploitation. He exploited the lepers of Anand Nagar.

Not content merely to collect rent for their miserable shacks, he forced them to pay him a daily tax of one or two rupees in exchange for his "protection" and a place to beg on the pavement at Howrah Station. Substantial political backing was necessary for the godfather actually to be able to implement such exactions with impunity. Rumor had it that he was a generous contributor to the coffers of the party in power, for whom he also acted as a diligent electoral agent. Ballots in the City of Joy, even those held between wasted stumps, formed part of his trafficking. Strangely, the residents were rather happy with this state of affairs and, since there existed no other uncontested body of authority in the slum, they even sought out frequent recourse to the godfather. In the course of years he had thus become a redresser of wrongs, a kind of Robin Hood.

Of course, he rarely intervened personally. Instead he delegated that role to his eldest son Ashoka or to some other member of his family. Nevertheless, it was he who pulled the strings and he was never short of tricks to establish his authority. He would send his henchmen, for example, to provoke an incident in one of his drinking dens. Then he would dispatch Ashoka or, in cases of extreme delicacy, would himself appear to restore peace and order and thereby show the community exactly how good and how influential he was. Furthermore, when Ashoka or any of his other sons had gotten a slum girl into trouble, he showed himself to be so generous toward the parents that people hastened to hush up the affair. In short he acted the role of a proper nobleman.

The presence of the godfather's son's motorcycle outside Stephan Kovalski's door one morning caused a sensation in Nizamudhin Lane. Rumors quickly ran: "The godfather's picking a quarrel with Big Brother Stephan. The godfather wants to turn the 'Father' out . . ." At first sight this anxiety appeared unjustified. After prostrating himself before the priest with all the respect he would award the goddess Kali, the messenger of the Mafia boss addressed Kovalski, "Father, my father has asked me to deliver an invitation to you."

"An invitation?" marvelled the priest.

"Yes. He would like to discuss a small matter with you. Something altogether insignificant . . ."

Kovalski knew that nothing was "insignificant" to the godfather. He judged it useless to stall.

"Fair enough," he said, "I'll follow you."

Ashoka beat the air with his large, hairy hands.

"Not so fast! My father doesn't see people at just any time of day! He'll be expecting you tomorrow at ten o'clock. I'll come and get you."

Crossing the City of Joy on the bulky and noisy motorcycle of the heir to the throne, with all his sirens going, Stephan Kovalski found the experience somewhat comical. He could just imagine the parish priest's expression if he could only see him now. "I don't know how the Hindu and Mogul emperors received their subjects," he was to recount, "but it would be very hard for me to forget the princely fashion in which the godfather of the City of Joy received me."

His house was truly palatial. Outside the door were three

Ambassador cars complete with radio antennas and protective screens at the windows, plus several motorcycles like those the police use to escort ministers and heads of state. The hall on the ground floor opened onto a large room furnished with Oriental carpeting and comfortable cushions. A small altar with a *lingam* of Shiva, the images of numerous gods, and a little bell to ring the *puja* adorned one corner of the room. The sticks of burning incense spread about exuded a heady fragrance.

The godfather was seated on a kind of throne sculpted out of wood and encrusted with designs in mother-of-pearl and ivory. He was wearing a white cap and a black velvet waistcoat over a long white cotton shirt. Tinted glasses with very thick lenses completely concealed his eyes but his reactions could be discerned by the puckering of his bushy eyebrows. Ashoka motioned to the visitor to sit on the cushion placed in front of his father. Servants in turbans brought tea, bottles of iced lemonade, and a plate of Bengali pastries. The godfather emptied one of the bottles, then began to tap the arm of his chair with the fat topaz that adorned his index finger.

"Welcome to this house, Father," he said in a ceremonial and slightly hollow voice, "and consider it your own." Without waiting for a reply, he cleared his throat and dispatched a globule of spit into the copper urn which glistened next to his right toe.

At this point Kovalski noticed that he was wearing sandals with straps encrusted with precious stones.

"It is a very great honor to make your acquaintance," added his host. One of the servants returned with a tray of cigars tied together in a bundle. The Mafia boss untied the cord and offered a cigar to the priest, who declined it. The godfather took his time lighting his own.

"You must be an altogether special person," the godfather declared, exuding a puff of smoke, "because it has been reported to me that you have made an application . . . I can't actually believe it . . . for Indian citizenship."

"You are decidedly well informed," Kovalski confirmed.

The godfather chuckled and settled himself comfortably in his chair.

"You must admit that it might seem somewhat surprising that

someone should be tempted to exchange his affluent and privileged status of foreigner for that of a poor man in an Indian slum."

"We probably don't have the same understanding of wealth, you and I."

"In all events, I shall be proud to count someone like you among the ranks of my compatriots. And, if by any chance the response to your request is delayed, do let me know. I have connections. I shall try and intervene."

"Thank you, but I put my trust in the Lord."

The godfather made an effort to believe what he had just heard: was it possible that someone was refusing his support?

"Father," he said after a growl, "I have heard some strange rumors. It would seem that you intend to create a leper hospital in the slum. Is that right?"

" 'Leper hospital' is a very grandiose expression. It's to be more a dispensary to treat the worst cases. I've asked Mother Teresa for the help of two or three of her Sisters."

The godfather surveyed the priest sternly.

"You must know that no one can concern himself with the lepers in that slum without my authorization."

"In that case, what's keeping you from helping them yourself? Your assistance would be most welcome."

The godfather's eyebrows puckered above his thick glasses.

"The lepers in the City of Joy have been under my protection for twelve years, and that's probably the best thing that has ever happened to them. Without me the other inhabitants of this place would have thrown them out ages ago." He leaned forward with a sudden air of complicity. "My dear Father, have you asked yourself how the people next door to your 'dispensary' will react when your lepers start to show up?"

"I have faith in the compassion of my brothers," Kovalski said.

"Compassion? You holy men are always talking about compassion! All you'll get by way of compassion is a riot. They'll set fire to your dispensary and lynch your lepers!"

The priest gritted his teeth, preferring not to reply. "This scoundrel is probably right," he thought.

The godfather relit his cigar and took a long draw on it, throwing his head back. "I can see only one way for you to avoid all

these trials and tribulations," he said, throwing his head back
again.

"Which is?"

"That you subscribe to a protection contract."

"A protection contract?"

"It will cost you a mere three thousand rupees a month. Our
rates are ordinarily much higher. But you are a man of God and, as
I'm sure you realize, in India we are used to respecting what is
sacred."

Then, without waiting for any reply, he clapped his hands. His
eldest son came hurrying in.

"The Father and I have come to an amicable agreement," the
godfather announced with evident satisfaction. "The two of you
can agree on the terms and conditions of the arrangement."

The godfather was a nobleman. He did not concern himself
with details.

*

That evening the founders of the Committee for Mutual Aid in
the City of Joy assembled in Stephan Kovalski's room to discuss
the godfather's ultimatum.

"The godfather's family is all-powerful," declared Saladdin.
"Remember the last elections—the Molotov cocktails, the blows
with iron bars . . . the people killed and all those injured! Is it
really worth the risk of setting it all off again, for the sake of a few
crippled carcasses? We'll just have to agree to pay."

"All the same, three thousand rupees for the right to take in
and nurse a few lepers is exorbitant." Margareta was indignant.

"Is it the sum that bothers you," asked Kovalski, "or the
principle?"

She seemed surprised at the question.

"Why, the sum of course!"

"A typical answer," thought Kovalski. "Even here in the
depths of the slum, extortion and corruption sticks to their skin
like flies." All the others shared Saladdin's view, all, that was,
except Bandona, the young woman from Assam.

"May God damn this demon!" Bandona exclaimed. "To give
him one single rupee would be to betray the cause of all the poor."

Her words had the effect of an electric shock on Kovalski.

"Bandona is right! We must take up the challenge, resist it, fight it. It's now or never that we can show the people here that they are no longer alone."

Early the next morning, the bulbous, backfiring motorcycle belonging to the son of Kartik Baba came to a halt outside Kovalski's room. As his father had ordered, Ashoka had come to discuss the payment terms for the "contract." The meeting, however, lasted only a few seconds, just long enough for the priest to intimate his refusal to the young ruffian. This was the first defiance ever laid before the authority of the all-powerful head of the Mafia in the City of Joy.

One week later the little dispensary was ready to receive the first lepers. Bandona and a number of volunteers set out to bring back the six extreme cases Kovalski wanted to hospitalize first. He himself went at dawn to Mother Teresa's house to collect the three Sisters who were to nurse the lepers. Hardly had they reached the square on which the mosque stood, however, than Bandona's group was intercepted by a commando of young thugs, armed with sticks and iron bars.

"No one's going any farther!" shouted the leader, a pimply adolescent whose front teeth were missing.

The young Assamese girl tried to move forward but an avalanche of blows stopped her. At that same moment the priest arrived from the other end of the slum, accompanied by his three nuns. Seeing the commotion at the far end of the alley, he clenched his teeth. Then he heard a loud explosion and an outcry. A second gang had begun to use iron bars and pickaxes to ransack the old school that was to serve as the leper clinic. Terrified, the neighborhood shopkeepers hastily barricaded their shop windows. On the Grand Trunk Road, the shrill grinding of dozens of metal shutters could be heard as traders rushed to lower them. When the destruction of the dispensary had been completed, a third gang appeared. They were carrying bottles and explosive devices in knapsacks strung over their shoulders. The street emptied in a flash. Even the dogs and the children, who were always swarming everywhere, took off. A series of deflagrations shook the entire neighborhood, their echo resounding far beyond the boundaries of the City of Joy, as far as the railway station and beyond.

At Kovalski's side, Mother Teresa's Sisters began to recite the rosary aloud.

The priest led them into Margareta's compound, entrusted them to the protection of Gunga, the deaf mute, and ran in the direction of the explosions. A voice begged him to come back. He stopped and turned around only to find that Margareta was hurrying after him.

"Stephan, Big Brother," she pleaded again. "For the love of God, don't go any nearer! They'll kill you!"

At that moment they saw emerging from the road that skirted the slum a procession, with flags and banners stripped with slogans proclaiming in Hindi, Urdu, and English: "We don't want a leper hospital in Anand Nagar!"

A man with a megaphone marched at the head and chanted out other slogans that the horde behind him repeated. One of them said, "No lepers here! Father Sahib go home!"

These people didn't actually belong to the neighborhood. There was nothing very surprising about that. Calcutta held the largest reserve of professional demonstrators in the world. Any political party or organization could rent a thousand of them, for five or six rupees per head per day. The same people who one morning shouted revolutionary slogans under the red flags of the Communists might well parade that evening or the next morning behind the banners of the Congress supporters. In a city that was a permanent boiling pot of tensions, any opportunity to let off steam was a good one. As soon as he spotted the emblem of Indira Gandhi's party on the banners demanding the expulsion of the lepers, the thirty-two-year-old local Communist party representative, a former foreman for Hindustan Motors, named Joga Banderkar, was also seized with the sudden impulse to demonstrate. Running as fast as his crippled leg would allow, he went to alert a few comrades. In less than an hour, the Communists in the slum had succeeded in assembling several hundred militants for a counterdemonstration. Thus the godfather's response to Stephan Kovalski's defiance was to result in a political confrontation.

There was nothing new about this sequence of events. Simple altercations between neighbors degenerated into scuffles between compounds, and those scuffles into battles waged between the residents of an entire neighborhood, in which people were wounded and sometimes killed. On the day when he had saved the unfortunate mad woman from being lynched, old Surya had explained the mechanics of such violence to Kovalski. "You bow your head, you shut up, you put up with everything indefinitely. You bottle up your grievances against the owner of your hovel who is exploiting you, the usurer who's bleeding you dry, the speculators who push up the price of rice, the factory bosses who won't give you a job, the neighbor's children who won't let you sleep for coughing their lungs out all night, the political parties who suck the life out of you and couldn't give a damn, the Brahmins who take ten rupees from you for a mere *mantra.* You take all the mud, the shit, the stink, the heat, the insects, the rats, until one day, wham! you're presented with an opportunity to shout, ransack, kill. You don't know why but it's stronger than you are, and you just pile on in there!"

Kovalski never ceased to be amazed and impressed by the fact that in so harsh an environment, outbreaks of violence were not more frequent. How many times had he seen scuffles in the compounds dissolve unexpectedly into a torrent of insults and invective, as if everyone concerned wanted somehow to avoid the worst; for the poor of Anand Nagar knew what the price of fights really was. Recollections of the horror of Partition and of Naxalite terrorism still haunted their memories.

Yet, that morning, nothing seemed to restrain the fury of the men and women stampeding through the slum. The two processions ran into each other on the corner of the Grand Trunk Road. There was a savage clash under a deluge of tiles, bricks, and Molotov cocktails thrown from the roof tops. Stephan Kovalski saw before him again the bleeding face of his father on that evening in the summer of 1947, when police and striking miners had fought around the pits. The confrontation today was even more vicious. "For the first time I read on their faces something which I had believed was extinguished," he was to explain. "What I discovered there was hatred. It twisted their mouths, inflamed their eyes, drove them to perform monstrous acts, like throwing a bottle of explosives at a group of children trapped in the confusion, or setting fire to a coach full of passengers, or throwing themselves on some wretched old men incapable of escaping. There were plenty of women among the most heated fighters. I recognized some of them, although their contorted features rendered them almost unidentifiable. The slum had lost all reason. I realized then what would happen on the day the poor of Calcutta resolved to march upon the districts of the rich."

All of a sudden there was a whistle, then a detonation followed by a blast of air so fierce that Kovalski and Margareta were thrown against each other. A bottle of gasoline had exploded just behind them. Immediately they were enveloped in dense smoke. By the time the cloud had dispersed, they were in the thick of the throng. It was impossible to escape without risking being struck down on the spot. Fortunately the combatants seemed to be observing a pause in order to conduct a ritual as old as war itself—pillaging. Then it began to rain down bricks and bottles once more.

The ferocity reached a state of paroxysm. Dozens of wounded had fallen on all sides. Kovalski saw a child of four or five pick up one of the projectiles lying beside a drain. The device exploded, tearing off his hand. A few seconds later, he saw an iron bar flash above Margareta's head. He had just time enough to throw himself in front of her and deflect the blow. Already another assailant was bearing down on them with a cutlass. At the very instant he was about to strike, Kovalski saw a hand seize his attacker by the collar and hurl him backward. Beyond the hand he recognized Mehboub, his Muslim neighbor who was himself armed with an iron bar. After his wife's death, the Muslim had entrusted his elderly mother and his children to the care of his eldest son, Nasir, and then he had disappeared. Now here he was back again as a henchman for the godfather. His forehead and nose were scarred with gashes and his mustache matted with blood; he looked more than ever like the picture of the Sacred Shroud before which he had so often collected himself. Meanwhile, all around them, blows rained down with redoubled savagery.

The most unrestrained fighters were the very young men. They seemed to be fighting one another for the sheer pleasure of it. It was terrifying. Kovalski saw one teenage boy plunge his knife into a woman's stomach. Then, he noticed the thickset silhouette and dark glasses of Ashoka, the godfather's eldest son. Until that moment neither Ashoka nor his father had appeared on the battlefield. Now Ashoka was issuing orders. The priest realized that something was going to happen.

He did not have to wait long to find out what. "The carnage stopped as if at the wave of a magic wand," he was to recount. "The assailants put up their arms, turned on their heels, and walked away. In a matter of minutes everything was almost back to normal. The groans of the wounded, the bricks and other bits of debris cluttering up the thoroughfare, and the acrid smell of smoke were the only signs that a battle had just taken place here. A reflex of reason had prevented the irreparable."

The godfather was satisfied. He had inflicted the desired lesson and still kept control of his troops. Stephan Kovalski had been given due notice: no one in the City of Joy could defy the godfather with impunity.

47

"WITH ALL THEIR speeches, their promises, and their red flags, we were snared like pigeons in glue. No sooner had we elected them than all those left-wing *babus* turned their backs on us," Hasari Pal was to recount, referring to the elections that had brought the left to power in Bengal. "They started off by voting a law that obliged the judges to order, not just the seizure of any rickshaws operating without official permission, but their actual destruction. These were the so-called defenders of the working class, the ones whose mouths were always full of 'rights' and 'justice,' the ones who spent their time setting the poor against the rich, turning the exploited against their bosses, attacking the very means by which a hundred thousand of us were able to stop our wives and children from dying of starvation! To destroy the rickshaws of Calcutta was like burning the crops in the fields! And who would be the victims of such madness? The owners of the carts? Hell no! They didn't need the five or six rupees each old crate brought them per day to fill their bellies. Whereas for us, God knows, it meant death!"

As always, Hasari was after an explanation. The man they called Scarface had one. According to him, if the government *babus* wanted to burn all unlicensed carriages it was because those "gentlemen" did not appreciate competition. He had discovered that several *babus* had their own rickshaws to exploit, for which they of course had arranged to obtain licenses. As for Golam Rassoul, the union secretary who looked like a sparrow fallen from its nest, he had another explanation. Ever since he had been militating with the Communist *babus*, his head was packed with all sorts of theories that simple souls like Hasari often had difficulty in understanding. "Because we had more opportunities to cultivate our calves than our brains," Hasari was to admit.

Rassoul claimed that the people responsible for the persecutions were really the technocrats among the municipality officials. According to him, the *babus* in question begrudged the rickshaw pullers the fact that they worked on the fringes of the government system, in other words, they were not dependent on either the *babus* or the state. "As if the state were in the habit of doing the rounds of the pavements and slums offering work to the starving unemployed," Hasari was to retort. "In any case," Rassoul went on to explain, "rickshaw pullers had no place in those technocrats' tomorrow's vision of Calcutta. The Calcutta of these visionaries would be one of machines, not human horses. Five thousand more taxis and buses would be better for everybody than the sweat of a hundred thousand poor bums." In Rassoul's view, it was not all that difficult to understand why. "Let us suppose," he explained, "that the government orders five thousand more taxis and buses to transport the one and a half million people who travel about in our old rattletraps each day. Well, you can imagine what an order like that would mean to the automobile manufacturers, the tire makers, the garages, and gasoline companies, not to mention the pharmaceutical laboratories, because of all the lung disease the new pollution would provoke."

For whatever reason, the newly elected *babus* decided to go after unlicensed rickshaws. The law was implemented and unauthorized carriages were confiscated. No puller dared to use the main avenues where there were policemen directing traffic. Other cops began to check on them at the stands.

"Let me see your license," an officer would order the first puller in line.

"I haven't got a license," the puller would apologize, the poor fellow, taking a few rupees out of the folds of his *longhi.*

This time, however, the policeman would pretend not to see the notes. He was under strict orders: the time for baksheesh was simply over. Sometimes the puller did not even reply. He'd just shrug his shoulders with resignation. He was used to a rotten karma. The cop would have the carriages slotted into one another and dragged to the nearest *thana,* the local police station. Soon, on the pavements outside all the *thanas* there were long snaking lines of rickshaws stacked up against each other, their wheels shackled with chains. Thus immobilized, the old carts presented a sad picture of desolation. They were like the trees in an orchard uprooted by a cyclone, like fishes caught in a net.

"What a calamity," lamented Hasari with his companions. "But as long as they were there, chained up outside the *thanas*, there was still the hope that one day they would be restored to those for whom they provided a livelihood." Even that hope was soon to be crushed, however.

As the law prescribed, the judges ordered the destruction of the confiscated rickshaws. One evening they were all loaded onto the yellow municipality garbage trucks and taken to an unknown destination. Rassoul managed to have the trucks followed by a union spy and soon the pullers discovered that their carriages had been collected on the city's public dump, behind the tanners' quarter, very probably to be burned.

Because they were so widely dispersed, it generally took a fair amount of time to gather a significant number of pullers together. But on this occasion, it took less than one hour for them to form a formidable procession on Lower Circular Road, with banners, posters, and all the usual trappings of that kind of demonstration. Led by Rassoul, Scarface, and all the union general staff, the column set out on a march to the dump, shouting, "Our rickshaws are our rice!" As they advanced, other workers joined them. In Calcutta demonstrating helped to forget an empty stomach. At every crossroad, policemen stopped traffic to let them pass. In Calcutta that was the norm. Those asserting their rights always took priority over other citizens.

They marched like that for miles, through the outermost suburbs, until finally they reached a deserted area. "And it was then," Hasari was to say, "that the shock came. First there was a stench that burned your lungs out, as if thousands of decaying carcasses were engulfing you, as if heaven and earth were decomposing under your nostrils. It took several minutes for us to get a grip on our nausea and go on." About a few hundred yards ahead laid an enormous mound from which the smell arose—the city's dumping ground. On a mattress of garbage as vast as the Maidan, dozens of trucks and bulldozers moved about in a cloud of pestilential dust.

A myriad vultures and crows circled above the putrescence. There were so many of them that the sky was as black as a monsoon day. Most astounding of all, however, was the number of ragpickers wriggling about like insects among the refuse.

As they reached the garbage platform, the pullers noticed their carriages on the far side of the wretched, stinking place. The rickshaws formed a long snake of wheels and arches slotted into one another. "How could the god ever have allowed those purveyors of rice to end up in a place like this?", wondered Hasari and his comrades. It was totally incomprehensible. "The god must have been in the arms of some princess the day the *babus* voted their law," thought the former peasant. "Either that or he just doesn't give a damn about us."

What happened next was to remain for Hasari the most terrible sight of his life. Behind the rickshaws and below the level of the mound, three police vans were concealed. When the procession spilled onto the dump, the policemen rushed out of their vehicles to block its way. They were not traffic policemen but specialized, antiriot cops with helmets, guns, and shields. They had been given the order to drive back the demonstrators and carry out the total destruction of all the rickshaws.

Rassoul armed himself with his loudspeaker and shouted that the rickshaw *wallahs* had come to oppose this destruction. In the meantime press photographers had arrived. They looked somewhat out of place in these surroundings, with their shoes and trousers, but the dump was soon black with people. The ragpickers had stopped scrabbling among the garbage and other people had come running from nearby villages. The policemen advanced, brandishing their guns, but not a single puller stirred. "In view of the enormity of the crime about to take place, we were all prepared to fall under the guns of the cops rather than back off," Hasari would say. "All these years had really hardened us and our last great strike had shown us that we could make our bosses tremble if only we remained united. We felt as solidly bound to one another as our shafts were to our carriages."

It was then that the real drama began. A policeman struck a match and lit a torch which he then plunged into the body of a rickshaw, right in the middle of the line. The flames immediately set the hood and seat ablaze, then spread to the next vehicle. After one stunned second, the people in the foremost ranks of the procession hurled themselves at the barrage of policemen. They wanted to push the burning vehicles out of the way to save the others, but the policemen formed an insurmountable wall.

It was at precisely that moment that Hasari noticed Scarface. He had managed to hoist himself up onto a friend's shoulders. Letting out a shout, he reared up and, with a formidable thrust of his haunches, managed to leap over the policemen. He literally fell into the flames, and from there his comrades saw him launch himself onto the burning carriages to topple them into the ravine. It was a crazy thing to do. Even the policemen turned around in astonishment. A scream went up from the blazing mass. Hasari spotted an arm and a hand grasping one of the shafts, then smoke enveloped the scene and the smell of scorched flesh mingled with the stench of the whole surroundings. Silence fell over the dump. All that could be heard now was the crackling of the flames as they consumed the rickshaws. The *babus* had won.

When at last the fire had died down, Hasari asked one of the garbage pickers for a tin. With it, he went and collected up Scarface's cinders from the embers. He and his comrades would scatter them on the waters of the Hooghly, the branch of the sacred river Ganges.

48

IN WINTER, the same phenomenon occurred each evening. No sooner had the women set fire to the cow dung cakes to cook their dinner than the reddening disk of the sun disappeared behind a grayish filter. Held there by the layer of fresh air above, the wreaths of dense smoke hovered stagnantly over the rooftops, imprisoning the slum beneath a poisonous screen. Its inhabitants coughed, spat, and choked. On some evenings, visibility was reduced to less than six feet. The smell of sulphur overrode all others. People's skin and eyes burned. Yet no one in the City of Joy would have dared to curse the wintertime, that all too short a respite before the summer's onslaught.

Summer, that year, struck like a bolt of lightning. In a matter of seconds, night fell in the very middle of day. Crazed with panic, the slum people rushed out of their compounds and into the alleys. From the terrace where he was sorting medicines, Stephan Kovalski saw an atmospheric disturbance of a kind that was totally unknown to him. At first sight it could have passed for the Aurora Borealis. What it in fact consisted of was a wall of suspended particles of yellow sand bearing down upon the slum with lightning speed. There was no time to take shelter. The tornado had already reached them.

It devastated everything in its path, tearing off the roofs of houses and tossing their occupants to the ground. In their sheds the cow buffalo bellowed with terror. The slum was instantly covered with a shroud of yellow dust. Then a succession of flashes lit the darkness, the signal for a cataclysm which this time bombarded the slum with hailstones succeeded by a torrential downpour of rain. When finally the rain stopped and the sun came out again, a cloud of burning vapor descended over the slum. The thermometer rose from fifteen degrees to a hundred and four degrees Fahrenheit. Stephan Kovalski and the seventy thousand other inhabitants of the City of Joy realized that the short winter truce was over. The blazing inferno was with them once more. That March 17, summer had come to the city.

Summer! That beloved season of all temperate zones inflicted upon the occupants of this part of the world unimaginable suffering and, as always, it was the most destitute people, the miserable slum dwellers, who were most cruelly stricken by it. In the windowless hovels crammed with up to fifteen people, in those tiny compounds scorched for twelve hours a day by the sun, in the narrow alleys where never the slightest breath disturbed the air, while extreme poverty and the absence of electricity prevented the use of fans, the summer months that preceded the arrival of the monsoon were as atrocious a form of torture as hunger itself.

In the avenues of Calcutta people simply did not move without the protection of an umbrella. Even the policemen directing traffic were equipped with linen shades attached to their crossbelts, so as to leave their hands free. Other people sheltered themselves from the sun beneath attaché cases, wads of newspaper, piles of books, the tails of their saris or *dhotis* raised over their heads. The furnace-like heat was accompanied by humidity that could sometimes reach 100 percent. The least movement, a few steps, going up a staircase, induced a shower of perspiration. From ten o'clock in the morning on, any physical effort became impossible. Men and beasts found themselves petrified in the incandescence of the unmoving air. Not a breath stirred. The reflection off the walls of the buildings was so bright that anyone imprudent enough to go out without dark glasses was liable to a sensation of melted lead in his eyes. Venturing barefoot onto the asphalt of the streets was even more painful. The liquified tar scorched strips of flesh from the soles of the feet. Pulling a rickshaw on this fiery carpet was an act of pure heroism— running, stopping, setting off again with wheels that stuck fast in the burning tar. To try and protect his feet already ulcerated with cracks and burns, Hasari Pal resolved to wear a pair of sandals, an act which millions of barefooted Indians had never accomplished. Thus for the first time in his life, Hasari put on the beautiful pair of sandals received in his wife's dowry on the occasion of his marriage. His initiative was to prove disastrous. The sandals parted company with his feet at the first patch of burning asphalt, sucked off by the melting tar.

For six days the inhabitants of the City of Joy held out; then the hecatomb began. With lungs charred by the torrid air and bodies dried of all substance, those who suffered from tuberculosis and asthma and a whole host of babies began to die. The members of the Committee for Mutual Aid with Stephan Kovalski, Margareta, and Bandona at their head, ran from one end of the slum to another to help the most desperate cases. "Ran" was not really the word, because they too were compelled to move slowly for fear of falling unconscious after only a few steps. Under the torment of such temperatures, a body dehydrated in a matter of hours. "The slightest effort," Kovalski was to recount, "and all your pores exuded a flood of sweat that drenched you from head to toe. Then you experienced something like a shiver and almost instantaneously your head began to swim. So numerous were the victims of sunstroke and dehydration that the alleys were soon strewn with helpless people incapable of standing on their feet."

Strangely enough, it was the Pole who, although used to a more temperate climate, seemed the best able to resist the rigors of such blazing heat. With his burning metal crucifix dancing about on his bare chest, his waist and thighs swathed in a cotton *longhi*, and his head covered with an old straw hat, he looked like a Devil's Island convict. On the tenth day, however, the temperature broke the record for the last quarter of a century. On the thermometer at the old Hindu's tea shop, the mercury touched a hundred and fourteen degrees Fahrenheit in the shade. Taking into account the humidity, it was the equivalent of a hundred and thirty degrees in the sun. "The worst part about it was the perpetual dampness in which you were steeped," Kovalski would comment. "It soon caused a series of epidemics that decimated many families. On top of that, malaria, cholera, and typhoid made their appearance again. But it was gastroenteritis that claimed the most victims. It was quite capable of killing a man in less than twenty-four hours."

Yet this was only the beginning. Further trials lay in store for the Pole. Outbreaks of boils, carbuncles, whitlow, and mycosis hit the slum. Thousands of people caught them. The blight reached many other parts of Calcutta, and certain professions like those of the rickshaw *wallahs* and the *telagarhi wallahs* who were used to walking barefoot through the muck were particularly vulnerable. Because of the lack of dressings and antibiotics, such skin diseases spread like wildfire. Next door to Kovalski, the bodies of Mehboub's children became open sores. Mehboub himself, having returned home, fell victim to a very painful crop of carbuncles, which the priest had to lance with a penknife. At the end of March the temperature rose again, and as it did so something quite extraordinary happened. The flies began to die. Next it was the mosquitoes' turn; their eggs perished before they hatched. All the centipedes, scorpions, and spiders disappeared. The only vermin to survive in the City of Joy were the bugs. They came forth and multiplied as they made it a point to fill the vacuum left by the others. Every evening Kovalski gave a furious chase to them, yet still they flourished. Several of them had even taken refuge behind the picture of the Sacred Shroud. The frenzy with which he attacked and killed them gave the priest a measure of the lack of serenity to which he had been reduced. "After all that time in India, the result was bitterly disappointing. Despite the litanies of *Oms* and the example of detachment that Surya, the old Hindu opposite, set me, I was still rebelling against the inhuman conditions inflicted upon my brothers here."

One morning as he was shaving, the mirror cast back at him yet another shock. His cheeks were even more sunken and two deep furrows had appeared around his mouth and his mustache, accentuating the comical snub of his nose. His skin had assumed a waxlike hue. It was stretched over his bones like a piece of old shining oilcloth.

The real martyrs of the heat, however, were the workers in the thousands of little workshops and rooms scattered throughout the City of Joy and other slums. Lumped together with their machines in huts without ventilation, they were like the crews of sinking submarines. The women's conditions were pitiful too. Trammeled in their saris and veils at the back of hovels transformed into ovens, the least household chore made them perspire all the sweat their bodies could muster.

Oddly, in a heat so suffocating that it prostrated even the most robust, it was inactivity that was most arduous. "The heat seemed even more unbearable when you stopped moving," Kovalski was to say. "It came down on you like a leaden mantle, stifling you as it did so." To stop themselves from suffocating, people tried to create a minute turbulence of air on their faces by waving a piece of cardboard or newspaper back and forth. "The extraordinary thing was that they went on fanning themselves while they dozed, even while they slept." The Pole tried to do the same but as soon as sleep overtook him, his hand would let go of the improvised fan. He realized then that that kind of ability must be "an adaptation of the species, a reflex acquired in the course of generations of combating the rigors of the climate."

One night in April, Stephan Kovalski felt under his armpits and on his stomach the beginnings of an itch that within a few hours extended to every part of his body. "It felt as if millions of insects were gnawing away at me." The irritation became so intense that he could not resist scratching himself. Soon his entire epidermis was one big sore. Suffocating and drained of all strength, he remained prostrate in his room. A slum is not, however, like one of those Western dormitory cities where a man can disappear or die without his neighbor noticing. Here, the slightest deviation from the norm aroused curiosity.

The first person to be perturbed by the "Father's" failure to emerge was Nasir, Mehboub's eldest son, who lined up for him each morning at the latrines. He alerted his father who ran to inform Bandona. In a matter of minutes the whole neighborhood knew that Big Brother Stephan was sick. "Only a place where men live in such close contact with death could offer so many examples of love and solidarity," thought the priest on seeing Surya, the old Hindu from across the way, coming into his hut with a pot of tea and milk and a plate of biscuits. A few moments later Sabia's mother brought in a bowl of "lady's fingers," green vegetables that look like large beans. To give them a little more flavor, she had garnished them with a piece of gourd and some turnips, a real extravagance for a woman as poor as she. Bandona arrived next. The young Assamese girl diagnosed the ailment at a glance: it was indeed insects that were biting Stephan Kovalski, but not the bugs and other small creatures that generally infested the hovels in the City of Joy. The Pole was being devoured by tiny parasites called "acarus," whose invasion beneath the epidermis produced a painful skin disease that was ravaging the slum.

"Stephan *Daddah,*" clucked Bandona with a smile, "You've got scabies!"

At the end of April the thermometer rose several more degrees, and with this new assault a sound that usually formed part of the decor of the City of Joy was silenced. The only birds in the slum, the crows, ceased to caw. Some days later, their corpses were found on the roofs and in the compounds: A thin trace of blood trickled from their beaks. The heat had burst their lungs. The same fate was soon to befall other animals. First in their tens and then in their hundreds the rats began to die. In the hovel next to Kovalski's, Sabia's mother had stretched an old sari over the low ledge on which her youngest daughter who had chicken pox used to sleep. Finding a number of maggots on her child's forehead one day, the poor woman realized they must have dropped through a hole in the material. When she looked up at the framework, on a bamboo beam above her, she saw a dead rat.

It was at this juncture that the municipal workers responsible for emptying the latrines and cleaning the manure from the cattle sheds chose to strike. In a few days the slum was submerged beneath a lake of excrement. Blocked by mountains of dung from the cattle sheds, the open drains overflowed, spilling out a blackish, stinking stream. Into the torrid, static air, there soon rose an intolerable stench, borne upward on the smoke of the *chulas.* To top it all, the month of May ended with a terrible premonsoon storm, during which the level of the drains and the latrines rose by almost two feet in one night. The corpses of dogs, rats, scorpions, and thousands of cockroaches began to float around in the foul sludge. People even saw several goats and a buffalo drifting through the alleyways with bellies inflated like a balloon. The storm activated another unforeseen phenomenon: millions of flies hatched out. Naturally the floodwater invaded most of the hovels, transforming them into cesspools. Yet, in the very midst of the horror, there was always some kind of miracle to be found. The one which Stephan Kovalski experienced in the depths of his hut that Sunday in Pentecost took the form of "a little girl in a white dress, with a red flower in her hair, who picked her way through all that dung, with the regal air of a queen."

PART THREE

Calcutta My Love

49

A SHARP DECELERATION thrust him backward in his seat. The wing of the Boeing had just tipped toward the ground, unveiling a lush landscape of cultivated fields and coconut palms. After flying for two hours over the parched expanse of central India, it seemed to Max Loeb as if he were arriving in the middle of an oasis. Everywhere there was water: canals, shimmering pools, stretches of marshland covered with wild hyacinths and looking like floating gardens retained by narrow dikes. He thought of the Everglades of Florida and of the Mexican marshland borders of Xochimilco. The somber shapes of a host of buffalo emerged from out of the green. Then the airplane righted itself, revealing in one swoop the city.

It was an enormous city, devoid of either limits or horizon, traversed by a brownish colored river on which the ships at anchor looked like petrified ducks; a city with contours rendered indistinct by the shroud of smoke that blanketed its entanglement of roofs. The glittering outline of a gasoline tank, the silhouette of a crane on the riverbank, the metallic structure of a factory, pierced through the thick layer.

As the hostess announced that the aircraft was about to land in Calcutta, Max could just make out the Gothic bell tower of a cathedral, the stands of a racecourse, and red double-decker buses moving along an avenue set in the middle of a park. Finally the Boeing drew level with the runway and landed.

As soon as the door was opened—the furnace outside surged into the plane. "I felt as if I was being hit by a blast from a giant hair dryer," the American was to recount. "I recoiled under the shock and for a moment found myself struggling to get my breath back. When at last I did get out onto the gangway, I was blinded by fierce reflection and had to hang on to a rail."

A few moments later, in the confusion of the arrival terminal, Max spotted a garland of yellow flowers held aloft. It was Kovalski, brandishing the welcoming garland bought to welcome the American visitor in traditional Indian style. The two men recognized each other instinctively. Their greetings were effusive but brief.

"I suggest I take you to the Grand," said Kovalski, climbing into a taxi. "That's the local luxury hotel. I've never actually set foot inside it but I imagine it's a more suitable place than the City of Joy for a first encounter with the realities of this dear city."

The young American was perspiring more and more heavily. "Unless, of course, you want to plunge straight in," Kovalski added with a wink. "And I really mean plunge. The sewer workers are on strike again. You realize that what you're coming into isn't exactly Florida!"

Max checked a grimace. He was just considering the proposed alternatives when his gaze fell on his companion's arm. "What have you got there?" he asked, indicating the skin covered with scabs.

"I caught scabies."

The young doctor grunted. No doubt Kovalski was right: it would make better sense to take a little time to acclimatize himself. To go straight from a millionaire's playground to the depths of hell might well do irreparable damage. Max was realistic enough to be wary of that sort of traumatic shock. How many hulking men from the Peace Corps had had trouble adjusting to real poverty! It would be wiser to adapt himself bit by bit, in the comfort of an air-conditioned room, and with the help of a few generous glasses of Scotch and some mellow Montecristo cigars. After all, there was no real rush.

After a moment, however, Max turned abruptly to his companion. "I'd rather come with you to Anand Nagar," he announced.

An hour later, the new friends were facing each other across a table, under the flickering light of one of the slum's eating places. A fan, apparently on the point of expiring, was stirring up a torrid atmosphere, heavy with the smell of frying.

"Buffalo stew?" asked the American, daunted by the looks of the strange mixture one of the young serving boys had placed in front of him.

"Not real 'stew,'" corrected the Pole, mopping greedily at his plate. "Just the sauce. There isn't any meat in it. But the bones, skin, marrow, and gelatine have been so well simmered that it's full of protein. It's just like eating a New York sirloin. And for thirty *paisas* (three U.S. cents) you can hardly expect them to serve duck and olives, can you?"

Max made a face that spoke eloquently of his repugnance.

"I think you should realize that we were lucky to get a table," added Kovalski, eager to portray his slum in the best possible light. "This is actually the Maxim's of the neighborhood!"

The American stopped frowning but he continued to examine his plate, the squalor of the decor, and the clientele. About twenty or so customers were engaged in eating their meals amid the din of voices. They were all factory workers without families, or employees from the workshops, condemned to live near their machines because of power cuts. The establishment belonged to a fat, bald-headed Muslim called Nasser, who presided over his steaming caldron like a Buddha behind an incense burner. Nasser was the leader of the local Marxist-Communist party cell. No madness of the thermometer could shift him from his observation post. He oversaw a dozen employees, who called the Pole "Father," "Uncle," or *"Daddah* Stephan." Five of them were slum children, the eldest no more than eight years old. They worked from seven in the morning till midnight for their food and a monthly salary of ten rupees (one U.S. dollar). Barefooted, dressed in rags, they ran to fill buckets at the well, wash the tables, clean up, chase the flies away, serve the meals, sort out the customers. They were tireless and ever joyful little men. Three others in charge of cleaning the vegetables were mentally deficient. Nasser had picked them up when they were begging on the Great Trunk Road among trucks that only narrowly avoided flattening them. They lived on the restaurant's premises, sleeping on perches their employer rigged up for them out of planks suspended from the bamboo of the building framework. A blind man and a one-eyed man presided over the washing up. The blind man sported a small white goatee and sang verses from the Koran. Kovalski never went past the restaurant without going over to talk with him. "Like Surya, the old Hindu in the tea shop, that man had the gift of recharging my batteries. He gave off good vibrations."

How could anyone bring all these nuances to the attention of an American who had just landed from a different world? Kovalski knew from experience that the City of Joy was a place that had to be discovered in homeopathic doses—and which had, above all, to be deserved. It would be a long and difficult undertaking.

An exceptional event was to take place that first evening, however, which would accelerate the process and plunge Max Loeb into the very heart of his new surroundings. The Pole had given his companion a dessert to sample—a piece of *barfi*, the delicious Bengali nougat eaten in its thin sliver of silver paper—when a small man burst in, rushed over to Kovalski, threw himself at his feet, and spoke to him in Bengali, his hands joined together in a gesture of supplication. There was an air of urgency and deep emotion about him, and Max Loeb noticed that several fingers were missing from both his hands.

"How much do you know about obstetrics?" asked Kovalski as he got to his feet.

The American shrugged his shoulders.

"Only what I learned at school . . . not much."

"Come on! It's got to be better than nothing. It seems our friends here have been keeping a little welcoming surprise in store for you."

The American's astonishment delighted the Pole. "Yes, Doctor, they want to give you a brand-new baby!"

"And I'm supposed to help?"

"How did you guess?"

They hurried off behind the messenger, who was growing impatient in the street. Wading up to their calves through sludge, they moved cautiously forward. From time to time they stumbled on something soft—the carcass of a dog or a rat. Darkness falls early in the tropics and the night was as black as ink.

"Try not to fall into one of the main sewers," observed Kovalski, alluding to the six-foot-deep gutters that ran through the slum.

"It'd be one good way of making me miss the Florida beaches!"

"Provided you came out alive! In this filth, you'd die in seconds because of the gas."

For half an hour they picked their way along, past the astonished gazes of people who obviously wondered where these two *sahibs* might be going, through the muck, at such an hour.

"Duck your head!"

This warning saved the American from cracking his skull against a fat bamboo beam.

"You'll have to get used to bending down around here . . . Just bear in mind how good it is for your humility!"

Max bent his large body to enter a courtyard full of people; they were chattering noisily but the arrival of the two foreigners brought silence. With the fugacious light of a candle, the American made out noseless faces, the stumps of limbs moving about like marionettes. He realized that he was in the leper quarter.

The worst aggressor was the smell, an indefinable odor of rotten meat, of putrefying flesh. Like Stephan Kovalski on his first visit, Max could hardly believe his eyes. At the feet of those mutilated bodies, children were playing, splendid chubby children who looked as if they'd stepped straight out of an advertisement. A gray-haired old man led Kovalski and his companion toward a miserable room from which feeble groans were issuing. As they were about to cross the threshold, two very wrinkled old women tried to block their way, a flood of invectives bursting from their betel-reddened mouths.

"Midwives." explained the Pole, turning back to Max. "Our arrival is an insult to them."

The old man pushed the women unceremoniously out of the way and led the visitors inside. Someone brought a candle, whereupon Kovalski discovered a pale face with deep-sunken eyes that he recognized.

"Meeta!" he exclaimed, astonished.

The young wife of his crippled friend looked exhausted. She was bathed in a sea of blood. Only with difficulty did she open her eyes, but when she saw the turned-up nose and familiar forehead with its receding hairline above her, her mouth formed a faint smile.

"Stephan, Big Brother!" she sighed feebly.

Her withered hands reached out for him, as Max removed the rags that served as a compress.

"We'll have to hurry!" the American declared. "If not, they've both had it!"

Between the thighs of the leper woman he had just discovered the tip of a small blood-covered skull. The baby was wedged half-way out of the uterus. Its mother could not manage to push it out. Possibly it was dead already.

"Have you got anything to sustain her heart?" asked Max as he tried to find the young woman's pulse. Kovalski foraged in the bag that was his constant companion, in which he always carried a few emergency medicines, and took out a bottle.

"I've got some Coramine."

Max grimaced. "Nothing stronger? An intravenous cardiac stimulant?"

The question seemed so incongruous to the priest that, despite the circumstances, he could not help laughing.

"What do you think I am, a Miami drugstore?"

The American apologized with a slightly forced smile, and Kovalski asked for a cup of water into which he poured the medicine. Kneeling at the bedside of the young leper woman, he supported her head and helped her to drink slowly, involuntarily adding to her cup the droplets of sweat pouring off his own forehead. It was at least a hundred and ten degrees inside the hut.

"Tell her to start pushing again, as hard as possible," Max ordered.

Kovalski translated this into Bengali and Meeta contracted her body, panting with the effort. Tears of pain rolled down her cheeks.

"No, not like that! She's got to push *down*."

"Tell her to take a deep breath first and then push hard as she breathes out. Hurry!"

Max was dripping with sweat. He mopped his face and neck. A rancid taste rose up in his throat. Was it the heat, the buffalo stew that wouldn't stay down, the stench, or the sight of all those mutilated bodies? He was gripped by an incoercible desire to vomit. Seeing him turn as white as a sheet, Kovalski emptied the remainder of the bottle of Coramine into the cup from which the leper woman had just been drinking.

"Get this down quickly!"

Max started at the sight of the receptacle.

"Are you out of your mind?"

"You've got no choice. They're all looking at you. If you show your revulsion, they might turn nasty. You never know with lepers."

Seeing Max turn more livid in color, however, he said, "There's nothing to worry about. You can't catch her sort of leprosy. It's not contagious."

Max raised the cup to his lips, closed his eyes, and drank the contents down in a gulp. A little girl with black eyes made up with kohl came and fanned him with a piece of cardboard. He felt better. Bending over to examine the woman in labor more closely, he could see that the child was coming out the wrong way. It wasn't the upper part of the head that was emerging but the nape of the neck. Max knew that there was only one way of extricating the baby: he would have to turn it.

"Do you think the baby's still alive?" Kovalski asked.

"How can I tell without a stethoscope?"

The young doctor put his ear to the leper woman's stomach. He straightened up with an expression of disappointment.

"No heartbeat. But that doesn't mean much. He's turned the wrong way. For God's sake, tell her to push harder!"

The Coramine was taking effect; the leper woman's contractions were coming with increased vigor. Max knew that he must take advantage of every thrust. There could be no doubt about it; this was his last chance.

"Go around the other side," he said to Kovalski. "While I try to turn the baby, you massage her stomach from top to bottom to help the downward motion."

As soon as Kovalski had stepped over the body, the doctor slid his hand in behind the baby's neck. Meeta groaned at the movement of his fingers.

"Tell her to breathe deeply and to push evenly, without jerking."

All the leper woman's muscles tightened. Her head thrown back, her mouth contorted, she made a desperate effort.

What happened next might well seem improbable. The American's hand had just reached the baby's shoulder when two balls of

fur brushed against his head and rebounded on the stomach of the
mother. In the framework of the hovel, some of the rats had survived the heat wave. They were as large as cats. In his surprise, Max
withdrew his hand. Was it his abrupt movement or the shock of the
creatures' landing? One thing was certain: the baby's body righted
itself.

"Push, push, push!" cried Max. Ten seconds later, a bundle of
flesh enveloped in mucus and blood passed into his hands. He
lifted it up like a trophy.

It was a magnificent boy weighing at least six pounds. He saw
the baby's lungs inflate and his mouth open to let out a cry that
unleashed an amazing echo of joy in the courtyard of the compound. One of the midwives severed the cord with a sharp blow
and tied it off with a piece of jute. The other brought a basin to
begin the ablutions.

The American's heart missed a beat at the color of the infant's
clothing. "This people must be tougher than steel," he thought to
himself. Since no Brahmin would agree to enter into a leper compound, the honor of undertaking the first rite that follows the birth
of a child fell to Stephan Kovalski. Suddenly he felt someone
touching his feet and, looking down, found Anouar who had just
arrived on his piece of wood on wheels. Having wiped the dust off
Kovalski's sneakers, the crippled man then raised his stumps to his
forehead as a mark of respect. He looked overjoyed.

"Stephan, Big Brother, you've given me a son! A son!" Paralyzed with anxiety, Meeta's husband had kept out of the way until
this triumphal moment. Now he brought a bowlful of grains of rice.
Wedging it between his stumps, he raised it up as an offering to the
priest. "There," he said, "put the rice next to my boy, that the gods
may grant him a long and prosperous life." Then he took an oil
lamp from one of the midwives. According to ritual, its wick must
burn without interruption until the following day. If it went out,
the newborn baby would not live.

In his first letter to his fiancée, Max Loeb would report of the
demonstrations of enthusiasm that followed. "All the lepers were
overwhelmed with joy. It was impossible to restrain them.
Withered hands flung themselves round my neck. Pitted faces embraced me. Cripples brandished their crutches and clapped them
together like drumsticks. 'Daddah, Big Brother, God bless you!' the

people cried. Even the midwives joined in the celebration. Children brought biscuits and sweetmeats which we had to eat on pain of breaching the rules of hospitality. I was suffocating, nauseous. The smell of decay was even more unbearable in the courtyard than inside the hovel. Yet Stephan, my companion, seemed completely at home. He grasped the fingerless hands held out to him, while I confined myself to joining mine together in this beautiful gesture of greeting that I had seen people use at the airport. The cries of that newborn baby filled the night—my first night in Calcutta."

50

"THERE AREN'T just tigers and snakes in the jungle of Calcutta," mused Hasari Pal. "You also meet lambs and doves there, even among taxi drivers." The latter were generally real villains who had no sympathy whatsoever for human horses. Riding along like rajahs in their black-and-yellow motor palanquins, they never missed an opportunity to assert their superiority.

One day in a traffic jam, one of these "rajahs" had nudged Hasari and his carriage into a gutter. It was then that the miracle occurred. The driver, a small, bald man with a scar around his neck, actually stopped to apologize. This was no *sardarji* from the Punjab, with a rolled beard, a turban, and a dagger, but a Bengali like Hasari, originally from Bandel, a little place on the banks of the Ganges, some twenty miles from the Pals's village. He hastened to help Hasari extricate his rickshaw from the gutter and even suggested sharing a bottle of *bangla* with him. Next day he turned up during a torrential downpour. Abandoning their respective vehicles, the two men took refuge in a dive at the back of Park Street.

The taxi driver was called Manik Roy. He had started out as a bus driver, until one night a gang of *dacoits,* thieves who worked the highways, stopped him on the road. Having made his passengers get out and having relieved them of their possessions, the robbers then proceeded to slit their throats. By what miracle Manik had been found still alive, the following day, he could not say, but as a reminder of that horrific night, he still bore an impressive scar on his neck. This was how he had come to be nicknamed *Chomotkar* which means literally, "Son of Miracle."

In Hasari's eyes that man was indeed the "son of miracle," but for quite another reason. Instead of gripping the shafts of a rickshaw, his hands caressed a steering wheel; instead of treading asphalt and holes, his feet traveled deftly between three small rubber pedals; instead of straining and sweating, he earned his children's rice seated calmly on the seat of a chariot more noble than Arjuna's. A taxi! What rickshaw puller had not dreamed that one day the four arms of the god Viswakarma would gently touch his rattling cart and transform it into one of those black-and-yellow vehicles that streaked through the avenues of Calcutta.

One day Son of Miracle invited Hasari for a ride in his taxi. He could not have offered him a finer gift. "It was like going off to Sri Lanka with the army of monkeys," Hasari was to say, "or inviting me to take my seat in the chariot of Arjuna, king of the Pandavas." What a treat it was to settle himself on a seat so well upholstered that the back sank in at the slightest pressure of his body; to discover before his eyes all kinds of dials and pointers that provided information about the state of health of the engine and other parts. Son of Miracle put a key into a slot and instantly there was a joyful backfire beneath the hood. Then he depressed one of the pedals with his foot and maneuvered a lever under the steering wheel. "It was fantastic," Hasari would say. "Those simple actions were enough to set the taxi in motion. It was fantastic to think that all you had to do to get it going and then give it more and more speed was to press the toe of your foot on a tiny little pedal." Dumbfounded, Hasari watched his companion. "Could I, too, manage those actions?" he wondered. "Had Son of Miracle already been a taxi driver in a previous incarnation? Or had he only learned to drive a car in his present existence?" The driver noticed his companion's perplexity.

"A taxi is much easier to drive than your carriage," he affirmed. "Look, one simple touch of this pedal and you stop dead." The vehicle came to such an abrupt halt that Hasari was flung against the windshield. Son of Miracle burst out laughing.

The rickshaw puller had discovered another world, a world that called on mechanical slaves not muscles, a world in which there was no such thing as fatigue and where you could talk, smoke, and laugh while you worked. Son of Miracle knew all the high spots, the luxury restaurants, nightclubs, and hotels in the

Park Street area. He was in business with a whole network of hotel procurers who kept the best fares for him. These middlemen were themselves in partnership with doormen and waiters. The system worked like a dream.

Son of Miracle picked up the day's first two clients in front of the Park Hotel. They were foreigners. They asked to be driven to the airport. "Then something happened that gave me quite a shock," Hasari was to recount. "Before moving off, my friend got out of his taxi, went around and tipped up a sort of small, metal flag on a box affixed to the left of the car windshield. On this box I discovered a sight that seemed so extraordinary that I couldn't take my eyes off it. As we went along, every five or six seconds a new number wrote itself up on the box. I could virtually see the rupees tumbling into my companion's pocket! Only the god Viswakarma could have invented such a machine, a machine that manufactured rupees and made its owner richer by the instant. It was incredible. We rickshaw *wallahs* never saw money falling into our pockets like that. Each of our journeys had a corresponding fare that was fixed in advance. You could talk it over and ask a little more or accept a little less but the idea that all you had to do was press on a pedal and rupees would rain down on you like wild roses on a windy day was as inconceivable as that of bank notes growing in a paddy field." When Son of Miracle stopped his taxi outside the airport, the meter was showing a sum that seemed so astronomical to Hasari that he began to wonder whether it really represented rupees at all; but it did. That one journey paid a full thirty-five rupees, almost as much as Hasari earned in half a week. On the way back, Son of Miracle stopped off at a large garage on Dwarka Nath Road.

"When you've saved up enough rupees," he announced, "this is where you'll come for your nirvana."

The passport to this nirvana was a small booklet with a red cover and two pages containing stamps, an identity photograph, and a fingerprint. Son of Miracle was right: this slip of cardboard was the brightest jewel of which a rickshaw puller could dream, the key that would enable him to rise above his karma and open the door to a new incarnation. This document was a West Bengal motor vehicle driver's license, and the garage was the most important driving school in Calcutta, the Grewal motor training school.

Inside, a spacious yard harbored trucks, buses, and instruction cars, and a kind of classroom with benches under a covered area. On the walls, pictures depicted the various parts of a car, traffic signs found on the streets and highways, and sketches of every possible accident. There was also a vast colored map of Calcutta including a whole list of routes for the information of prospective taxi drivers. There were so many things to attract his attention that Hasari didn't know where to look first. What humble rickshaw puller could ever hope one day to cross the threshold of this dream school? To follow a course of instruction and pass the test involved an impossible expense, almost six hundred rupees, more than four months' worth of money invoices to his family back home in the village.

Yet, as he climbed back into the taxi, Hasari Pal felt as if that dream was suddenly tattooed upon his flesh. "I shall try to get my full strength back to work even harder. I shall reduce my food to save even more, but one day, I swear on the heads of my sons Manooj and Shambu, I shall pack my rickshaw bell away in the box with our festival clothes and I shall hand back my shafts and my old crate to Musafir and install myself with my beautiful red booklet behind the steering wheel of a black-and-yellow taxi. Then I shall listen with pride to the rupees raining down in the meter like the fat raindrops of a monsoon storm."

51

"IT'S NOT EXACTLY the Miami Hilton," Kovalski apologized, "but just keep telling yourself that people here live twelve to fifteen into rooms twice as small as this."

Max grimaced as he inspected the lodgings the Pole had found for him in the very heart of the City of Joy. Yet by comparison with many others, it was indeed a princely lodging, complete with a brand new *charpoy*, a cupboard, a table, two stools, a bucket, a jug, and on the wall a calendar with the face of a fine, chubby baby. The room even boasted a window opening onto the alleyway. Another of its advantages derived from the fact that the floor had been raised about one foot and was thus, in theory at least, protected from the monsoon floods and from the currently overflowing drains.

"And the john?" asked the American, anxiously.

"The latrines are at the end of the alleyway," Kovalski replied apologetically. "But it's better not to use them too often at the moment."

Max's perplexed expression amused Kovalski. With a straight face he added, "And the best way not to have to go too often is to eat nothing but rice. That way your intestines are bound up with concrete."

The arrival of Bandona interrupted their joking. Max was charmed by the Oriental beauty of the young Assamese girl. In her bright red sari she looked like a princess in a miniature painting.

"Welcome to Anand Nagar, Doctor," she said shyly, offering the American a bouquet of jasmine.

Max breathed in the very strong scent exuded by the flowers

and for a second, he forgot his surroundings, the noise, and the smoke from the *chulas* that was stinging his eyes. He was transported thousands of miles away. The perfume was identical to that of the tuberose bushes, which in springtime embalmed the terrace of his house in Florida. "How strange it was," he would recall, "to smell that fragrance in the middle of so much shit."

It took the young woman only a few minutes to make the American's room more welcoming. Moving about as noiselessly as a cat, she unrolled a mat on the strings of the *charpoy*, lit several oil lamps, set alight some incense sticks, and put the flowers in a copper pot on the table. This done, she looked up at the ceiling.

"And you up there, I'm ordering you to let the doctor sleep. He's come from the other end of the world and he's *very* tired."

That was how Max discovered that he was, in fact, to share his room. He would have rather done it with this pretty Oriental girl, or with some goddess of the *Kama Sutra*, rather than with the furry creatures he had already encountered in the leper woman's house. Suddenly a kind of croaking made itself heard. Bandona laid a hand on Max's arm with an expression of joy that brought crinkles to her almond eyes.

"Listen, Doctor," she urged, straining her ears. "It's the *tchik-tchiki*. He's greeting you."

Max looked up at the roof and saw a green lizard looking down at him.

"That's the best omen you could have," announced the young woman. "You will live for a thousand years!"

*

Since the Mafia boss' Molotov cocktails had reduced to ashes the building in which Kovalski had hoped to nurse the lepers and set up an operating room for other inhabitants of the slum, it fell to the American's room to become during daytime the City of Joy's first dispensary. From seven in the morning till ten at night and sometimes even later, this single room was to become reception room, waiting room, consultation room, nursing ward, and operating theater all combined, a room full of suffering and of hope for several hundred of the seventy thousand slum dwellers. "The setup was primitive in the extreme," Max was to say. "My table and

bed were used for both examining and treating. There was no
sterilizer and my instruments were reduced to three or four tweezers and scalpels contained in my student's case. God, this was far
away from our Bel Air clinic in Miami!" The stock of bandages,
gauze, and cotton was on the other hand rather well supplied.
Kovalski had even passed on to Max a gift from one of his Belgian
lady admirers: several boxes of sterilized compresses for the treatment of burns. The priest had spent three agonizing days discussing with the customs officials before obtaining their release without paying four hundred rupees in duty and the baksheesh
solicited. It was medicines that they lacked most. All the American
had at his disposal was contained in a small metallic trunk: a small
quantity of sulphone for the lepers, Ryfomicine for tuberculosis
patients, quinine for malaria, a small stock of ointments for skin
diseases, and a few vitamins for those children who were suffering
most acutely from malnutrition. Finally there were about ten antibiotic tablets for cases of virulent infection. "There was nothing
to brag about," Max would recount, "but as Kovalski kept telling
anyone prepared to listen, love would make it up for all."

The Indian word-of-mouth telephone was a supremely efficient news system. No sooner had the dispensary opened, than the
entire slum knew of its existence. In the alleys, compounds, and
workshops people talked of nothing else but of the "rich Big
Brother" who had come from America to alleviate the misery of
the poor. The City of Joy had received the visit of a "great sor-
cerer," a "big *daktar,*" a "worker of miracles," who was going to
cure the inhabitants of all their ailments. Kovalski allocated
Bandona to assist Max in his task. It would take someone as shrewd
as the young Assamese girl to identify those who were really sick
from those who were pretending, and to sift out the urgent and
most extreme cases, the chronically ill and the incurable.

A tidal wave! Dozens of mothers rushed to the dispensary with
children covered in boils, abscesses, anthrax, alopecia, scabies, sick
from every possible disease caused by the heat wave and the staph-
ylococci which ran rampant about the City of Joy. At least two out
of every three children were affected by gastroenteritis and parasites. What a training ground it was for a young doctor, with the
additional premium of dealing with many diseases that were virtu-

ally unknown in the West! Without the aid of Bandona, Max would never even have been able to identify them.

"You see those chalky traces on the pupils, Big Brother Max," she would say, showing him the eyes of some small child. "That's a sign of xerophthalmia. In one or two years this kid will be blind. They don't know that where you come from."

Max Loeb was out of his depth, drowned, submerged. Nothing he had learned at school had prepared him for this confrontation with the physiological poverty of the third world at its very worst. Manifestations such as eyes that were extremely yellow, chronic weight loss, painfully swollen ganglions in the throat corresponded with nothing he knew or recognized. Yet these were the symptoms of the most widespread disease in India, the one that caused by far the most mortality: tuberculosis. The National Institute for Tuberculosis affirmed that some two hundred and sixty million Indians were exposed to it.*

During the first week, the American examined and treated as best he could 479 sick people. "They arrived in an interminable, pathetic procession," he was to recount. "Sometimes there was a touch of folklore about it. Most of the children were naked with a thin cord about their loins, holding a small bell at the level of their navel. It made examining them by auscultation more practical, but made treatment less easy because their little bodies slipped through your fingers like eels. Many of the women were tattooed, some of them from head to toe. They turned up decked out with all their wealth: a single bangle made out of colored glass or real jewels in some delicate setting, earrings, a semi-precious stone pinned to a nostril, gold or silver ornaments on their wrists, fingers, ankles, and occasionally their toes. Sometimes they wore necklets ornamented with religious symbols: for Muslims a miniature Koran or a crescent; for Hindus a Shiva's trident; for Sikhs a small silver sword; for Christians a cross or a medallion. As for the animists, they wore all kinds of other gris-gris and amulets.

"The ocher and bright red dye with which the women and young girls plastered their hands and feet, together with the stains from the red betel chewed not only by men but also by many women to stifle their hunger, didn't make my diagnoses any easier.

* *India Today*, November 30, 1982.

How was I supposed to distinguish changes in skin color or inflam-
mation of the mucous membranes in the mouth or throat under all
that dye? Some patients tried to make up for it by helping me a bit
too much—like this wizened old man who obligingly coughed up a
great clot of blood into his hand and showed it to me with supreme
satisfaction. Oh, the millions of bacilli that were swimming about
in that palm! From my very first day, I strove to apply a few rudimentary principles of asepsis and hygiene. It was by no means easy.
I didn't even have a washbasin to disinfect my hands between each
patient. And here, germs, sickness, and death were so much a part
of everyday life! I saw one woman wipe the running ulcer suppu-
rating on her leg with a corner of her sari. Another spread the
ointment I had just applied so delicately to her wound with the flat
of her hand.

"Fortunately, there were comic interludes too, like the time
when a jet of urine from one infant hit me straight in the face. His
mother tried to dry me quickly by rubbing my eyes, mouth, and
cheeks energetically with the tip of her veil. Then there was the
hilarious character who turned up with a prescription that was
several years old, on which Bandona read that, as he was suffering
from a general cancer in its terminal stages, he should take six
aspirin tablets a day. Or this other man who arrived, bearing with
as much solemnity as if he were transporting a sacred picture of
god Shiva, an X ray of his lung cavities that was at least twenty years
old.

"But it was the tragic cases that were most prevalent. One day
I was brought a little girl whose body was atrociously burned all
over. A locomotive had released its steam when she was picking up
remnants of coal along the railway line. On another occasion, a
young Hindu girl showed me a light patch on her pretty face. The
mere prick of a needle in the center of the patch was enough for
Bandona to be able to diagnose an illness hardly studied in the
American medical faculties: leprosy. Again there was the young
father of a family who was suffering from acute syphilis. I had to
explain to him, via my young Assamese assistant, the dangers of
contagion involved for his wife and children. Or this mother who
brought me a lifeless bundle of flesh to which diphtheria had
reduced her baby. Not to mention all those who came because a
miracle effected by the 'great white *daktar*' was their only hope:

people with cancer, severe heart conditions, madmen, blind men, the mute, the paralyzed, the deformed.

"Most unbearable of all, and something I thought I would never get used to, was the sight of those rickety babies with their inflated stomachs, tiny monstrosities placed on my table by their supplicant mothers. At a year or eighteen months they weighed not so much as nine pounds. They were suffering so acutely from deficiency that their fontanels hadn't closed. Deprived of calcium, the bone structure of their heads had been deformed and their dolichocephalic features gave them all the look of Egyptian mummies. With this degree of malnutrition, the majority of their brains' gray cells had probably been destroyed. Even if I did manage to pull them through, they would most probably be idiots—medically classified idiots."

Max was subsequently to learn that all those little victims only represented a sad sample of an affliction that was striking the country as a whole. A great Indian scientific authority on the subject, the director of the Nutrition Foundation of India, asserts that India is producing today more and more "subhumans" because of inadequate nourishment.* According to this expert, the health of generations to come will find itself in jeopardy. A hundred and forty million Indians at least, that is, nearly half the population of the United States, are likely to suffer from malnutrition. Of the twenty-three million children born each year, only three million, according to this same authority, have a chance of reaching adulthood in good health. Four million are condemned to die before the age of eight or to become unproductive citizens because of mental and physical defects. Because of nutritional deficiencies, 55 percent of all children under the age of five will manifest psychic and neurological problems occasioning behavioral disorders, while several million adults suffer from goiters, causing similar disorders.

On the second day, a young Muslim woman in a black tunic and veil placed a baby wrapped in a piece of rag on Max's table. Fixing on the doctor a wild look, she unfastened her tunic, bared her chest, and cupped her two breasts in her hands.

"They're dry!" she exclaimed. "Dry! Dry!"

* Dr. C. Gopalan, "The Nutrition Factor," *Indian Express*, January 9, 1983.

Then her gaze fell upon the calendar hanging on the wall. At the sight of the chubby baby displayed on the piece of cardboard she let out a shriek. "Nestlé makes your children healthy," the slogan on it read. The young mother hurled herself at the calendar and tore it to shreds. At that moment another woman burst in. Pushing aside the young Muslim mother, she rushed at the American and thrust her baby into his arms.

"Take him!" she wailed. "Take him away to your country! Save him!"

It was an inconceivable action that translated the enormity of the despair these mothers felt. "For nowhere else," Kovalski would say, "had I seen women adore their children in quite the way that they did here, where they deprived themselves, sacrificed themselves, gave their life's blood that their infants might live. No, it was not possible: so much love could not be lost."

As for Max Loeb, he was sure that for the rest of his life he would see "those flames of distress burning in the eyes of the mothers of the City of Joy, as they witnessed impotently their children's agony." That evening Calcutta provided him with yet another unforgettable memory. "CALCUTTA DOCTORS BRING A TEST-TUBE BABY INTO THE WORLD" announced with a huge headline a local newspaper.

52

"THEY SAY THE COBRA always strikes twice," Hasari Pal was to recount. "In other words, no disaster occurs on its own. I already had the red fever in my lungs. And now it was another blow. Early one morning, I was awoken by the noise of an engine and the grinding of a caterpillar. 'I'll bet those bastards have come,' I said to my wife as I got up."

Adjusting his *longhi*, he rushed outside. Already the whole slum was in an uproar. For several days there had been rumors about eviction. The "bastards" had indeed arrived: a bulldozer and two vans bursting with policemen armed with *lathis* and tear-gas cylinders. A black Ambassador car arrived to join them, out of which stepped two *babus* in *dhotis*, wearing waistcoats over their shirts. They conferred with the police officer in charge and then, after a moment, advanced upon the group of slum dwellers.

The elder of the two, who was holding some papers in his hand, was the first to speak. "The municipality has directed us to carry out the destruction of your settlement," he announced.

"For what reason?" asked a voice.

The *babu* appeared disconcerted. He was not accustomed to the poor asking questions.

"Because your settlement is impeding construction work on the future subway line."

The inhabitants looked at one another, flabbergasted.

"What is this 'subway'?" Hasari asked his neighbor Arun, who claimed to have traveled as far away as Afghanistan.

Arun was compelled to admit that he did not know. The *babu* consulted his watch and began to speak again.

"You have two hours to get your things together and leave. After that . . ."

Without going to the trouble of providing more expansive explanations, he gestured toward the bulldozer. The official had spoken without raising his voice, as if he had come to communicate the most banal information. Hasari observed his neighbors' responses. They said not a word, and the silence was so surprising that even the *babus* appeared embarrassed by it. Without a doubt, they had anticipated protestations, threats, some kind of reaction. "But no. They had come to chuck us out just as you would turn out rats and cockroaches, and we—we said nothing," would recall Hasari. "True enough: no one could really miss the slum. All the same, in the pyramid of disaster, that heap of shacks was a better bargain than the pavement. Here at least people had a piece of canvas and some scraps of cardboard over their heads."

In fact the lack of reaction was due to quite another reason. "We simply had no more resources," Hasari would add. "This city had finally broken our capacity to react and in this rotten tenement we had no one to come to our defense—no union, no political leader. As for those thugs of the Mafia who had managed so well to extract rent from us, they were nowhere to be seen. And why not admit it also: we had all been hit by so many blows that one blow more or less didn't really matter. That vicious wheel of karma never lost its grip."

The two *babus* joined their hands in farewell and got back into their car, leaving the occupants alone to face the police and the bulldozer. It was then that something totally astonishing happened. Hasari saw his neighbor Arun grab the bamboo beams that supported the roof of his shack and run at the forces of law and order. With this signal something snapped; the initial stupor lifted, everyone felt a sense of rage wash over them. One by one, the shanties collapsed as a deluge of building materials hit the police. Several policemen fell to the ground, whereupon the fury of the assailants redoubled. They fell on the policemen, beating them with planks, bricks, and tiles. Women and children cheered the men on. Hasari saw someone take a nail and puncture the eyes of an injured policeman. He saw one of his neighbors sprinkle another with a bottle of kerosene and set fire to him. Some of the cops tried to shoot at the mob before retreating to their vans, but other occupants of the slum ran after them with bottles of gasoline; the police vans took fire. Then someone threw a bottle at the bulldozer and it exploded. A cloud of blackish smoke enveloped the battlefield. When the fighting finally stopped, people paused to survey the extent of the disaster. Several badly burned policemen lay huddled in the middle of a chaos that defied description.

As for the slum itself, it was as if a cyclone had reduced it to dust. There was no need now for a bulldozer; the anger of the poor had done the job, and work on the subway could begin as planned.

Hasari, his wife, and children prepared for a hasty escape before the police returned in full force. They had lost virtually everything. Hardly had they reached the first junction when the shriek of whistles and sirens filled the sky. Like hundreds of other fugitives in search of a patch of pavement, Hasari and his family could do nothing now but hope for the mercy of the gods. "But that day the gods of Calcutta had run out of ears."

All morning they wandered through the city before they eventually ended up near the portal of a church, on the pavement in Lower Circular Road. There, a makeshift settlement of several families belonging to an Adivassi tribe lived. The Adivassis, who came from the North of India, were the country's aborigines, and their plight was a particularly wretched one. The site in question had the advantage of being near to a fountain. Above all, however, it was close to Park Circus, where Hasari went to pick up his rickshaw each morning. The puller with whom he shared his vehicle was a young Muslim with fuzzy hair who came from Bihar. His name was Ramatullah, and around his neck there hung a miniature Koran on a small chain. He worked from four until midnight and sometimes even later if he could find passengers. In order to save as much money as possible for his family, he slept on his carriage, his head and legs dangling over either side of the shafts. It was not very comfortable, but at least while he was doing that, no one could steal the rickshaw.

Ramatullah was a marvelous companion. Ever since he had seen Hasari coughing and spitting blood, he had made frequent gestures of friendship. If Hasari did not turn up in the morning at the usual time, he would run all the way to Harrington Street to collect the two children his friend was supposed to take to school every day, because he knew that to lose a "contract" like that, so sought after by the other pullers, would have been a catastrophe. In the afternoons he would come a little earlier to save Hasari the fatigue of a last run, and each time he did so, he gave the sick man the money he had earned in his place.

By the frightened look with which Ramatullah greeted him that morning, Hasari understood he must have really harbored a dejected expression. He told Ramatullah about the battle in the slum and the eviction of its residents; but nothing, it seemed, would divert the compassionate eyes of the Muslim from his friend's face.

"You ought to go and see a doctor at once," Ramatullah said. "You're as green as an underripe lemon. Go on, get in the rickshaw. Today, you are the first *marwari* of the morning!"

"A featherweight *marwari!* You're in luck," observed Hasari, settling himself on the seat.

Ten minutes later, the Muslim steered his Hindu friend into the cramped shop of a specialist in Ayurvedic medicine in Free School Street. Two other patients were already waiting on a bench. The doctor, a fat, bald man in an impeccable white *dhoti,* was seated at the rear of the room in an armchair. It was as if a *zamindar* or a rajah were giving an audience. On shelves that ran around the room, all the pharmacopoeia of India's Ayurvedic medicine, a range of jars and bottles full of herbs and powders, were on display. After each consultation the doctor would get up, select several jars, and go and sit at a table behind a set of scales similar to those used by jewelers, where, after weighing each ingredient with meticulous care, he made up mixtures.

When it came to Hasari's turn, the physician considered him with a skeptical air and scratched his bald head. All he asked Hasari was how old he was. Then he took down at least ten jars from his shelves. It took him a long time to work out his different preparations. In addition to various pills and tablets, he also concocted a potion to restore Hasari's strength. In payment he asked for twenty rupees. This price was considerably more expensive than a pavement quack's would have been, but Ramatullah assured his companion that there could be nothing better than the drugs of this man of science when it came to getting rid of the red fever. He knew two friends who had been cured by him. "I pretended to believe him, but in the bottom of my heart, I knew there was no cure for the red fever. The fact that it had taken a diehard like Ram Chander was proof enough."

On his way back to Park Circus, Hasari heard the squeak of tires beside him. It was Son of Miracle who had been driving past in his taxi. He had a wild expression on his face, as if he had just downed three bottles of *bangla*. "When you can hardly stand up and your morale is really bottom low, suddenly meeting up with a familiar face smiling at you is as comforting as seeing Surya's ball of fire appear after a week of the monsoon," Hasari was to say.

"Just the person I was looking for!" his friend called out. "I've got great news for you, but first you'll have to buy me a drink."

Son of Miracle swept Hasari and Ramatullah into an alley behind Free School Street where he knew a clandestine drinking den. There he ordered up two bottles of *bangla*. After his first glass his eyes began to sparkle.

"One of my neighbors is leaving my slum and going back to his village," Son of Miracle said at last. "So his room will be free. It's a solidly built room, with a real roof, walls, and a door. I thought of you right away . . ."

"I didn't even hear the rest," Hasari would remember. "My vision suddenly blurred and rickshaw bells began to jangle furiously in my head. Then I saw the blurred shape of a man burning like a torch and I felt my skull knock against something hard. I don't know how long it lasted, but when I opened my eyes, I was stretched out on the ground and above me I saw the crimson faces of Son of Miracle and Ramatullah. Their heavy hands were slapping me as hard as they could to bring me back to life."

53

OF ALL THE ANIMALS and insects with which Max Loeb had to share his new lodgings, he found none more repugnant than the cockroaches. There were hundreds, thousands of them—creatures that managed to resist all insecticides and devoured absolutely everything, including plastic. By day they remained more or less inactive, but as soon as night fell they came out in full force, moving about at breathtaking speed, zigzagging in all directions. They had no respect for any part of your body, not even your face. Hardiest of all were the black beetles. They had a more elongated shape and a smaller girth than the fat brown cockroaches. Their only enemies were the giant hairy spiders that clung like octopuses to the most substantial pieces of bamboo in the framework.

On the second evening Max was able to witness a performance that was to become one of his main sources of evening entertainment. By the light of his lamp he spotted a lizard as it launched itself onto a beam in hot pursuit of a beetle. On the brink of capture, the insect made a fatal mistake and took refuge under a spider's stomach. Max then saw the spider seize the intruder with its legs and sink the two hooks with which its abdomen was armed into the beetle's body. In a few minutes it had emptied the beetle like an egg. Executions of this kind were frequent. Every morning Max had to shake his pajamas to rid himself of the empty carcasses of beetles that had fallen on him in the course of the night.

Shortly after his arrival, Max Loeb was to be the victim of an incident that would enable him to get to know his neighbors far better than if he had spent a whole year with them. One evening he was sprawled out on his string bed reading, when he noticed a

small creature, slightly bigger than a grasshopper, moving swiftly
down the pisé wall next to him. He hardly had time to leap to his
feet before the little beast had sunk its stinger into his ankle. Max
let out a shriek, more of fear than of real pain, and crushed the
aggressor with his sandal. It was a scorpion. He immediately put a
tourniquet around his thigh to prevent the poison spreading, but
the precaution had hardly any effect. Overwhelmed by violent
nausea, icy sweats, shivering, and hallucinations, he collapsed onto
his bed.

"I can't remember anything about the hours that followed,"
he would recount. "All I can recall is the sensation of a damp cloth
on my forehead and the vision of Bandona's almond eyes above
me. The young Assamese girl was smiling at me and her smile was
very reassuring. There was a crowd in my room and it was broad
daylight. People were busy all around me. Some were massaging
my legs, children were fanning me with pieces of cardboard, others
were making me sniff little balls of cotton impregnated with a
strange smell that was nauseatingly pungent. Others brought me
cups of potions, and yet others were advising goodness knows
what."

The incident provided an opportunity for the entire neighborhood to get together and talk, to comment and demonstrate its
friendship. What surprised the young American most, however,
was that no one seemed to take the matter very seriously. Here a
scorpion sting was something quite banal. Someone explained to
Max that he had been stung seven times. Another man exposed his
thigh, repeating "Cobra! Cobra!" in a way that suggested that a
scorpion sting was nothing. Yet those small creatures killed between ten and twenty slum people every year, particularly children.

"How did you get to know about it?" Max asked Bandona.

"Big Brother Max, when your neighbors didn't see you go out
to attend to 'the call of nature,' they wondered whether you were
sick. When they didn't see you at the fountain, they thought you
must be dead, so they came to get me. You can't hide anything here
—not even the color of your soul."

54

To say that Stephan Kovalski received the news with transports of joy would be an exaggeration, but he was convinced that it was a sign from God, confirming the meaning of his mission at a time of distress. It came at an instant in his life when this man who had shared everything and accepted everything had begun to feel his strength deserting him. To add to the excessive heat, the strike of municipal workers who cleaned the latrines had transformed the City of Joy into a cesspool more difficult than ever to tolerate. At night, desperate for sleep in the oppressive humidity, Kovalski dreamed of the vast wheat plains of his native Poland or of the deserted beaches of Brittany. He dreamed of space, of rural fragrances, forests, flower beds, and animals in the wild. When he first arrived in the slum he had plugged up his ears in order not to hear the cries of suffering. Now he found himself yearning to veil his face in order that he might no longer see or feel anything. In short, he was in the depths of a depression, and even the presence of Max Loeb did not alleviate it. It was at this point that Ashish and Shanta came to tell him the news.

"Stephan, Big Brother, we've found you a room in our compound," announced Shanta in a trembling voice. "No one wants to live in it because the previous owner hanged himself from the framework. People call it the 'hanged man's room.' But it's right next door to ours."

Kovalski was being offered a room in one of those little courtyards where something like a hundred people lived together, were born and died together, ate and starved together, coughed, spat, urinated, defecated, and wept together, where they loved each other, insulted each other, helped and hated each other, where they suffered together and hoped together. For a long time now Kovalski had been wanting to leave the relative anonymity of his alleyway to go and live in a compound, to devote himself even more completely to others. Now, Ashish and Shanta had arranged everything. As ritual required, they presented their protégé to the senior man in the compound, a former sailor and a Hindu who had been stranded in Calcutta by a drinking bout during shore leave. Krishna Jado had lived in Anand Nagar for twenty-seven years. His extreme thinness, his wheezing breath and husky voice betrayed the fact that he had tuberculosis. The head man in his turn introduced the Pole to the other tenants, who welcomed him warmly. As Shanta commented, "A Father *Sahib* landing in a compound, it was like Santa Claus coming to you."

Eleven families, nearly eighty people, lived in a rectangle, about thirty-five feet long and nine feet wide. They were all Hindus. That was the rule: people of different religions avoided cohabiting in the same compound, where the slightest difference in custom could assume major proportions. How could it be conceivable for a Muslim family to grill a piece of beef on their *chula* immediately next door to the devotee of a religion that declared the cow as sacred? The reverse was true for pork. In a society where religious practices were endowed with such importance, it was better to forestall any potential conflicts. Every hour of every day was the opportunity for some form of festival or celebration. Hindus, Sikhs, Muslims, and Christians seemed to compete with each other in their imagination and fervor. Aside from the major religious festivals, the births and the marriages, all kinds of other commemorative celebrations kept the compounds in a perpetual state of excitement. One day it might be a girl's first period that was being celebrated; the next, all the girls who were due to be married might be paying tribute to the lingam of the god Shiva, to ask him for a husband as good as he. At some other time a prospective mother would be celebrating the first month of her pregnancy, or then again a huge *puja* might be made, complete with Brahmin, musicians, and banquet to glorify the moment when a baby received his first mouthful of rice from the hands of his father.

The ceremony that was in full swing when Stephan Kovalski arrived at his new dwelling was no less astonishing. Assembled behind the well, some fifteen women were singing canticles at the top of their voices. Metal dishes placed before them overflowed with offerings: mounds of rice grains, bananas, flower petals, incense sticks. Noticing the surprise of his new tenant, the head man explained: "They are imploring Sitola to save little Onima."

The child had caught chicken pox and Sitola is the goddess of variola. All the occupants of the compound joined in the *puja*. They had embarked on a three-day fast. After, no one would eat either eggs or meat—insofar as they ate them anyway—or any other food that wasn't boiled, until the child was better. None of the women would wash or hang out her linen on pain of annoying the deity. Thus there was no *bara khana**to celebrate Stephan Kovalski's arrival, but the warmth of his reception compensated for the absence of the traditional celebratory meal. All the other residents of the compound waited for the new arrival with garlands of flowers. Shanta and the neighboring women had decorated the threshold and floor of his room with *rangoli*, the magnificent geometric compositions designed to bring good fortune. In the middle of them, Kovalski read a message of welcome from his brothers in the City of Joy. It was a sentence quoted from the great Bengali poet, Rabindranath Tagore, "You are invited to the festival of this world and your life is blessed." He made his entrance escorted by many of the neighbors from his former home. Old Surya, little Sabia's mother, the coal man from across the way, Nasir, Mehboub's eldest son, most of the adults and children from the alleyway where he had spent the last hard years were there, weeping freely. Although distances in the slum were only small, their Big Brother Stephan might just as well have been leaving for another planet. It was perhaps Sabia's mother who gave the most articulate expression to the grief they all felt: "Before you go away, give us your blessing, Big Brother Stephan. In a way, from now on we shall all be orphans."

The priest raised his hand and slowly made the sign of the cross over their heads, repeating softly in an undertone the words of the Beatitudes, "Blessed are you, for you are the children of my Father, you are the light of the world."

* Banquet.

Then he made his way to "the hanged man's room" to put down his knapsack and his rolled mat made out of rice straw.

"Is that all you own?" asked one woman, surprised.

He intimated that this was the case. Immediately one of his neighbors appeared with a stool, another brought him some cooking utensils, a third wanted to give him his *charpoy* but this Kovalski declined. He wanted to continue living as one of the poorest of the poor. From this point of view his new lodgings were the perfect answer to his wishes. "During the fifteen months that no one had lived there, a colony of rats had settled in. Small ones, fat ones, enormous males with tails one foot long, baby rats that emitted strident cries—there were dozens of them. They infested the framework, ran down the walls, ferreted in all the corners. Their droppings covered the floor. Nothing seemed to daunt them. By some miracle, they had survived the heat and the latest storm appeared only to have decupled their energy. In the "hanged man's room," they were the masters. The new resident's first move was to claim from them a piece of the wall, by hanging up his picture of the Sacred Shroud, and also a piece of floor space on which to sit in his meditation position and thank the Lord for having granted him this new opportunity for love and for sharing.

Love and sharing! These few square feet of communal court-yard were an ideal place for the realization of a program of that kind. Here people lived in a state of complete transparency. The slightest emotion, deed, or word was immediately seized, interpreted, and made the subject for comment. Such a promiscuous environment forced you to take special precautions. You had to learn to wash while holding the corner of your *longhi* between your teeth to conceal your nudity. You had to clean the bowl of the latrines in a particular fashion and walk without letting your gaze stray onto a woman engaged in urinating in the gutter. The shock really hit him that evening. Driven out of his room by the rats, Kovalski sought refuge under the little veranda outside his door, only to stumble across the several bodies that were already occupying it. During those blisteringly hot nights nearly everyone slept outside. Fortunately a low brick wall erected at the entrance to the compound protected it from the drains that overflowed into the alley. Kovalski created a space for himself between two sleepers.

"There was so little room that I had to lie down head to foot alongside my neighbors, like sardines in a can."

He was to retain two memorable impressions of that first night. Neither of them related to his neighbors' snores, the cavalcade of beetles and bats across his face, the bouts of coughing and spitting to which the tuberculosis sufferers around him were subject, the barking of the pariah dogs at the rats, the vociferations of drunks trampling over sleeping bodies, the metallic clatter of buckets being brought back from the fountain by the womenfolk. The first indelible impression of that night was the crying of infants prey to nightmares. Their cries, intercut with snippets of sentences, made it possible to understand the terrifying visions that haunted the slumbers of those little Indian children. There was a strong preoccupation with tigers, spirits, and *bhuts*, or ghosts. "That was the first time I had heard a tiger actually referred to by its name," Kovalski was to say. "In India people always called it 'the big cat,' 'the great wild beast,' 'the great feline,' but never 'the tiger,' for fear of attracting the attention of its spirit and thereby making it appear. It was a taboo that had been brought originally from the countryside where tigers still devoured more than three hundred people a year in Bengal alone. The threat of them haunted many a child. What mother in the City of Joy had not said to her offspring at some time or other, 'If you're not good, I'll call the big cat.' "

The second striking memory was of a "vociferous cock-a-doodle-doo sounding in my ears, from a cockerel at four-thirty in the morning, when I had only just gotten to sleep." Kovalski had not noticed the bird tied to a post of the veranda when he laid down the night before. It belonged to the occupants of the room next door. They were the only tenants he had not yet met, because apparently their activities frequently took them out of the compound. They had returned only late that night. Kovalski sat up and saw "four women sleeping head to foot, swathed in veils and multicolored saris." Remarking to himself that he had never seen such tall Indian women before, when he heard them speak, he was so surprised at their low gruff voices he thought perhaps he was dreaming. Finally he understood. His neighbors were eunuchs.

55

MAX LOEB HAD just taken a cigar out of his box of Montecristo No. 3s and was about to light it when he heard something bombarding the roof of his room. It was the tenth night after his arrival. He had experienced tropical tornadoes before but never before had he witnessed quite such a downpour of rain. A fresh premonsoon storm had just hit Calcutta.

Max poured himself a double Scotch and waited. He did not have to wait long. The disaster began with a cataract between two tiles, then the rain began to penetrate from all sides. In seconds the room was transformed into a lake, the level of which rose with menacing rapidity. In the hovels nearby families were fighting to save their few possessions. People were shouting, calling to each other. At the first drops the American had piled onto his bed the canteen of medicines, his case of instruments, his personal effects, and the three boxes of milk powder that Kovalski had brought him to save babies suffering from the fourth- and fifth-degree of malnutrition. At the very top of the pyramid he placed what he called his "survival kit": three bottles of whiskey and three boxes of cigars. The deluge was at its worst when Max heard a faint knocking at his door. Paddling up to his ankles, he went to open it and discovered in the beam of his torch, "the reassuring vision of a young girl dripping with rainwater. She was holding a large black umbrella her father was sending me." A few moments later the unemployed fellow from the hovel next door arrived with his arms loaded with bricks to raise the level of the low wall at the entrance and the *daktar*'s bed and table. Solidarity in a slum was no empty word.

After about an hour the downpour eased up a little. The

marvelous dream of taking refuge "in the luxury of a suite with a private bathroom in the Grand Hotel" had just crossed Max's mind when his door was shattered to pieces. Three figures burst in. Immediately two hands grabbed his shoulders and pushed him up against the wall. Max felt the point of a knife pricking him in the stomach. "A holdup," he thought. "That's all I needed."

"Milk!" snarled the big fellow with the broken nose who was threatening him with his knife, "Milk, quick!"

Max was determined not to play Buffalo Bill in the depths of this slum. He pointed to the three cartons of milk.

"Help yourself!"

Each thief grabbed a box and they ran off. As he went out of the door, the man with the broken nose turned around and announced in English, "Thank you! We'll be back!"

It had all happened so quickly that the American found himself wondering whether he had been dreaming. He made an attempt to put the planks from the door back in position but as he did a horrible smell brought him to a halt. Something wet touched his calf. He heard a gurgling sound and realized then that, swollen by the rain, the pestilential waters from the drains in the alley were in the process of overflowing into his room.

A night of horror thus began. There were no more matches, no torch, not a glass to be had. Everything had been submerged in the floodwater. What malevolent creature, Max wondered, had bitten him the day he had responded to Stephan Kovalski's appeal? He thought of Sylvia's velvety skin, of her breasts that tasted of peaches, of the touching childlike air she had about her when she recited her poems. He looked at his watch. It was afternoon in Miami. The jasmine would be sweet-scented on the veranda and people would be listening to the lapping of the water against the boats on the canal.

At dawn, Bandona appeared in the frame of the dismembered door. It was difficult to read the expression on her face in the dim light of a flooded morning, but the young Assamese seemed very upset. Her small almond eyes were set, her features rigid.

"Max, Big Brother, come quickly. My mother is feeling very bad. She's bringing up blood."

A few moments later they were both wading up to the middle of their thighs in slime. Bandona proceeded with caution, sounding the ground beneath with a stick because some of the open sewers actually cut across the alley. Every now and then she would stop to avoid the corpse of a dog or a rat, or to prevent Max from being splashed by the reckless flounderings of children who were laughing and swimming about in the putrid floodwater. The surprising thing about it was that nowhere in this nightmare had life come to a halt. At one crossroad they encountered a comical little man in a turban, perched on the seat of a carrier tricycle. A dozen children, up to their chests and sometimes even their shoulders in water, were milling around him. The carrier tricycle was equipped with a cogwheel which rotated against a set of numbers. "Roll up, roll up, a grand lottery prize for ten *paisas!*"

"A grand lottery prize in this filth?" marveled Max. And why not? Two biscuits and a piece of candy were a maharajah's reward for youngsters with empty stomachs.

Contrary to expectations, Bandona's mother was up on her feet. She was a small woman with a bun, all wizened like an elderly Chinese country woman. She was chatting and joking with the neighboring women who had squeezed themselves into her very clean and meticulous room. On the wall, behind the low ledge that served as a bed for her and her five children, there were two pictures of Buddhist wise men, their heads covered with yellow bonnets, and a photograph of the Dalai Lama. In front of these icons burned the flame of an oil lamp.

"*Daktar*, you shouldn't have gone to this trouble!" she protested. "I'm very well. The great God doesn't want me yet."

She ordered the American to sit down, and she served him tea and sweetmeats. Reassured, Bandona recovered her smile.

"All the same, I'd like to examine you," insisted Max.

"It's not worth the trouble. I tell you again, *Daktar*, I am very well."

"Mother, the doctor has come especially from America," Bandona intervened.

The word "America" had a magical effect. But there was no question of having all the people leave the room. In a slum anything and everything is undertaken in public, even a medical examination.

Half an hour later Max laid his stethoscope down.

"Bandona, your mother is as sound as a rock," he affirmed in a comforting tone.

It was then that tragedy struck. The old woman was trying to stand up to pour some water into the teapot when a sudden fit of coughing took her breath away. She collapsed. A flow of blood issued from her mouth. Max rushed to help Bandona lift her onto the bed. As Bandona mopped up the blood, Max could tell by the movement of her lips that she was praying. The aged Assamese woman surveyed all the people around her. There was not a trace of fear in her expression, only total serenity. Max prepared a syringe containing a cardiac stimulant but he had no time to inject the needle. The old Assamese woman stiffened abruptly. She let out a sigh and it was all over.

A howl rang out through the room. It was Bandona. She was clasping her mother in her arms and sobbing. For a few minutes there was the heartrending sound of weeping, wailing, and lamentation. Women tore their faces with their nails, men beat their skulls with their fists. Distraught children imitated their parents. Other manifestations of grief rose from the compound and the neighboring alley. Then, just as suddenly as she had broken down, Bandona stood up again, dusted off her sari, and rearranged her braids. Dry-eyed and solemn-faced she took control of the situation.

"What I witnessed next was a riot of orders and injunctions," the American was to recount. "In the space of ten minutes that young woman had organized and arranged everything. She sent her brothers off to the four corners of Bengal on a mission to alert relatives, she dispatched neighbors and friends to the bazaar to buy what was necessary for the funeral: a bier—white according to Buddhist tradition—vermilion powder for the ritual decoration of the corpse, candles, incense, *ghee*, cotton *khadi*, and bunches of jasmine, marigolds, and lilies. To cover the cost of all this she had her two gold bracelets and her pendant taken to the Afghan usurer at the end of the alley to obtain a loan of a thousand rupees. To welcome, feed, and thank the dozens of relatives and friends who would come for the occasion, she arranged to buy a hundred pounds of rice, as much flour for *chapatis*, vegetables, sugar, spices, and oil. Finally she had a hundred rupees taken to the bonze at the pagoda in Howrah for him to come and recite Buddhist *slokas* and perform the appropriate religious rites."

Three hours later everything was ready. Swathed in white cotton, Bandona's mother reclined on a litter embalmed with jasmine. Her feet and hands, duly streaked with vermilion, were visible, as was her face, from which death had wiped away nearly every wrinkle. She looked like an Egyptian mummy. All around her, dozens of incense sticks gave off the sweet scent of rosewood. Things went on very quickly. The bonze in his saffron robe pronounced prayers, striking a pair of cymbals as he did so. Then he anointed the deceased's forehead with *ghee* and camphor, and he sprinkled grains of rice over her body to facilitate the transmigration of her soul. Then four men belonging to the family took hold of the stretcher. When Bandona saw her mother leaving the hovel where they had both lived and struggled for so many years, she could no longer conceal her grief. Immediately the other women began to wail, sob, and moan once more. Already, however, the litter was receding into the flooded alleyway.

Only the men accompanied the deceased to their funeral pyres. They sang canticles with a syncopated rhythm to Ram, God, for in the absence of a specifically Buddhist place of cremation, Bandona's mother was going to be burned according to Hindu ritual. It took the little procession an hour to wend its way to the funeral *ghats* on the banks of the Hooghly. The bearers set the litter down under a banyan tree while Bandona's eldest brother went to negotiate the hiring of a pyre and the services of a priest. When his mother was placed on one of the piles of wood, the Brahmin poured a few drops of Ganges water between her lips. Her eldest son then walked five times around her remains before plunging in a flaming torch. As the flames engulfed the pyre, there rose the sound of voices singing.

Knowing that a body takes four hours to be consumed, Max slipped discreetly away to go and bring a little comfort to Bandona. Just before he got back to her hovel, however, he suddenly felt the ground give way beneath his feet. A blackish stream rushed into his mouth; then his nostrils, ears, and eyes were submerged beneath the gurgling filth. He struggled against it but the more he floundered, the more he was sucked down toward the bottom of the cesspool. Two or three times in the course of his existence, his life had been saved by virtue of his prowess as a swimmer. This time, in this unholy slime, he was paralyzed: the density and consistency of the liquid made his attempts to surface ineffective. He realized then that he was going to drown.

It is said that at such an instant you see your life pass before you in a flash. In this eddy of putrefaction, he had only time to glimpse a strange vision: "that of my mother carrying an enormous birthday cake out onto the terrace of our house in Florida." It was at that moment that he lost consciousness.

What followed was told to Max Loeb by others. The body of a *sahib* swirling about in the sewers of the City of Joy could not pass unnoticed for long. Some people had seen him disappear. They had rushed over and, without hesitation, had plunged in after him, had retrieved his inanimate form and taken him to Bandona's house.

For the second time that day, the young Assamese woman took charge of the operation. She got everyone moving. Kovalski, Margareta, and the others came running. She even succeeded in inducing a doctor to come from Howrah. Artificial respiration, cardiac massage, injections, the washing out of his stomach—everything possible was done to try and bring Max back to life. After three hours of relentless efforts, Max finally opened his eyes to be greeted by "a whole collection of marvelous faces, who seemed to be pleased at my awakening! In particular there were two almond eyes gazing at me fondly, eyes that were still red from having cried much that day."

56

"YOU COULD DO with a good clean up," Kovalski announced the next day to the survivor of the sewers of Anand Nagar. "What would you say to a little chlorophyll bath? I know a magnificent place."

Max looked hesitant. "To be honest with you, I'd prefer a bubble bath in a five-star luxury hotel."

Kovalski raised his arms to the heavens.

"That's really banal! Whereas the place I want to take you to . . ."

An hour later a bus dropped the two *sahibs* outside the entrance to an oasis that seemed improbable so close to the most prodigious urban concentration on earth. It was a tropical garden, several dozen acres in size, with thousands of trees of every variety in Asia. The universe of lush vegetation they entered more than warranted their surprise. There were huge banyan trees ensnared by interwoven creepers; many hundred-year-old cedars with trunks as thick as towers; clusters of mahogany and teak trees; pyramid-shaped ashok trees; gigantic magnolias with beautiful leaves like the glazed tiles of Chinese pagodas. "The garden of Eden had just sprung up before my eyes still stinging as they were from the filth and fumes of the City of Joy," Max Loeb was to say. Even more extraordinary were the number and variety of birds that populated the park. There were bright yellow orioles; splendid woodpeckers as large as pigeons, with golden backs and conical beaks; majestic black kites with forked tails, circling in the sky before swooping down on their prey. There were proud sandpipers with long incurved beaks perched on the tall stilts of migrating birds. Flying from one clump of bamboo to the next were magpies, russet wagtails, and large parakeets with yellow plumage. Suddenly a kingfisher with bright violet-red feathers and a large red beak came and landed in front of the two visitors. They stopped to avoid frightening him, but he was so tame that he moved to another piece of bamboo to be even nearer to them.

"What a release it is to watch a bird in the wild!" enthused Kovalski. "A creature in his natural state, his free state. He takes no notice of you. He just hops from one branch to another, catches an insect, calls out. He shows off his plumage."

"He does what birds are supposed to do," Max said.

"That's exactly what's so great about it; he isn't even looking at us."

"If he were looking at us, everything might become contrived."

"Absolutely. He's truly a free spirit. As in the kind of environment where we live we never meet truly free spirits. People are always in the grip of some problem or other. And as you're there to help, you're obliged to ask yourself questions about them, to try and understand their predicaments, study their antecedents, and so on."

Max thought of the arduous day he had just been through. "It's true. The least encounter in a slum is an occasion for tension."

Kovalski pointed to the bird.

"Except when it comes to the children," he said. "Only a child is a creature devoid of tension. When I look into the eyes of a child of the City of Joy, I see God. A child doesn't assume an attitude, doesn't seek to play a role, doesn't change to suit events, he is open. Like that bird; a bird that lives out his bird's life to perfection."

Max and Kovalski had sat down on the grass. To both of them it was as if they were millions of miles away from Anand Nagar.

"I think it is here that I drew the strength to hold out over these last years," admitted the Pole in a confidential mood. "Here and in praying. Every time I felt too depressed, I jumped on a bus and came here. A dragonfly fluttering on a bush, the cooing of a brown woodpecker, a flower closing as evening approaches—

those are the things that have been my life-buoys in this experience."

There was a long silence. Then suddenly the Pole asked, "You're a Jew, aren't you?"

Seeing Max's surprise, Kovalski apologized. "It's a typically Indian reflex to ask that question. Here a man is determined by his religion. Religion conditions everything else."

"Yes," Max said, "I am a Jew."

Kovalski's face lit up.

"You're privileged. Judaism is one of the world's most sumptuous religions."

"That hasn't always been the view of all Christians," Max observed calmly.

"Alas no, but what millenary heroism that has inspired in you! What unshakable faith! What dignity in suffering! What tenacity in listening to the one God! Haven't you inscribed the Shema Israel on the doors of your homes? What a lesson that is to the rest of humanity! For us Christians in particular."

Kovalski laid a hand on the American's shoulder. "Spiritually, you know, we Christians are Jews," he went on. "Abraham is the father of us all. Moses is our guide. The Red Sea is part of my culture—no, of my life. Like the tablets of the Law, the desert, the Arch of Alliance. The prophets are our consciences. David is our psalmist. Judaism brought us Yahweh, the God who is all-powerful, transcendent, universal. Judaism teaches us to love our neighbor as we love God! What a wonderful commandment that is. Eight centuries before Christ, you realize, Judaism introduced to the world the extraordinary notion of a one, universal God, a notion that could only be the fruit of revelation. Even Hinduism, despite all its intuitive, mystical power, has never been able to envisage a personal God. It was the exclusive privilege of Israel to have revealed that vision to the world and never to have strayed from it. That's really fantastic. Just think, Max, the same luminous moment of humanity that saw the birth of Buddha, Lao-tzu, Confucius, Mahavira, also witnessed a Jewish prophet called Isaiah proclaiming the primacy of Love over Law."

Love! It was in India that both the Jew and the Christian had discovered the real meaning of the word. Two of their brothers from the City of Joy were to remind them of it that very evening on their return. "A blind man of about thirty was squatting at the end of the main street in front of a small boy struck with polio," Max would recount. "He was speaking to the boy as he gently massaged first the youngster's needle-thin calves, then his deformed knees and thighs. The boy held on to the man's neck with a look submerged with gratitude. His blind companion was laughing. He was still so young, yet he exuded a serenity and goodness that was almost supernatural. After a few minutes he stood up and took the boy delicately by the shoulders to get him on his feet. The latter made an effort to support himself on his legs. The blind man spoke a few words and the lad put one foot in front of him into the murky water that swamped the street. Again the blind man pushed him gently forward and the child moved his other leg. He had taken a step. Reassured, he took a second. After a few minutes they both were making their way down the middle of the alley, the little boy acting as guide for his brother in darkness and the latter propelling the young polio victim forward. So remarkable was the sight of those two castaways that even the children playing marbles on the curbstones stood up to watch as they passed."

57

WITH HER GAUDY bracelets and necklaces, brightly colored saris, dark eyes circled with eyeliner, eyebrows penciled in, and her pretty mouth reddened with betel juice, twenty-year-old Kalima was the pinup of the compound. Even Kovalski was disturbed by a presence that spread sensuality and gaiety into the dark hole in which he now found himself. Above all, he admired the wide blue ribbon and the jasmine flower with which this creature ornamented her thick waist-length black hair. Such refinement in the midst of so much ugliness delighted the Pole. The only problem was that Kalima was not a woman, but a eunuch.

Kovalski had seen the proof of this while he was washing on his second morning. The "young woman" had let her veil fall for a fraction of a second and the priest had caught sight of his penis, or at least what was left of it. Kalima was not a man dressed in woman's attire. He was indeed an authentic representative of the secret and mysterious caste of the *hijras,* which had communities scattered throughout India. He had been castrated.

A few days later an impromptu celebration was to give Kovalski the opportunity to discover what functions this picturesque person and his companions served in the slum. Night had just fallen when the cries of a newborn baby suddenly filled the compound. Homaï, the wife of the one-eyed Hindu who lived on the other side of the courtyard, had just brought a son into the world. At once his grandmother in a white widow's veil rushed across with the other women of the family to the eunuch's room to invite him urgently to come and bless the child. Kalima and his friends hastily put on their makeup, changed into their festival saris, and adorned themselves with their baubles. Kalima also fastened on several strings of bells around his ankles while his companions smeared their *dholaks,* the small drums from which they never separated, with red powder. Thus arrayed, the five eunuchs emerged jangling their instruments and singing in their gruff voices, "A newborn baby has appeared on the earth. We have come to bless it. *Hirola! Hirola!"*

The eldest of the little troupe, a eunuch with fuzzy hair and prominent cheekbones, was called Boulboul—the Nightingale. Dressed in a bright red skirt and bodice, with a gold ring through his nose and gilded earrings in his ears, he led the ceremony, swaying his hips as he did so. He was the guru of the group, its master, its "mother." His disciples, with Kalima at their head, followed, skipping and singing. "Sister, bring me your child," called out Boulboul, "for we wish to share in your joy. *Hirola! Hirola!"* The grandmother in the white widow's veil hastened to go and fetch the baby, then offered it to Kalima. The eunuch took the little body gently in his arms and began to dance, hopping from one foot to another, to the sound of bells, turning and swaying to the jerky rhythm of the drums. With his gruff voice he intoned:

> *Long live the newborn child!*
> *We bless you,*
> *That you may live for a long time,*
> *That you may always have good health,*
> *That you may earn lots of money.*

The singing had attracted the inhabitants of the neighboring compounds. The courtyard had filled. Clusters of children had even scaled the roofs. No one appeared to be daunted by the crushing temperature. This was an occasion for celebration. While Kalima and his companions went on dancing, the guru Boulboul went off to collect the fee for his troupe. Eunuchs charged a good deal for their services and no one dared to haggle for fear of incurring their maledictions.

"Our newborn baby is as strong as Shiva," the dancers next proclaimed, "and we beg the all-powerful god to transfer the sins of all his past lives to us." In a way this appeal was the eunuchs' credo, the justification of their role in society. Mystical India had sanctified the most underprivileged of its pariahs by granting them the role of scapegoat.

The guru returned with a bowl of rice sprinkled with pieces of ginger. With the tip of his index finger he dabbed up the red powder from one of the drums and marked the baby's forehead with it. This symbolic gesture transferred onto his person, onto his companions and onto all the *Hijra* caste the past sins of the newborn child. For eunuchs, the red powder, which is the emblem of marriage among Hindu wives, represents their ritual union with their drums. Next the guru scattered a few grains of rice onto the instrument, then threw one whole handful at the door of the infant's home to bless the mother, and then another over the child. After that, raising the bowl above his head, he began to spin around on the spot.

Accompanied by the others striking their drums and clapping their hands in time, he sang, "We shall bathe in the sacred rivers to wash away all the sins of the newborn child." Then, before the admiring eyes of the onlookers, Kalima began to dance, cradling the infant in his arms. His fine features and the femininity of his movements perfected the illusion. Pathetic in the realism of his performance, the eunuch smiled maternally at the little bundle of flesh which was making his entry into the world of the City of Joy. The ceremony concluded with a display of mime. Kalima restored the baby to his grandmother and fixed a cushion under his sari. Personifying a woman in the final stages of pregnancy, he began to dance around in a circle. Then he aped the first pains of childbirth. Uttering cries that grew ever more heartrending, he fell to the ground while the other eunuchs patted him on the shoulders and back as if to help him give birth. When finally he was completely exhausted, his guru fetched the newborn baby and deposited him in his arms, whereupon Kovalski saw Kalima's face light up with happiness. He saw his lips addressing the child words of love. Then his bust and his arms began to move in a rocking motion. The eunuch was tenderly cradling the new addition to the compound.

58

"GOOD GOD," thought Max Loeb suddenly, "there is such a thing as paradise!"

A servant in a white turban and tunic, with the hotel coat of arms blazoned on his breast, had just come into his room. He was bearing on a silver tray a double whiskey, a bottle of soda, and a bowlful of cashew nuts. The American had been unable to resist the temptation to recharge his batteries. The chlorophyll bath in the tropical garden had not been enough. He had taken refuge in an air-conditioned suite in Calcutta's luxury hotel, The Grand. A foaming Niagara of perfumed froth was already tumbling into the bathtub of his marble bathroom. The nightmare of the City of Joy had receded to another planet. He slipped a ten-rupee note into the servant's hand. Just as he was leaving, however, the servant swung around in a half circle. He was a very wrinkled little man with a gray beard.

"Would you like a girl, *Sahib?* A very pretty young girl?"

Startled, Max put down his glass of whiskey.

"Very pretty and sweet-natured," elaborated the servant with a wink. The American swallowed another mouthful of alcohol. "Unless you'd prefer two girls together," urged the Indian, "young girls but very, very skillful. The entire range of the *Kama Sutra, Sahib.*"

Max thought of the erotic sculptures in the temples of Khajurao which he had admired in a photograph album. He remembered too, his fiancée's words during their last dinner together. "They're lovers without equal, those Indian girls," Sylvia had said. The Indian plucked up his courage. He knew his clientele all too well. As soon as they arrived in Asia, Europeans and Americans turned into devils. No temptation seemed spicy enough for them. "Perhaps you'd prefer a boy, *Sahib*? A fine looking young boy, sweet and . . ." The servant made an obscene gesture and matched it with another wink. Max nibbled at a cashew nut. The servant remained undaunted by the American's silence. With the same air of complicity, this time he suggested "two young boys," then after a few moments, he volunteered "two young boys and two girls together," then a eunuch, and finally a transvestite. "Very clean, *Sahib*, very safe."

Max could just imagine the face Kovalski would make when he described this scene to him. He got up to turn off the faucet in the bathroom. When he returned the servant was still there. His catalog of pleasures was not yet exhausted.

"If sex doesn't tempt you, perhaps you'd like to smoke a little grass?" he suggested. "I could get you the best in the country. It comes straight from Bhutan." Next he added, "Unless of course you prefer a really good pipe"—a gleam came into his watery eyes —"our opium comes from China, *Sahib*." Quite undeterred by the lack of enthusiasm inspired by his merchandise, the servant then ventured to suggest "a nice syringe full of coke," along with various other locally manufactured drugs, like *bhang,* the local hashish. Quite obviously, however, the honorable foreigner wasn't buying.

Not wanting to leave the room as a complete failure, the man in the turban finally suggested that most banal of all transactions that resounds like a litany in the ears of every tourist in this world. "Would you like to change some dollars, *Sahib*? For you I can manage a special rate: eleven rupees to the dollar."

Max emptied his glass. "I'd rather you brought me another double whiskey," he ordered as he stood up.

The servant surveyed him with a look of sadness and pity.

"You don't appreciate the good things of this life, *Sahib.*"

Of course Max Loeb appreciated the "good things" in life. Especially after weeks of doing penance in the cesspool of the City of Joy. After downing his second double whiskey, he asked the beturbaned servant to send him one of those *Kama Sutra* princesses he had been offered. This first experience with one of the descendants of the sacred prostitutes who had once inspired the temple sculptors did not, however, develop at all in the way he had ex-

pected. Brought to his door by the owner of the cabaret into which
she had been sold, the girl, a tiny thing outrageously made-up,
looked so terrified that Max did not dare even to caress her long
dark oily hair. Instead he decided to put on a feast for her. He
called room service and had them bring up a lavish assortment of
ice cream, pastries, and cakes. The young prostitute's eyelashes
began to flutter like the wings of a moth around a lamp. Never
before had she seen such marvels. To her it was quite obvious: this
client was none other than the Lord Shiva in person.

"We gorged ourselves to bursting point," Max was to tell
Kovalski, "like two school kids who wanted to believe in Santa
Claus."

Several evenings later Max's taxi passed through a grand portal guarded by two armed sentries, and along a drive lined with
jasmine bushes which infused the night with a penetrating tropical
scent. "I've got to be dreaming," he told himself when he caught
sight of the colonnades of a vast Georgian residence at the end of
the driveway. On either side of the steps and along the roof of the
terrace burned a garland of oil lamps. "It's Tara," he thought in
amazement, the Tara of *Gone with the Wind,* on a night given up to
festivity. The magnificent structure really did seem to have
emerged from a dream.

Built at the beginning of the last century by a British magnate
in the jute industry, it was one of the residences that had earned
Calcutta its nickname, "the City of Palaces." Besieged on all sides
by slums and overpopulated neighborhoods, today it was an
anachronism. Yet some of the attractions of this vestige of a vanished era still remained—not least of them the lady of the house,
the statuesque and charming Manubaï Chatterjee, a thirty-five-
year-old widow and a great lover of modern painting, Indian music, and horseback riding. Gracious and slender like a poor peasant
woman—so many of India's women put on weight as soon as they
become rich, often losing all grace and natural beauty—Manubaï
was active in a number of cultural organizations and charitable
works. It was in her capacity as president of the Indo-American
Friendship Society that she was giving this evening's party. Tomor-

row the United States would celebrate the bicentennial anniversary of its Declaration of Independence.

It took Max a moment to acclimatize himself. Even after an evening feast with a prostitute and a few nights between the expensive sheets of a five-star hotel, he was so impregnated with the reality of the City of Joy that it had become like a second skin to him. Was it true that only a few minutes' taxi ride away from this oasis there were newborn babies with stomachs blown up, mothers with tragic eyes, exhausted men, death ever present in the form of a bier borne on four sets of shoulders, workshops like convict prisons, the noise of weeping, cries, quarrels.

On the lawn of the floodlit grounds several hundred guests thronged. The entire business community from Dalhousie Square was there: everyone who was anyone in industry, people in the import and export business, fat *marwaris* in embroidered *kurtas* and their wives no less fat in sumptuous saris encrusted with gold, representatives of the Bengali intelligentsia—the great filmmaker Satyajit Ray who had made *Pater Panchali,* a film the whole world hailed as a masterpiece; the famous painter Nirode Najundar, whom international critics had called the Picasso of India; the celebrated composer and performer of sitar music Ravi Shankar, whose concerts in Europe and America had accustomed the ears of Western music lovers to the subtle sonority of the Indian lyre.

Barefoot servants in white tunics with red velvet cummerbunds and turbans were offering the guests trays laden with glasses of whiskey, Golconde wine, and fruit juices; others presented silver platters overflowing with cocktail snacks. At the far end of the lawn, Manubaï had had a vast, vividly colored *shamiana* erected to provide cover for a buffet table overloaded with the finest dishes the rich Bengali cuisine could offer. To the left of the tent, musicians in braided uniforms played themes from Gilbert and Sullivan operettas and American swing music. "It was all deliciously nostalgic," Max would later recount. "At any moment I expected to see the viceroy and vicereine of India arrive in a white Rolls-Royce escorted by Bengal Lancers."

Draped in a sari of colors suited to the occasion—blue and red scattered with a dusting of little golden stars—Manubaï was moving from one group to another. Like the two or three hundred other guests, Max was dazzled by the grace and beauty of this

Indian lady who received people like a sovereign. Yet what a difficult path had been hers before she reached the point where she
could create this illusion! Although nowadays widows no longer
throw themselves into the flames of their deceased husband's funeral pyre, a widow's position in Indian society is still far from
enviable. How many battles Manubaï had had to fight after the
death of her husband who had been the owner of Calcutta's leading house of commerce, simply in order to remain in her princely
mansion and continue to enjoy there a decent revenue. The flames
of the funeral pyre had hardly died away before her in-laws had
given her notice of her expulsion. For two years, anonymous telephone calls had called her a money grabber and a whore. Insults
and threats—she had borne them all, treating her enemies with
silence and contempt, devoting herself to the education of her two
children, traveling, furthering the careers of young artists, supporting charity organizations. She had just bequeathed her emer-
ald-colored eyes to the first eye bank in Bengal, an institution
which she herself had founded to help some of the victims of
blindness that were so numerous in that part of the world.

Suddenly Max felt an arm slip through his.

"You must be Doctor Loeb?"

"That's right," he said, slightly disturbed by the young woman's odorous perfume.

"I've heard all about you. It seems you're a truly remarkable
fellow. You live in the slums and you've set up a dispensary to care
for the sick . . . Am I wrong?"

Max felt himself blush. The faces of Saladdin, Bandona, Margareta, of all his Indian companions from the City of Joy passed
before his eyes. If there were really remarkable people anywhere,
they were the ones—people who never even had a chance to spend
a night in a luxury hotel to forget the horror of their life's surroundings, people for whom there were never receptions or com-
pliments.

"I only wanted to spend some time doing something useful,"
he replied.

"You're too modest!" Manubaï protested. She took his hand
in her long fingers and steered him forward. "Come," she said,
"I'm going to introduce you to one of our most learned men, our
future Nobel Prize for medicine."

Forty-six-year-old Professor G. P. Talwar was a lively, smiling man. He had done part of his studies at the Pasteur Institute in Paris. Head of the biology department of the Institute for Medical Sciences in New Delhi, the shrine of Indian medical research, he had been working for several years on a revolutionary vaccine capable of altering the shape of India's future. He was about to invent the world's first contraceptive vaccine. A single prick of a needle would be enough to make a woman sterile for a year. Max thought of the hundreds of little bundles of flesh deposited on his table by desperate mothers. There was no doubt about it. He had just met one of humanity's benefactors. Already, however, Manubaï was leading him over to another of her protégés.

With his curly fair hair and jovial face, the Englishman James Stevens looked more like an advertisement for Cadum soap than a disciple of Mother Teresa. Yet, this thirty-two-year-old man dressed like an Indian in a full shirt and white cotton trousers was, like Stephan Kovalski and doubtless other unknown people, a kind of anonymous Mother Teresa. He had dedicated his life to the poor, in this case Calcutta's most underprivileged and neglected people, the children of lepers. Nothing would have predestined this prosperous haberdasher for his mission in India, had it not been for the fact that one day his taste for travel had led him to Calcutta. This visit had moved him so profoundly that it transformed his life. Back in England, he had liquidated all his assets, then returned to India where he married an Indian girl. Using his own funds to rent a large house with a garden in the suburbs, he started to comb the slums in an old van, gathering up sick and starving children. By the end of the year his home harbored about a hundred little inmates. He gave it the symbolic Indian name of *Udayan*, meaning "Resurrection," and into it he sank all his savings. Fortunately, generous people like Manubaï helped. Stevens would not for all the world have missed one of her parties. For this connoisseur of good whiskey and sherry they were exotic escapades onto some other planet.

Max Loeb's own escapade would that night end in a place of which he would never have ventured to dream: the canopied bed of Calcutta's first hostess. How did this come about? He had enjoyed too many whiskeys and too much Golconde wine to be able to recall exactly. He remembered only that when, toward midnight,

he had joined his hands together in front of his heart to take leave
of Manubaï, she had rejected his gesture.

"Max, stay a little longer. The night is deliciously cool." Her
emerald green eyes seemed to implore him.

Two hours later, after the last guest had gone, she had led him
to her bedroom, a huge room that took up almost all of the first
floor of her house. The parquet flooring shone like a mirror. Furniture made out of tropical woods exuded a delicious smell of camphor, and at the far end of the room stood a bed with posts of
twisted teak supporting a velvet canopy, from where tumbled the
delicate stitching of a mosquito net. The walls were hung with
brightly colored floral wallpaper. On one of them was displayed a
collection of old yellowing prints depicting views of the colonial
Calcutta of yesteryear and scenes from life in Bengal. The opposite
wall was entirely bare except for a huge portrait of a man with a
stern face. It was not a painting but a photograph, and the face it
featured occupied the room just as intensely as if the man had been
alive.

Max remembered that Manubaï had turned on a record
player, and suddenly the voice, the poignant, grainy voice of Louis
Armstrong, accompanied by the stirring sonority of his trumpet,
had invaded the room. Neglecting the Indian woman for one instant, Max fell back happily onto the couch in front of the bed. A
barefoot servant brought whiskey and bottles of soda. Manubaï
settled herself beside him and they kissed. Max recalled that at a
certain moment the sounds of birds had come in through the
window, mingling their trilling with the brilliance of the trumpet. It
was fantastic.

The young woman had extinguished all the lights except for a
large Chinese lamp. It bathed the room in a voluptuous half-light,
and the portrait of her husband was as if erased from the wall.

What followed would become for Max a succession of confused and exciting images. Having danced a few steps, the Indian
woman and the American had drifted gently toward the soft cushions and silken sheets of the four-poster bed. They had shut themselves away together behind the invisible wall of the mosquito net.
Stretched out side by side they had waited for the voice of the
unforgettable black musician to die away. Then they surrendered
themselves to pleasure.

*

It was broad daylight when the sound of knocking at the door
made Max leave Manubaï's arms and go to open it.

"*Sahib*, there's someone wanting to see you. He says it's urgent."

Max slipped on his clothes and went downstairs behind the
servant.

"Stephan! What the hell are you doing here?"

"I suspected that after your party, you'd want a lie in," replied
the Pole, laughing, "so I came to dig you out." Then, more seriously, he added, "The leper bus is due. We need you, Max. There'll
be some amputations to be done."

"The leper bus" was the nickname Kovalski had given to the
ambulance that Mother Teresa sent him every Wednesday, with
three of her Sisters. Having been unable to open his small leper
clinic in the slum, this was the only means he had been able to find
of caring for the worst cases. To avoid any further confrontation
with the godfather and his hoodlums, he parked the ambulance on
the pavement of the avenue leading to the railway station, well
outside the boundaries of the City of Joy.

Those Sisters of Mother Teresa were real driving forces. The
eldest of the three, a tall girl with very clear skin, beautiful and
distinguished in her white sari with a blue border, was not yet
twenty-five. Her name was Gabrielle. An Indian from Mauritius,
she spoke the picturesque, lilting French of the islands. Swallowing
her *R*s, she had nicknamed Kovalski "*Dotteu* Stef." "*Dotteu* Stef,
here," "*Dotteu* Stef, there"—Sister Gabrielle's calls made Kovalski
laugh. "They were like orchids scattered over putrefaction." Yet
the Wednesday sessions were harsh trials indeed.

That morning, as always, there was a massive rush as soon as
the red-and-white bodywork of the small van "donated to Mother
Teresa by her co-workers in Japan" appeared on the avenue. Lepers came from the City of Joy and from the nearby pavements
where they had spent the night. Clinging to their crutches, to their
crates on wheels, dragging themselves along on planks, they
swarmed around the three folding tables the Sisters set up right
there on the sidewalk. One table was used for the distribution of

medicines, another for injections, and a third for dressing wounds and for amputations. Gently but firmly, Sister Gabrielle tried to sort the mass of cripples into some kind of orderly line. By the time Max and Kovalski arrived, the line stretched back more than a hundred feet.

The stench! Max saw some passers-by hurry off, their noses buried in their handkerchiefs. On the whole, however, the spectacle was a big attraction. Dozens of people congregated around the two *sahibs* and the three Sisters, to watch. Soon the avenue was completely blocked, "I felt like a magician at a fair," the American would say, still caught up in the euphoria of his night of pleasure; but his euphoria was to be short-lived.

The scene was straight out of Dante's *Inferno*. Hardly had a leper placed his stump on the table than a swarm of maggots would come crawling out of it. Bits of flesh fell away from limbs that were completely rotten. Bones crumbled like worm-eaten pieces of wood. Armed with a pair of forceps and a metal saw, Max cut, trimmed, pared. It was butcher's work. Amid a sticky swirl of flies and sudden squalls of dust, in the overpowering heat, he shed streams of his own sweat over the wounds. Sister Gabrielle acted as anesthetist. She had nothing to relieve the pain of certain amputations—no morphine—no curare or *bhang*. She had only her love. Max would never forget the vision of that Indian girl "taking a leper in her arms and pressing him to her as she hummed him a lullaby as I cut off his leg."

Yet, as it was so often the case, in the midst of the worst trials there were scenes that were unbelievably funny. Max would always remember "the compassionate face of a helmeted policeman, furiously inhaling the smoke of two sticks of incense that he had stuck right into his nostrils, as he watched the amputations." Taking advantage of the large audience, several lepers began to give a performance of somersaults and clownish antics which was greeted with laughter and the dropping of small coins. Other lepers preferred to attract attention with outbursts of anger. Brandishing their crutches at the Sisters, they demanded medicine, food, shoes, clothing. Sister Gabrielle and "*Dotteu* Stef" constantly had to calm their onslaughts. It is sometimes harder to give than to receive, as Kovalski had often found it to be.

Max had been operating for three hours when two lepers

deposited on his table a bearded crippled man whose hair was covered with ashes. Kovalski instantly recognized his old friend.

"Max, it's Anouar!" he shouted to the American. "Anouar whose wife gave birth the evening you arrived."

"I thought I knew the face from somewhere. And it couldn't have been from Miami!"

Despite the tragedy of the situation, they broke into laughter. Almost instantaneously, however, Kovalski's gaiety dissolved. Poor Anouar seemed in the worst of states. His eyes were closed. He was perspiring. He was speaking incoherently. His fleshless torso swelled almost imperceptibly with his uneven breathing. Max had great difficulty in finding his pulse.

"Gangrene," said Kovalski, examining the dirty, malodorous dressing which enveloped his forearm. "It's got to be gangrene." Helped by Sister Gabrielle, they carefully undid the bandaging. Anouar seemed to be insensible. When they got down to the bare flesh Max felt his legs "sink suddenly into a sea of cotton." Anouar's rotten arm, the crowd of faces before him, the penetrating whistle of passing buses, Kovalski's voice, all suddenly toppled over into a maelstrom of colors and sounds. Then, all at once, everything went blank. There was a dull sound on the pavement. Max Loeb had collapsed in a faint. Letting go of the leper's arm, Sister Gabrielle and Kovalski grabbed hold of him and laid him in the ambulance. The priest saw Gabrielle's hand rend the overheated air and crashed down onto Max's cheek.

"Wake up, *Dotteu! Réveille-toi!*" she cried as she redoubled the smacks delivered to his face. Finally the American opened his eyes. He was amazed to find the faces bending over him. Memories of his night welled into his mind.

"Where am I?" he asked.

"On a pavement in Calcutta in the middle of cutting off leprous arms and legs," Kovalski replied sharply, somewhat annoyed by the incident.

He was immediately angry with himself for this reply.

"It's nothing, old friend. Just a little tiredness because of the heat."

A moment later Max took up his forceps and his butcher's saw once more. This time he had to cut off a whole arm up to the shoulder—Anouar's arm, rotten with gangrene. No doubt there was nothing else to do; the man had been stricken for so long. In the absence of antibiotics, the infection must already have run through his whole system. Kovalski and Gabrielle laid the poor fellow on his side. A murmur of voices came from the onlookers as Max's pair of forceps, rose above the prostrate man. Max himself had the impression of cutting into a sponge, so putrefied were the skin, muscles, and nerves. The severing of a blood vessel induced a spurt of blackish blood which Sister Gabrielle mopped up with a compress. When he reached the bone just below the shoulder joint, Max changed instruments. Everyone could hear the grinding of the teeth as they bit into the wall of the humerus. After a few strokes of the saw, Max felt his legs "sinking into cotton" again. He clenched his fingers on the handle and pressed with all his might. To avoid thinking, feeling, seeing, he talked to himself. "Sylvia, Sylvia, I love you," he repeated as his hands accelerated mechanically back and forth. Like a tree, felled by a final stroke of an ax, the limb came away from the body. Neither Kovalski nor Sister Gabrielle had time to catch it before it fell onto the ground. Max put down the saw to wipe his forehead and the nape of his neck. It was then that he witnessed a scene that was to haunt him for the rest of his life: "a mangy dog carrying off in its mouth a human arm."

59

HE WAS THE object of such veneration that peasants placed offerings of milk and bananas outside his hole. His entry into a hut was considered a divine blessing. Hindu Scriptures were full of fables and stories about him. Temples had been constructed in his honor and all over India, at the beginning of each month of February, the great festival dedicated to him gathered together millions of worshippers. Despite the fact that he claimed more victims per year than cholera, no devout person would ever have committed the sacrilege of raising a hand against him, for the cobra snake was one of the thirty-three million gods in the Hindu pantheon.

Poor Kovalski! His entire compound in the City of Joy would long remember the shriek of terror he let out when he went into his room one evening. Rearing up on shining coils with its tongue vibrating and its fangs exposed, a flat headed cobra was waiting for him beneath the picture of the Sacred Shroud. Neighbors came rushing to the scene. The Pole had already seized hold of a brick with the intention of crushing the creature, when Shanta Ghosh, his pretty neighbor whose father had been devoured by a tiger, stayed his arm: "Big Brother Stephan, don't kill him, whatever you do, don't kill him!" Alerted by these cries, more people came running with hurricane lamps. "We could have been in the middle of a scene from the Ramayana," Stephan Kovalski was later to say, "the one where the army of monkeys hurl themselves into the lair of the demon Ravana." In the end Ashish, Shanta's husband, with the help of two other men managed to capture the reptile in the folds of a blanket. Someone brought a basket and put the snake in it. A short while afterward calm once more prevailed in the compound.

Kovalski had understood the message. "That cobra was not put in my room as a token of welcome," he said to himself. "Someone here does not wish me well." But who? That night he could not close his eyes. One detail in particular had not escaped his notice. Whereas all the other residents had come rushing to his rescue, the door to the adjoining room occupied by the eunuchs had remained closed. This fact was all the more strange because during those sultry nights everyone fled the furnace of their rooms to sleep in the courtyard. The priest extracted the lesson from his adventure without bitterness. Despite the demonstrations of affection his life of sharing and compassion among his disinherited brothers had afforded him, he knew that for some he remained a white-skinned *sahib* and a priest—a foreigner and a missionary. Until now the relative anonymity of an alley had protected him. But in the restricted world of a compound, things were very different. In this concentration camp atmosphere, anything that did not conform with the group became a foreign body with all the dangers of rejection that that implied.

At daybreak, when the Pole returned from the latrines, a squat little man with short-cropped, curly, white hair, a jet black complexion, and a slightly flat nose, entered his room. Kovalski recognized the occupant of a hovel on the other side of the well.

"Father, we too were eligible for the cobra's strike," he declared with a wink. "Your cobra was for your white skin and the cross you wear on your chest. Ours was for our curly hair and because we came from the forests."

"And also because you're a Christian," added the priest, indicating the medal of the Virgin Mary hanging around the Indian's neck.

Kovalski had adopted the Indian habit of first defining a man by his religion.

"Yes, because of that too," admitted the man with a smile. "But primarily because we're from the forests," he insisted.

The forests! The mere mention of the word in the depths of this leafless, flowerless slum amid all the noise and acrid smoke of the *chulas* conjured up before Kovalski's eyes a whole sequence of magical images: images of freedom, of life that was primitive but wholesome, of happiness and stability achieved at a price but none the less real.

"Are you an Adivasi?" he inquired.

The visitor nodded his head. Kovalski thought of all the accounts he had read of the aborigine people. They had been the first to settle in India. When? No one really knew. Ten, twenty thousand years ago. Nowadays there remained some forty million aborigines, divided up into several hundred tribes, dispersed over the entire subcontinent. This man was one of them. Why had he left his forest to come and live in this slum? Why had he exchanged his jungle for this one? It was some weeks before Kovalski was able to reconstruct the path fifty-eight-year-old Boudhou Koujour, his Adivasi neighbor, had trod.

"The drums had been beating all night," Boudhou would recount. "It was festival time. In every village in the forest, beneath the ancient banyans, the giant tamarinds, and the lofty mango trees our women and girls were dancing side by side in long rows. How beautiful our womenfolk were with their tattoos, their shining skin, their supple bodies, and their rhythmically swaying hips! From time to time a group of men with turbans and bare chests, carrying bows and arrows and wearing bells around their ankles and peacock feathers on their foreheads, would leap into the moonlit circle of dancing women and break into a frenzied dance. The women had begun to chant wildly. It was no longer possible to think of tomorrow or of anything else. Your heart pounded to the rhythm of the drums. Problems and difficulties ceased to exist. All that mattered was life, the life that was joy, impulse, spontaneity. The effect was intoxicating. The supple bodies stooped, rose again, dipped, uncoiled, stretched. Our ancestors were with us and the spirits too. The tribe was dancing. The drums were beating, responding to each other, now softly, now more loudly, blending into the night."

That festive night, the aborigines of Baikhuntpur, a jungled valley on the borders of the states of Bihar and Madhya Pradesh, renewed their thousand-year-old rites. At dawn next day, however, a surprise awaited them. Toward six in the morning, two hundred henchmen sent by the area landowners descended like a cloud of

vultures. After setting fire to all the huts, they demanded payment
of outstanding farm rent and all interest on loans. They arrested
the men with the help of the police, sequestrated the cattle, raped
the women, and seized all the inhabitants' goods. This raid
brought to a climax several centuries of confrontation between the
people living in the forest and the large landowners who wanted to
take possession of their fields and crops. The ancient law inscribed
upon the memory of humanity that determined that whoever clears
the jungle becomes its owner should have been enough to safe-
guard the aborigines against such covetousness. At one time no-
mads, then semimobile, in the course of a few centuries the aborigines had become small-scale peasants. Their agriculture was
strictly for their subsistence, intended to feed their families. Products that grew wild in the forest were there to supplement their
diet. Boudhou told the priest how he and his children used to
climb trees to shake the berries off the branches, how they used to
scratch the ground to unearth certain roots, how they knew how to
peel off a particular bark, decorticate certain tubers, extract marrow, squeeze certain leaves, locate edible mushrooms, pick succu-
lent lichen, draw off sap, gather buds, collect wild honey. He
spoke, too, of how they used to set snares, traps, nooses, and bait
for small game, and automatic traps equipped with clubs or arrows
for bears and other larger animals. How they caught various insects, worms, ants' eggs, and giant snails. Each family gave the
community anything they caught that was surplus to their needs to
be passed on to widows, orphans, and sick people. "It was a hard
life but we were free and happy."

One day, however, the drums were reduced to silence. He and
his family and the other households in the valley were compelled to
move on. First they went to Patna, the capital of Bihar, then to
Lucknow, the great Muslim city, but nowhere could they find work.
Thus it was that, like so many others, they had taken the road to
Calcutta. Put off by the close confinement of the slums, at first they
had installed themselves on the outskirts of the city with other
aborigines. They had worked hard at baking bricks and they had
lived like dogs. Then one day a room fell vacant in the City of Joy.
On that day India suffered a fresh defeat: a man who had been Man
par excellence, primitive Man, free Man, was integrated into a
slum.

Some evenings later Kovalski arrived home to discover that tragedy had struck the compound. At first all seemed quiet. Even the laughter of the children and the shouting of the drunks were stilled. A few steps farther on he heard the sound of groaning. In the half-light he could just make out figures squatting outside the eunuchs' door. Under the veranda there was a *charpoy* on which he could see a shape enveloped in a white sheet. Several small oil lamps were burning around about it and in the brightness of their flames he noticed two feet. "Someone in the compound has died," he told himself. Beside the *charpoy* he recognized Kalima's dark tresses with their distinctive blue ribbon and white flower. The young dancer was sobbing. The priest slipped into his room and prayed as he waited on his knees before the picture of the Sacred Shroud. A moment passed and then he heard feet treading softly on the cement behind him. It was his neighbor Ashish.

"Stephan, Big Brother, there's been a fight," he explained in a low voice. Boudhou, the Christian Adivasi, has killed Bela, one of the eunuchs. It was an accident but the poor thing is well and truly dead. It was because of your cobra."

"My cobra?" stammered Kovalski, abashed.

"For several days the Adivasi had been conducting a secret inquiry to find out who put the cobra in your room," Ashish went on. "He had found out that a snake charmer had given a performance to celebrate a marriage in a compound not far from here. The eunuchs were all engaged to dance at the same wedding. The Adivasi managed to find the snake charmer, who admitted that one of the *Hijras* had insisted he sell him a cobra. The *Hijra* had offered him two hundred rupees, a truly fantastic price for a small creature like that. The *Hijra* explained that he wanted to perform a sacrifice so eventually the snake charmer agreed and that's how the cobra came to be in your room. By having it kill you, Bela no doubt wanted to expiate some obscure sin. Who knows? There are those who say that by killing you, he hoped to appropriate your sex for a future incarnation."

Kovalski wanted to speak but his voice was strangled in his throat. He could hardly breathe. The Indian's words eddied in his head like acid bubbles. Ashish recounted how that evening the Adivasi had turned up at the eunuch's hovel to punish him. He had only wanted to teach him a lesson, but Bela had gone demented. He had seized a knife to defend himself. An effeminate eunuch, even of substantial build, was no match for a forest dweller used to hunting bear with a spear. In the ensuing set-to the *Hijra* was impaled on his own knife. No one had had time to intervene. In a compound, the tensions are so great that, like a thunderbolt, death can strike at any moment.

Kovalski was shattered. He could hear the sound of the eunuchs' sobbing through the open door. Soon the sobbing stopped. He heard footsteps and voices and realized that his neighbors were preparing to carry their companion to the cremation pyre on the banks of the Hooghly. He knew how expeditiously funeral ceremonies were conducted in India because of the heat. What he did not know, however, was that tradition would not allow eunuchs to bury or burn their dead other than at night, out of sight of "normal" people. What was more, India denied in death what it granted its eunuchs in life: the status of women. Before swathing their "sister" in his shroud, Bela's companions had been obliged to dress him in a *longhi* and man's short-sleeved shirt, and Boulboul, the sad-faced guru, had cut off his long braids.

Ashish had just left when Kovalski heard a scratching at the casing of his door. Turning around, he saw Kalima's necklaces and bangles gleaming in the darkness.

"Big Brother Stephan, we would like to ask you to do us the honor of taking our sister to her funeral pyre," declared the young eunuch in the very deep voice which never ceased to come as a surprise.

As he delivered his request, his companions were addressing three other men in the compound. Once again the appeal was rooted in respect for tradition; in India women do not have the right to accompany a funeral cortege. Deprived of the comfort of this last homage, the *Hijras* gave their "sister" a poignant farewell. As Kovalski, Ashish, and the two other bearers took hold of the funeral litter, the guru Boulboul fell to his knees, uttering a succession of *mantras*. Crazed with grief, Kalima and the other eunuchs tore at their faces with their nails and gave voice to the most heartrending wailing. Then the four *Hijras* bared their feet and began to beat the corpse with their sandals "to prevent our sister from being reincarnated as a eunuch in her next life."

60

THERE WAS NO longer any doubt in Kovalski's mind: the eunuchs' attitude toward him had changed. The carrying out of the funeral rites had created a bond between them. Since he had borne to the funeral pyre the corpse of the *Hijra* who had tried to kill him by putting a cobra in his room, the four other eunuchs in the neighboring room had stepped up their tokens of friendship. Often, as he came home in the evening, he would now find some trace of their passing: a wick for his oil lamp, a dish of delicacies, the wall on which he hung his picture of the Sacred Shroud freshly whitewashed. These gestures both touched and embarrassed him. "I certainly had gotten used to all forms of cohabitation. Nevertheless, the presence of this strange 'family' on the other side of the wall made me uneasy. And yet of all the neglected, despised, rejected people in the slums, weren't they those who should be pitied most? Ah, what a long way I still had to go before attaining that true spirit of charity and acceptance."

Ultimately, it was Kalima's credit to dispel Kovalski's prejudices. Every morning after his ablutions, the young dancer came to chat with the man whom in his deep voice he called "my Big Brother Stephan." Although the language of the *Hijras* was a secret tongue known only to them, Kalima knew enough Hindi to make himself understood, and of all the destinies that had come together on this wretched place, his was assuredly one of the most curious.

Kalima was the son of a rich Muslim merchant in Hyderabad, a city in the center of India. When he was a child, his genital organs were only slightly developed, yet there was no doubt about the fact that he was a boy. Very soon, however, his femininity revealed itself. At an age when his classmates were battling it out on the cricket or hockey field, he devoted himself to learning dancing and music. Instead of Boy Scout uniforms and sportswear, he preferred *shalwars* with their baggy trousers and the long tunics young Muslim girls wear. He liked to put on perfume and makeup. To curb what they considered evil inclinations, his parents had married him off at the age of fourteen to the daughter of a rich jeweler. Kalima had tried to fulfil his conjugal duty, but the result had been so disastrous that his wife had run back to her parents on the morning after their wedding.

One day, among the crowd of worshippers who had come on pilgrimage to the tomb of a local Muslim saint, an old *Hijra* with short hair and a gaunt face had spotted the youth and followed him back to his home. Less than a week later, Kalima left his family forever and went off with the eunuch. He confided a few details of the strange ritual of his adoption ceremony to Kovalski. His "godmother," or rather his guru, was called Sultana. Like the majority of *Hijras*, Sultana had no breasts and so she had pressed a piece of cotton soaked in milk onto her chest and obliged her godchild to suck it. This was a condition of acceptance into his new family. Kalima then received one hundred and one rupees, silver and brass utensils, clothes, saris, petticoats, glass bracelets, and *chotis*—threads of black cotton which, once knotted in the hair, would become like the triple braid of the Brahmin, the hallmarks of his new caste. After his adoption, Kalima was subjected to a grand initiation ceremony, to which all the members of the community and the leaders of the other *Hijra* castes in the area were invited. His "godmother" and the other gurus dressed the new disciple in a skirt and blouse previously blessed in a sanctuary. Kalima then dressed his "godmother" in the same way and kissed his feet and those of all the other gurus present, who in return gave him their blessing.

It was after this ceremony of ritual transvestism that Kalima received his female name. All the gurus were consulted as to the choice. Kovalski was surprised that they had christened the boy with the name of the most bloodthirsty goddess in the Hindu pantheon. With his fine features and his carefully plucked eyebrows, Kalima had nothing demoniac about him. It was true that his rugged voice gave him away but, because of his delicate bone structure, the proud bearing of his head, and his flowing walk, he could easily pass for a woman.

Kalima's initiation was not yet complete. The worst was yet to come, for a real *Hijra* must not be confused with a transvestite. Transvestites belonged to another caste, a pariah caste even lower on the social ladder. In the muddy alleyways of the City of Joy, Kovalski had often come across these tragic individuals disguised as women, outrageously over made-up, fitted out with false breasts —ridiculous actors who sang, danced, and wriggled their rumps at the head of wedding marches and religious processions, pathetic, obscene clowns, employed to make others laugh at their own expense and to transform the most sacred rites into grotesque parodies. Those men, however, managed to carry out their profession without sacrificing their masculinity. Some of them had several wives and whole streams of children. The deception was part of the game.

The *Hijras'* position in society was entirely different. They must be neither men nor women. Mothers, who called them to take upon their shoulders the sins committed by their newborn babies in previous lives, had the right to verify this fact. And be damned those guilty of deception!

The ceremony took place in the middle of the first winter. Castrations were always carried out in winter in order to reduce the risk of infection and allow the wound to heal more rapidly. The risks were by no means negligible. No statistics really revealed how many *Hijras* died each year from the aftermath of emasculation. Still, the Indian press never missed the opportunity to denounce dramas like that of a Delhi hairdresser, aged about thirty, who died after his emasculation carried out by eunuchs who had persuaded him to join their group. At one time the operation was performed in particularly atrocious conditions. *Hijras* took away their victim's masculinity with a horsehair which was tightened progressively each day until the genital organs were severed completely.

One day Kalima was taken by Sultana, his godmother-guru, to an isolated village where a small community of eunuchs lived. The community's astrologer selected an auspicious night for the operation. The *Hijras* called such nights when castrations were carried out "black nights." Sultana made his young disciple drink several glasses of *todi,* an alcoholic drink made from palm tree juice into which some powder of *bhang,* a narcotic with analgesic properties, had been dissolved. While Kalima lost consciousness his guru lit a great fire. A priest recited *mantras* and poured a bowlful of *ghee* into the flames. Tradition required that the flames flare up if the castration was to take place. This night the flames leaped into the sky like fireworks. That signified that Nandni-na and Beehra-na, goddesses of the *Hijras,* would accept the new recruit. The officiant could now tie a thread around the young man's penis and testicles and draw the knot progressively tighter to anesthetize the organs. Then, with a slash of a razor blade, he sliced straight through.

A scream rent the night air. The agonizing pain had woken Kalima. Immediately a saraband of drums struck up and all the eunuchs began to dance and sing round the flames, while a soloist intoned a canticle intended to chase away all maleficent powers and evil spirits. The other *Hijras* punctuated each phrase with a resounding *Hanji!* Yes!

> *A new Hijra has been born!*
> *Hanji!*
> *A sari without a woman!*
> *Hanji!*
> *A cart without wheels!*
> *Hanji!*
> *A stone without fruit!*
> *Hanji!*
> *A man without a penis!*
> *Hanji!*
> *A woman without a vagina!*
> *Hanji!*

Sultana himself applied the first dressing to his disciple's wound. It consisted of a kind of plaster made of ashes, herbs, and oil mixed together. The recipe dated back to the days of the Mogul conquest, a time when the eunuch caste had undergone a veritable Golden Age. That was the era when, all over India, poor parents sold their children to traders who emasculated them. One nobleman at the court of one of the Mogul emperors possessed twelve hundred eunuchs. In those days some *Hijras* raised themselves to elevated positions, not merely as guardians of the harem, court dancers, or musicians, but even as confidants of kings, provincial governors, and army generals.

Once Kalima had recovered from his mutilation, Sultana entrusted him to the care of professional musicians and other gurus, who taught him the traditional songs and dances. They also taught him how to mime a mother cuddling her child or breast-feeding a baby, to act the part of a young bride or a woman expecting a child or in labor. Soon he was awarded the title of *"Baï,"* or "dancer and courtesan," and then began a period of traveling for the young eunuch. *Hijras* travel a great deal from one end of India to another to visit their "relatives." Kalima's guru had a "sister" in New Delhi, "aunts" at Nagpur, and "cousins" in Benares. Links between eunuchs and their "relatives" are much stronger than any of those they might maintain with their real parents. It was in Benares, on the banks of the Ganges, that tragedy suddenly struck. At dawn one day as he was on his way to the *ghats* to dip himself in the waters of the sacred river and worship the sun, Kalima saw his "godmother" collapse in the street. The *Hijra* was dead, struck down by a heart attack.

Fortunately for Kalima, it was the time of the year for pilgrimages and there were many *Hijras* in the holy city. Almost immediately a guru volunteered to take him as his disciple. He had prominent cheekbones and a doleful expression. He came from Calcutta, his name was Boulboul, and he was Stephan Kovalski's neighbor.

61

TO SLEEP! Sleep for fifteen, twenty hours at a stretch! On cement, with rats, scolopendras, scorpions, *anywhere*, but just sleep! Since his arrival in the compound, Stephan Kovalski's dream was turning into an obsession. His nights had been reduced to three or four hours of relative silence punctuated by outbreaks of coughing and spitting. As early as four-thirty the musical squalling of a transistor sounded the reveille. Garuda, the eunuchs' cockerel, then preened himself to let off his volley of cock-a-doodle-doos. Other such birds answered him from every corner of the slum, and from all around the veranda there burst forth a concert of tears and cries from children whose stomachs were empty. Shadows armed with tins full of water rose in haste to go in search of a latrine or some gutter spared by the cesspool emptiers strike. Little girls were already lighting the *chulas*, scouring the pots and pans from the previous evening, putting the mats away, bringing buckets of water from the fountain, making up cow dung cakes, or delousing their elder sisters' hair. They were the first to set to work.

Every morning at about five o'clock, Kovalski saw little Padmini, the youngest daughter of the Adivasi who killed the *Hijra* with the cobra, set off for somewhere. He wondered where so tiny a girl might go at such an early hour. One morning he followed her. After padding across the slum behind her, he saw her scale the railway embankment. It was the time of dawn when the passenger trains arrived in Calcutta from the various towns in the Ganges valley. As soon as Kovalski heard the sound of the first train, he saw the child take a stick from under her patched blouse. The tip of it had been split so that she could fix a one-rupee note to it. As the locomotive slowly passed her, she held out the stick. A blackened hand grabbed the note. Then Kovalski saw the driver go into the tender and throw out a few pieces of coal. Padmini scrambled to pick up the miraculous manna and ran off with it in her skirt. Her father would keep half of it, religiously breaking it up into small pieces for use on the family *chula*. The other half would be resold. This trade was only one of innumerable tricks invented by the underprivileged people of the City of Joy in order simply to survive.

Yet, despite his lack of sleep, Kovalski did not miss his alley. The compound was a matchless observation ground for one who felt himself, as he did, married to the poor. What a hive of activity the place was from daybreak till night. There was no end to the comings and goings: at every moment there seemed to be some bell ringing, a gong, a whistle, or a voice announcing the arrival of a vendor of this or that, a Brahmin priest who had come to sell a few drops of Ganges water, or an entertainer of some kind. The most popular visitor was the exhibitor of bears, especially among the children. As soon as his drum was heard, the entire courtyard would come running. Nor was there any lack of enthusiasm for the monkey, goat, mongoose, rats, parrot, or scorpion trainers, or the viper and cobra charmers. The same was true of the chroniclers, puppet shows, poets, storytellers, troubadours, fakirs, mimers, strongmen, dwarfs, conjurers, illusionists, contortionists, acrobats, wrestlers, madmen, saints . . . indeed all the Zampanos and Barnums that a special hunger for entertainment and celebration could invent to enable the slum people to escape the sadness of their lot.

The compound was first and foremost the children's domain. "Marvelous children of the City of Joy," Kovalski would say. "Little innocent beings nourished on poverty, from whom the life force never ceased to burst forth. Their freedom from care, their zest for life, their magical smiles and dark faces set off by luminous gazes colored the entire world in which they lived with beauty. If the adults here managed to retain some spark of hope, was it not because of them, because of their dazzling freshness, because of the earnestness of their games? Without them the slums would have been nothing but prisons. It was they who managed to turn these places of distress into places of joy."

Kovalski counted seventy-two children in those few square feet of space so rarely penetrated by the sun's rays. It was in the rough-and-ready school of life that they learned their lessons, discovering how to fight their own battles as early as the age of three. Even before that age there were never any intermediaries between them and their world. They did everything directly with their little hands: eating with the right hand; sweeping, cleaning, going to the latrines with the left. A stone or a piece of wood served as their first toy. Right from the start this direct link with objects encouraged their relationship with all things and nurtured their creative instincts. With their hands as their only tools, their communion with nature was immediate and deep-rooted and would influence their entire lives. So too would their games, games that were concrete and simple. No Lego sets or electric or automatic objects for them. The children of the compound invented their own toys. The piece of string that Padmini, the little girl who went to fetch the coal from the railway embankment each morning, attached to her left foot with a stone on the end of it made a perfect skipping rope. The skipping left her hands free for the simultaneous composition of a dance or piece of mimicry. Kovalski was enchanted by her display: the child's postures were those of the temple divinities. All the genius of Indian dance was contained in that frail poverty-stricken body in the depths of the compound. For the boys, a simple piece of plank became a Ben Hur chariot on which the older enthusiasts pulled the smallest ones about. A few pebbles and fruit pits provided for heated marble games played from one end of the courtyard to the other and even right into Kovalski's room. One day Mallika Ghosh, the little girl next door who always came running to him with a bowl of milky tea, made a doll out of rags. But realizing all of a sudden that there were quite enough real babies in the compound for them to play at being mothers, she and her friends decided to turn their doll into an object of worship. The rag doll became Lakshmi, goddess of prosperity, to whom the poor of the slums pledge a very special veneration.

Hopscotch, spinning tops, yo-yos, hoops . . . the energy, the fervor, the ingenuity, the zest for play displayed by those small beings with their distended stomachs, never ceased to amaze

Kovalski. One day the neighboring woman's little boy ran between
the priest's legs in hot pursuit of a hoop. Kovalski caught hold of
the toddler's arm and asked him to teach him how to operate his
toy. The toy in question was a simple scrap iron wheel propelled
along by a stick with a hook. After three attempts, the Pole gave up
to a deluge of laughter. Mastery of the Indian hoop requires a long
apprenticeship and it takes the dexterity of an acrobat to keep it
balanced among so many people and obstacles.

The toy par excellence, however, the game to crown all games,
and the one that unleashed as much enthusiasm among the parents
as it did among the children, the one that aroused most competition, rivalry, and conflict, the one that carried with it all the dreams
of freedom and escape harbored by these immured people, was a
toy made out of a simple wooden framework and paper and string.
Here the kite was more than just a game. It was the reflection of a
civilization, of the joy of being borne along, guided, mastered by
the forces of nature. It was an art form, a religion, a philosophy.
The shredded remains of the hundreds of kites that dangled from
the electric cables across the slum were the decorative emblems of
the people of the City of Joy.

The tiniest children tried their hands with bits of packing
paper. By the age of six or seven they were already seeking to
perfect their aircraft. By that time, they were quite capable of
turning a piece of *khadi*, an end of a shirt, or a rag into a real
airship. They decorated them with geometric designs and asked
their "big brother Stephan" to write their names in calligraphy on
the wings. The most sophisticated devices, complete with tail and
drift, were the work of the eldest boys. Sometimes the pieces of
string that secured them were coated with paste and powdered
glass to sever the strings of rival kites.

One evening, a premonsoon squall precipitated the launching
of one of these aircraft. The whole compound was caught up in a
fever. "It was like being at Cape Canaveral on the brink of a space
launching," Kovalski was to say. Twelve-year-old Jaï, one of the
sons of the onetime sailor from Kerala, climbed onto the roof and
ran across the tiles to launch his cloth bird into an ascending gust
of air. Buffeted by the squall, the kite took off, each upward lurch
encouraged by a burst of cheers. "It was as if every mouth were
blowing heavenward to help it climb more quickly." The boy

leaped from one roof to another to steer his creation, restrain it, and direct it toward a stronger current.

Dozens of youngsters from the slum had broken their bones performing these kinds of acrobatics. "Up, up, up!" yelled the people. Jaï had maneuvered it so well that the great white bug with the two pink ribbons trailing behind its tail, rose above the electric cables. There was a tremendous burst of applause. Gaiety had taken over. The eunuchs banged frantically on their drums. Even Kovalski felt himself carried away by the general exultation. It was then that a second kite appeared in the air. The adjoining Muslim compound was offering a challenge. From then on the business became far too serious to be left in the hands of the children. Jaï's father and Ashish Ghosh, the young therapist who was preparing to leave the slum to go back to his village, sprang onto the roof. They took charge of the aircraft's string. The rival was to be shot down and captured no matter what the price. Men from the other compound also hoisted themselves up onto the tiles. A savage duel ensued, punctuated by the enthusiastic yells of the onlookers. The game had become a battle. For long minutes the result remained undecided. Each team maneuvered to try and hook the other's string. A sudden reversal of the wind direction instantly exploited by the team from Kovalski's compound, enabled them to block the ascent of the Muslim kite and push it onto the electric cables. Pandemonium broke out. In their fury, the Muslims hurled themselves at the two Hindus. Tiles began to fly in all directions and the saraband of drums was redoubled. More men clambered onto the rooftops and from below in the compounds the women urged the combatants on. The two flying machines collided, became entangled with one another, and eventually tumbled like dead leaves onto the electric cables. All the same, down below on the rooftops the fierce confrontation did not stop. Bodies rolled down into the courtyard and the bamboo frameworks shattered, scattering panic-stricken rats.

Powerless to intervene, Kovalski took refuge in his room. Through the open doorway, he could see young Jaï, little Padmini, and other adolescents looking incredulously at "the grown-ups who had stolen their children's game and were fighting each other like wild beasts."

62

"KEEP OUR LEAVING a secret?" exclaimed Ashish Ghosh. "In an ants' nest where all spend their time spying on everyone else? Impossible!"

Son of Miracle wagged his head. The taxi driver knew very well that his young neighbor was right. A slum was a cooking pot in which people simmered together from one end of the year to the other. Every life activity, even the most intimate, like making love or talking in your sleep, was accomplished here with the full knowledge of everybody else. Nevertheless, the taxi driver would have preferred that the word that an accommodation was about to become vacant be kept a secret until he had had time to negotiate its reallocation for Hasari Pal with the landlord. He might just as well have tried to prevent the day from dawning!

The impending departure of the Ghoshs soon became the sole topic of general conversation. It was not so much the imminent vacation of a room that provoked so much interest, as the news of the departure itself. After a few years in the slum, everyone's dream, the dream of returning home to the village, became so much a mirage that it seemed insane for anyone to even attempt it. That a couple should decide to give up two salaries to go and plant rice was inconceivable. Strangely too, the reactions back in the Ghoshs's village were equally negative. "When the goddess, Lakshmi, has put oil in your lamp, it's a crime to extinguish the flame and go elsewhere," the boy's parents repeated angrily, threatening to prevent him from returning by force.

All the same, aspiring successors to the hovel crowded around the Ghoshs's door in such large numbers that the landlord himself turned up unexpectedly. He was a corpulent Bengali with hair that shone like a statue of Vishnu coated with *ghee*. Even the foulest hovel in the City of Joy had a legitimate owner. Some of them even had four, one for each wall. Many of these landlords owned several houses, and sometimes a whole compound.

"The fact that the fat Bengali has appeared in person does not bode well at all," thought Son of Miracle and, sure enough, it was not long before his worst fears were realized. The owner blithely informed him that he was going to double the rent for the next tenant. Instead of thirty rupees a month, the room would cost sixty, six U.S. dollars, an outrageous price for a rabbit hutch with no electricity and no windows, and certainly quite incompatible with the miserable means available to a rickshaw puller stricken with the red fever. Hasari's beautiful dream had just been shattered.

Yet the taxi driver would not admit defeat. "My nickname was Son of Miracle and, bent on living up to my name, I decided to put up a fight to get that dwelling for Hasari," he was to recount. "So I said to my wife, 'Prepare a dish of rice with a banana and a little jasmine, and we'll go and see the Brahmin about making a *puja*.'" The Brahmin was an extremely thin little man. He lived with his family in the enclosure of a small temple, in one of the poorest parts of the slum, between the railway tracks and the boarded shacks of a community of people originally from Tamil Nadu. Son of Miracle paid him two rupees. The Brahmin put a *tilak* on the visitors' foreheads and likewise on the foreheads of Shiva and Nandi, the bull of abundance, enthroned beside the deity in its little shrine. Then he took his ceremonial tray, incense sticks, a pot of *ghee*, a small bell, a five-branched candlestick with little cups in which there burned small flames known as *panchaprodip*, and a pitcher containing Ganges water. He recited *mantras*, rang the bell, and proceeded to the ceremony of fire, walking his candlestick around the statues. He put particular emphasis on the bull, for it is to Nandi that Hindus attribute the power to grant any desire.

After his *puja* to the gods of the heavens, Son of Miracle decided to address himself to the gods of the earth.

"We must get the godfather to help," he announced to Ashish Ghosh. "He's the only one who could cut down that pirate's demands."

"Do you really think the godfather would put himself out over so trivial a matter?" asked Ashish.

"Of course he will! In fact it's exactly the kind of intervention that he likes. After all, doesn't he call himself the 'defender of the little ones,' the 'protector of widows and orphans,' the 'guru of the poor'?"

Accordingly, Son of Miracle requested an audience. Two days later an envoy from the godfather came to fetch him, whereupon he underwent the same ritual as had Kovalski. The taxi driver was ushered first into a kind of anteroom where bodyguards were playing cards and dominoes and smoking cigarettes. Then the godfather's eldest son appeared to conduct the visitor into the vast reception room. Son of Miracle stared, wide-eyed with wonder. The godfather was in truth a nobleman. He sat enthroned like the great Mogul at the far end of the room on his armchair encrusted with precious stones, but his dark glasses and the heavy folds of his jowls gave him the air of an aging toad. Without a word, he projected his chin in the direction of the taxi driver to indicate that he was ready to listen.

Son of Miracle presented his request powerfully. After three minutes the godfather raised his fat, hairy hand covered with rings. He had understood. Any further explanation would be superfluous. He signaled to his son to approach the throne and whispered in his ear the price of his intervention. "Irrespective of the fact that the godfather was the protector of the poor and the oppressed, he was like a race horse: he didn't run without his oats," the taxi driver was to say. "Much to my surprise, however, this time it wasn't a question of money. Instead, he gave me to understand through his son that in exchange for his intervention with the overdemanding owner, he intended to set up a drinking dive in the compound. Not bad, eh? And there was no question of raising the slightest objection. You don't refuse hospitality to someone who's giving you a roof over your head."

*

One of the most notable events that could ever occur in the life of a slum—a family's departure and return to its village— passed off completely unnoticed. Having given up the idea of leaving separately, the Ghoshs and their three children piled their things into a rickshaw and left the compound one morning at dawn. There was no farewell banquet or celebration, only a few emotional displays from neighbors who had lived and suffered with them in the same prison for years. The young people of the compound had, however, prepared a going-away present for them. It was Padmini, the little girl who collected coal from the locomotive, who actually presented it to Mallika, the Ghoshs's eldest daughter. The gift was the rag doll which some weeks earlier they had metamorphized into Lakshmi, goddess of prosperity, now coated with *ghee* and garlanded with rose petals.

Kovalski accompanied the departing family to the station. After a two-hour train journey as far as the small town of Canning, then three hours on a steamboat on the River Matla, a branch of the Ganges delta, followed by an hour's bus journey and two hours across the dikes on foot, they would be home again at last—after six years in exile! They were living proof that the tide of exodus could turn, that the tragedy of Calcutta was not ineluctable, that it need not be forever. That was how Kovalski wished to look upon their departure. Yet his grief at losing his brother and sister was immense. Since that distant evening when Margareta had first shown them into his room in Nizamudhin Lane, a profound affection had grown up between him and these two bright young people who were ever ready, day or night, to fly to the rescue of anyone in distress and constantly prepared to devote themselves to the most neglected. On the point of putting his family in the train, Ashish paused and faced the priest.

"Big Brother Stephan," he said in a voice taut with emotion, "as you know we are Hindus, but it would please us if you would give us the blessing of your Jesus before we go."

Much moved, Kovalski raised his hand above the five heads clustered together in the midst of the throng and slowly made the sign of the cross.

"May the blessing and the peace of Christ be with you," he murmured, "for you are the light of the world."

It was only when the train had pulled away and the faces at the window had vanished into the scalding air at the end of the platform that Kovalski became aware that he was crying.

*

How the fat Bengali landlord knew the exact date of the Ghoshs's departure was something of a mystery. At about six o'clock on that very same morning, however, he burst into the compound accompanied by half a dozen thugs. In Calcutta anyone could recruit a small army to keep his personal affairs in order. It cost less to engage a man than to hire a bullock to pull a cart. The landlord came armed with an enormous padlock to secure the door of the vacant hovel.

Just as the battle of Hastinapur brought luster to the Mahabharata epic, so the battle which now ensued was to become a striking page in the history of the City of Joy. On this occasion, however, the adversaries were not mythological warriors disputing the glorious capital of a kingdom but vulgar good-for-nothings, ready to tear each other's guts out for the possession of a miserable rat hole in the heart of a slum. The godfather had sent his son, Ashoka, at the head of a commando unit armed with clubs. Pushing the owner and his guards aside, they took up their position in front of the Ghoshs's former home. Fighting broke out. Kovalski saw someone brandish a knife and slice off one of the combatant's ears. The occupants of the compound were seized with panic. Women fled, screaming. Others barricaded themselves in with their children. Terrified, the eunuchs' cockerel emitted cock-a-doodle-doos that assembled the entire neighborhood. The tiles from the roofs began to fly, followed by *chulas*, buckets, and bricks. Wounded people crawled away, groaning. It was like a scene out of a play, except that here people were really fighting, and with unparalleled ferocity.

It was at this point that the godfather made his appearance. Dressed in an immaculate white *dhoti* with gilded sandals on his feet and an ivory-handled cane in his hand, he looked more than ever like a Grand Mogul between the two bodyguards who fanned him. "It's the emperor Akbar coming to appease the anger of his subjects," thought Kovalski. Instantly the fighting stopped. No one, not even the *gundas* engaged at the docks, would have dared to dispute the authority of the lord of the City of Joy. Reassured, the residents returned to their homes in time to witness an extraordi-

nary scene. The godfather advanced toward the fat Bengali landlord, entrusted his cane to one of his guards, raised both his hands
to the level of his face and joined them in a gesture of salutation.
Then, taking back his cane, he pointed the tip of it at the large
black padlock the proprietor was gripping. With an imperceptible
movement of the head, he invited one of his guards to take possession of it. Not a word was spoken and the Bengali put up not the
least resistance. On the contrary, he bade the godfather a respectful farewell and withdrew with what was left of his escort, whereupon the godfather did a tour of the compound to savor his triumph and caress the cheeks of a number of children in their
mothers' arms.

Son of Miracle was exultant. He had lived up to his name.
True, the victory had been expensive—he had had to hand out
quite a lot of money to the neighbors to induce them to accept the
idea of the drinking den, the price of the godfather's intervention
—but the result was well worth the sacrifice. Hasari would at last be
able to escape the degradation of the pavement and settle with his
family in a compound near Son of Miracle's own: a four-star compound where the slum houses were built out of mud and bricks,
and topped with proper roofs. Even better, it had the bonus of an
authentic white-skinned holy man and no fewer than five authentic
eunuchs as immediate neighbors. The godfather had lost no time
in making sure this outstanding event would be celebrated in the
proper fashion. The bottles of *bangla* and *todi* for his new clandestine drinking den were already awaiting the revelers.

63

THERE WAS NO doubt in Max Loeb's mind: the incredible vision was an effect of the heat. "I'm delirious," he thought to himself. He put down his scalpel and rubbed his eyes but the vision was still there, planted in the murky water in the middle of the alleyway.

"Daddy!" he finally yelled, dashing out of his room.

The tall figure with the russet hair was indeed Arthur Loeb, although with his trousers rolled up to his knees, the surgeon looked more like a fisherman after shrimps. For a moment father and son stood facing each other, unable to utter a word, until finally Arthur held out his arms and Max rushed into them. The sight of the two *sahibs* embracing each other provoked much hilarity among the crowd that thronged the door of the dispensary room.

"Is that your hospital?" asked Arthur Loeb at last, pointing to the mud-walled room.

Max nodded his head and they laughed together, but Arthur Loeb's features became suddenly set. His gaze had just encountered all the pitted faces, the skeletal babies in their mothers' arms, the protruding chests of tuberculosis sufferers coughing and spitting as they waited for their consultation.

"It's a real gathering of the lame, the sick, and the dying here," he stammered, stricken by what he saw.

"I'm sorry this is all I can offer you by way of a reception committee," apologized Max. "If you'd warned me in advance, you'd have qualified for a band with dancing girls, transvestites,

eunuchs, garlands of flowers, welcoming *tilak*, and all the trimmings! India is a lavish land!"

"Welcoming *tilak?*"

"That's the red dot they put on your forehead. It's known as
the third eye and it enables you to see the truth beyond appear-
ances."

"For the moment what I can see is staggering enough," Arthur
admitted. "Surely there must be a place less alarming in this city to
celebrate our reunion."

"What would you say to a Punjabi dinner? I think it's the best
cuisine in India. And the best restaurant is right in your hotel. I
take it you are staying at the Grand Hotel?"

Arthur nodded.

"Eight o'clock at the Tandoori restaurant of the Grand then!"

Max pointed to the line of sick and crippled people who were
beginning to grow impatient. "And tomorrow, you can come and
give me a hand! Respiratory illnesses are your specialty, aren't
they? Well, you are going to have fun!"

As soon as they could afford it, Calcutta residents would
avenge themselves from the excesses of the heat with excesses of
the inverse kind. To defy the madness of the temperature, one city
industrialist had even gone so far as to install an ice-skating rink in
his garden. Like all up-to-date places equipped with air-conditioning, the restaurant Max had chosen was like an icebox. Fortunately
the beturbaned headwaiter had dug out a magnum of Dom Peri-
gnon which quickly warmed the two frozen table companions and
whetted their appetites. Max knew all the Punjabi dishes. He had
first discovered them in this very place, in the company of Manubaï
Chatterjee, the beautiful Indian woman who had supervised his
gastronomical initiation.

Arthur raised his glass. "Here's to your speedy return home,
Max!"

"First let's drink to your discovery of Calcutta!" suggested
Arthur's son, clinking glasses with his father.

They drank several mouthfuls.

"What a shock that was this afternoon, damn it," said Arthur.

"And yet you didn't really see anything tragic."

The surgeon looked incredulous.

"Do you mean to say there's worse?"

"I know it must be hard to imagine when you've come straight from a paradise like Miami," said Max, thinking of his father's luxurious clinic. "In fact, no one can really have any idea of the living conditions of the millions of people here without actually sharing them like the Polish priest I told you about in my letters. And like me, to a lesser extent."

Arthur listened with a mixture of respect and astonishment. Images of his son as a child and as an adolescent flooded into his mind. Nearly all of them related to one salient feature of his character: a morbid fear of dirt. Throughout his life, Max had changed his underwear and clothes several times a day. At high school, among his friends, his mania for washing had earned him the nickname of "Supersuds." Later at medical school, his obsessive fear of insects and all forms of vermin had occasioned some memorable practical jokes, like his finding a colony of cockroaches between his sheets or a whole family of tarantulas in his dissection kit. Arthur Loeb couldn't get over it. The gods of the City of Joy had metamorphosed his son. He wanted to understand.

"Didn't you want to run away when you first landed in this cesspool?" he asked.

"Sure I did," replied Max without hesitation. "Especially as Kovalski, sadist that he is, had kept a hellish surprise in store for my arrival: one of his leper friends in labor. You should have seen my face! But that wasn't the worst of it."

Max told his father of the infernal heat, of the hundreds of living dead who invaded his room in the hope of some impossible miracle, of the cesspool emptiers' strike that had transformed the slum into a sea of excrement, of the tropical storms, the flood, the holdup in the middle of the night, the scorpion sting, and his tumble into the sewer.

"From my very first week onward the City of Joy offered me its complete catalog of charms," he concluded. "So, it was bound to happen. I cracked up. I jumped in a taxi and cleared out. I took refuge here and indulged myself. But after three days I felt a kind of nostalgia and I went back."

The waiters brought several aromatic dishes laden with a mountain of orange-colored pieces of chicken and mutton.

His father grimaced.

"Don't worry. That color is typical of dishes from the Punjab," explained Max, delighted to be able to show off his knowledge. "To begin with, the pieces of meat are macerated in yoghurt steeped in all kinds of spices. Then they're coated with a kind of chili paste. That's what gives them their color. After that they're baked in a *tandoor*, that's a special clay oven. Have a taste, they're marvelous."

Arthur Loeb took a bite, but almost immediately Max saw his father's cheeks turn crimson red. He heard him stammer a few words. The poor man was asking for some champagne to put out the fire in his mouth. Max quickly filled his glass and ordered some *nan*, the delicious oven-baked wheaten bread that was ideal for soothing burning palates. Arthur chewed his way through several pieces in silence. Suddenly, after five minutes had passed, he looked up again.

"Supposing I were to buy your City of Joy?"

Max nearly swallowed his chicken bone.

"You mean the slum?"

"Precisely. I could raze it to the ground, rebuild it anew with running water, provide the whole lot with drains, electricity, even television. And give the residents their homes as a present. What do you say to that, my boy?"

Max emptied his glass slowly and thoughtfully.

"Dad, it's a brilliant idea," he said at last. "The only trouble is that we're in Calcutta, not in South Miami or in the Bronx. I'm afraid a project like that would be difficult to implement over here."

"If you're willing to pay the price, you can implement anything," replied Arthur, slightly irritated.

"I'm sure you're right. It's just that over here, money isn't enough. All kinds of other considerations come into play."

"Such as?"

"First of all no foreigner is allowed to purchase real estate. It's an old Indian law. Even the British at the height of their power had to submit to it."

Arthur swept away the objection with a wave of his hand.

"I'll use Indian front men. They can buy the slum for me and the end result will be the same. After all, it's the end result that matters, isn't it?"

Either as a consequence of the spicy cooking or of the trau-

matic memory of his first visit to Anand Nagar, the surgeon was
very excited. "An achievement like that would have a more direct
impact than all the nebulous programs of aid to underdeveloped
countries discussed in the United Nations," he finished up by
saying.

"No doubt," acknowledged Max with a smile. He could just
imagine the expressions on the faces of the government *babus*
when they learned that an American *sahib* wanted to buy up one of
Calcutta's slums. There remained, however, a more serious objection. Since immersing himself in the poverty of the third world,
Max had been induced to revise a fair number of his bright theories
on how the problems of the poor should be solved. "When I first
arrived in the slum," he told his father, "one of the first thoughts
Kovalski shared with me came from a Brazilian archbishop struggling shoulder to shoulder with the poor out in the country and the
favelas. According to him, our help serves only to make people
more dependent *unless it is supported with actions designed to wipe out the
actual roots of poverty.*"

"Does that mean that it's no use taking them out of their
hovels full of crap and setting them up in new housing?"

Max nodded his head sadly.

"I've even come to learn the validity of a strange reality here,"
he said. "In a slum an exploiter is better than a Santa Claus . . ."
Confronted by his father's stupefied expression, he went on to
explain, "An exploiter forces you to react, whereas a Santa Claus
demobilizes you."

"It took me several days to understand exactly what Max
meant," Arthur Loeb was later to admit. "Every morning I climbed
into a taxi and went to join him in his slum. Hundreds of people
had been lining up outside the door of his dispensary since dawn
or even since the night before. Bandona, the delightful Assamese
girl, cleared a corner of the room for me. It was she who sorted out
the patients. With an infallible eye she directed the most serious
cases to me, generally patients in the terminal stages of tuberculosis. In all my career I had never seen such ruined systems. How
those specters ever found the strength to take even the few steps to
my small table, I do not know. As far as I was concerned, they were

already dead. But I was wrong. Those walking dead were really *alive.* They jostled each other, argued, and joked. In the City of Joy the life force always seemed to prevail over death."

Above all, these daily plunges into the very heart of the poverty and suffering of an Indian slum would enable Dr. Loeb to better understand what form effective help should take. "I had been prepared to give tens of thousands of dollars to buy a whole slum and build it anew," he was to say, "when in fact the urgent need was for a ration of milk to be distributed to rickety babies whose fontanels were still open, for a people who ran a high risk of epidemics to be vaccinated, for thousands of tuberculosis sufferers to be rescued from fatal pollution. That experience shared with my son and Bandona made me appreciate a fundamental truth. It's at grass roots level that gestures of solidarity are really noticed and appreciated. A simple smile can have as much value as all the dollars in the world."

A simple smile! Every Wednesday morning, Max hired a minibus at his own expense. Into it he piled ten or so rickety children, youngsters suffering from paralysis, from polio, from physical and mental handicaps. Some of the mothers, together with Bandona and Margareta, accompanied the young doctor and his pitiful little troop. On one Wednesday morning the bus contained an extra passenger, Max's father. The vehicle crossed the large metal bridge over the Hooghly and, with great blasts of its horn, tackled the madness of the traffic jams. No. 50 Circus Avenue was a decrepit old two-story building. A simple painted sign at the entrance announced: Estrid Dane Clinic, 1st Floor. Could this vast, dusty, and badly lit room, furnished only with two large tables, really be a clinic? wondered the American professor as he allowed his bewildered gaze to roam over the austere decor. The scene he was about to witness, however, was to give him one of the greatest medical thrills of his life.

Once all the children were in their places, the mistress of the establishment appeared. She was an elderly lady with bare feet, small in build, and almost insignificant in appearance. She was wearing the white sari and very short hair of a Hindu widow. One detail struck the American instantly: her smile, a luminous smile that encompassed the whole of her wrinkled face, her bright eyes, and her delicate mouth reddened with betel juice. Hers was a smile of communion, life, hope. "That smile alone," Arthur Loeb was to say, "lit up the wretched refuse dump we were in with a supernatural brilliance and consolation. It was pure charisma."

At the age of eighty-two, Estrid Dane was one of the glories of Indian medical science. Yet she was neither doctor nor healer nor bonesetter. For forty years in the clinic she had opened in London, her long, slender hands, her gentle voice, and angelic smile had cured more physical ailments than many a specialist institution. The greatest professors sent her their hopeless cases. The press and television reported on her activities. "The old Indian lady with the miraculous hands," as she was called, was known throughout almost all of England. In the twilight of her life, Estrid Dane had decided to return to her homeland and dedicate her final years to her fellow countrymen. She had settled in this run-down old building in Circus Avenue and it was here that, each morning, with the help of a few young students whom she was training in her technique, she performed her miracles anew.

Margareta and Bandona deposited the inert body of a small, emaciated boy of five or six on the first table. His arms, legs, eyes, head, everything about him was devoid of life. Arthur Loeb could not help thinking of "a little corpse that had kept its freshness." His name was Subash. He was a polio victim. On the previous day his mother had brought him to Max. "Take him," she had implored with an expression that was heartrending. "I can't do anything for him." Max had examined the child, then returned him to his mother's arms. "Bring him back tomorrow. We'll take him to Estrid Dane."

"The old Indian lady's hands were placed gently on the child's thorax and fleshless thighs," Arthur Loeb would recount, "and her eyes, her mouth, the dimples of her cheeks, all wrinkled as they were, broke into a fresh smile. To me it was as if that smile struck the patient like a laser beam. His eyes shone, his little teeth appeared between his lips. His lifeless face lit up a shade. Incredible as it seemed, he too was smiling." Then Estrid's hands began their awe-inspiring ballet. Slowly and methodically the Indian woman probed Subash's muscles, his tendons, his bones, to try and distinguish the dead areas from those where there might still be a spark of life. "You sensed that this woman was searching with her brain and her heart as much as with her hands," the American was to

continue, "that she was constantly asking herself questions. Why
was such and such a muscle wasted? Because of the breakdown of
its link with the nervous system or because of undernourishment?
Why had this particular area lost all sensation? In brief, what were
the possible causes of each lesion? Her hands stopped continually
to seek out the fingers of one of her students and guide them to a
deformity or a sensitive area. Then she would give a long explanation in Bengali to which all the girls listened with religious respect.
The truly magical part of her treatment came only after the
stocktaking. Throughout the entire half hour that followed, Estrid
Dane's palms, firm and tender by turns, kneaded the body of the
little polio victim, forcing him to react, rekindling in him the flame
apparently extinguished. It was absolutely spellbinding. Each
movement seemed to say to him, 'Wake up, Subash, move your
arms, your legs, your feet. Live, Subash!' "

Squatting in the shadows behind the Indian woman, Subash's
mother kept watch on the slightest movement near her child. Like
all the other onlookers, the two Americans held their breath.
There was not a sound to be heard but the friction of Estrid's
hands on the cracked skin of her small patient.

No miracle really occurred. No one saw the paralyzed boy
suddenly get up and rush into his mother's arms. Nonetheless what
did happen remained for the Doctors Loeb, father and son, a
demonstration of what they did not hesitate to qualify as "exceptional medical prowess." "Suddenly," the professor was to recall,
"a series of vibrations seemed to shake the child's body. His right
arm came to life first, then his left. The head that had seemed for so
long to be soldered at his chin to his chest in a prone position gave
a slight movement. Timidly, weakly, the life was being breathed
back into that mummified body. It was obvious that the fingers of
the old Indian woman in the widow's sari had somehow set the
engine moving again. They had reawoken the nervous system,
compelled it to send its impulses through that little living corpse.
This was only a first result and the road to complete recovery was, I
knew, a long one. Nevertheless that terrible city of Calcutta had
taught me the most beautiful lesson in hope of my life."

64

"THEY LOOK AS a herd of goats being led to the slaughter-house," thought Stephan Kovalski watching the family entering the compound. "With his cotton loincloth tucked up between legs that were as thin as matchsticks," the priest was to recount, "the father walked in with a basket on his head containing the family possessions: a *chula*, a few cooking utensils, a bucket, a pitcher, a little linen, and their festival clothes wrapped up in newspaper secured with strands of jute. He was a frail man with a large drooping mustache, a thick mop of salt-and-pepper hair, and a face that was unshaven and furrowed with wrinkles. A certain suppleness about his bearing suggested that he was younger than he looked. Behind him, with lowered eyes and her veil pulled down over her forehead, trotted a woman with a light complexion dressed in an orange sari. She was holding on her hip the family's last born child, a bony little boy with close-cropped hair. A young girl with her head uncovered and two long braids followed with two boys in vests, aged fourteen and ten. Their heads were bowed and indeed they looked as timorous as a herd of goats being led to the slaughter."

Son of Miracle was waiting for Hasari and his family at the entrance to the hard-won trophy that was to be their new home. He had had the floor decorated with a *rangoli* covering. The residents of the compound immediately formed a circle around the somewhat dazed newcomers and the taxi driver began the introductions. He had bought several bottles of *bangla* from the godfather's clandestine supply, and glasses circulated from hand to hand. The head of the compound pronounced a few words of welcome and

clinked glasses with Hasari, who could not get over the warmth of
the reception. "After all those years of suffering it was as if the
great god Bhagavan had suddenly opened the gates of paradise."

Stephan Kovalski was by no means the last to join in this little
celebration. Along with the eunuchs, the Pals would now be his
nearest neighbors, and his stomach had survived so many onslaughts that now it could certainly put up with a few mouthfuls of
alcoholic poison, even in the blazing heat. Not everyone, however,
had the same powers of endurance. Kovalski saw Hasari's pupils
dilate suddenly and turn a strange whitish color. Before anyone
had time to react, the rickshaw puller staggered and fell to the
ground. His body was shaken by a series of convulsions, his throat
and cheeks distended as if he were about to vomit. Kovalski fell on
his knees and raised the sick man's head.

"Spit it out. Spit all that poison out," he urged him. In response to these words he saw the lips half open beneath the bushy
mustache. "Spit, old brother, spit," he repeated. The Pole heard a
gurgling in the depths of Hasari's throat and saw a stream of
reddish froth appear from between the corners of his mouth. The
residents of the compound realized then that it wasn't the *bangla*
from their welcoming festivities that was making their new neighbor vomit. He too had the red fever.

That evening, as the sun's disk was vanishing beyond the
mantle of smoke that imprisoned the slum, the sound of a horn
tore the priest away from his meditation before the picture of the
Sacred Shroud. The sound was as familiar to him as the cawing of
the hooded crows. As soon as he regained consciousness, Hasari
had decided to honor his new hovel with a *puja*. He had placed
incense sticks in the hinges of the door and in the four corners of
the room. Then, as thousands of millions of Indians had done each
evening since the dawn of humanity, he had blown into a conch to
draw down upon himself and his kinsfolk "the beneficent spirits of
the night." Kovalski prayed with a particular fervor that this cry
might be heard. "But for some time now the gods of the slum had
seemed to be suffering from a cruel deafness."

Although he would much rather have shared his sleeping spot
with a couple of eunuchs than with a bacillary tubercular, Big
Brother Stephan did not hesitate: he invited Hasari and his eldest
son to share the bit of veranda outside his room. There were too

many Pals to lie down outside their own hovel, and the stifling heat of the premonsoon weeks made sleep inside the slum houses impossible. Kovalski would never forget the first night he spent lying beside his new neighbor, not only because of the sound Hasari's lungs made with each breath—like the noises coming from a blacksmith's forge—but primarily because of the confidences he was to hear. Hardly had the priest lain down on the cement than Hasari turned to him.

"Don't go to sleep yet, Big Brother," he entreated. "I need to talk to you."

Many times Kovalski had heard appeals of that kind, sometimes from complete strangers.

"I'm listening, brother," he said warmly.

Hasari appeared to hesitate.

"I know that my *chakra* will soon cease to turn for this life," he declared.

Kovalski knew well the meaning of those words. Hasari was expressing foreknowledge of his impending end. The Pole protested, but only as a matter of form. After the crisis of the afternoon, he knew, alas, that neither Max nor anybody else could save the unfortunate man. "I am not afraid of death," continued the rickshaw puller. "I've had such a tough time since I left my village that I am almost sure . . ." Again he hesitated, "Almost sure that today my karma is less heavy and will have me born again into a better incarnation."

Kovalski had often discerned this hope in the confidences of the people he had helped to die in the slum. It had a calming effect on them. Tonight, however, it was of other things that his new neighbor wanted to talk. "Big Brother," he went on, propping himself up on his elbows, "I do not want to die before I've . . ." He choked, shaken by a fit of coughing. Kovalski thumped him on the back. All around them there rose the snores of sleeping people. In the distance they could hear the sound of shouting and the blaring of a loudspeaker; somewhere there was a celebration going on. Long minutes passed, during which the Pole wondered what sudden concern could be preoccupying his neighbor at so late an hour. He did not have to wait long for an answer. "Big Brother, I cannot die before I've found a husband for my daughter."

For an Indian father there was no more powerful obsession

than that of marrying off his daughter. Amrita, the rickshaw puller's daughter, was only thirteen years old but if the cruel years on
the pavement and in the shantytown had not tarnished her freshness, the gravity of her expression bespoke the fact that she had
long since ceased to be a child. The role of a girl in Indian society is
a thankless one. No domestic task, no drudgery is considered too
much for her. Up before everyone else and last to go to bed, she
leads the life of a slave. A mother before ever having children of
her own, Amrita had brought up her brothers. It was she who had
guided their first steps, foraged for their food in the hotel refuse,
sewn together the rags that served as their clothes, massaged their
fleshless limbs, organized their games, deloused their heads. Right
from her earliest years, her mother had unflaggingly prepared her
for the one big event of her life, the one which for a day would
transform a child of poverty into the subject of all the conversation
in the small world of the poor who surrounded her: her marriage.
All her education was directed toward that end. The shanty of
cardboard and planks in their first slum, the pavement squats, had
been for her places of apprenticeship. It was there that the skills of
a model mother and perfect wife had been passed on to her. Like
all Indian parents, the Pals were aware that one day they would be
judged on the manner in which their daughter conducted herself in
her husband's house and, as her role could only ever be one of
submission, Amrita had been trained from the very first to re-
nounce all personal inclinations and relinquish all play in order to
serve her parents and brothers, something that she had always
done with a smile. Ever since she was a small child she had accepted the Indian idea of marriage, a conception that meant that
Hasari would one day say to Kovalski, "My daughter does not
belong to me. She has only been lent to me by God until she
marries. She belongs to the boy who will be her husband."

Indian custom generally requires that a girl should be married
well before puberty, hence the occurrence of the child "marriages"
that seem so barbaric to Westerners. In such cases it is only a
question of a ceremony. The real marriage takes place only after
the girl's first period. Then the father of the "bride" goes to the
father of the "groom" and informs him that his daughter is now
capable of bearing a child. A more definitive ceremony is subsequently arranged and it is then that the young girl leaves her

parents' home to go and live with the boy to whom she has been "married" for years.

The daughter of a poor rickshaw puller not being a particularly desirable match, Amrita's first period had come before she was married, almost on the eve of her eleventh birthday. As tradition would have it, the little girl had then abandoned the skirt and top of a child and put on an adult's sari, but there had been no celebration on the piece of pavement occupied by the Pals. Her mother had simply wrapped up in a sheet of newspaper the piece of rag that had absorbed the first blood. When Amrita would marry, she and her entire family would take the piece of linen to the Ganges and immerse it in the sacred waters so that the young wife might be blessed with fertility. In order to make this glorious occasion come without further delay, Amrita's father had first to resolve a problem, a very crucial one indeed.

As his father before him had done for his sisters and as millions of other Indian fathers had done for their daughters, Hasari had to get together a dowry. Indira Gandhi might well have forbidden this ancestral custom but that did not prevent its continuing in modern India in a way that was even more tyrannical. "I can't give my daughter to a man who is paralyzed or blind or a leper!" the rickshaw puller was to lament to Kovalski. Only such disinherited people would agree to take a girl in marriage without a dowry. The poor man never stopped doing all kinds of calculations but they all came back to the same fateful figure. Five thousand rupees was the sum he had to collect before the very humblest of boys would accept his daughter. Five thousand rupees! That meant two whole years of running about between the shafts of his rickshaw or a lifetime of being indebted to the slum's *mahajan*. But what lifetime and how much running about? "When you cough red," he was to go on to say, "you watch the sun rise each morning and wonder whether you'll see it set."

Kovalski entrusted his new neighbor to Max, who put him on a powerful treatment based on antibiotics and vitamins. The effect on a virgin metabolism, totally unaccustomed to medicines, was spectacular. The attacks of coughing became less frequent and he recovered enough strength to start pulling his carriage again in the humid heat of the weeks that preceded the monsoon. The imminent arrival of the annual deluge enhanced his prospects of increased income since rickshaws were the only vehicles that could get about the flooded streets of Calcutta. Still, even that would not be enough to guarantee the indispensable five thousand rupees.

It was then that fortune intervened in the form of a new encounter with one of the vulturous procurers that prowled the streets in search of business. The meeting took place outside the agency for the SAS airline company on the corner of Park Street where the exhausted puller had just set down two ladies and their heavy suitcases. Struck by an attack of coughing that shook him like a reed in a tornado, Hasari was so unwell that two other pullers rushed to help him lie down on the seat of his carriage. Suddenly a face pockmarked from smallpox appeared above Hasari's. The eyes were full of sympathy.

"Well now, my friend," volunteered the stranger. "You don't look too well!"

This friendly remark comforted Hasari. There were not many people who treated you like a "friend" in this inhuman city. He wiped his bloodied mouth with a corner of his vest.

"It must really be a tough job to have to pull one of those carriages when you're coughing your head off!" continued the stranger.

Hasari nodded. "You bet your ass!"

"What would you say if I were to offer you as much money as you earn in two months sweating between your shafts, without your having to do anything," the stranger then inquired.

"As much money as . . ." stammered Hasari at a loss for words. "Oh, I would say that you were the god Hanuman in person." Then suddenly he remembered the middleman who had accosted him one day in the Bara Bazar: "If it's my blood you're after, you're on the wrong track," he announced sadly. "Even the vultures wouldn't want anything to do with my blood. It's rotten."

"It's not your blood I'm after. It's your bones."

"My bones?"

The puller's expression of horror brought a smile to the procurer's face.

"That's it," he explained calmly. "You come with me to my boss. He'll buy your bones for five hundred rupees. When you kick off he'll collect your body and take your skeleton."

This man was one of the links in a singular trade that made

India the prime exporter of human bones in the world. Each year, some twenty thousand whole skeletons and tens of thousands of different carefully packed bones departed from India's airports and seaports, destined for medical schools in the United States, Europe, Japan, and Australia. This extremely lucrative business brought in approximately one and a half million dollars a year. Its center was Calcutta. The principal exporters—eight in number—all had a house of their own and their names featured in the register of the local customs headquarters. They went under the names of Fashiono & Co., Hilton & Co., Krishnaraj Stores, R. B. & Co., M. B. & Co., Vista & Co., Sourab and Reknas Ltd., and finally Mitra & Co. Precise administrative regulations governed the exercise of this trade. A special manual entitled the *Export Policy Book* specified in particular that "the export of skeletons and human bones is authorized upon the furnishing of a certificate of origin from the corpse signed by a police officer of at least substantive superintendent rank." The same document stipulated that the bones could not be exported except for the purposes of study or medical research. It did, however, provide for the fact that exportation could be effected "for other reasons, upon examination of individual cases."

The fact that Calcutta was the center of this strange activity had nothing to do with the mortality rate in its slums. This commerce owed its prosperity to the presence in the city of a community of several hundred immigrants from Bihar who belonged to an extremely low caste, that of the *Doms*. *Doms* are destined from birth to take care of the dead. Often they are also looked upon as footpads, pillagers of corpses. They usually live near the funeral pyres of the Hooghly and near cemeteries or hospital morgues and they do not mix with other residents. It was they who provided the exporters with most of the remains necessary for their activities. They came by their macabre merchandise in a variety of ways: primarily by picking up the bones and corpses cast up on the bank of the Hooghly, for tradition determined that many bodies—those of certain *Saddhus*, lepers, or children less than a year old, for example—should be committed to the river rather than cremated. At the entrance to the cremation area they would also intercept families who were too poor to buy wood for a pyre or pay for the services of a priest. The *Doms* would offer to undertake the funeral rites themselves for a more advantageous price. Such poor people were completely ignorant of the fact that their relative's remains would be cut up in a nearby hut, that his bones would be sold to an exporter, and that one day his skull, his spinal column, perhaps even his complete skeleton would be exhibited for the edification of American, Japanese, or Australian medical students. Hospital mortuaries provided another reliable source of bones. In the Momimpur morgue alone, more than twenty-five hundred unclaimed bodies fell into the hands of the *Doms* each year. When demand was exceptionally great, they would even go and compete with the jackals for the bones of the dead buried in the Christian and Muslim cemeteries. In short, there was never any real danger of running out of merchandise. Yet the ingenuity of the traffickers had just conceived of a fresh means of supply. The idea of buying a man while he was still walking about, in much the same way that you might purchase an animal for slaughter, in order to secure the right to dispose of his bones when he died, was as diabolical as it was ingenious. It made it possible to accumulate unlimited stock for there was certainly no shortage of poor or moribund people in Calcutta.

"Five hundred rupees!" The sum tumbled about in Hasari's head like the balls in a lottery barrel. The procurer had not been mistaken. He knew how to spot his prey at a glance. The streets were full of poor devils coughing their lungs up, but not all of them were in a position to provide the necessary guarantees. For the purchase of a man to represent a profit-making venture, he must have a family, an employer, friends, in other words an identity and an address. How else could his body be retrieved after his death?

"Well, friend, do you agree?"

Hasari looked up into the pockmarked face awaiting his response. He remained silent but the man showed no sign of impatience. He was used to this, "Even a fellow with his back against the wall doesn't just sell his body like a piece of *khadi.*"

"Five hundred rupees, no less! What do you say to that?" In the company of Ramatullah, the puller who shared his rickshaw, Hasari was still marveling at the astonishing offer he had just been made. He had asked the procurer for time to think it over until the next day. Ramatullah was a Muslim. Persuaded that when he died, Allah would come to drag him straight into paradise by the hair, any idea of bodily mutilation after death was repugnant to him. The mullahs of his religion even forbade the donation of organs to science, and the few Indian eye banks had not one single Muslim on their files. Nevertheless the sum was so considerable that he could not fail to be dazzled by it.

"Hasari, you've got to do it," he eventually advised. "Your great God will forgive you. He knows you've got to get your daughter married."

The former peasant was equally anxious not to offend the gods. The Hindu faith required that, for the soul to "transmigrate" into another form after death, the body should first be destroyed and reduced to ashes by the fire that purifies all. "What will become of my soul if my bones and my flesh are cut up by those butchers instead of being burned in the flames of a funeral pyre?" lamented the rickshaw puller. He resolved to confide in Kovalski. In principle the priest's attitude fell into line with that of the Muslim Ramatullah. The Christian idea of resurrection implied the existence of an intact body coming to life again in all its vigor and beauty to take its place alongside its Creator in its original state of wholeness. Years of living in the poverty of a slum, however, had led Kovalski to accept occasionally compromises between the ideals of faith and the imperatives of survival.

"I think you should take this opportunity to further the completion of your mission here below," he declared reluctantly, drawing the rickshaw puller's attention to his daughter who was busy delousing her little brother at the other end of the compound.

As a two-story building eaten away by the humidity, next door to a kind of warehouse, there was nothing to distinguish the appointments of "Mitra & Co." from those of hundreds of other small-scale enterprises scattered throughout the city, except that this company bore no notice to indicate the nature of its undertakings. The procurer with the pockmarked skin knocked several times at the door of the warehouse and soon a face appeared in the half-open door. The procurer indicated Hasari.

"I'm bringing a client," he announced.

The door opened wide and the porter motioned to the two men to enter. The smell that hit them was a suffocating stench of the kind that tears at the throat, overpowers, and flattens. Hasari had never smelled anything like it before. For a moment he wavered in his resolve, but his companion pushed him forward. It was then that he saw the source of the stench. He had just entered a place such as only the imaginations of Dante or Dürer could have conceived, an unbelievable catacomb for the next world in which dozens of skeletons of all different sizes were ranged upright along the walls like a parade of phantoms, where rows of tables and shelves were covered with human remnants. There were thousands of bones from every part of the body: hundreds of skulls, spinal columns, thoraxes, hands and feet, sacrums, coccyxes, whole pelvises, and even hyoids—those little U-shaped bones in the neck. Perhaps most astonishing of all, however, was the supermarketlike display of this macabre bazaar. Every skeleton, indeed every bone, bore a label on which the price was marked in U.S. dollars. An adult skeleton for demonstration purposes, with movable bones and metal articulation, was worth between two hundred and thirty and three hundred and fifty dollars, according to its size and the quality of workmanship. For a mere hundred or a hundred and twenty dollars, you could acquire a child's skeleton without articulation, a complete thorax for forty dollars, a skull for six. The very same "items" could cost ten times more, however, if they had been subject to special preparation.

Mitra & Co. maintained a whole team of specialist bone extractors, painters, and sculptors. These craftsmen worked in a poorly lit room at the end of the gallery. Crouched among their mountains of human remains, they looked like the survivors of some prehistoric cataclysm, scraping, decorticating, assembling, and decorating their funereal objects with precise gestures. Sometimes real works of art emerged from their hands, like the collection of articulated skulls with jaws that could be dismantled and movable teeth, ordered by the dental faculty of a large American university in the Midwest. Of all the precious merchandise exported from India, doubtless none was packaged with more care. Each item was first protected by a small cotton pad, then wrapped in a carefully stitched piece of linen before being placed in a special cardboard box and then in a packing case covered with labels marked "Very Fragile. Handle with Care." "Dear God," thought Hasari, flabbergasted by what he saw. "Those poor chaps' bones were never given such celebrity treatment when they were alive."

Not all the merchandise delivered up by the *Doms* was necessarily destined for such dignified use. Thousands of skulls, tibias, collarbones, femurs, and other pieces that had been gnawed by jackals or had spent too long in the water, ended up more prosaically between the teeth of a crushing mill and then in a boiling pot where they were turned into glue. It was from precisely that subsidiary process that the stench arose.

In a cabin at the far end of the gallery, they found the man who negotiated the purchase of "living" skeletons. In his white overalls he presided over a dusty table heaped with files, paperwork, registers, and folders, threatened every fifteen seconds by the motion of a rotating fan. Actually, not a single paper ever flew away, thanks to an entire collection of paperweights made out of the skulls of newborn babies and decorated with red and black tantric symbols. Mitra & Co. also exported thousands of skulls to Nepal, Tibet, and even China, to be used for devotional purposes. Other countries imported them to make them into votive cups or ashtrays.

The toothless employee examined the rickshaw puller attentively. The latter's prominent collarbone, his lean thorax, and vertebrae protruding like a catfish's spine reassured him. There was no doubt about it: the merchandise was bona fide. It would not be unduly long before what was left of this poor fellow enriched the stocks of Mitra & Co. He gave the procurer a satisfied wink. All he had to do now was draw up a formal purchase agreement and inform the *Doms* who lived closest to the slum where Hasari resided so that they knew where to recover the corpse when the time came.

These various formalities took three days, at the end of which Hasari was entitled to a first payment of one hundred and fifty rupees. Like all the other companies engaged in the same trade, Mitra & Co. were reluctant to invest their money on too long-term a basis. Hasari was, therefore, informed that the sum outstanding would be paid as soon as his state of health would show further deteriorating signs.

65

SOME RUDIMENTARY scenery on trestles was enough. It was as if all the grayness, all the mud, the stench, the flies, the mosquitoes, the cockroaches, the rats, the hunger, the anguish, the sickness, and the death had faded away. The time for dreams had come once more. With their eyes starting out of their heads and their emaciated bodies racked with laughter or with tears, the imprisoned people of the City of Joy were rediscovering the thousand enchantments and dramatic episodes of the ancient folk story that had molded them. The epic Ramayana was to India what the Golden Legend, the Chanson de Roland, and the Bible had been to the crowds assembled on Europe's cathedrals' steps. For three months the troupe of actors and strolling musicians had installed itself and its carts bulging with drapes and costumes in between the two large buffalo sheds at the very heart of the slum. News of their arrival had spread from one compound to the next like the announcement of a kindly monsoon. Thousands of people flocked to the site. Children who had never seen such a thing as a tree, a bird, or a hind came to delight in the cardboard forest where the handsome prince Rama and his divine Sita would experience the joy of love before being torn from each other's arms. Hours before the presentation of the first tableau, the little esplanade in front of the stage was already covered with a sea of brown heads and motley veils. All the nearby roofs accommodated clusters of spectators. The audience trembled in anticipation of the curtain rising, impatient to let themselves be borne away from their existence in garbage for a few hours by their heroes, eager to find in the song's

twenty-five thousand verses fresh reasons for continuing to live
and to hope.

Written, so tradition has it, by a sage at the dictation of the
gods two and a half thousand years ago, the Ramayana opens with
a marvelous love story. The handsome young Rama, the only one
of all the princes to be able to bend the bow of the god Shiva,
receives as his reward the princess Sita. Her father wishes to give
his throne to the young couple but, succumbing in his weakness to
one of his favorite ladies, he exiles them instead to the wild forests
of central India. There they are attacked by demon brigands whose
leader, the terrible Ravana, harbors a lustful passion for Sita.
Tricking her husband into leaving her alone, the demon succeeds
in seizing the princess and lifting her onto his winged chariot
drawn by flying, carnivorous donkeys. He transports her to his
fabulous island of Lanka—none other than Ceylon—where he
shuts her up in his quarters, seeking in vain to seduce her.

In order to win back his wife, Rama forms an alliance with the
king of the monkeys who places at the prince's disposal his principal general, Hanuman, and the whole army of monkeys aided by
bands of squirrels. With one single prodigious leap across the sea,
the monkey general reaches Ceylon, finds the captive princess,
reassures her, and after a thousand heroic and comic reversals
reports back to Rama. With the help of the monkey army, the latter
manages to sling a bridge across the sea and invade the island. A
furious battle is then waged against the demons. Eventually Rama
personally defeats the odious Ravana and good thus triumphs over
evil. The freed Sita appears, overwhelmed with joy.

Complications, however, set in, for Rama sadly pushes her
away. "What man could take back and cherish a woman who has
lived in another's house?" he exclaims. The faultless Sita,
wounded to the quick, then has a funeral pyre erected and casts
herself into the flames. Virtue, however, cannot perish in the fire:
the flames spare her, testifying to her innocence, and all ends with
a grand finale. The bewildered Rama takes back his wife and returns with her in triumph to his capital, where he is at last crowned
amid unforgettable rejoicing.

The ragamuffins of the City of Joy knew every tableau, every
scene, every twist and turn of this flowing epic. They followed each
move made by the actors, the mimes, the clowns, and the acrobats.

They laughed, cried, suffered, and rejoiced with them. Over their rags they felt the weight of the performers' costumes, on their cheeks they felt the thickness of their makeup. Many of them even knew whole passages from the text word for word. In India it is quite possible for a person to be "illiterate" and still know thousands of verses of epic poetry by heart. Old Surya from the tea shop, the children of Mehboub and Selima, Kovalski's former neighbors, the coal man from Nizamudhin Lane, Margareta and her offspring, the lovely Kalima and the other eunuchs, the former sailor from Kerala and his aborigine neighbors, Bandona and her Assamese brothers and sisters, the godfather and his thugs, hundreds of Hindus, Christians, and even Muslims packed themselves in side by side, night after night, before the magic stage. Among the most assiduous spectators was Hasari Pal. "That broken man went every night," Kovalski was to say, "to draw new strength from his encounter with the exemplary obstinacy of Rama, the courage of the monkey general, and the virtue of Sita."

To the rickshaw puller "those heroes were like tree trunks in the middle of raging floodwaters, life buoys that you could cling to!" He could remember how when he was a small child, carried on his mother's hip as she walked the narrow dikes across the rice fields, she used to sing softly to him the verses of the mythical adventures of the monkey general. Later, whenever bards and storytellers passed through the village, his family would gather along with all the others in the square, to listen for nights on end to the extravagant recitations always so rich in resilience, which had nourished the beliefs of India since time immemorial and given a religious dimension to its everyday life. There was not one infant on that vast peninsula who did not fall asleep to the sound of his elder sister intoning a few episodes from that great poem, not one children's game that did not derive its inspiration from the confrontations between good and evil, not a single schoolbook that did not extol the exploits of the heroes, not a marriage ceremony that did not cite Sita as an example of the virtues of fidelity. Each year, several grand festivals commemorated the victory of Rama and the benevolence of the monkey god. Each evening in Calcutta, thousands of dockers, coolies, rickshaw pullers, laborers, and starving people would assemble around the storytellers on the embankments of the Hooghly. Squatting for hours, their eyes half-closed, these people whom happiness seemed to have somehow overlooked, exchanged the harshness of their reality for a few grains of fantasy.

Above the multitudes squeezed around the trestled boards, there often rose the slightly balding skull of Stephan Kovalski. Despite his difficulties in grasping the subtleties of the language and the little free time he had, he greatly loved to watch the performances. "It was the perfect way to get to know the memory of a people," he was to say. "The Ramayana is a living encyclopedia. There, in my slum, I suddenly went back in time. The perfumes, gifts, weapons, court life, music, the habits of wild elephants, the forests of India soon held no secrets from me. But above all, that great popular epic was an ideal means to marry the mentality of my brothers and enter more completely into my new skin. Marrying their mentality meant no longer thinking of the Red Sea when you talk of a dry passage across the waters, but rather of the straits of Ceylon. It meant no longer citing one of our miracles as evidence of a supernatural event, but rather the exploit of the monkey general Hanuman who transported the Himalayas in his hand just so that the captive Sita could smell a flower. It meant wishing a woman about to give birth that she will be the mother of one of the five Pandavas. Entry into the mentality of a people involves using its imagery, its myths, and its beliefs. That applied to the Muslims too. What smiles I brought to their faces when I mentioned the name of the emperor Akbar, when I referred to Mohammed, or compared a little girl to the princess Nur Jahan or to some other Mogul queen, or when I deciphered an Urdu text on a calendar hanging at the back of one of their hovels."

66

HIS NAME WAS NISSAR. He was twelve years old and he was a
Muslim. The whole compound agreed: that boy was an archangel.
His luminous face, the keenness of his gaze, his natural authority
made him a being apart. The harelip that revealed his dazzling
teeth and the small monkey with the sad eyes that never left his
shoulders further accentuated how different he was. "Nissar was a
diamond with a thousand facets, a firework, a glittering light in the
world," Kovalski was to comment. Yet the skinny little boy with
short hair was not the son of any of the families in the compound.
He had been found one evening half-dead on a pavement in Dalhousie Square and picked up by Bouddhou Koujour, the aborigine
who killed the eunuch with the cobra. Driven away from his village
in Bihar by parents who could no longer feed him, Nissar had
traveled on the roofs of trains to get to the mirage city. After
wandering around for a few days, feeding himself on scraps, he
found in an alleyway of the Bara Bazar, the object that was to
become both a means of earning a living and his talisman: a
patched old jute sack. Like thousands of other starving youngsters,
Nissar became a ragpicker. Every evening he went to deposit his
pitiful findings in the den of a ragpicker wholesaler and received in
exchange a few small coins, sometimes one or two rupees. One day
a secondhand dealer gave him a monkey. Christened Hanuman,
the animal slept with him on the pavements and they became
inseparable companions. On monsoon nights, Nissar would shelter them both as best he could under the awning of a shop or in the
arcades on Chowringhee Avenue. His great love were the movies.
As soon as he had earned a few *paisas,* he would rush off with his

monkey to one of the caravansaries, purveyors of dreams to the poor of the slums. His favorite actor was a certain Dilip Kumar, who always took the parts of princes and maharajahs draped in brocade tunics, jewels, and beautiful courtesans.

The integration of this young abandoned Muslim into the little Hindu world of the compound posed very few problems. His two years of drifting on the asphalt of the great city had endowed him with a special kind of aura. This fact was in itself remarkable for the living conditions of the other youngsters in the compound were hardly less harsh. As soon as they could walk, they were expected to do their bit, just like adults, toward their collective survival. They were spared no task, not even the drudgery of fetching water which, because of the weight of the buckets, often caused irreparable damage to their fragile, undernourished bone structure. Two or three out of fifty were lucky enough to go to school. (The evening classes subsidized by Kovalski did not yet involve anyone in this compound.) By the time they were seven or eight they were nearly all working. Some of them were salesmen or assistants in a grocer's store, a cobbler's workshop, or a *pan* or *bidi* shop. Others toiled from dawn to dusk in one of the eating houses in the main street. Others knew the slavery of the small factories found in such profusion in the slums. The two sons of the former sailor from Kerala earned their food and the twenty rupees a month, which enabled their parents to buy just sixteen pounds of rice, by making chains for ships for ten hours at a stretch in one of the innumerable sweatshops.

Before Nissar arrived, three boys from the compound had already been working as ragpickers. It had not, however, proved to be a very profitable occupation. In a slum nothing is ever thrown away. Anything that can be salvaged—the smallest bit of coal, the remains of a cow dung cake, a shred of shirt, a broken bottle end, a coconut shell—can become the object of covetousness.

"You won't find anything here but small fry. To bring back a good catch you have to go where the real fish are," the young Nissar announced one evening to the three little Hindu ragpickers.

Hasari had overheard the remark. "That kid must know where there's gold to be struck," he told himself. Obsessed as he was with the idea of finding the money for his daughter's dowry, the idea of a secret source of wealth excited him. "Whatever happens he's got to take Shambu with him," he confided to Kovalski, pointing to his second son who was flying a kite up on the roof. Hasari never stopped computing figures: "Suppose I add the five hundred rupees of my bones to the eight hundred I can expect to earn wading about with my rickshaw in the monsoon slush. If, on top of that Shambu brings back two or three hundred rupees from rag picking with the young Muslim, that makes . . . that makes (since he had had the red fever Hasari's reckoning had slowed down) . . . that makes it close to two thousand rupees! Just think, Big Brother Stephan! All I'd have to do then would be to pay a little visit to the *mahajan* with the earrings belonging to the mother of my children and that'd be it!" Hasari could already see the Brahmin binding his daughter's hand to that of her husband.

A gold mine! The rickshaw puller had not been dreaming. It was indeed for an El Dorado, a land of milk and honey, that the Muslim boy with the harelip set off each morning with his monkey. Yet in that same place, on a bed of trash the police had one day set fire to all unlicensed rickshaws. The name under which it appeared in the municipality records and plans did not instantly evoke the idea of wealth, but in a city where even a poster taken off a wall or a bent nail was of some value, the Calcutta dumping ground might well seem like a promised land to the thousands of human ants that scrabbled about on it. Young Nissar was among their number and henceforth the three other little ragpickers from the compound would accompany him together with Shambu Pal whom he had agreed to take with him.

"Get your son up tomorrow at the first crow of the eunuchs' cockerel," Nissar ordered the rickshaw puller. "We leave at dawn."

*

Nissar led his comrades to the mouth of the great Howrah Bridge. Pointing to one of the overloaded buses, he directed Shambu to cling onto the spare wheel. The others climbed onto the rear bumper. Every day tens of thousands of people made use of Calcutta's public transport in this way without paying. They were not the only defrauders. The real champions of this system were some of the conductors themselves who, it was said, pocketed part of the takings by selling passengers false tickets. In the hellish traffic, a journey undertaken balancing on the bumpers or the spare tire, or clinging onto the clusters of humanity that hung from the windows, was a dangerous acrobatic feat. Nearly every week there was some mention in the papers of the death of an illicit passenger squashed between the metalwork, crushed by the wheels of a truck, or electrocuted by a streetcar.

"Off, fellows!"

Nissar's order rang out through the already scorching early morning air. The five children let themselves drop onto the asphalt. The bus had just emerged from the last suburb to the east of the city and the road now ran across a vast, flat expanse of marshy land. Shambu rubbed his eyes still heavy with sleep. A mile and a half away to the east, the sky was black with clouds of vultures.

"Is it over there?" he asked.

Nissar wagged his head. With his old jute sack slung over one shoulder and his monkey on the other looking for nits in his hair, he took the head of the group. He was happy in his role as a ragpicker. Ragpickers were free and each day brought with it new hope of some outstanding discovery. They walked for half a mile until suddenly, just as his father had done on the evening the rickshaws were burned, Shambu experienced the shock of the stench rising from the dump; but the nostrils of a child reared on the pavements of Calcutta are less sensitive than those of a peasant used to the aromas of the countryside. Shambu followed Nissar and the others without faltering. Apart from the vultures and the cows that grazed on the refuse, large numbers of men, women, and children were already at work on the huge mound. Nissar stopped his party three hundred yards short of the approach ramp used by the dump trucks.

"We're going to have to be quick," he announced in a voice that his harelip turned into a whistle. "It's the hotels and hospitals day. Mustn't miss out on their goods."

Sure enough, once a week the municipal dump trucks brought the refuse from the establishments mentioned. Their arrival was always greeted with a frantic onslaught. It was only to be expected. Real treasure often lay concealed in their loads, the kind that represented top value on the dumping ground exchange: flasks, bandages, syringes, remnants of coal, scraps of food.

"You, Shambu," ordered the young Muslim, pointing to a kind of low burrow, "park yourself in that hole. As soon as you see a bit of red rag in the window of a truck, give a whistle to let me know. That means it's coming from a hospital or a hotel." Nissar took a five-rupee note out of his belt. Showing it to his companions, he went on, "I'll run over to the truck waving this note. The driver will slow down to grab it. That's when we all have to jump onto the back. The driver will make for a distant corner of the dump and ditch all his load as quickly as possible. We'll really have to look quickly before the others get there."

The young Muslim with the harelip had spoken with all the calmness and authority of a commando leader. They all rushed to their respective positions to await the first truck. Most of the other ragpickers already foraging about in the mound lived in the small number of hovels that stood nearby. The ragpickers were mostly women and children, for the local men were otherwise occupied, macerating the guts of animals and vegetable scraps in watertight jars, which they submerged at the bottom of foul reservoirs of green, stagnant water. They subsequently distilled these concoctions and the juice extracted was put into bottles and delivered to the clandestine gambling dens of Calcutta and the drinking places in the slums. "That puts the life back into a man!" Hasari used to say, remembering his libations with Ram Chander and Son of Miracle. Yet the forbidden alcohol, the famous *bangla*, had killed more Indians than had any number of natural disasters.

The first yellow truck arrived, then another, then a third. None of them, however, was carrying the red signal. Nobody moved. Hasari's son felt as if his pupils were about to burst. He had never seen such a spectacle. Just above him in the searing early morning light, an extraordinary ballet was unfolding. A host of barefoot women and children were scouring the hill of refuse with baskets in one hand and spikes in the other. The arrival of each vehicle unleashed a frenzied seething of activity as everyone scrambled after it. A suffocating cloud of sulphur dust enveloped each unloading. Even more mind-boggling was the flurried searching that went on around the bulldozers there to level out the mountains of refuse. Children slipped without hesitation under the mastodons to be the first to explore the manna turned over by their steel scoops. How many had perished, suffocated by their solid bulk or

crushed by their caterpillar bands? Shambu felt a cold sweat break
out on his back. "Would I be capable of such courage?" he wondered. Just then a fourth truck appeared, but still there was no red
rag at the window. Above him, the ballet continued. To protect
themselves against the sun and the dust, the women and girls had
covered their heads and faces with old but colorful pieces of cloth
which made them look like harem princesses. As for the boys, with
their felt hats, their caps full of holes, and their worn-out shoes that
were far too big for them, they all looked like Charlie Chaplin in his
early films. Each had his speciality. The women tended to look for
bits of coal and wood. The children preferred things made out of
leather, plastic, or glass as well as bones, shellfish, and papers.
They all picked up anything edible with equal enthusiasm: rotten
fruit, peelings, crusts of bread. This kind of picking was the most
difficult and often the most dangerous. Shambu saw a vulture bear
down like a torpedo on a small boy to snatch the piece of meat he
had just found. Vultures were not the only creatures to compete
with men for grazing ground. Pigs, cows, goats, pariah dogs and, at
night, even hyenas and jackals had chosen to make their homes on
the dump, as had millions of other small creatures and insects. The
flies were the most aggressive. Greenish in color, they buzzed
about in their myriads, clinging to men and beasts, even to their
eyes, mouths, or the inside of their noses and ears. Those flies were
completely at home among all that decaying matter and they made
quite certain that everyone knew it.

The most surprising factor about this nightmare was that all
the ingredients of normal life had been established here. Among
the heaps of stinking rubbish, Shambu could see ice-cream salesmen on their decorated carrier tricycles, water vendors laden with
large goatskin bottles, fritter makers squatting under sunshades
behind their smoking braziers, *bangla* retailers surrounded by bottles set out like bowling pins. So that mothers could forage more
effectively among the refuse, there were even baby-sitters to look
after their children, usually very young girls seated under old black
umbrellas with holes in them, with several fly-covered babies in
their laps.

The dumpsite was also a busy trading center, a bazaar, a
money market. A whole tribe of secondhand salesmen and scrap
iron merchants had grafted themselves onto that of the ragpickers.

Each one had his speciality. Using archaic scales, traders in vests and *longhis* would buy by the weight anything the foragers had unearthed. Every evening wholesalers would come with trucks to harvest the various treasures which, once cleaned and sorted, would be resold to factories for recycling.

Shambu felt his heart begin to pound. He had just seen the tip-off color in the window of a truck. Stuffing his fingers into his mouth, he whistled in the manner agreed. Instantly he saw Nissar, straddled by his monkey, loom up in the cloud of dust and jump onto the running board to hand over his five-rupee note. The driver put on his brakes. This was the signal. With the agility of lizards, the five little ragpickers from the City of Joy climbed aboard the dump truck full of refuse.

"All of you, flat on your bellies!" Nissar ordered.

The truck accelerated to climb the access slope to the dump. Half-submerged in the filthy cargo the five ragpickers were well out of sight of any onlookers. "That garbage was sticky and burned you at the same time," Shambu was to recount, "but worst of all, I felt as if thousands of creepy-crawlies were coming out of it and jumping onto me. The enormous cockroaches were the most frightening. They ran over my legs, my arms, my neck."

Instead of heading for the bulldozers, the driver veered off in the opposite direction. This was part of the "deal." Nissar and his band would have ten minutes in which to forage alone. It all went off like a holdup in the films. The truck pulled up sharply. The five boys leaped down and the dump truck unloaded its avalanche of garbage. They scrabbled, located, sorted, and stowed their booty away as fast as they could. With bottles, stray bits of cooking utensils and crockery, broken tools, pieces of tile, old tubes of toothpaste, run-down batteries, empty tins, plastic soles, scraps of clothing, and papers, their bags were filled in a trice.

"Let's hurry, fellows! Here come the others."

Nissar knew only too well that they had to scram from there before the furious crowd of other ragpickers fell upon them. Caught up in the fever of the search, Shambu sank his spike into the stinking mass for one last time and let out a cry. "I had just seen something glinting among all that shit. I thought it was a coin and struck out frenziedly to free it. What I brought out on the end of my hook was a bracelet, and on the end of the bracelet was a watch."

*

"At first an expression of total stupefaction came over Hasari Pal's face," Kovalski was to say. "Then he took the object in his hands and lifted it up with so much emotion and respect that we thought he wanted to offer it to some deity. All he actually wanted to do was put it to his ear." The voices in the compound fell silent. For several seconds Hasari remained like that, immobile, incapable of uttering a word, as if transfigured by the jewel that ticked in unison with the beating of his heart.

It was at this point that something very strange occurred. Propelled by some mysterious force, an eddy of scorching air suddenly surged off the rooftops to shower the compound with the sound of broken tiles. Immediately thereafter a series of thunderbolts rolled across the sky. Hasari and all the other residents looked up at the heavens. Above the smoke of the *chulas* appeared great waves of black clouds. The rickshaw puller felt tears obscure his vision. "That's it," he thought. "The monsoon has come. I am saved. I shall be able to die in peace. Thanks to this watch and to the downpour that is about to fall, thanks to the five hundred rupees for my bones, my daughter will have a good husband."

67

"THE CITY HAD changed our eyes," Hasari was to recount. In the village we would scrutinize the sky for days on end, waiting for the first clouds to come bearing water. We would dance and sing and implore the goddess Lakshmi to make our fields fertile with a beneficent downpour. But in Calcutta there was nothing to make fertile. Neither the streets, nor the pavements, the houses, buses, nor trucks could be rendered fruitful by the water that makes the rice grow in our countryside. That doesn't mean that here we did not yearn for the monsoon; we yearned for it because of the appalling heat that reduced you to a state where you could have stopped in the street and just lain down and died. Sometimes there wasn't any need to stop to wait for death. Instead it would take you by surprise in midaction, when you were taking a schoolboy to school or a *marwari* to the movies. You just collapsed suddenly. Sometimes your own carriage would run over you before tipping over onto a bus or the pavement. That was known as the 'stroke of Surya', the stroke of the Sun-god.

"All that night and throughout the next day big, black clouds rolled across the sky, plunging the city into almost total darkness. The clouds mingled with the fumes and the dust. Soon, above the rooftops, there appeared a kind of blackish mantle. It was as if Sani, the planet that augurs ill, wanted to punish us with asphyxiation. People were suffocating. They fought in the streets over nothing. The cops' sticks began to twitch without your even knowing why. I was having more and more difficulty breathing. Even the crows and the rats scavenging among the piles of garbage in Wood Street had a peculiar look about them. The children never stopped crying.

Dogs barked ceaselessly. I found myself wondering whether, rather than the monsoon, this might not be the end of the world that was approaching.

"Lots of people begged me to take them to the hospital. They wanted someone to help them breathe. But I knew that in the hospitals they wouldn't even help people to die. At the entrance to Lower Circular Road, I picked up an old woman groaning on the pavement. She was all dried out. Her skin was like cardboard. I bought a coconut and made her drink the tepid, slightly sweet milk from it. Then I took her to the hospital, where such a long time ago, our coolie friend had died.

"After three days had gone by, a violent wind blew up, a tornado of sand and dust such as we had already had during the premonsoon storms. In a matter of minutes the whole city was covered in a sheet of yellow sand. Apparently that sand comes from the Himalayan Mountains and from the plateaus on the Chinese side. It was terrifying. Sand and dust permeated everything. People's eyes and mouths were full of it. I don't know whether it was because of those gusts of wind or because of the red fever, but all of a sudden I felt quite unable to lift the shafts of my old cart. I was reduced to nothing by some force from the beyond. I lay down on the canvas seat with my legs in the air, trying to get my breath back. My head was buzzing, my eyes hurt, and my stomach was knotted with cramps. How long did I lie there like that? In the absence of the sun, hidden as it was by black clouds, I completely lost all track of time."

The nightmare lasted for several days. In the City of Joy the drought began to dry up the wells and fountains. The number of victims of dehydration multiplied and Max exhausted his small supply of serum in the space of a few hours. On the sixth day, toward noon, the thermometer rose to one hundred and seventeen degrees Fahrenheit. The wind had dropped and the slum stifled beneath a blanket of fire. Yet still no drop of water fell. Persuaded that this year the monsoon would not come, many of the residents lay down in their hovels to wait for the wheel of their karma to put an end to their torment.

The next day, a few short squalls restored a little hope. Towards midday, however, despite all the offerings placed on the altars to the gods, the thermometer went wild again. Its excesses were a harsh test of strength for Max, Bandona, and all the other members of the Committee for Mutual Aid. An SOS could summon them at any moment to the bedside of the latest heat victim.

Returning from one of these visits, Max had just gotten back to his room, exhausted, when he felt a damp, perfumed cloth on his sweating face. Bandona was gently mopping his brow. He grasped her hand and raised it to his lips. The unexpected contact with her skin, so fresh and so alive, in those sordid surroundings that smelled of ether and alcohol, threw him completely. The patients crowding at the door were dumbfounded. This kind of public demonstration of affection was quite uncommon in India.

He let go of the young woman's hand but kept the piece of linen, delighting in its perfume. The scent reminded him of something. He sought in his mind and suddenly the vision of Manubaï Chatterjee came to him. Hers was an unwonted, unreal image in this stricken slum. Despite the furnacelike heat, he shivered. The beautiful, rich Indian woman had brought so much embellishment to his life since that memorable night not so long ago, when for awhile he had forgotten his slum on the pillows of her muslin-draped four-poster bed. The very incarnation of the India of tales, myths, and spells, Manubaï had reminded him that luxury too was part of creation, that even in Calcutta it was possible to live surrounded by floral gardens, to eat and drink to repletion, and to rejoice in the pleasures of existence. Careless of what people might say about her, she had thrown several dinners in his honor in her sumptuous dining room decorated with paintings of tropical birds. She had taken him to diplomatic evenings, to receptions on the verdant lawns of the Tollygunge Golf Club, to bridge parties at Government House. Caressing her body vibrant with sensual fragrances, listening to the exhilarating sound of her laughter had given him a taste of the pleasures and refinements of an India of thousand-year-old enchantments.

Yet it was from another woman that he had drawn the will and the strength to pursue his task among the poor of the City of Joy. Bandona had no house, no servants, and no four-poster bed. She had never known anything but sweatshops, hovels, mud, and hunger, but her illuminating smile, her availability to others, her magical ability to bring relief and comfort were worth any amount of riches. In a world where tortured people every day besieged the door of his dispensary, bringing him their wounds, their illness, and their misery, in the face of all that suffering, naked despair, and death, it was this angel of mercy who had given Max the courage to stand firm. How could the shared experience of so much horror and the giving of so much love have failed to create an exceptional bond between them?

In this concentration camp where never a wink could pass unnoticed, it was quite inconceivable that such a bond should be outwardly manifested. Kovalski had warned Max: a slum was a pot boiling in a constant state of ferment. Any event that was the slightest bit out of the ordinary risked blowing the lid off and causing an explosion. Unlike Manubaï Chatterjee who, by virtue of her social position, could cast off her chains and defy the existing order, Bandona had not the least hope of ever being incarnated as Radha, the divine love of Krishna, the herdsman god and flutist. She was a prisoner of the rites and taboos that governed relationships between men and women in India. Like all the other young girls in her position, her destiny was to be given as a virgin to a husband, whom others—her father, an uncle, or a grandmother— would choose for her. Emotional and physical attraction would play no part in her union. She would see her husband for the first time at the ceremony. As for her wedding night, like all the future couplings of her married life, it would be primarily a ritual intended to conceive a male heir.

The circumstances of this ritual never failed to take Kovalski by surprise. "Suddenly I would hear a strange stirring among the people sleeping around me. Then in the darkness, I would make out people getting up discreetly. There would be the sound of doors, then stifled cries. The couples of the compound were making love. I knew then that it was *purnima,* the full moon."

At midday, three days after the episode with the perfumed handkerchief, when a further rise of the thermometer was subjecting the hovels of the City of Joy to a white heat, Bandona came into Max's room. She was holding an offering so rare in a slum that it was reserved for the gods.

"Doctor, Big Brother," she said kindly as she laid a bouquet of jasmine on the table, "don't be afraid. You're not alone. I am here to share it all with you."

Max took the flowers and sniffed at them. So intoxicating was the perfume they exuded that it was to him as if the decay, the stench, the blazing heat, the rat-infested framework, the mud of the walls, and the cockroaches were all borne away in a dream. All that remained of that damnable cesspool was the bouquet of happiness and the young girl in a bright pink sari, as motionless and meditative as a madonna in a cathedral.

"Thank you, sweet Bandona," he murmured at last, before borrowing Kovalski's favorite compliment. "You are a light of the world."

Max could not remember clearly the events that followed. The heat and fatigue had distorted his faculties. "I think," he was later to tell Kovalski, "that I went over to her and pressed her to me in an irrepressible need to possess that light. Bandona did not repulse me. On the contrary, with an embrace full of infinite tenderness, she offered me her love."

It was then that they heard a strange pattering noise on the roof. Max thought people were bombarding the tiles of his room with pebbles. Then he heard shouting in the neighboring buildings, immediately followed by a great commotion on all sides. A mighty thunderclap shook the walls and roofing of the little room. Max saw a troop of crazed rats emerge from the framework. Almost immediately all the tiles began to vibrate with a dull, powerful, regular sound. Bandona gently pulled away from Max's chest and looked up at the roof. Her small, almond eyes were brimming with tears of joy.

"Max, Big Brother, do you hear? The monsoon has arrived."

68

"IT MUST HAVE been late afternoon when I saw the first drop of water fall," Hasari was to recount. "It was enormous, but as soon as it hit the asphalt, the heat caused it to evaporate instantaneously." To the former peasant, banished forever from his land by drought, every year that first drop of water was like "manna from the heavens and proof that the gods could still weep for the plight of mankind on this earth." He thought of the singing and shrieks of joy that would be erupting in his village at that very moment. He imagined his father and his brothers squatting on the small dike at the edge of the rice field and gazing with wonder upon the young shoots, endowed with new vigor by dew from the heavens. "Will I ever see them again?" he sighed.

That first downpour of the monsoon was exceptionally violent. The water was battering the ground with the sound of drums beaten by a million fingers. Swiftly, Hasari put up the hood of his rickshaw, then gave himself up to the sheer joy of being soaked by the flood. "After a moment a breath of air blew through the warm shower, bringing with it a touch of coolness," he would say. "It was as if the portals of some giant icehouse had opened onto the city to release a little coolness into the overheated air stirred up by the tornado. By this time the beating of the water obscured all other sounds. All you could hear was the noise of the sky emptying itself. Instead of seeking shelter, people had rushed out into the rain. Children, completely naked, danced and laughed and performed somersaults. Women let themselves be drenched and their saris clung to their bodies like the thin bark of bamboo canes.

"At the rickshaw stand on Park Circus and elsewhere, the

pullers had begun to sing. Other workers joined them from the neighboring streets and took part in the thanksgiving. It was as if the whole city had gone down to the river to bathe and purify itself, the only difference being that the river was falling from the heavens instead of flowing over the ground. Even the old palm trees in the Harrington Street gardens trembled with joy. Trees that had looked like dusty old men were now all shiny with vitality, freshness, and youth.

"The euphoria lasted for several hours. While this communal bathing went on, we all felt like brothers. Coolies and *sadarjis*, rickshaw *wallahs*, *babus*, *marwaris* from the Bara Bazar, Biharis, Bengalis, Hindus, Muslims, Sikhs, Jains—all the different people of this great city were taking part in the same grateful *puja* by letting ourselves be soaked in the same saving deluge.

"The rain stopped suddenly to reveal the most extraordinary sight: in the sunlight the entire city began to steam like a gigantic boiling washtub. Then the downpour began again."

In the slum Max could hardly believe his eyes. "A whole race of people who only a second earlier had seemed half-dead had just been resurrected in a fantastic explosion of happiness, exuberance, and life," he would remember. "The men had torn off their shirts, women rushed out fully clothed, singing. Swarms of naked children were running about in all directions under the magical shower and shrieking for joy. It was a real festival, the carrying out of some ancestral ritual." At the end of his alleyway, he noticed a tall figure with white skin. Amid all the general levity, Kovalski was dancing unrestrainedly in a circle with the other residents of the City of Joy. On his streaming chest his metal cross jumped about as if to beat out the time. "He looked like the god Neptune under the waters of some celestial spring!"

69

FOR THREE DAYS the deluge continued, a deluge such as Bengal had not known for several years. From one compound to the next and throughout the alleyways of the City of Joy there soon rang out the word that had haunted the memory of India, for as long as the monsoon had existed. *"Barha!"* "Flood!" The jubilation of the initial moments was succeeded by a frantic hunt for umbrellas, bits of canvas, cardboard, or plastic, for anything that might serve to patch up the roofs and hold back the water invading the slum houses. There followed a search for containers and any utensils that could be used for bailing.

The water, however, always came back. It welled from out of the ground, for the slum was built on marshland. Finally, people went after bricks and any other materials they could use to raise the *charpoys* in the hovels, the only refuge on which the castaways could shelter their children and their few possessions. The situation grew rapidly worse and soon the dreaded noise was heard. The lapping of the water rose above the general commotion. Voices assumed a distinctive resonance because the sheet of water made them echo. One evening Max made out a feeble cry coming from the room next door. Intrigued, he went to investigate. The little girl who had brought him the umbrella during the premonsoon cataracts had slipped into the blackish floodwater and was in the process of drowning. He grabbed her by the hair and carried her back to his room.

His room by now was more a pestilential bog. Awash with the downpour, the latrines, the sewers, and the drainage channels from the cattle sheds were overflowing, and their vile tide had just spilled over the small protective wall outside his door. To save the cartons of milk and the medicine chest, Bandona had suspended a sheet from the four corners of the framework to form an improvised hammock which looked like the sail of painter Delacroix's Medusa's raft. Elsewhere umbrellas had come to the rescue. The trick was to hang them upside down under the gutters in the roof and empty them as soon as they were full.

Hunger soon added itself to the discomfort caused by the overflowing excrement, the stench, and the humidity. Their cow dung cakes reduced to sponges, the women could no longer cook food. Striking a match had become a real survival feat. "Look here, Big Brother," Kalima explained to Kovalski, "You rub the match vigorously under your armpit to warm the sulphur and then you strike it!" Sure enough, the miracle occurred: in the middle of the deluge a small flame emerged from between the eunuch's fingers. Kovalski tried to repeat the performance, but the armpit of a Polish Catholic priest, it would appear, does not secrete the same fluids as that of a *Hijra* from the India of the fakirs: the attempt ended in failure.

Kovalski set out in search of Margareta, Saladdin, Bandona, and other members of the Committee for Mutual Aid, groping his way through the darkness and wading up to his waist in the foul flood. Help had to be organized urgently. The rain was still falling. The water level was rising. The situation was becoming desperate.

*

The rest of Calcutta was experiencing a similar nightmare. In the lower districts to the East, on the Topsia, Kasba, and Tiljala side, thousands of residents had been compelled to flee or take refuge on the rooftops. The entire city was plunged into darkness: the cataracts had drowned the transformers and the electric power cables. No trains could reach the stations anymore. The traffic on the roads had come to a standstill and supplies had begun to run out. One pound of potatoes was already worth the astronomical sum of five rupees (fifty U.S. cents), an egg was nearly thirteen U.S. cents.

Much to the delight of the rickshaw pullers, there was no longer any other form of urban transport. Hasari, who had been counting on these catastrophic days to make up his daughter's dowry, was ecstatic. "What a joy it was to survey the spectacle of disaster presented by the proud red double-decker buses of Calcutta, the blue-and-white streetcars, the *Sadarji* Sikhs's arrogant yellow taxis, and the privately owned Ambassador cars with their uniformed drivers. With their engines flooded, their chassis up to the doors in mud, abandoned by their passengers, deserted by their crews, they looked like wreckage from the boats on the banks of the Hooghly. What a glorious opportunity we had been given at last to avenge the brutality we had taken from drivers and all the humiliating haggling the clients had inflicted on us. For once we could ask for the fares our efforts warranted. Our carts with high wheels and our legs were the only vehicles that could get about the flooded streets. To my dying day I shall hear the desperate appeals of people wanting me to carry them in my rickshaw. All of a sudden I had ceased to be a despised, insulted animal, whose sides people pummeled with their feet to make me go faster, and from whom people lopped ten or twenty *paisas* off the agreed price once they reached their destination. Now people fought with each other, offered two, three, or even four times the usual price just to be able to sit on the drenched seat of the only boats still afloat on the sea of Calcutta."

The shortest of trips made the former peasant a small fortune —almost an entire day's earning's before the monsoon. Yet how much suffering it cost him! Obscured by the floods, every obstacle became a trap. The bits of old iron on which his bare feet risked impaling themselves at any moment were just one example. "Wading up to your thighs through the slime, stumbling over the corpses of rats and dogs was a joke," Hasari was, however, to say, "by comparison with the torture the rain inflicted on our carcasses. Sweating in those cataracts without ever being able to dry yourself off, doesn't do wonders for your system. It was no use wringing out my *dhoti* and vest after each fare, and rubbing my hands and feet down, I was constantly bathed in moisture. Steeped in the infected water, many of my colleagues contracted skin diseases. Some of their feet looked like the lumps of old meat you see in butcher's stalls. They were covered with ulcerations and wounds. But the real danger lay in the bouts of intermittent heat and cold—especially in my case. Many of my colleagues left their lungs somewhere in the monsoon. They called it pneumonia or something like that. That's when you caught a raging fever, then shivered with cold and split open without even coughing. Ramatullah, the Muslim friend with whom I shared my rickshaw, claimed that it was much more pleasant than the red fever because it was all over with very quickly and you didn't have to spew your lungs out."

When Hasari showed his friend Son of Miracle the proceeds from his first two days in the monsoon, the taxi driver, condemned to unemployment by the flood, let out a hoot of admiration. "Hasari, as far as you're concerned, that's not water pouring out of the sky, it's gold nuggets!"

The rickshaw puller's joy was to be short-lived. The next day when he arrived at the Park Circus stand to pick up his rickshaw, he found his colleagues gathered around an old cart. He recognized his carriage and looked for Ramatullah among the group, but in vain. It was only then that one of the pullers, one of the oldest on the rank, said to him, "Your pal is dead, Hasari. He fell down a man hole. That's the third fellow to drown since yesterday. Apparently some *babu*'s given the order to take off all the drain covers to make it easier for the water to flow away."

*

Kovalski was passing in front of his former room in Nizamudhin Lane when he felt a small hand brush against him. He grabbed hold of it only to find that it was inert. He tugged at the little body floating on the surface of the water and hoisted it onto the platform of the tea shop belonging to Surya, the old Hindu. He called out, paddled over to Mehboub's house and tried his onetime neighbor's door, then knocked at Sabia's mother's hovel. There was nobody around. The alleyway looked like a film set deserted by its extras. All he could hear was the beating of the rain, the lapping of the water, and the piercing cries of the rats as they fled from their lairs. From time to time one of them would drop into the water with a splash. Testing the ground with every step to avoid falling into the deep drains that cut across the alley, Kovalski covered several hundred feet. Suddenly a voice rose from the cesspool, his voice, a deep, powerful voice which soared upward through the pouring rain to the opaque vault of a sky streaked with lightning. "Nearer my God to thee, nearer my God to thee . . ." sang the priest at the top of his lungs as had the shipwrecked passengers of the *Titanic* on the night their liner sank beneath the waves.

The Indians belonging to the Committee for Mutual Aid were waiting in Max's room. Everyone was up to his knees in water. The atmosphere was gloomy.

"Big Brother Stephan, panic has broken out," announced the old man Saladdin who was used to the slums being flooded. "Everywhere people are running away. At least five hundred occupants have already taken refuge in the great mosque."

The Jama Masjid was the only building with several stories.

"And this is only the beginning," said Margareta whose soaked sari was clinging to her skin. "Apparently the Ganges is overflowing its banks."

"That's enough bad news!" interrupted the Anglo-Indian Aristotle John. "We're not here to whine but to decide how we can help."

"Aristotle John is right!" said Kovalski, whose sneakers full of water were sending up a steady flow of bubbles.

A silence ensued. Each one was conscious of the enormity of the task. Max was the first to speak.

"We ought to vaccinate people quickly—against cholera, typhoid . . . There's a risk of epidemics . . ."

"How many doses have you got?" asked Kovalski, pointing to the medicine chest in the hammock.

"Pathetically few. We'll have to try and get some from the hospitals."

The young doctor's candor made the assembly smile. "This American is incorrigible," reflected Kovalski. "After all these months in Calcutta, he still thinks as if he's in Miami."

"Shouldn't we start by organizing emergency provisions for the refugees?" suggested Saladdin. "Thousands of people are going to find themselves without food and water."

"Definitely!" said Kovalski.

It was at this point that Bandona's voice was heard. "Big Brother Stephan, our first priority must go to the old and infirm who have stayed in their homes," she said gently but firmly. "Many of them will drown if someone doesn't go and find them."

When it came to need, no one knew the order of priorities better than the young Assamese girl. On this occasion, however, she was wrong. Her appeal had suddenly reminded Kovalski of something even more urgent.

"The lepers!" he exclaimed. "The lepers! You three go for the sick and the elderly," he directed Bandona, Max, and Saladdin. "I'll go with Aristotle John and Margareta to the lepers. We'll all meet at the Jama Masjid!"

The Jama Masjid, the great Friday mosque! That night the rectangular building with four modest minarets at its corners was like a lighthouse in a storm. Hundreds of escapees clutched at the Arabian latticework of its windows, jostling each other and calling out. Others were still arriving. Fathers, sometimes with three or even four children perched on their shoulders, mothers carrying pitiful bundles on their heads and frequently babies in their arms, waded through the filthy water to try and get near the only door. Inside, the spectacle was another scene out of Dante's *Inferno*. Children, frightened by the darkness, screamed with terror. Women shouted, bickered, and wept. Everyone was trying to reach the galleries on the first floor because the flood water had already invaded the ground level and was rising rapidly. Suddenly, however, a torrent was released from the roof and submerged the galleries. Some young men managed to break down the doors leading onto the terrace and set up a barricade. The atmosphere became more and more suffocating and some of the refugees fainted. Babies suffering from dysentery emptied their bowels. The first dead were evacuated, passed from arm to arm over the heads of the crowd. It was not long before the rumors spread: eroded by the water, hundreds of hovels were in the process of collapsing all over the slum.

The little leper colony situated below the level of the railway lines was completely submerged. In order to cover the last few feet, Margareta had to hoist herself onto Kovalski's back, an acrobatic feat that was somewhat delicate in a sari. Not a single inhabitant had left. The parents had put their children up on the roofs and the relatively able-bodied lepers had piled *charpoys* one on top of another to protect the sick and the infirm. Kovalski discovered Anouar perched on one of these improvised pyramids, half-immersed in water. The crippled man had survived his amputation. He was smiling.

"Anouar, old friend, I've been looking for you," said the priest breathlessly.

"Looking for me? But why? This isn't the first time the monsoon has gotten our feet wet!"

Again Kovalski was amazed at the leper's stoical, almost cheery attitude. "These lights of the world really deserve their place next to the Father," he thought. "They have been to the very ends of suffering."

"The rain is still falling. You could all be drowned." Even as he spoke these words, the priest became aware of the vanity of his intentions. How could he hope to evacuate these poor people when he himself and his companions had several times nearly disappeared into the eddies of dark water that engulfed the whole area. He must get reinforcements. Reinforcements? The idea seemed somewhat comical in a night of general panic. It was then that he saw before him the image of a man with small cruel eyes behind thick-lensed glasses, a man with protruding ears and the fat jowls of a pleasure seeker. He called out to Margareta and Aristotle John.

"I'm heading for the godfather," he shouted to them. "He's the only one who can help us to get everyone out of here."

With its four stories of solid masonry, its flights of steps built out of brick, and its stone balconies, the godfather's house emerged like a fortress out of the flood water. Lit up *a giorno* by a powerful generator, its numerous rooms illuminated the waves that beat against its walls with an unusual clarity. "It's the doges' palace!" Kovalski remarked to himself, not without a certain admiration. Nothing, not even this deluge, could modify the behavior of the doge of the City of Joy. Insensible to what was going on outside, to the cries and appeals of residents fleeing their collapsing hovels, he remained as impassive as ever, enthroned in his chair encrusted with precious stones. Even the abrupt entrance of a figure dripping in putrid slime, led by his son, unleashed not the faintest shadow of surprise on his toadlike face.

"Good evening, Father," he said in his hissing voice and fixed his old adversary with a stare. "What kindly breeze brings you here in weather like this?"

He clapped his hands and a beturbaned servant brought tea and soft drinks on an engraved copper tray.

"The lepers," said Kovalski.

"Them again?" marveled the godfather and his forehead puckered. "It would seem that it's always to the lepers that I owe the honor of an encounter with you. What is it this time?"

"They will probably all drown if they're not evacuated urgently. We need men and a boat immediately."

Whether out of the fear of losing an appreciable source of income or out of an unexpected upsurge of human solidarity, Kovalski could not say, but the City of Joy's Mafia boss reacted in a manner that was quite spectacular. He stood up and clapped his hands, whereupon Ashoka, the little thug with the big motorcycle, came rushing back. An initial private conference was held, then other members of the family appeared. Less than ten minutes later, a boat set out with Kovalski and a team of *mafiosi* on board. As the first strokes of the oars bore the vessel away into shadows reverberating with the sound of shouting and other noises, Kovalski heard again the hissing voice of the godfather. Turning back, he saw the squat little man framed in a lighted window. He would never forget the words of the Mafia boss, ringing out across the swirling water.

"Ashoka," he shouted to his son at the top of his lungs. "Bring all the lepers back here. Tonight, our house is for the wretched ones."

*

Max Loeb's bulky, wet body collapsed onto the pile of milk cartons. Exhausted by the hardest night of his life, he was back in his room in the first light of dawn. The downpour was now being succeeded by lighter rain that was warm and more restrained, and the rise of the water seemed to have relented a little. All through the night he had accompanied Bandona on her rescue operations, carrying his medicine chest at arm's length above the flood water. The head and heart of the little Assamese girl contained a complete list of all the most flagrant distress cases in the slum. With the help of a team of young men who had placed themselves spontaneously at their disposal, they had waded from one hovel to the next to rescue blind and paralyzed people, bedridden patients with

tuberculosis, beggars, and even a deaf and dumb madwoman with
her newborn baby. Only once had they arrived too late. When they
entered the shack occupied by the old blind leper woman to whom
Kovalski took Communion every week, they found her wasted
body already afloat in her widow's shroud. Her rosary was twined
about her wrist and her mutilated face looked unaccountably se-
rene.

"Her torment is over now," murmured Bandona as she
helped Max to hoist the body onto the low ledge. "The god she
used to call upon has heard her at last. He has taken her to be with
him."

The simplicity of this explanation in the midst of such a nightmare moved the American deeply. "It was that night that I realized
that I could never be quite the same again," he was to write a few
days later to Sylvia, his fiancée in Miami.

The arrival of the first boatload of lepers at the godfather's
house was the occasion for deeds that even a heart as full of love as
Kovalski's would not have imagined. He saw Ashoka take Anouar
in his arms and carry him carefully to the *charpoy* in his room. He
saw the women of the house strip off their beautiful muslin veils to
rub down naked children shivering with cold, for the temperature
had suddenly dropped ten degrees. He saw the godfather's wife, a
plump matron with arms jingling with bracelets, bring in a cooking
pot full of rice and steaming pieces of meat. Above all, he saw a
sight that would obliterate forever the horrifying spectacle of Molotov cocktails exploding outside his small leper clinic: the godfather himself reaching out his gold-ringed fingers to receive the
castaways, helping them to disembark, drying their mutilated
limbs, serving them tea, and offering them dishes of sweetmeats
and pastries.

"In that catastrophic flood," Kovalski was to comment, "all
the people of the City of Joy had become brothers. Muslim families
took Hindus into their homes, young people nearly drowned carrying the elderly on their shoulders, rickshaw pullers transported the
sick free of charge in vehicles that were three-quarters submerged,
owners of eating houses did not hesitate to risk their lives to get
provisions to the refugees shut up in the mosque."

In the midst of disaster God was not forgotten. Stopping off at
his room, now invaded by more than three feet of water, Kovalski

discovered two candles burning in front of his picture of the Sacred Shroud. Before escaping with the other residents of the compound, Kalima, the eunuch, had lit them "to greet the deity of Big Brother Stephan and ask him to make the rain stop."

All the same, the god of the Christians, the Bhagavan of the Hindus, and Allah the merciful appeared to be deaf to all entreaty. The torment of the flood victims of Calcutta was to go on for days. As Max had feared, cholera and typhoid began to break out. There were no medicines and no chance of evacuation. People died. Corpses that could not be incinerated or buried were simply abandoned in the flooded streets. In the space of only a few hours Max stumbled upon three bodies drifting about in the current. Paradoxically, with all that liquid around, there was not a drop of drinking water left. The inhabitants hung up rags and umbrellas to try and collect a little rain, but some had to drink directly from the infected strait of water that engulfed them. The food situation was just as tragic, despite the fact that teams of rescue volunteers were working miracles. Saladdin had managed to dig out a boat and two large pots. Paddling as hard as his strength would permit, the old man did the rounds of the eating houses to fill up his receptacles with rice and wheat flour and to take this precious cargo to the people marooned in the mosque.

The strangest thing about this cataclysm was that life still went on as before. On the corner of a submerged alleyway, Max remained rooted to the spot, confronted by a scene that would never leave him: that of a group of children up to their shoulders in water, laughing and splashing in front of a tiny platform on which an old man was selling little plastic cars and dolls, oblivious to the rain.

For eight days and eight nights the anger of the heavens remained unrelenting. Then gradually it did begin to wane, but it took more than a month for the tide to retreat altogether. Slowly Calcutta began to hope again. A few buses ventured out into the collapsed avenues. More than four hundred miles of streets had been destroyed or damaged. Half a million citizens had lost everything. Thousands of houses and buildings, either decayed or still under construction, had crumbled away. Whole neighborhoods were without electricity or telephones. Hundreds of water mains had burst.

It was in the slums, however, that the full horror of the disaster was most readily apparent. When the water subsided, the City of Joy was nothing but a polluted marsh. A glutinous, stinking mud covered everything, interspersed with the decaying carcasses of dogs, cats, rats, lizards, and even humans. Millions of flies soon hatched out of the putrefaction and made straight for any survivors. Epidemics broke out in various quarters. To try and contain them, Bandona and Aristotle John distributed tons of disinfectant provided by the municipality. Alas, the operation caused heavy losses among the volunteers. Max had to amputate several hands and feet burned to the bone by corrosive substances.

By the time Kovalski, concealed behind a two-week beard and covered with dirt and vermin, finally regained his compound, all the other occupants had already returned. They were all busy clearing away traces of the inundation. Kalima and his eunuch companions from the room next door were quick to come to greet him.

"Welcome back, Big Brother Stephan," said Kalima warmly, "We've been waiting for you."

What was his emotion when Kovalski discovered that in his absence the eunuchs had washed, scrubbed, and completely repainted his hovel! Before the picture of the Sacred Shroud, a pattern of *rangoli,* the attractive auspicious motifs traced on the ground in colored powder, paid homage to his God. Before resting, the priest gave thanks for so much love shown in the depths of his wretched slum. He was deep in meditation when a bearded figure burst in. Hasari had lost so much weight that the priest hardly recognized him.

"Now I can die," announced the former peasant, brandishing a bundle of bank notes in his triumph. "Look how much I've earned. I'm going to find a husband for my daughter."

70

H IS ENTIRE WEALTH lay heaped together on a small copper
tray: a conch, a little bell, a pitcher full of Ganges water, a pot of
ghee, and the *panchaprodip,* the five-branched candlestick used in the
ceremony of the offering of fire. Forty-three-year-old Hari Giri, a
puny little man with pale skin and an enormous wart on his forehead, was the neighborhood *pujari,* the Hindu priest. He lived in a
humble dwelling near the huts occupied by the Madrasis, the most
poverty-stricken inhabitants of the slum. In front of his dwelling
stood the small temple dedicated to Sitola, goddess of variola.
With her scarlet head and black eyes, her silver diadem and necklace of cobras and lions, she looked even more terrifying than Kali
the Terrible, patron goddess of Calcutta. It was primarily, however, for his devotion to another divinity that the Brahmin was
renowned among the residents of the slum. Daughter of the elephant-headed god Ganesh, Santoshi Mata was the goddess with
the power to grant a husband to every young Indian girl. The cult
devoted to her provided the *pujari* with a not inconsiderable source
of revenue. Of all the ceremonies in Hinduism, that of marriage is
in fact the most profitable for a Brahmin, so much so that Hari Giri
had studied astrology in order to set himself up as a professional
matchmaker. Hasari's anxiety could not leave him entirely untouched. One evening he paid the rickshaw puller a visit to ask him
the time and date of his daughter's birth. "I shall be back soon with
some good news for you," he assured him.

A few days later he did indeed return.

"Your daughter's horoscope and caste are in perfect harmony
with those of a boy with whom I am acquainted," he announced

triumphantly to Hasari and his wife. "The family concerned are *kumhars*. * They have two potteries in the neighboring slum and are highly respectable people." Then, addressing himself exclusively to Hasari, he added, "The boy's father would like to meet you very soon."

Profoundly moved, Hasari prostrated himself on the ground to wipe the Brahmin's bare feet, then raise his hands to his forehead. No self-respecting *pujari* would be satisfied with this kind of gratitude, however. Holding out his hand, he claimed an advance on his fee. This visit was to mark the beginning of a tragicomedy with many a twist of plot, of which Kovalski was to become, by force of circumstances, one of the principal protagonists. Although it is customary for the long and detailed negotiations that precede a marriage to be conducted in public in the middle of the courtyard, the parties concerned often prefer a more discreet place when it comes to the discussion of financial matters.

"My room was always at everyone's disposal," the priest was to say. Thus it was there, in front of the Sacred Shroud, that the two parties met. As to the "parties" concerned, that certainly did not mean either young Amrita or her prospective husband, who would not meet until the evening of their nuptials. Rather, it meant the father of the prospective boy, a surly man of medium build with hair matted with mustard oil, Hasari, the Brahmin with the wart on his forehead, and Kovalski. After a long exchange of greetings and social niceties, the primary issues were broached.

"My son is an exceptional boy," declared the father unhesitatingly. "And I want his wife to be no less so."

Naturally everyone correctly understood the exact meaning of this line of approach. He was not referring to moral qualities or even to physical ones, but to the price that must be paid for so "exceptional" a son. "This character's after the moon," Hasari remarked to himself. He turned to Big Brother Stephan, seeking reassurance. He had insisted upon Kovalski agreeing to be present at the debate. "In front of the *sahib,* they won't dare to exaggerate" he told himself. For once, however, the former peasant had made a psychological error. Contrary to Hasari's expectations, the *sahib*'s presence was to become a source of security for the opposite camp:

* Potters by birth.

"If the girl's father can't pay, the *sahib* will just have to pay instead."

"My daughter is just as exceptional as your son," retorted Hasari, not wishing to be outdone.

"If she is such a jewel, you will no doubt have anticipated giving her a generous dowry," said the father of the boy.

"I have anticipated doing my duty," assured Hasari.

"Well, let's see then," said the father, lighting up a *bidi.*

An Indian girl's dowry is made up of two parts. One part consists of her trousseau and personal jewels that remain in principle her property. The other part is made up of the gifts she will take to her new family. Hasari's reckoning was intended to take in both. The whole list was not very long, but each item represented so many trips through the waters of the monsoon, such deprivation, so many sacrifices, that the rickshaw puller felt each concession he was giving away meant a little of his own flesh and blood. The list included two cotton saris, two bodices, a shawl, various household utensils, and a few imitation jewels and ornaments. As for the presents for the groom's family, they were made up of two *dhotis*, as many vests, and a *punjabi*, the long tunic that buttons up to the neck and goes down to the knees. It was true that it was a poor man's dowry but it represented some two thousand rupees, a fabulous sum for a poverty-stricken rickshaw *wallah.*

The boy's father's eyebrows wrinkled. After a silence, he inquired, "Is that all?"

Hasari shook his head sadly, but he was far too proud to try and play upon the pity of his interlocutor.

"My daughter's qualities will make up for what is lacking."

"Maybe," growled the boy's father, "but it does seem to me that one or two toe rings would not be entirely superfluous. And also a nose brooch and a gold *matthika.** As for the gifts for my family . . ."

The Brahmin interrupted to declare, "Before continuing with your bartering, I would appreciate it if you could come to an agreement on the price of my services."

"I had thought two *dhotis* for you and a sari for your wife," replied Hasari.

---

* An ornament worn on the forehead.

"Two *dhotis* and a sari!" guffawed the *pujari,* beside himself. "You must be joking!"

Kovalski saw great beads of sweat break out on his friend's forehead. "Dear Lord," he thought, "they're going to fleece him down to the very last hair."

Kalima and some of the other neighbors were glued to the opening to the little room, trying not to miss any of the palavering and keeping the rest of the compound informed.

The discussion went on for a good two hours without achieving anything; they all maintained their positions. Marriage negotiations were traditionally very long-winded affairs.

The second meeting took place three days later in the same place. As was customary, Hasari had prepared small gifts for the father of the boy and for the *pujari.* Nothing very much: a *gamcha** each. Nevertheless those three days of waiting seemed to have sapped the rickshaw puller's strength. He was having more and more difficulty in breathing. His coughing fits, provisionally suppressed by Max's emergency treatment, had started up again. Haunted by the fear of dying before he had fulfilled his duty, he was ready to concede to any demands. He might never be able to implement them. This time it was the *pujari* who opened fire, but his claims were so excessive that for once the two fathers were in agreement. They rejected them.

"In that case, I shall withdraw," threatened the Brahmin.

"That's too bad. We shall just have to find another *pujari,"* responded Hasari.

The Brahmin burst out laughing.

"The horoscopes are in my possession! No one will ever agree to take my place!"

His reply provoked general hilarity in the compound. Women exchanged comments on the proceedings. "This *pujari* is a true son of a bitch," announced one of the matrons. "What's more he's sly! I'll bet he's in connivance with the boy's father!" another replied. Inside the room, they had reached an impasse. Suffering from a surge of fever, Hasari had begun to shake. "If you muck up my daughter's marriage, I'll skin you alive," he stormed inwardly, his bloodshot eyes fixed upon the Brahmin. The *pujari* went through

---

* A kind of large handkerchief.

the motions of getting up to leave, but Hasari caught hold of his wrist. "Stay!" he begged.

"Only if you pay me a hundred rupees right away."

The two helpless fathers exchanged glances. After a few seconds' hesitation they each foraged in the waistbands of their *longhis*.

"There you are!" said Hasari tartly, tossing a bundle into the hand of the man with the wart.

The latter instantly became all sweetness and light. The negotiations could recommence. No king's or millionaire's marriage could have been the subject of keener discussion than this proposed union of two ragamuffins in a slum. It took no fewer than eight sessions to settle the question of the dowry. Crises of weeping alternated with threats; ruptures with reconciliation. There was always some new requirement. One day the boy's father claimed on top of everything else, a bicycle; next day he wanted a transistor radio, an ounce of gold, an additional *dhoti*. Six days before the wedding, a misunderstanding threatened to end everything. The groom's family swore that they were supposed to receive twelve saris and not six, as Hasari claimed. Having run out of arguments, one of the young man's uncles came rushing to Kovalski.

"*Sahib*, all you have to do is provide the six missing saris. After all, you're rich! They say you're even the richest man in your country!"

This marathon completely exhausted the poor rickshaw puller. One morning when he had just collected his carriage he felt the ground dissolve beneath his feet.

"I felt as if with every step I was sinking into a drainage hole," he was to tell Kovalski. "I saw the cars, trucks, and horses revolving around me as if they were attached to a merry-go-round at a fair. I heard the screech of sirens, then everything went blank, a great dark blank." Hasari let go of his shafts. He had fainted.

When he next opened his eyes, he recognized the thin face of Musafir, the representative of the owner of his rickshaw, looming over him. Musafir had been doing his rounds, collecting the rent, when he noticed the abandoned rickshaw.

"Hey there, fellow, have you drunk a bit too much *bangla?*" he asked in a friendly way, patting the puller's cheeks.

Hasari indicated his chest.

"No, I think it's my motor that's giving out."

"Your motor?" inquired the man anxiously, suddenly on the alert. "Hasari, if your motor's really giving out, you're going to have to hand in your machine. You know how adamant the old man is about things like that. He's always saying, 'I want buffalo between my shafts, not baby goats.' "

Hasari nodded. There was neither sadness nor revolt in his expression, only resignation. He knew too well the laws of the city. A man whose motor failed him was a dead man. He had already ceased to exist. He thought of the poor coolie he had transported to the hospital during the first days of his exile. He thought of Ram Chander and of all those whom he had seen die in the arms of their rickshaws, their strength sapped, consumed, annihilated by the climate, by hunger, and by their superhuman effort. He looked with tenderness upon the two great wheels and the black bodywork of his old cart, the punctured canvas seat, the hoop and material of the little hood, in the shelter of which so many young people had loved each other and so many of the city's inhabitants had braved the excesses of the monsoon. Above all, he looked at those two instruments of torture between which he had suffered so much. How many thousands of miles had his ulcerated feet traversed on the molten asphalt of this mirage city? He did not know. He knew only that every step had been an act of will to induce the *chakra* of his destiny to complete just one more turn, an instinctive gesture aimed at survival and escape from the curse of his condition. Now, that *chakra* was going to stop once and for all.

He looked up at the owner's representative astride his bicycle. "Take your rickshaw back," he said. "It will make someone happy."

He got to his feet again and for one last time he pulled rickshaw No. 1999 back to the stand on Park Circus. While he was saying goodbye to his friends, Hasari saw the representative call out to one of the young men waiting on the edge of the pavement. They were all refugees, part of the last exodus that had emptied the Bengal and Bihar countryside, ravaged by a fresh drought. All of them longed for the opportunity to take a turn at harnessing themselves to a rickshaw. Hasari went over to the one the representative had chosen and smiled at him. Then he took the small copper bell from his finger.

"Take this little bell, son," he said, jangling it against a shaft. "It will be your talisman to keep you safe from danger."

Before going home, Hasari made a detour to call on the skeleton salesman and claim the second part of the proceeds from the sale of his bones. The cashier examined the visitor with care and, judging that his state of decline was well under way, he agreed to a further payment.

It took three more days of heated arguing before everyone agreed upon the size of the dowry. As tradition required, this agreement was sealed with a special ceremony in the Pals's compound, with all the other residents as witnesses. Coconuts, incense, and a whole carpet of banana leaves were laid on the ground to enable the *pujari* to carry out the various rites and pronounce the *mantras* for the occasion. Hasari was invited to announce that he was giving his daughter away in marriage and to enumerate the list of goods that would constitute her dowry. Much to Kovalski's fury, this formality immediately provoked a further cascade of incidents. The groom's family demanded to see the goods in question. A real showdown ensued. "I might have been in the middle of the Bara Bazar," Kovalski was to recount. "They demanded proof of the cost of such and such a jewel, they protested that the wedding sari wasn't beautiful enough, they thought the transistor radio was pathetic. Each recrimination took away a little more of the small amount of breath left in Hasari's chest." On the eve of the wedding, a new drama erupted. The groom's father, uncles, and a whole group of his friends came bursting in to check the preparations for the celebrations.

"There will be at least a hundred of us," declared the father. "And we want to be sure there'll be enough to eat."

Kovalski saw Hasari start.

"A hundred," he protested. "But we agreed that there wouldn't be more than fifty of you."

There followed an argument, to the amusement of the entire compound. The visitors dissected the menu, demanding that a vegetable was added here, a fruit or a sweetmeat there. With his back to the wall, Hasari tried to front it out.

"All right, if you reduce the number of guests by twenty," he eventually conceded.

"Twenty? Never! By ten at the very most!"

"Fifteen."

"Twelve and not one more."

"All right, twelve," sighed Hasari, to put an end to the matter. But his agony was not yet over.

"What about the musicians?" One of the groom's uncles was concerned. "How many will there be?"

"Six."

"Only six? But that's pathetic! A boy like my nephew warrants at least ten musicians!"

"It's the best orchestra in the slum," protested Hasari. "They've even played at the godfather's house!"

"Best or not, you'll have to add at least two more musicians," retorted the uncle.

It was then that a further demand was made. For some mysterious reason, connected, it seems, with subtle astrological calculations, Indian weddings nearly always take place in the middle of the night. Anouar, the leper, and Meeta had gotten married at midnight. Amrita's horoscope and that of her future husband determined the same hour. So the *pujari* had decided, after reading the celestial cards.

"Where's the generator?" asked the groom's father. "It's dark at midnight and a wedding without lots of lights is not a proper wedding."

Hasari remained dumbfounded. His own sweat had glued his back to the wall. His mouth opened in response to a desire to vomit and with his breath painful and wheezing, he felt the ground once more dissolve beneath his feet. Faces, walls, sounds all swam together in a haze. Clasping the post of the veranda, he groaned. "I'm not going to make it. I know I won't make it. They're going to do me out of Amrita's marriage." Yet the groom's father's requirement was justified.

For the millions of slum people condemned because of the lack of electricity to live in perpetual obscurity, there could be no celebration without illuminations. An orgy of light, like the one provided on the evening of Anouar's wedding, was a way of defying misfortune. Hasari shook his head sadly, showing them his empty palms. This man who felt his end so very close at hand had had no reservations about incurring debts for generations to come in order to execute his final duty. He had taken the two rings and

the small pendant that had formed part of his wife's dowry, plus
the watch his son Shambu had found among the refuse, to the
usurer. He had killed himself working. He had sold his bones. He
had exceeded the possible. Yet now he must submit to the supreme
humiliation.

"If you persist in your demands," he said, pausing after each
word to regain his breath, "there is only one solution: we shall have
to cancel the wedding. I have no more money."

So it was that less than fourteen hours before the ceremony,
they had reached an impasse of the kind that might mean total
breakdown. For the first time Hasari appeared resigned. "The man
who had struggled so hard had the look of one who was already
elsewhere," the Pole was to say. Bluff or no, the other camp maintained the same attitude. "Surely to God," Kovalski said to himself,
"they're not going to let the whole thing cave in over a little matter
of lighting." Alarmed, he decided to intervene.

"I know a compound not very far away where they have electricity," he said. "A cable could easily be led off it to here. With
four or five lamps, there would be plenty of light."

For the rest of his life Kovalski would carry with him the sight
of the gratitude in his friend's face.

The contest was still not won, however. Less than seven hours
before the ceremony, a new crisis erupted. But this time the person
responsible was the rickshaw puller himself. Recollecting suddenly
that the standing of a wedding was assessed as much on the munifi-
cence of the nuptial procession as on the opulence of the festivities, he inquired of the groom's father as to the manner in which he
intended to have his son arrive at the domicile of his future wife.
Even in this slum of mud and pestilence, such a journey was usually
undertaken on a horse caparisoned with gold and velvet.

"In a rickshaw," replied the father. Kovalski thought Hasari
was going to suffocate.

"In a rickshaw?" he hiccuped. "You did say 'in a rickshaw'?"
The groom's father nodded his head.

Hasari gave him a withering look. "My daughter will never
marry a man who comes to her wedding in a rickshaw, as if she
were a common poor man's daughter," he thundered. "I demand a
taxi. A taxi and a procession. Otherwise I shall take my daughter
back."

Providence was once more to call upon Son of Miracle. Informed of the latest point of difference between the two families, the taxi driver was quick to offer his car to transport the cortege. His generosity moved the former peasant in a very special way. After all, it had been in that same car that he had once experienced the greatest revelation of his life. It was as he sat in that vehicle that he had watched the rupees on the meter "fall like the monsoon rain." "That taxi will bring luck to my daughter and her household," he said to himself, his cheerfulness and confidence restored.

A few hours later, Hasari would at last witness the marvelous sight toward which all his arduous efforts had been directed. "Look, Big Brother Stephan. How beautiful my daughter is," he murmured ecstatically. Swathed in a scarlet sari sprinkled with golden stars, her head bowed, her face concealed behind a muslin veil, her naked feet painted red, her toes, her ankles, and wrists sparkling with the jewels that were her dowry, Amrita, led by her mother and the women of the compound, was going to take her place on the rice straw mat placed in the center of the courtyard, just in front of the little brazier in which the sacred and eternal flame burned. In sheer happiness, his lips parted in a smile that rose from the very depths of his soul, Hasari rejoiced in the most beautiful spectacle of his life, a magical scene that wiped out so many nightmare images at a single stroke: Amrita crying of cold and hunger on the winter nights spent on their piece of pavement, foraging with her little hands through the refuse from the Grand Hotel, begging under the Chowringhee arcades . . . This was a moment of triumph, of apotheosis, of final revenge on a rotten karma.

A brass band burst into sound, accompanied by singing and shouting. Preceded by a troupe of transvestite dancers, outrageously made up with rouge and kohl, the procession made its grandiose entry into the courtyard filled with the smoke of the *chulas*. "It was as if a prince out of *A Thousand and One Nights* had just dropped out of the sky," Kovalski was to say. "With his cardboard diadem encrusted with bits of colored glass, the groom looked like one of the maharajahs you see in engravings, surrounded by his courtiers."

Like Anouar, before taking up his position the boy had to

submit to the ritual of *parda*, the imposition of a veil, so that the eyes of his betrothed would not be able to see his face before the moment prescribed by the liturgy. Then the *pujari* motioned to him to go and sit beside Amrita. So began the interminable and picturesque ritual of a Hindu wedding ceremony, punctuated with *mantras* in Sanskrit, the language of sages and men of letters, which of course no one in this slum could understand, not even the Brahmin who recited them.

The congregation had not failed to notice that the best man's place to the right of the bride had remained vacant. Hasari had offered this place, the first in the hierarchy of precedence, to his brother in poverty, the Big Brother from the hovel next door, the man of God who, together with Son of Miracle, had been his providence, his friend, his confidant. Kovalski, however, had not been able to occupy the place. At the very moment the groom and his procession made their entrance, a series of convulsions had brutally shaken Hasari's chest. The priest had rushed to carry the poor man into his room. The eyes and mouth that only a moment previously had been exultant with joy had closed again in an expression of intense pain. When the convulsions stopped, his body remained stiff and motionless. Then, as if under the influence of an electrical impulse, his chest and all his muscles contracted anew. His lips parted. They were completely blue, a clear indication of respiratory difficulties.

Kovalski straddled the body and, putting all his weight on the thorax, started to massage it vigorously from bottom to top. The rickshaw puller had been reduced to skin and bone to such an extent that it was like getting hold of a skeleton. The sternum and ribs creaked under the pressure of his fingers. Soaking his beautiful white best man's *punjabi* with perspiration, the Pole worked away with all his might and, miracle of all miracles, a very feeble, almost imperceptible breath soon quivered through the fleshless form. Kovalski realized that he had succeeded in restarting the motor. To consolidate this victory, he gave his brother the most beautiful demonstration of affection he could. Bending right over him, he put his lips to Hasari's mouth and began to blow rhythmic puffs of air into lungs consumed with the red fever.

Kovalski was to write of the events that followed in a letter to the superior of his fraternity. "Hasari opened his eyes. They were swimming with tears and I realized he must be in pain. I tried to give him a drink but the water trickled over his lips without his being able to swallow it. He was breathing very faintly. At one point he seemed to be straining to listen. He appeared to be able to hear the noises coming from the courtyard, the voices and the music of the festivities. He smiled weakly at the joyous commotion. Hearing the wedding going on had such a curative effect that he wanted to speak. I put my ear closer to his mouth and heard, 'Big Brother, Big Brother,' then some words that I could not make out.

"A few moments later he took hold of my hand and squeezed it. I was amazed at the strength with which he clasped my fingers. The hand that had grasped the shafts of his rickshaw for so many years was still like a vise. He looked at me then with eyes that were full of supplication. 'Big Brother, Big Brother,' he repeated, then murmured some words in Bengali. That time I understood that he was referring to his wife and sons, that he was asking me to take care of them. I tried to reassure him. I knew that the end was near and he must have been thinking the same thing because with several movements of his hand he conveyed to me that he wanted to leave the compound without anybody noticing. No doubt he was afraid that his death would disrupt the celebrations. I had foreseen such an eventuality and asked Son of Miracle to have Hasari transferred to his compound as soon as possible.

"Toward three o'clock in the morning, with the help of Kalima and Hasari's son Shambu, the little ragpicker, we were able discreetly to move the rickshaw puller. The revelers noticed nothing. The godfather had sent along an extra supply of *bangla* and many of the guests were already drunk. Hasari must have been conscious that he was leaving his home because he joined his hands across his chest in a gesture of Namaskar as if to bid everyone farewell.

"After that, it all happened very quickly. At about five in the morning, Hasari was shaken by a violent attack. Then his lips parted and a jet of foaming blood spurted out. Shortly afterward his chest caved in with a rattle. It was all over. I closed his eyes and recited the prayer for the dead."

Less than an hour later a series of heavy blows shook the door to the room where Son of Miracle and Kovalski were watching over the mortal remains of their friend, now enveloped in a white *khadi* shroud and adorned with a garland of marigolds. The taxi driver went to open it. In the shadows he could just make out two very dark-skinned faces.

"We're the *Doms*," announced the elder of the two. "The deceased was under contract. We've come to collect his body."

71

"BROTHERS, SISTERS, LISTEN!" Stephan Kovalski raised
a finger in the direction of the ringing bells and closed his eyes to
absorb fully the crystalline notes that came cascading across the
fume-hung sky. "Christ, our Savior is born" announced the peal
from the illuminated church of Our Lady of the Loving Heart. It
was midnight on Christmas Eve.

At that instant, from one end of the immense metropolis to
the other, other chimes sounded out the same news. Despite the
fact that Christians represented a small minority in Calcutta, the
birth of Jesus was celebrated with as much devotion and display as
that of Krishna, Muhammad, Buddha, the guru Nanak of the Sikhs,
or Mahavira, saint of the Jains. Christmas was one of approximately twenty official religious festivals marked with a general
holiday in a city where such a miscellany of faiths and such devotion to God prevailed.

Filled with decorations, in the darkness the church looked
more like a maharajah's palace on a coronation night. In the courtyard, only a few feet away from the pavements where thousands of
homeless people slept huddled in the bitter cold, a monumental
crib with life-size models reconstructed the birth of the Messiah in
the straw of a Bethlehem stable. A colorful crowd, the women in
magnificent saris, their heads covered with embroidered veils, the
men and children dressed like princes, filled the vast nave adorned
with banners and garlands. The splendid bouquets of tuberoses,
roses, and marigolds that decorated the altar and choir had been
brought by a Christian woman from the City of Joy in gratitude for
the miraculous healing of her husband, who had recovered from

cholera. All around the pillars, before the innumerable plaques
recording the names of the British men and women who had been
buried in this church since its construction two centuries earlier,
wreaths of foliage and flowers formed a triumphal arch.

Suddenly a burst of firecrackers shook the night. To the accompaniment of the organ, the congregation joined in singing a
hymn celebrating the advent of the holy infant. The rector, Alberto
Cordeiro, looking more opulent than ever in his immaculate alb
and his red silk vestments, made his entrance. Escorted by his
deacons and a double row of choirboys, he processed through the
nave and ceremoniously approached the altar. "So much pomp
among so much poverty," marveled Max Loeb who attended midnight Mass for the first time in his life. The Jewish doctor did not
know that the good priest had once tried to dissuade Kovalski from
going to live among the poor of the City of Joy, for fear that he
might "become a slave to them and lose their respect."

Similar services were beginning in churches elsewhere in Calcutta. All around St. Thomas, the smart parish in the Park Street
area, dozens of private cars, taxis, and rickshaws were unloading
worshippers. Park Street and the neighboring streets glittered with
garlands and luminous stars. The night was resonant with Christmas carols. On the pavements children sold little Santa Clauses
they had made and decorated in their slum workshops. Others
offered cardboard fir trees glistening with snow, or cribs. All the
shops were open, their windows full of presents, bottles of wine,
alcohol, and beer, baskets bursting with fruits, confectionaries,
and special preserves. Wealthy Indian ladies escorted by their servants did last-minute shopping for the midnight supper. Whole
families besieged Flury's, the celebrated ice-cream and pastry
shop. Others swept into Peter Kat, Tandoor, or into the restaurants at the Moulin Rouge, the Park Hotel, or the Grand Hotel.
This last was declared to be fully booked. Its dinner, with entertainment and souvenirs, cost three hundred rupees for two, almost
the price for which Hasari Pal had sold his bones.

Deep in the alleyways of the City of Joy, Christmas was no less
lively. Garlands of lights and streamers had been strung up wherever there were Christian homes. Loudspeakers spread the sound
of carols and hymns. Each family had decorated its home. Taking
advantage of Kovalski's absence, Margareta had put a new coat of

paint on the walls of his room, drawn a *rangoli* pattern on the floor, placed a small crib under the picture of the Sacred Shroud, opened up the Gospels at the page of the nativity, and lit candles and sticks of incense. From the framework she had hung garlands of marigolds and roses that formed a kind of canopy above the little oratory.

For all the Christians of the City of Joy, however, it was the enormous luminous star poised on the end of a bamboo cane above Kovalski's hovel that was the most beautiful symbol of that magical night. The Hindu Ajit and the Muslim Saladdin had had the idea of hoisting the emblem into the sky over the City of Joy, as if to say to the despairing people of the slum: "Be not afraid. You are not alone. On this night when the God of the Christians was born, there is already a Savior among us."

That night the "savior" in question had remained, with the agreement of the parish priest, among his brothers. With his head and shoulders wrapped in a shawl because of the biting cold, Kovalski was celebrating the mystery of the Eucharist for some fifty worshippers who had assembled in Margareta's compound. How many years had gone by since his first Mass, celebrated on that same piece of plank supported on two crates? Five, six, seven? How could anyone measure the passing of time in this world without past or future? In this world where the life of so many hinged upon surviving the present minute? Listening to the carols that filled the night, he thought, "This concentration camp is a monastery." The thought had often come to him and on this Christmas night, one conviction impressed itself upon him more forcefully than ever: nowhere was the message of a God who was made man to save humanity more alive than in this slum. The City of Joy and Bethlehem were one and the same place. Before uplifting to the heavens the fragment of unleavened bread that took the place of the host, the priest felt the need to speak a few words.

"It is easy for any man to recognize and glorify the riches of the world," he said, seeking out faces in the shadows. "But only a poor man can know the riches of poverty. Only a poor man can know the riches of suffering . . ."

Hardly had he spoken these words than a strange phenomenon occurred. First there was a sudden gust of wind, then a mass of hot air swept into the compound, tearing down the garlands and streamers, extinguishing the luminous stars and bringing the tiles off the rooftops. Almost immediately after that, a formidable thunderclap rent the night. Kovalski could not help wondering if the monsoon was on its way back. After a few seconds, however, all was calm once more.

"And it is because the poor are the only ones to be able to know such riches that they are able to stand up against the wretchedness of the world, against injustice, against the suffering of the innocent," he said. "If Christ chose to be born among the poor, it is because he wanted the poor to teach the world the good news of his message, the good news of his love for mankind.

"Brothers and sisters of the City of Joy, it is you who today are the bearers of that flame of hope. Your Big Brother can promise you that the day will come when the tiger shall lie down with the young child, and the cobra will sleep with the dove, and all the peoples of all the nations will be as brothers and sisters."

Kovalski was to relate how as he spoke these words he saw again a photograph of Martin Luther King, Jr., meditating in front of a Christmas crib. In the caption to this photograph, King told how before that crib he had had a vision of an enormous banquet on the hillsides of Virginia, where slaves and the sons of slaves sat down with their masters to share in a meal of peace and love. That evening Kovalski felt himself impelled by the same dream. One day, he was quite certain, the rich and the poor, slaves and their masters, executioners and their victims, would all be able to sit down at the same table.

The priest picked up the morsel of griddle cake and raised it to the heavens. What he then saw above the rooftops seemed so extraordinary to him that he could not take his eyes off it. Sheaves of lightning were streaking the sky, lighting up an enormous mass of black cloud scudding past at great speed. A fresh cannonade of thunder immediately rolled across the night, followed this time by a burst of wind so forceful that, in the depths of their compound, Kovalski and his congregation felt as if they were being literally sucked up into it. A few moments later the clouds shed a deluge of lukewarm water. It was then that Kovalski heard the voice of Aristotle John shouting above the uproar, "A cyclone, it's a cyclone!"

*

On the other side of the city, in an old colonial mansion with balusters in the residential district of Alipore, a man was listening to the rising howl of the tornado. His interest was of a professional nature: T. S. Ranjit Singh, a thirty-eight-year-old Sikh originally from Amritsar in the Punjab, was on duty that Christmas night at the meteorological center for the region of Calcutta. Situated among hundred-year-old banyan trees beneath which Rabindranath Tagore had composed some of his poems, the center's antennae received and collated weather bulletins from all the stations planted along the shores of the Bay of Bengal, in the Andaman islands, and even as far away as Rangoon in Burma. Similarly, twice a day the station laboratory picked up photographs of the Indian subcontinent and the seas that bordered on it, taken from the upper stratosphere by the American satellite *NOAA7* and by its Soviet counterpart *Meteor*. The Arabian Sea to the west and the Bay of Bengal to the east had always been areas with a predilection for giving birth to the savage hurricanes known to meteorologists as cyclones. Caused by harsh variations in temperature and atmospheric pressure between sea level and higher altitudes, the whirlwinds unleashed forces comparable to those of hydrogen bombs of several megatons. From time to time they ravaged the shores of India, causing thousands, sometimes tens of thousands, of deaths, destroying and submerging in one fell swoop regions as vast as New England or Louisiana. India's whole memory had been traumatized by the nightmare of its cyclones.

On the night in question, however, Ranjit Singh had no particular reason to be alarmed. Not all tropical depressions became cyclonic whirlwinds, particularly when they occurred as late in the season as this. The photograph transmitted by the American satellite at seven in the evening was even somewhat reassuring. The Sikh examined it attentively. The diffused zone of stratocumulus it showed had little chance of becoming dangerous. Situated more than eight hundred miles south of Calcutta, it was tracking northeast, in other words, in the direction of Burma. The last readings from the weather stations, transmitted by teleprinter, had come in barely an hour ago. It was true that they indicated areas of low pressure all over the region but the wind speed everywhere was less than thirty miles an hour. Reassured, the Sikh decided to spend his Christmas Eve as pleasantly as possible. Opening his attaché case, he took out the two tin boxes his wife had prepared. They contained a real midnight feast: fish curry with cubes of white cheese in a sauce, little balls of vegetables, and baked *nan*. He also took out a small bottle of rum he had brought back from an inspection in Sikkim and filled a glass. Oblivious to the squalls that were banging at the shutters, he swallowed a first mouthful with relish. Then he began his meal. When he had finished eating, he poured himself a fresh glass of rum, got up, and appeased his conscience by casting an eye over the teleprinter roll in the adjoining room. With some satisfaction he confirmed the absence of any message and went back to his seat. "There we go," he remarked to himself as he savored his drink. "Yet another uneventful night."

At two in the morning, he awoke with a start to the rattle of the teleprinter. The Vishakhapatnam station to the north of Madras was announcing gusts of wind of one hundred and twenty knots, a little more than one hundred and thirty miles per hour. Shortly afterward the station on the Nicobar islands confirmed this information. The mild depression of the previous day had transformed itself into a major cyclone. The anger of the god Indra was raging across the Bay of Bengal.

One hour later, an SOS from an Indonesian cargo boat caught up in the storm confirmed that danger was imminent. Its position, latitude 17°25' north, and longitude 91°10' east, indicated that the cyclone was located about three hundred and fifty miles away from the coast of Bengal. It had changed direction sharply and was heading toward Calcutta.

The Sikh lost not a second. Instantly he informed his superior, the chief engineer, H. P. Gupta, who was sound asleep with his family in his government flat situated in a wing of the building. Then he called the local station for All India Radio, the national broadcasting network, and the cabinet office of the Minister for Internal Affairs in order that the people living in the delta area might be immediately informed of the imminence of a "cyclonic wind of very severe intensity." Next he turned to a radiotelephone positioned on a console behind his table. The apparatus relayed his H.Q. directly to an ultramodern piece of equipment on top of the highest building in Calcutta. From beneath its fiberglass dome the parabolic antenna for the radar of the Indian meteorological department could locate a cyclone over four hundred miles away, trace its course, determine the dimension of its "eye," and calculate the volume of torrential rain it was liable to dump on hitting its target. That night, however, the radar was switched off and the great sky-blue room, decorated with photographs of all the cyclones that had ravaged Bengal in the course of the previous ten years, was deserted. The next tour of observation was not due to begin until seven on Christmas morning.

72

ASHISH GHOSH, the young peasant who had been daring enough to return to his village after six years of exile in the City of Joy, had not gone to bed that night. Together with his wife and their three children he had struggled against the onslaughts of the wind and pouring rain which were gradually demolishing his mud and thatch hut. His village, Harbangha, consisted of an assembly of small dwellings in the middle of infertile rice fields, inhabited for the most part by refugees from what had once been East Pakistan and was now Bangladesh. It was one of the world's poorest regions, a marshy area without roads, traversed by rivers, creeks, canals, and estuaries; an inhospitable expanse of land constantly beset by some calamity, by floods, for example, or tornados, tropical storms, droughts, the collapse of its banks, the bursting of its dikes, the invasion of salt water. This was unproductive ground which did not yield even an annual harvest of fifteen hundred pounds of rice per acre for its two million peasants. Life was even harder for the one million inhabitants who possessed not even a paddy field. Risking their own lives, the fishermen tried to keep their families from perishing in a region that was enormously rich in fish, but where all fishing was rendered aleatory by the poverty of means. Half a million dayworkers offered their labor for hire but only at harvest and tilling time did they actually find any work. For the rest of the year they cut down wood and gathered wild honey in the enormous virgin forests of the Sundarbans, an area as large as Mississippi but almost as impenetrable as the Amazon, infested with snakes, crocodiles, and man-eating tigers that each year devoured three or four hundred people among them.

Ashish Ghosh had brought back with him from the City of Joy one of the primary symbols of economic ascent for a poor refugee, a transistor radio. At about six in the morning he switched it on. The static caused by atmospheric disturbance impaired his reception. Nevertheless, through the crackling, he could make out a voice relentlessly repeating the same message. He jammed the appliance to his ear and instantly understood. A few minutes later the Ghoshs were fleeing into the downpour, leaving behind them the fruits of their six years of exile, deprivation, saving, and suffering in the inferno of their slum: their house with its store of seeds and fertilizer, their field, the large pool so arduously dug out, where the first carp had just been born, their two bullocks bellowing in their thorny enclosure, the three goats and Mina, their beautiful cow with her swollen udders and her horns curved like those of the wild sheep of the Himalayas. Ashish turned around to look back at it all through the tornado. Squeezing the arm of his sobbing wife, he promised, "We'll be back." It was then that with eyes lashed by the pouring rain he saw his hut borne aloft "like a flycatcher's nest carried away by a monsoon squall."

*

The image of a large whitish snail pierced in the center by a black hole suddenly appeared on the green-tinted screen. At the top, on the left, the digital chronometer announced the time in orange letters. It was seven thirty-six. The Calcutta radar had just detected the monster. Its position—latitude 19° north, longitude 89°45' east—its breadth—three hundred and five miles—and the dimension of its eye—twenty-two miles—confirmed the alarm messages being issued by all the weather stations in the region. They were evidently dealing with a major whirlwind, with what the Indian meteorologists refer to in their jargon as a "severest cyclonic storm." Half an hour later a detail was to further reinforce their concern. Although the eye of the cyclone, the black hole in the middle, remained perfectly visible, a series of milky spirals had begun to form around the cavity, gradually obscuring it behind a whitish veil. This was evidence that the whirlwind was in the process of becoming swollen with millions of tons of water.

Without losing a second, Haresh Khanna, the frail little technician who had just taken up his post in charge of the radar that Christmas morning, picked up his radiotelephone to alert the meteorological center. Originally from Bombay, the other great Indian metropolis frequently visited by cyclones, Khanna had followed the progress of whirlwinds on his screen on dozens of occasions. Never yet, however, had he seen the eye cover itself with this milky veil. After transmitting his observations, he climbed to the building's terrace. From up there it was possible to embrace the whole city at a glance. Holding his old umbrella firmly over his head, Khanna could distinguish through the sheets of rain the metallic latticework of the Howrah Bridge with, just behind it, the rooftops of the City of Joy and, to the left, the imposing pink mass of the railway station, then the brown waters of the river with its hundreds of barges, the green expanse of the Maidan, the long brick façade of the Writers' Building, and finally the entanglement of thousands of terraces and roofs that formed the gigantic metropolis which All India Radio was slowly wresting from its holiday slumbers.

Fortunately the monster was still far, very far away, over the sea. The wind and rain that had been lashing Calcutta since the previous night were only precursory signals, the prodromes of the cataclysm.

*

Fisherman Subash Naskar, twenty-six, owed his life to an extraordinary reflex action. Instead of trying to take shelter from the wall of water about to engulf his village, he turned around, plunged into the huge tidal wave, and let himself be carried inland. He would never be fully aware of what really happened, but the next thing he knew, he was six miles away, clinging to the window of a temple. All around him lay disaster: he was the only survivor. It was a little after ten in the morning. The monstrous spinning top had just struck the land.

It was sheer hell, a hell of wind, water, and fire. It had begun with a blinding light like a colossal ball of fire that streaked across the horizon and lit up the landscape. Caused by the accumulation of electricity up among the clouds, this extremely rare phenomenon scorched the tops of all the trees within an area one hundred

and twenty miles wide and thirty deep. Then, siphoning up the
relatively shallow sea along the coast, the whirling column impelled the resulting freak wall of water forward. Under the combined effect of the wind and the tidal wave, houses, huts, and trees
were pulverized, pounded, mangled; fishing boats were sucked up
and ejected miles away; buses and railway carriages were picked up
and tossed about like bundles of straw; tens of thousands of people
and animals were borne away and drowned; thousands of square
miles were submerged under a magma of salt water, sand, mud,
debris, and corpses. In the space of a few seconds, an area as large
as Guatemala with a population of three million inhabitants had
been expunged from the map.

Caught in midflight by the raging torrent, like thousands of
others, Ashish Ghosh and his family owed their safety only to the
proximity of a small mosque perched on a hill. "My wife and
children hung on to me," he was to recount, "and I managed to
drag them all as far as the building. It was already packed with
survivors. All the same I was able to clamber onto a window ledge
and glue myself to some bars, still clinging to my family. We remained there, suspended above the flood, all through that day and
the following night. By the next morning there were only about
twenty of us still alive." At one point Ashish saw in the distance a
family of six people, clinging as best they could to a tree trunk, but
it was not long before an eddy engulfed the fragile skiff together
with all its castaways.

Terror reigned for ten hours before the whirlwind veered
away and headed out to sea. Two days later Ashish and his family,
and the first escapees, reached the approach to the small town of
Canning, thirty miles farther inland. Haggard and hungry, clinging
to each other for support, they walked like sleepwalkers, without
looking right or left. For miles they had struggled through a landscape of devastation and ruin, stumbling everywhere over corpses.
The nurse who ran the little local dispensary would never forget
the pitiful sight of "that column of survivors silhouetted against
the dark line of the sky. Even at a distance you could sense their
dreadful distress," she would say. "Some were carrying small bundles or a few utensils. They were propping up the injured, shuffling
along with their children clutched in their arms. All of a sudden I
caught the smell of death. Those people had seen their parents,

wives, and husbands drown before their very eyes. They had seen their children carried away by the floods, their houses collapse, their land disappear."

*

For three days Calcutta remained ignorant of the magnitude of the disaster. The whirlwind had destroyed telephone lines, radio transmitters, roads, and seaborne transport. Anxious not to find themselves accused of lack of foresight or negligence, the authorities deliberately prolonged this state of ignorance. The first announcements minimized the seriousness of the tragedy. It had been an ordinary tornado, so it was claimed, of the kind that occurred every year anywhere along the Indian coast! And just in case anyone was tempted to take a look for himself, the area was cordoned off by police and border guards.

What a shock it was, therefore, when the first accounts of the escapees began to filter through! The press went wild. It talked of ten or twenty thousand dead, of fifty thousand head of cattle drowned, of two hundred thousand houses razed to the ground, of a million acres rendered barren by seawater, of fifteen hundred miles of dikes demolished or damaged, of three or four thousand wells made forever unusable. It also revealed that at least two million people were in danger of dying of hunger, thirst, and cold because of the lack of an immediate organized relief effort.

All world catastrophes have had their petty disputes and wranglings over relief and aid. But here a desperate poverty made the need for aid more urgent than anywhere else. Yet it took another three days for the Calcutta and New Delhi authorities to agree on the first rescue operations, three days of which certain individuals were quick to take advantage. The people in question wore the ocher robes of monks belonging to the mission of Ramakrishna, the Bengali saint who in the last century preached mutual aid and love between Hindus and other communities. As soon as the cataclysm was announced, they rushed from Madras, Delhi, and even Bombay. The policemen cordoning off the area let them pass: barefoot angels of charity must not be intercepted. Going about in pairs, they mingled with the survivors and offered to take in as many orphans as they could. So much generosity did not fail to touch the hearts. Children abruptly deprived of their parents by the disaster were quickly rounded up. "Those men were generosity itself," one thirty-five-year-old widow was to testify. "One of them said to me, 'Whatever you do, don't worry about your little girl. She will be quite safe. We shall find her work and in two months' time we shall bring her back to see you together with her four or five hundred rupees in wages. In the meantime, here are a hundred rupees in advance.' I knelt down and kissed the feet of my benefactor and gave him my daughter." Like so many other victims of the tragedy, that poor woman would never see her child again. She did not know that these purported monks were pimps.

The genuine solidarity of the inhabitants of Calcutta, however, would compensate a thousandfold for such imposters. Max would never forget "the explosion of generosity" the catastrophe engendered throughout the city, and especially among the poor of the slums. People rushed in thousands to the headquarters of the various health organizations, to the clubs, the mosques, and even to the door of his dispensary, to offer a blanket, clothing, a candle, a small bag of rice, a little oil, some sugar, a bottle of paraffin, some cow dung cakes, or matches. "A country capable of so much solidarity is an example to the world," thought the young American doctor on seeing all those poor people spontaneously giving the little they had to their brothers in misfortune. Dozens of organizations, most of them unknown, were galvanized into action, hiring trucks, motorized tricycles, taxis, and even handcarts to convey the first relief to the survivors. Together these organizations formed a prodigious Indian mosaic, representing as they did churches, sects, confraternities, unions, castes, sports teams, schools, and factories. Kovalski, Max, Bandona, Saladdin, Aristotle John, Margareta, and the whole team of Indian volunteers from the City of Joy's Committee for Mutual Aid were naturally in the front line of this humanitarian mission. Even Gunga, the deaf mute, was there. They had filled up a whole truck with medicines, milk powder, rice, blankets, and tents. Their load also included two inflatable rafts and two outboard motors, the personal and combined gifts of the godfather and Arthur Loeb, Max's father. The only thing that prevented them from leaving was a slip of paper: the road permit from the authorities. All week Kovalski and Max dashed from office to office, trying to extract the precious magic document. Contrary to what might have been expected, their status as *sahibs,* far from facilitating proceedings, aroused the suspicion of many officials. Kovalski knew all too well that the bugbear of the CIA was always suspected of lurking behind a foreigner. Despairing of his cause, the Pole decided to resort to a lie. "We're working with Mother Teresa," he announced to the man in charge of delivering the permits.

"Mother Teresa?" the *babu* repeated respectfully, drawing himself up behind his ocean of paperwork. "The Saint of Calcutta?"

Kovalski nodded.

"In that case you and your truck can leave immediately," declared the man, initialing the pass with a stroke of his pen. "I am a Hindu, but we Indians all respect saints."

The delta road was a journey to the far reaches of hell. A mere ten miles away from the city, the way was already immersed in a sea of mud. The wreckage of overturned trucks was everywhere. "It was like looking at a naval cemetery," Kovalski was to recall. Wearing a turban of a scarlet red that contrasted sharply with the lividity of his complexion, the driver maneuvered as if engaged in a slalom competition. He cursed, braked, and sweated. With water up to its hood, the heavy vehicle was constantly skidding. Soon the first columns of survivors came in sight. "There were thousands of them, tens of thousands of them," Max was to write to his fiancée. "They were up to their chests in water, carrying their children on their heads. Some had taken refuge on ledges where for six days they had been waiting for help. Dying of hunger and thirst, they cried out, throwing themselves into the water and wading towards our truck. About twenty of them managed to clamber onto it. To make them listen to reason, Kovalski and Saladdin shouted that we were doctors and were carrying only medicines, and by some miracle they let us pass. A little farther on another miracle occurred. Among the hordes encircling us, Kovalski recognized a regular customer from the little restaurant he frequented in the City of Joy. He was a militant Communist sent by the party to organize the refugees. He allowed us to continue. Aristotle John and Saladdin walked ahead to guide the truck. Soon, however, the engine hiccuped, coughed, and stopped once and for all—drowned.

"We put the rafts in the water and piled our cargo into them. A new night had fallen. There was not a single light for hundreds of square miles around us, but a myriad of fireflies lit up a spectral landscape of shredded trees, gutted huts, and bushes draped with detritus carried there by the whirlwind. Here and there, torn down electric wires had already electrocuted several ferrymen. Suddenly we heard shouting and the roll of drums in the night. Hundreds of escapees who had taken refuge among the ruins of a village perched on a little mound were waiting anxiously in the darkness for help. I shall never forget the triumphal welcome they gave us. Before even showing any interest in what we had brought, Muslim mullahs led us to the little mosque that had survived the catastrophe. In the very midst of disaster, we had to first give thanks to Allah!"

That night, the young doctor was to be particularly struck by one detail as he first set foot on the ground: the bellies of all the children who came running toward him, clapping their hands, singing, and dancing. They were huge, protruding, inflated bellies, empty bellies full of worms. As for Kovalski, he was to be seized by the vision of a "woman holding herself erect among all the wreckage, her baby in her arms. She did not beg or moan but stood as dignified and motionless as a statue, with all the poverty of the world inscribed on her expression. Poised beyond time, or rather at the very heart of time, a time that is an eternity to those in distress, that mother with her child was the Bengal Mother, a symbol of that Christmas of misfortune."

Poor Kovalski! There he was, the man who thought he had seen everything, shared in everything, and understood everything about the suffering of the innocent, condemned to take a further step toward the heart of the mystery. Why had the God of love, the God of justice allowed these people, who were among the world's most disinherited, to be so cruelly afflicted? How, he asked himself, will the incense of our temples ever be able to efface the smell of the death of all these innocents?

The smell of death! Despite the generous premiums offered in return for the destruction of the corpses, the professional grave-diggers sent by the authorities had fled after only two days. How could Hindus be distinguished from Muslims in such a charnel house? How could some be burned and others buried without mistakes arising? Teams of convicts from a penitentiary sent to take their place exhibited no more enthusiasm for the task. Soldiers had to be sent in as a last resort. They were duly equipped with flamethrowers. The entire delta was thus transformed into one gigantic barbecue, the stench of which could be smelled as far away as Calcutta.

There remained only the living to be dealt with. For four weeks Kovalski, Max, and their Indian companions kept combing several miles of one isolated sector. Going from one group of survivors to the next, they vaccinated them with compressed-air Dermo-jets, treated fifteen thousand sick people, vermifuged twenty thousand children, distributed some twenty-five thousand food rations. It was a drop of water in the ocean of need, the Pole would admit, but a drop of water that would be missed if it were not there, he added, citing Mother Teresa's famous remark. On the morning the committee's team packed its bags to return to the City of Joy, the survivors in the area gave their benefactors a small celebration. People who no longer had anything, poverty-stricken people stripped even of hope itself because the sea had rendered their fields unfertile, managed somehow to dance and sing and express their gratitude and joy. Overwhelmed, Kovalski thought of the words of Tagore: "Misfortune is great, but man is even greater than misfortune." As the celebration drew to a close, a little girl dressed in rags, with a water lily in her hair, approached the priest to offer him a gift on behalf of all the villagers. They were Muslims but they had made up a little Crucifix out of shells with the figure of Christ on it. Accompanying the gift, there was a piece of paper on which an uncertain hand had inscribed a message in capital letters. As he read the words aloud, Kovalski thought he could hear the voice of the Gospels.

"Blessings on you, brothers! Brothers, you came to our aid when we had lost everything, when the light of hope had been extinguished in our hearts. You fed the hungry, clothed the naked, cared for those who were suffering. Thanks to you we have rediscovered our taste for life.

"Brothers, from now on you will be our closest relatives. Your leaving fills us with sadness. We express our eternal gratitude to you and pray God that he will grant you a long life.

The survivors of the cyclone"

*

One morning, some weeks after this catastrophe, the City of
Joy and all the other districts of Calcutta seethed with an unaccustomed excitement. Woken with a start by the explosion of firecrackers and the sound of shouting, Max hurried out of his room.
Outside he found his neighbors singing, shouting, congratulating
one another, dancing, and clapping their hands. Children chased
one another with shrieks of joy. Exultant in their happiness, people
were offering one another sweetmeats and cups of tea. Youngsters
were exploding fireworks over the roofs. Since no festival had been
forecast for that day, the American could not help wondering what
the reason was for this sudden outburst of morning enthusiasm.
Then he saw Bandona racing toward him with a garland of flowers
in her hands. He had never seen the young Assamese girl so
cheerful. Her small almond eyes sparkled with joy. "These
scourged, humiliated, starved, broken people are truly indestructi-
ble," he thought with amazement. "Their zest for life, their capacity for hope, their will to survive enables them to triumph over all
the maledictions of their karma."

"Max, Big Brother, have you heard the news?" the Angel of
the City of Joy called out breathlessly. "We've won! Now we're as
strong as the people in your country, as strong as the Russians, the
Chinese, the British . . . We shall be able to irrigate our fields, to
harvest our rice several times a year, and to put lighting in our
villages and slums. We shall all be able to eat to our heart's content.
There will be no more poor people. Our great Durga Indira Gandhi has just made an announcement on the radio: this morning we
exploded our first atomic bomb!"

Epilogue

THE LIVING CONDITIONS of the inhabitants of the City of Joy have improved conspicuously since the events recorded in this book. A young French teacher went one day to visit the slum. On her return to her home city, she talked to her students with so much emotion about what she had seen that they helped her to found an organization whose members would undertake each year to send a sum of money to the Committee of Mutual Aid in the slum. The organization was soon to include three hundred people. An article subsequently appeared in the French magazine *La Vie*, which would multiply the number of members by ten. One year later, a second article again doubled the membership. Donations now provided by some seven thousand members of the organization made it possible to set up in the slum a proper medical-social infrastructure. Dr. Sen, a Bengali doctor with a generous heart, who had been treating the poor free of charge for thirty years, was to become the committee's president. Later two young French people, in love with India, went to live out there to bring new strength and impetus to the team. Dispensaries, homes for rickety children, maternity clinics, soup kitchens for the old and the needy, training centers for adolescents, and workshops to teach adults skills were gradually set up by the residents themselves with the help of funds sent out from Europe. Campaigns were launched to detect and vaccinate against tuberculosis. This action extended beyond the walls of the City of Joy: rural development programs also introduced irrigation, dug wells, and set up dispensaries in several impoverished and deprived areas of Bengal. It was naturally to the handful of Indians who had assembled one evening in

Kovalski's room to "think about the possibility of helping others" that people appealed to create and run all these centers. Today it is Bandona, Saladdin, Ajit, Margareta, Aristotle John, and some two hundred and fifty Indian social workers, nurses, and instructors, helped by local doctors and a few foreign volunteers, who form the mainsprings of this network of mutual help, aid, care, and education.

For their part, the Bengal government and the Calcutta municipality have not been sparing in their efforts. With the help of funds lent by the World Bank, a vast rehabilitation program was launched in the slums. The alleyways of the City of Joy were paved over, some of them were raised, new latrines were dug, piped wells were sunk, electric cables were extended. These benefits were to have unforeseen consequences. The fact that rickshaws and taxis could now gain access to the interior of the slum, encouraged employees, small business men, and traders to seek premises in the City of Joy. Indeed, situated only a ten minutes' walk away from the great Howrah Railway station and so close to the center of Calcutta, the slum constituted a much more convenient location than the new residential suburbs constructed fifteen to twenty miles out of the city. Rents suddenly shot up, and the number of jeweler-usurers multiplied tenfold in less than two years, a sign of certain economic change. Unscrupulous entrepreneurs became caught up in unbridled speculation. Three- or four-story apartment buildings began to crop up and many of the poor had to leave.

The first victims of this new situation were the lepers. The change of government in Bengal deprived the godfather of the support he had hitherto enjoyed. A new Mafia installed itself in the City of Joy and it decreed the expulsion of the lepers. They left in small groups, without protest or violence. Kovalski succeeded in rehousing Anouar, his wife and children, and the majority of his friends in one of Mother Teresa's homes. To compensate for the lepers' eviction, the eight thousand buffalo in the cattle sheds were allowed to remain. They still form part of the population of the City of Joy.

*

Three weeks after the cyclone, Ashish and Shanta Ghosh returned with their children to their devastated village on the edge of the Sundarban forest. With a courage and application strengthened by their hard apprenticeship in the slum, they rebuilt their hut, cleaned up their fields, and returned to their life as peasants. Their experience of sharing spurred them into taking an even closer interest in their neighbors' lot. Shanta started up several craft workshops for the women of the village while her husband founded an agricultural cooperative which was markedly to improve the resources of the people living in that particularly destitute area.

Sadly, the example of this family was to remain almost unique. Rare indeed were the occupants of the City of Joy who have to this day managed to escape their hovels and return to the countryside. Recent developments have, however, introduced certain elements of fresh hope. A distinct decline has been recorded in the number of poor peasants fleeing to Calcutta, a fact that may be explained in terms of a marked improvement in the yield provided by Bengali agriculture. Today, in more than half the province, two annual rice harvests are produced, and approximately a quarter of the territory even manages three. This transformation has enabled hundreds of thousands of landless peasants to find work where they live nearly all the year round. Furthermore, whereas twenty years ago Calcutta represented the only hope of finding work in the whole of Northeast India, the implantation of new industrial centers in Orissa, Bihar, and other provinces in that area has created new labor sites that have considerably reduced emigration to Calcutta. Thus, provided there are no further major catastrophes, it is possible to hope for a stabilization of the population of Calcutta, and perhaps even for the beginning of a future reflux of the slum dwellers to the countryside of their origin.

*

Max Loeb went back to America. Speaking of his experiences, he declared that except perhaps for a trip to the moon, a stay in an Indian slum was the most extraordinary adventure a man of the twentieth century could live through. Other young doctors, male and female, have continued to come from all over the world to give

several months of their lives to the residents of the City of Joy. As
for Max, his stay has transformed his perception of life and his
relationships with others. He continues to keep in close contact
with Kovalski. Together with Sylvia, now his wife, he has founded
an organization to send medicines and medical equipment to the
Committee for Mutual Aid. Above all, however, Max returns regularly to visit his friends in Anand Nagar. Again and again he likes to
say, "The smiles of my brothers in the City of Joy are lights that will
never be extinguished in me."

*

One day, Aloka, Hasari Pal's widow, brought Stephan Kovalski a brown envelope covered with official stamps.

"Big Brother Stephan, a registered letter arrived for you this
morning," she announced.

Kovalski saw instantly that it came from the Home Ministry.
With a pounding heart, he opened it. "Dear God," he shuddered,
"I'll bet the government is kicking me out." Anxiously he scanned
the type, until suddenly his eyes fell on words that he had to reread
several times before he grasped their meaning. "The Government
of India hereby grants the said Stephan Kovalski the certificate of
. . ." The letter went on to declare that after he had pledged his
loyalty at the time appointed and according to the regulations
prescribed by the law, he would be entitled to all the privileges,
prerogatives, and rights and would be subject to all the obliga-
tions, duties, and responsibilities of an Indian citizen.

"An Indian citizen," stammered the Pole. To him it was as if all
at once the heart of the slum were beating in his chest. Seized with
vertigo, he leaned against the pillar of the veranda and closed his
eyes. When he opened them again, he took hold of the cross he
wore around his neck and gazed at the two dates his mother had
had inscribed upon it, that of his birth and that of his ordination.
His vision dimmed by tears of happiness, he considered then the
little blank space in front of the Indian name he had had engraved
several years previously. This was the name that, on the day of his
citizenship, would replace that of Stephan Kovalski. In Hindi, as in
Bengali, *"Premanand"* meant "Blessed is he who is loved by God."
It summed up perfectly the meaning of his relationship with the

humble, the poor, and the broken individuals that were the people of the City of Joy. Next to the patronym which henceforth would be his, he would this very day add the date of his final entry into that great family of his Indian brothers, for this was the third most important day in his life.

ACKNOWLEDGMENTS

First and foremost, I would like to express my enormous gratitude to my wife, Dominique. She shared every moment of my extensive research in the City of Joy and she was my irreplaceable collaborator in the preparation of this book.

I would also like to acknowledge my great thanks to Colette Modiano, Paul and Manuela Andreota, and Gérard Beckers, who spent many hours correcting my manuscript and helping me with their encouragement and their extensive knowledge of India.

I also want to thank my friends in India, who with such generosity facilitated my research and made my numerous stays in India so enjoyable and fruitful. It would take several pages to name them all individually, but I would like to mention in particular Nazes Afroz, Amit, Ajit and Meeta Banerjee and Mehboub Ali; Pierre Ceyrac, Tapan Chatterjee, Ravi Dubey, Behram Dumasia, Pierre Fallon, Christine Fernandès, Georges and Annette Frémont, Leo and Françoise, Adi Katgara, Ashwini and Renu Kumar, Anouar Malik, Harish Malik, Aman Nath, Jean Neveu, Camellia Panjabi, Nalini Purohit, Gaston Roberge, Emmanuel and Marie-Dominique Romatet, James and Lallita Stevens, Baby Thadani, Amrita and Malti Varma and Francis Wacziarg.

A book that was especially informative about the past of Calcutta was *Calcutta* by Geoffrey Moorhouse.

I also wish to acknowledge my gratitude to those who sustained me with their encouragement and their affection during the long and difficult task of researching and writing this book, in particular, Alexandra and Frank Auboyneau, Jacques Acher, Gilbert and Annette Etienne, Jean and David Frydman, Louis and

Alice Grandjean, Jacques and Jeannine Lafont, Adélaïde Oréfice, Marie-Jeanne Montant and Tania Sciama.

Without the enthusiasm and faith of my friend and literary agent, Morton L. Janklow, and of my publishers, I would never have been able to write this book. My warmest gratitude goes to Robert Laffont and his assistants in Paris; Tom Guinzburg, Henry Reath, Sam Vaughan, Kate Medina, Betsy Nolan, Don Epstein and their associates in New York; Mario Lacruz in Barcelona; Giancarlo Bonacina and Carlo Sartori in Milan; Peter Gutmann in Munich; Antoine Akveld in Amsterdam; and, finally, to my friend, collaborator, and translator Kathryn Spink, herself the author of many remarkable books, one of which on Mother Teresa is entitled *The Miracle of Love*.

A very special thanks also goes to the team at the Médiatec computer agency in Marseilles and especially to its president and general manager, Mr. Jean-Claude Aubin, and the director of the Apple department, Mr. Hervé Bodez, for their technical help in the organization of my documentation and the presentation of my manuscript.

Finally, I would like to express my gratitude to all the friends in India who gave me so much of their time as I collected the material for this book, but who wish to remain anonymous.